Mind, Psychoanalysis and Science

Mind, Psychoanalysis and Science

Edited by
PETER CLARK AND
CRISPIN WRIGHT

Basil Blackwell

Copyright © Basil Blackwell Ltd 1988

First published 1988

Basil Blackwell Ltd
108 Cowley Road, Oxford, OX4 1JF, UK

Basil Blackwell Inc.
432 Park Avenue South, Suite 1503
New York, NY 10016, USA

British Library Cataloguing in Publication Data

Mind, psychoanalysis and science.
  1. Psychoanalysis
  I. Clark, Peter   II. Wright, Crispin
  150.19'5   BF173
  ISBN 0–631–14544–3

Library of Congress Cataloging in Publication Data

Mind, psychoanalysis, and science.
  Based upon papers presented at the International
Conference on Psychoanalysis and the Philosophy of Mind,
held Mar. 1985 at the University of St. Andrews.
  Includes index.
  1. Psychoanalysis – Congresses.   2. Psychology –
Philosophy – Congresses.   I. Clark, Peter A.   II. Wright,
Crispin, 1942–   .   III. International Conference on
Psychoanalysis and the Philosophy of Mind (1985:
University of St. Andrews)
  BF173.M5275   1988   150.19'5   87–26788
  ISBN 0–631–14544–3

Typeset by Hope Services, Abingdon
Printed in Great Britain
by T. J. Press Ltd, Padstow

Contents

Introduction

PETER CLARK AND CRISPIN WRIGHT

The University of St Andrews appointed Adolf Grünbaum, Andrew Mellon Professor of Philosophy at the University of Pittsburgh, as the 1984–5 Gifford Lecturer. His series of ten lectures, entitled 'Psychoanalytic Theory and Science', were given during February and March of 1985. The timing of the lectures was fortunate, since Grünbaum's book *The Foundations of Psychoanalysis: A Philosophical Critique* had been published in the United Kingdom in the previous autumn, attracting much scholarly interest. The conclusion of the lectures was thus a particularly suitable occasion for an international, interdisciplinary conference devoted to the foundations of psychoanalysis and to three specific groups of issues. These were: the relation of general psychology and the philosophy of mind to psychoanalysis; the appraisal of psychoanalytic theory in the light of clinical evidence; and the current state of the neurophysiological theory of dreaming and its relation to the psychoanalytic account.

Funding for the conference came from a variety of sources. The Department of Logic and Metaphysics at St Andrews is fortunate to be the beneficiary of a Trust Fund instituted by the late Anne Wright, daughter of Professor J. N. Wright, formerly Professor of Logic and Metaphysics. The trust generates a sum specifically for the holding of conferences in Logic and Metaphysics subjects every three years, and provided our basic funds on this occasion. Further generous support was given by our publisher, Basil Blackwell, and by the University of St Andrews. In this context we should like to express our special gratitude to the late Steven Watson, then Principal of the University and Chairman of the Gifford

viii *Peter Clark and Crispin Wright*

Committee. Finally, a grant was provided by the British Academy which allowed for the invitation of one further scholar from the United States of America. We would like to thank all those scholars (and their universities) who provided their own funds for travel to and from St Andrews, and to express our thanks and appreciation to all our sponsors. The conference took place in St Andrews on 19–21 March 1985 before an invited audience of recognized scholars in the field.

The present volume consists of (descendants of) the papers delivered by the symposiasts in the conference sessions, with three exceptions, the chapters making up part 1. The first of these is Grünbaum's own contribution. This consists in a précis of the main arguments and conclusions of his book. It is the only essay in this volume which has been previously published and is taken from *Behavioral and Brain Sciences*, 9, 1986, 217–28. We wish to thank Professor Grünbaum, the editor of the journal, and Cambridge University Press for permission to include the article here. Most chapters in the volume make reference to Grünbaum's book, and all either take up or take issue with claims pertinent to its central concerns. We therefore felt that, both as an aid to the reader and as a guide to much of the critical analysis which the volume contains, it was right to include what is a very effective and careful summary of Grünbaum's position on the scientific interpretation and scientific standing of psychoanalytic theory.

Of particular importance for this volume is Grünbaum's rejection of the hermeneutic construal of psychoanalysis proposed by Ricoeur and Habermas, and his claim that psychoanalytic theory is, as its founder Freud maintained, a scientific or causal theory. Grünbaum argues that the psychoanalytic explanation of behaviour cannot be counted as a form of intentional explanation, since the explanatory motive postulated by psychoanalysis does not include an unconscious belief that such behaviour is a means of realizing the repressed aim. While none of our contributors is prepared to defend the original hermeneutic interpretation of psychoanalytic theory, Hopkins, Dilman and Sharpe all suggest forms of interpretative construal in which intentional or motivational explanations of behaviour play the central role.

Grünbaum has made a case that Freudian theory is empirically testable, and thus a genuinely scientific theory by falsificationist criteria. Grünbaum himself, of course, does not accept the falsificationist demarcation criterion but relies upon a version of eliminative inductivism in the tradition of Bacon and Mill. Assuming the scientific status of Freudian theory, the question naturally arises, whether and to what extent did Freud manage to vindicate his method of clinical investigation. Grünbaum's answer is twofold: that Freud did produce an ingenious purported justification for employing specially selected clinical data in evaluating his theory, despite the problem of contamination by suggestion, but that this justification hinges on an empirical claim which, it turns out, has little or no support. The purported justification is provided by the so-called Tally Argument, to the effect that a patient will experience a lasting cure only if the psychoanalytic interpretations achieved in therapy tally with something real in him. However the well-known phenomena of spontaneous remission and placebo effect render the claim that genuine cure follows only on correct analytical interpretation extremely suspect.

Grünbaum's repudiation of the claim that psychoanalytic theory is unfalsifiable and his account of the methodological significance of the Tally Argument are the subject of Frank Cioffi's chapter. The question concerning exactly what empirical support Freudian theory actually gains from both clinical and experimental evidence is the issue to which part 4, by Edward Erwin and Paul Kline, is devoted.

Chapter 2 is by Jim Hopkins. It is essentially a critical notice of Grünbaum's book and was not as such read at the conference. It argues that psychoanalytic explanation can be regarded as a sound extension of explanation in common sense or – as it seems we shall all have to acquiesce in calling it – 'folk'-psychology, to which the application of neo-Baconian inductivist canons is anyway inappropriate. The explanatory inferences characteristic of much of psychoanalysis, Hopkins argues, are comparable to those in commonsense psychology in which a desire or motive is postulated as a cause of action. To be sure, in the explanation of action, motives together with beliefs produce actions aimed at the satisfaction of desire; whereas, in, for example, the psychoanalytic explanation of dreams, unconscious motives produce wishes and mere representations of satisfaction, like wishful imagining. But in both cases, Hopkins argues, there is a relation of shared content between the description of motive and the resulting action, be it overt or simply an episode of imagining that which one desires. This connection of content present in the explanations both of commonsense psychology and Freudian theory, Hopkins suggests, makes for a kind of explanatory achievement which is not possible in the case of the purely causal claims typical of scientific theory. If this is overlooked, Hopkins claims, the degree of support for Freudian theory will be systematically understated; and is, in the Hopkins's view, by Grünbaum.

Frank Cioffi's chapter, which concludes part 1, attacks Grünbaum's claim that Freud was highly sensitive to the scientific status of his theory and regarded early versions of psychoanalysis as refutable and refuted.

Cioffi criticizes Grünbaum's account of how Freud dealt with the problem of the epistemic contamination of clinical data by suggestion. In particular, he argues that Grünbaum greatly overestimates the power of the Tally Argument.

Part 2 explores the general theme of psychoanalysis and consciousness. It opens with a chapter by Morris Eagle on a neglected but important theme, that of psychoanalysis and *self*-consciousness. Eagle argues that the distinction between ownership and disownership of thought (in psychoanalytic terms, between the thought content of a coherent ego and the ego-alien disowned content of dysfunctional obsessive thought) is as fundamental in analysis as the famous distinction between conscious and unconscious mental states. John Haldane's chapter takes up Eagle's central concern by focusing on the question of what general form a philosophically viable account of mind must have if it is to take account of both the conscious/unconscious distinction and the ego/ego-alien distinction as they occur in psychoanalytic theory. Clearly the issue has considerable bearing on theories within the philosophy of mind; neither distinction would be acceptable to a Cartesian dualist, for example. Haldane proceeds to consider how well current philosophies of mind can accommodate these Freudian ideas.

Chapter 6, by Michael Moore, returns to the specific problem of the unconscious as treated in psychoanalytic theory and the philosophy of mind. Moore begins with the observation that there are at least two accounts of the unconscious in the Freudian corpus: first, the account provided by the clinical theory; second, that provided by Freud's metapsychological theory. The burden of his paper is threefold: to show that there is no absurdity or impossibility involved in a functionalist account of unconscious mental states; to argue that there is a clear, defensible account of metapsychological theory when conceived as distinct from the specific hypotheses of Freudian clinical theory; and, third, to show that this metapsychology is distinct from that based upon outmoded physiology and the hypothesis of 'universal conflict' that we have inherited from Freud.

Part 3 returns to the theme of the hermeneutic interpretation of Freudian theory. Ilham Dilman's chapter raises the question, pursued by Hopkins, of how psychoanalytic explanations and the intentional explanations of human behaviour familiar from commonsense psychology are related. Dilman argues that any paradox in the idea of unconscious intention is only apparent. Undoubtedly, the idea of an unconscious intention is an attenuation of the ordinary notion. But if it is possible to know something without recognizing that one knows it, it is possible for someone to have an intention without that intention being an object of knowledge. Focusing on examples of temporary forgetfulness – 'Why have I come to the kitchen?' – hypnotic suggestion, and others, Dilman argues that psychoanalytic explanations can be understood as invoking no crucial departures from the explanations of intentional action in commonsense psychology. Robert Sharpe, too, in his contribution to part 3, supports an 'interpretative' account of Freudian theory, though he is inclined to place more emphasis than Dilman on the differences between psychoanalytic and 'folk'-psychological explanations. Sharpe rejects the assumption of the scientific interpretation of Freudian theory: that there is a unique causally correct hypothesis concerning the aetiology of a given neurosis and argues for a 'narrative' interpretation of the theory – one which he argues, further, can explain the well-known placebo effect of therapy and also give an account of how a single aetiological hypothesis (a single narrative) can appear to be an unequivocally correct explanation of the origin of a neurosis.

Part 4 is devoted to discussion of the support for Freudian theory provided by clinical and experimental evidence. Edward Erwin begins by considering the special difficulties involved in the claim that uncontrolled clinical case studies can be used as evidential support for the causal hypotheses of psychoanalytic theory. He takes what he describes as a qualified sceptical view of this claim. In the second part of his chapter he reviews how far existing experimental studies support the crucial Freudian claim, in the light of the Tally Argument, that psychoanalytic therapy is more effective than can be accounted for as a pure placebo effect, and considers whether there is sufficient positive experimental evidence to conclude that the central components of the Freudian theoretical edifice have been confirmed. He argues against both claims. Indeed, in Erwin's view, an examination of the experimental studies so far undertaken fails to warrant any of Freud's theoretical hypotheses.

In his reply to Erwin, Paul Kline argues that there is, on the contrary, good experimental evidence for some of the Freudian theoretical claims and that in particular Erwin's, and Eysenck's and Wilson's, attacks on the confirmatory nature of this data are flawed. He concedes that it is hard to gather good evidence for the effectiveness of psychoanalytic *therapy* but argues that this is because the wrong approach has been taken to its evaluation. He proposes an approach based upon studying the process of therapy itself. Kline argues that the impression that the experimental evidence is non-confirmatory is often supported by the invention of rival explanations of the observed data which show themselves as spurious, untested and *ad hoc*. To illustrate his claim he considers various non-Freudian explanations of paranoid subjects' tendency to fixate longer over pictures of naked men than of women, and of the results of perceptual defence and repression studies. The data obtained from the latter, he argues, are just what are to be expected in the light of Freudian theory.

Part 5 contains two chapters, one by the literary critic Frederick Crews, and the other by Peter Lamarque. Crews argues that the real message of Frank J. Sulloway's *Freud, Biologist of the Mind* is that Freud's reputation as a scientist is entirely discredited. He claims that Freud, and indeed many of his intellectual heirs, were guilty of much scientific malpractice and that what Sulloway's book actually achieves is to destroy forever the legend of Freud's scientific integrity.

Lamarque's chapter is a sustained criticism of the widely held view that psychoanalysis is illuminating in literary criticism. He argues that, although psychoanalytic concepts have attracted many literary critics, neither psychoanalytic theory nor its clinical practice is at all pertinent to the special tasks of the critic who wishes to understand the creation, appreciation and reception of literature.

The final section of the volume, part 6, is devoted to the psychoanalytic theory of dreams. Chapter 13 is a very comprehensive three-part contribution by the Harvard physiologist J. Allan Hobson. In the first part of the chapter Hobson claims that the basis of Freud's *Interpretation of Dreams* lies in his unsuccessful 'Project for a Scientific Psychology', arguing that in his account of dreams Freud translated his neurobiology into a general psychological framework. In the second part of the chapter, Hobson describes and summarizes much of the modern physiological investigations into dreaming and its correlation with REM sleep. In particular, on the basis of investigations undertaken by himself and his co-author, McCarley, he proposes the 'activation-synthesis' theory as an explicit rival to the Freudian account. According to this hypothesis, the principal manifest elements in dreams arise from a synthesis performed by the forebrain on highly disparate disorganized information generated by the brainstem reticular system which is auto-activated (when all external stimuli are shut off) during periods of REM sleep. This hypothesis, the content and evidential support for which he develops in detail, is clearly superior, Hobson contends, to the disguise-censorship psychoanalytic account, both in explanation of the bizarreness of dreams (arising from the auto-activity of pontine generator neurons) and of the stable cognitive features of dreams (resulting from forebrain synthesis). The concluding part of Hobson's chapter is an extended attempt to evaluate the prospects for Freud's general project for a scientific psychology, with special reference to sleep and dreaming. In it Hobson proposes a thesis of psychophysical isomorphism and considers the conceptual issues raised by such an approach to the interpretation of dreams.

The problem of the relation between the neurophysiology of dreaming and the general psychological account of the content of dreams is the central issue raised by Roger Squires in his reply to Hobson. He points out that though the 'activation-synthesis' hypothesis would, if true, rule out the psychoanalytic interpretation of certain features of dreams, the question still would remain as to how the forebrain synthesizes the manifest dream content from the signals it receives during REM sleep. There is still the possibility that this synthesis is motivational, informed by unconscious wishes, and a core idea of the Freudian theory is thus still very much in play. To rule out this possibility would require very much more physiological detail as to the process of synthesis than is presently available. Squires then calls attention to two widely accepted but problematic claims for any thesis which seeks to draw connections between neurophysiology and dream reports; viz. the claim that there is typically a suppression of critical faculties during sleep, and the claim that the recollection of dreams may be selective. Both points, he argues, pose serious methodological difficulties for any neurophysiological theory of dreams which is based on correlations between neurophysiological activity and dream reports. The activation-synthesis model is such a theory, and makes claims about the relation between neurophysiology and dream content. But how are dream contents and dream reports related, and how are claims concerning that relation to be tested? Such problems, Squires contends, should be viewed positively, as an encouragement to the further elaboration of the 'activation-synthesis' model, and to further study of the exact physiological processes underlying dream production; only thereby is there any prospect of a way out from the threat of a self-confirming circle, the mechanism of synthesis simply being filled in in such a way as to suit the dream reports.

The 'madness' of dreams is the starting point of Helene Sophrin Porte's essay on Freud's dream theory, the burden of which is to expose what she sees as a deep incoherence in the theory. She begins with the observation that there is a tension in the account of the bizarreness of dreams proposed in *The Interpretation of Dreams*. Freud rejects the idea that the quality of 'illogicality', so familiar in dreams, could arise without repression of information from external sources; but he simultaneously holds to the *hypothesis of regression*, according to which the aetiology of dream contents resides entirely within the spontaneous activity of the nervous system. Here, she claims, there is not one dream theory in place but two and they are, despite Freud's intermingling of them, mutually irreconcilable. The second, which owes much, she argues, to Freud's work on aphasic misuse and distortion of speech (*paraphasia*), is a pre-psychoanalytic, biological theory. The first theory is genuinely psychoanalytic, deriving the 'madness' of dreams from the operation of a 'censor' blocking the access of unconscious wishes into consciousness, so crucially involving repressive mechanisms. Only the first theory will sustain an analogy between neurotic symptoms and dreams. But, in order to dream at all, the dreamer must be asleep! Psychoanalytic theory can provide no explanation of the functional role of this state. Such an explanation requires a biological theory which has no place for the concept of repression. Thus Porte argues Freud's complete theory is fatally flawed, despite his ingenious efforts, and the two accounts cannot be consistently combined.

The final chapter of the volume by Alessandro Pagnini seeks to summarize the current standing of the Freudian theory of dreams in the light of modern neurophysiological research and to sum up the current methodological and epistemological status of the theory. Broadly Pagnini endorses Porte's account of *The Interpretation of Dreams* but argues, mainly on the basis of the work of the Italian neurophysiologist Mancia, that physiology and psychoanalysis are not in principle irreconcilable, but that the specific theory of dreams as found in Freud and some of his commentators must be given up.

The conference ended with a short panel discussion among the main symposiasts and their commentators. Much of the success of the conference was due not only to the high standard of scholarship and argument displayed by the symposiasts, but to the general good will and positive attitude of all the participants. As organizers we would like to thank the Chairmen of Sessions for their efforts in allowing discussion to be wide-ranging while always to the point. A list of participants at the conference and brief biographical notes on contributors are included at the end of this volume. To Mrs Janet Kirk, our Departmental Secretary, we wish to express especial thanks for her patient administrative work both in the organization of the conference and in the preparation of this volume.

Throughout the book the pronoun 'he' is used in the generic sense. Where citations of Freud's writings in English are from the *Standard Edition of the Complete Psychological Works of Sigmund Freud*, trans. and ed. by J. Strachey et al. London: Hogarth Press, 1953–74, 24 volumes, the references use the abbreviation 'S.E.' followed by volume number, and page(s). The date given is the year of first appearance. We are grateful to Sigmund Freud Copyrights Ltd, The Institute of Psycho-Analysis and The Hogarth Press for permission to quote from this edition.

PART ONE

Foundations of Psychoanalysis

1
Précis of *The Foundations of Psychoanalysis: A Philosophical Critique*

ADOLF GRÜNBAUM

The Foundations of Psychoanalysis: A Philosophical Critique (Grünbaum 1984; henceforth *Foundations*) offers a philosophical assessment of the theoretical, epistemological and heuristic grounds of Freud's monumental clinical theory. The appraisal concentrates on the central arguments offered by the founding father, because his own reasoning, though deeply flawed, is considerably more challenging than most of the defences by his later exponents. The latter – orthodox and revisionist – are also subjected to critical scrutiny, with special attention to one such hermeneutic reconstruction of psychoanalysis.

INTRODUCTION: CRITIQUE OF THE HERMENEUTIC CONCEPTION OF PSYCHOANALYTIC THEORY AND THERAPY

During the past 15 years, the philosophers Paul Ricoeur (1970; 1974; 1981) and Jürgen Habermas (1970; 1971; 1973), as well as the psychoanalysts George Klein (1976) and Roy Schafer (1976), have put forward the so-called hermeneutic reconstructions of the Freudian corpus in order to supplant Freud's own view of the psychoanalytic enterprise as a natural science (S.E. 1933, XXII: 159; 1940, XXIII: 158, 282). Such influential latter-day analysts as Charles Brenner (1982: 1–5) also espoused Freud's scientific view.

Thus Ricoeur (1970: 358) tried to use the scientific weaknesses of Freud's clinical theory for a philosophical 'counterattack' against those who criticize it as poor science. Quite recently Ricoeur (1981: 259) endorsed anew Habermas's complaint that Freud had fallen prey to a portentous 'scientific self-misunderstanding'.

Habermas

According to Habermas, Freud incurred a 'scientistic self-misunderstanding' when he attributed natural science status to his own clinical theory. As seen by Habermas (1971: 246–52), and also by George Klein (1976: 42–9), this error arose from over-generalizing a projected reduction of the clinical theory to a neurobiologically inspired (i.e. scientific) 'energy' model of the mind. In my case against Habermas, the following five considerations are developed in detail:

1   Habermas (and Klein) misrepresent the mature Freud's notion of what is scientific as requiring reduction to the laws of the physical sciences, thereby making the scientific status of the clinical theory parasitic on Freud's energy model. Such a reading is contradicted by explicit and definitive texts (S.E. 1925, XX: 32–3; 1914, XIV: 77), showing that during all but the first few years of his psychoanalytic career, Freud's view of what is scientific was based on methodological features, not on reducibility to physical laws.

2   According to Habermas, the dynamics of psychoanalytic therapy exhibit a sort of causation not present in the causality of nature: the patient's psychoanalytic 'self-reflection' supposedly 'dissolves', 'overcomes', or 'subdues' the connection linking the neurosis to its cause (Habermas 1971: 256–7, 271; 1970: 302, 304). This is simply an error. There is no such causal dissolution according to psychoanalytic theory any more than there is in physical theory.

3   Important laws in electromagnetic theory and other branches of physics contradict Habermas's claim that law-based explanations in the natural sciences always rely on 'context-free' or unhistorical laws of nature. On the basis of this ill-founded claim, Habermas asserts that there is a fundamental contrast between law-based explanations in the natural sciences and those using psychoanalytic generalizations, which are applied to individual life histories in a personalized narrative (Habermas 1971: 272–3).

4   Habermas's thesis that the analysed patient has a cognitive monopoly on the proof or disproof of psychoanalytic hypothesis

completely begs the question. Many Freudian assumptions are testable without any recourse at all to the subjective judgements of patients in the treatment setting. Yet Habermas insists that there is a critical difference between the analytic patient's privileged knowledge and that of the objective observer in the natural sciences.

5 Habermas's (1971) book failed to take into account Pierre Duhem's insightful discussion of refutation in physics, written half a century earlier. Thus uninformed, Habermas relied on an incorrect notion of how physical hypotheses are refuted, and posited a false contrast with the logic of falsifying psychoanalytic interpretations.

Freud's 'scientistic self-misunderstanding' (Habermas 1971, ch. 10) is claimed to be demonstrated by just the theses that *Foundations* shows to be untenable. Habermas claims that this misunderstanding has had far-reaching consequences, if only because it prevented our recognizing that psychoanalysis was actually a depth-hermeneutic mode of inquiry, the only tangible example of a science incorporating methodical self-reflection, and potentially a prototype for the other sciences of man.

Ricoeur

In his 'hermeneutic' account, Ricoeur ignores the fact that observations in physics are already theory-laden and are then further interpreted theoretically, a point emphasized by Freud (S.E. 1915, XIV: 117). Ricoeur thereby creates a false contrast between the psychoanalyst and the natural scientist in the garb of the behaviourist: 'Strictly speaking, there are no "facts" in psychoanalysis, for the analyst does not observe, he interprets' (Ricoeur 1970: 365). In truth, well before the appearance of Ricoeur's (1970) book, Popper (1959), Sellars (1961) and Hanson (1958) – not to mention Kant with his 'percepts without concepts are blind' – had already discredited the crude observation–theory dichotomy that Ricoeur (1981: 247–8) uncritically assumes for the natural sciences. Thus, to the serious detriment of his case for hermeneutics, he is unaware that insofar as the interpretative activity of any observer already implies that there can be no 'pure' data – i.e. 'facts' to be explained – theory in the natural sciences is on the same epistemic footing as the clinical hypotheses generated by analysts.

Having run foul of this commonplace, Ricoeur goes on to restrict the application of psychoanalytic theory to the patient's speech from the couch: Its subject matter, he tells us (1970: 275), is 'analytic experience [in the dyadic clinical doctor–patient setting], insofar as the latter operates in the field of speech'. Again, the object of psychoanalytic knowledge is 'only that part of [analytic] experience which is capable of *being said*' (1981: 248). From this, Ricoeur draws the following conclusions: (1) unlike the behavioural 'facts' of scientific psychology, 'facts in psychoanalysis are in no way facts of observable behaviour' (1981: 248), and (2) the empirical scrutiny characteristic of the observational sciences cannot intrude on the hermeneutic construal of Freudian theory. The 'facts' dealt with in psychoanalysis, we are told, 'are not verifiable by multiple independent observers' (1974: 186). As partial grounds for (1), Ricoeur depicts Skinnerian behaviourism as the prototype for scientific psychology. Yet his use of behaviourism as the paradigm is incorrect and misleading, if only because cognitive psychology, for example, takes mental states into consideration, no less than psychoanalysis does. (See special issue on the work of B. F. Skinner: *Behavioral and Brain Sciences*, 7, 1984.)

Thus it emerges that Ricoeur's claims (1) and (2) are ill-founded, even if one does not challenge his restricting of psychoanalytic theory to the dyadic 'work of speech with the patient' in the treatment setting. It is extensively argued in *Foundations*, however, that this restriction is itself unwarranted. For example, it is unsound to infer that dreamers' verbalized recollections of their dreams, rather than the dreams themselves, are the domain of relevance for any theory of dreams, merely because these utterances are presumed to be the only available data for such a theory. Of course, Freud himself never made this inference, although he accepted its premise.

Ricoeur attempts in vain to strengthen his case on the basis of Freud's modification of the original seduction theory of hysteria. Freud had initially claimed that actual childhood seductions were the causes of this neurosis, but later he was driven to substitute imagined seductions: *'In the world of the neuroses it is psychical* [as contrasted with *material*] *reality which is the decisive kind'* (S.E. 1917, XVI: 369; italics in original). But ascribing this causal role to psychic reality does not help Ricoeur's hermeneutic thesis. Even for imaginary seductions, there remains the burden of showing that they have pathological effects. Nowhere does Ricoeur provide even a hint of evidence that children who fantasize seduction develop hysteria *because* of these fantasies. Gathering the requisite evidence would require precisely the scientific methods rejected by the hermeneuticist.

Thus, just as the free association method cannot show that actual childhood seductions have caused hysteria, it is unable to show that imagined ones have done so. Indeed, Freud's substitution of fantasies for real seductions only makes it harder to provide evidence of causation. By the same token, the very quest for the veiled 'meaning' that psychoanalytic explanation is expected to disclose cannot succeed without relying on methods of causal inquiry and validation that hermeneuticists declare inappropriate outside the natural sciences. A hydrophobic's fear of drinking is connected in thematic content to a repressed feeling of disgust for seeing a dog lapping water from a person's glass. But no matter how strong such a thematic affinity between a supposedly repressed thought and a neurotic symptom, this 'meaning connection' is not enough to-show that the repressed thought is the 'hidden intentionality' behind the behaviour. Thematic affinity itself is not sufficient for causation. Even analysts who do not consider themselves hermeneuticists are susceptible to what might be dubbed 'the thematic affinity fallacy'.

It would even be wrong to suppose that there is typically thematic affinity between the ideational or affective content of a repressed desire and the symptoms that provide an outlet for it. As Breuer and Freud emphasized at the outset (S.E. 1893, II: 5), 'the typical hysterical symptoms' or outcroppings of repressed ideation do not have any apparent thematic connection at all to their presumed causes. And, as Freud stressed later, the products ('derivatives') of the dynamic unconscious that are thrust back into consciousness usually have a relatively distant topical connection to the repressed motif in which they presumably originated (S.E. 1915, XIV: 149–51, 190–1).

The upshot of these observations is that, *pace* Ricoeur, neither the supposed causal role of seduction fantasies nor the explanatory role of 'meaning' exempts psychoanalysis from the modes of explanation and validation of natural science.

In a further futile effort to hermeneuticize psychoanalysis, Ricoeur offers a 'semiotic' construal of the various outcroppings of repressed ideation as linguistic communications, with the clinical theory providing a 'semantics of desire'. In psychoanalytic theory, both full-fledged neurotic symptoms and minineurotic ones (e.g. manifest dream contents, Freudian slips, jokes) are seen as *compromise-formations*, products of the defensive conflict between the repressed ideas and the repressing ones (S.E. 1896, III: 170; 1917, XVI: 358–9). As such, symptoms have also traditionally been viewed as 'symbols' of what is repressed. But they are 'symbols' in the non-semantic sense of being substitutive formations affording replacement satisfactions or outlets, not linguistic representations of their hypothesized unconscious causes. Vicarious wish-fulfilment in dreams, for example, hardly amounts to the *semantic* function of linguistic communication. As one might accordingly expect, Freud himself tells us that 'a dream does not want to say anything to anyone. It is not a vehicle for communication'

(S.E. 1916, XV: 231). Ironically, Ricoeur (1970: 5) bases his semantic construal on dreams.

To take another example, when paranoiacs give verbal or non-verbal expression (e.g. by suspicious glances) to their delusions of persecution, this distrustful behaviour is taken as good psychoanalytic evidence of repressed homosexual longings. Even assuming that this interpretation is correct, however, the behaviour still does not constitute communicative acts that refer semantically to the unconscious sexual feeings. More generally, even when symptoms and other derivatives are actually verbalized, and even if they are thematically connected to their unconscious causes, they do not linguistically designate the repressions that engender them (although they manifest them!).

In sum, it is incorrect to assimilate to one another the following two sets of relations: (1) the way an effect manifests its causes and can hence serve as evidence for its operation; and (2) the way a linguistic symbol represents its referent semantically or designates its attributes. Furthermore, to be a vicarious outlet for an ungratified, hidden desire is plainly quite different from being any kind of linguistic representation. In conflating the psychoanalytic and semantic uses of the term 'symbol', Ricoeur has wrongly assimilated inferability and vicariousness, on the one hand, to semantic reference, on the other. His 'semantics of desire' are themselves the result of a semantic error.

Reasons versus causes

The thesis that, in psychoanalysis, explanatory motives are reasons but not causes is shown to be untenable on the following grounds:

1   The thesis rests on the misconception of the relation of causal relevance between an antecedent X and an outcome Y; it overlooks that X may be physical, mental or psychological, so long as it makes a difference to the occurrence of Y, and affects the incidence of Y. But in psychoanalysis, explanatory unconsciousness motives are held to have just that kind of relevance to the phenomena they explain. Thus, the hypothesized unconscious motives X can be (partial) causes of human conduct Y, whether or not psychoanalytic explanations conform to the so-called practical syllogism (see below).

2   Explanations in terms of reasons normally do conform to the practical syllogism: An agent carries out an action A, because he desires to achieve a goal G, and also believes that doing A will achieve G. Thus the desire-cum-belief set supplies 'the reason' for doing A. And, in

virtue of (1), an explanatory reason for an action is causally relevant to its performance. Hence such reasons are causes.

3 Though explanatory reasons do qualify as (partial) causes, it is shown that unconscious motives do not constitute such 'reasons', because classical psychoanalytic explanations typically do not even conform to the practical syllogism. It turns out that the explanatory motives do not include an unconscious belief that the explained behaviour is a means of realizing the repressed aim. Therefore, such behaviour fails to be a species of intended action, although the impulse that instigates it can be said to be a repressed aim or 'intention'.

Thus, when Freud maintained that both unconscious and conscious motives qualify as causes (S.E. 1909, X: 199; 1910, XI: 38), he certainly was not erroneously supposing that all causes had to be physical. Yet Klein (1976: 56, also 12, 21) has claimed that *bona fide* psychoanalytic explanations provide 'reasons rather than causes' for human conduct. In the same vein, Roy Schafer (1976: 204–5) writes that the unconscious 'reasons' fail to qualify as causes. Apparently, the exponents of the reasons versus causes thesis are, in effect, contradicting Freud's views rather than explicating them.

Overall, it is difficult to avoid the conclusion that the 'humanistic' implementation of the Freudian enterprise by a hermeneutic reconstruction is just an investigative cul-de-sac and a negativistic ideological battle cry, hardly a promising prototype for the human sciences generally.

In view of the weakness of the arguments offered to hermeneuticize Freud, it is difficult to avoid making conjectures about underlying ideology. Proponents seem to want (1) to free the study of human ideation from the evidential burdens of the standard empirical sciences and (2) to draw an ontological boundary line between mental and other natural processes so as to strengthen the case for (1). Their motivation is likely to be religious, political, or the understandable desire to safeguard a lifetime professional investment in the practice of psychoanalytic treatment. What other stakes could the proponents of hermeneutic reconstruction have?

Freud's actual criteria for theory validation were essentially those of hypothetico-deductive inductivism (S.E. 1914, XIV: 77; 1915, XIV: 117; 1925, XX: 32). He regarded adherence to these as the hallmark of the scientific status he claimed for his theory. I undertook to appraise Freud's arguments for his clinical theory of personality and therapy by those very standards. Hence the verdict I reached was not based on imposing some extraneous methodological purism. Nor does my application of Freud's avowed norm of scientific rationality to psychoanalysis imply that

I consider it *the* criterion of demarcation between science and non-science. In short, I grant Freud his own canons of scientific status in addressing the following key question: Did his clinical[1] arguments vindicate the knowledge claims he made for his evolving theory in labelling it 'scientific'?

My answer has two parts. First, the reasoning on which Freud rested the major hypotheses of his clinical edifice was fundamentally flawed, even if the validity of his clinical evidence were not in question. Second, as it happens, far from deserving to be taken at face value, the clinical data are themselves suspect; more often than not, they may be the patient's responses to the suggestions and expectations of the analyst.

THE CLINICAL METHOD OF PSYCHOANALYTIC INVESTIGATION: PATHFINDER OR PITFALL? (PART I)

Is Freud's theory empirically testable?

Freud himself always claimed that the treatment setting is the arena *par excellence* for psychoanalytic research, experimental tests being essentially superfluous, if not inappropriate. By contrast, Eysenck (1963) asserted that Freudian theory is experimentally testable but denied that well-designed clinical tests are feasible. Others, such as Glymour (1980), have contended that there are after all viable strategies for supporting or refuting psychoanalytic hypotheses on the couch. Glymour allowed for both clinical and experimental tests. Thus, all of these writers do agree that at least some parts of the Freudian corpus are in fact testable by empirical findings of *some* sort.

Just this shared assumption of actual testability has repeatedly been denied by Popper, who has even rejected the *logical* possibility of testing psychoanalysis empirically. As recently as when he replied to his critics in 1974 (pp. 984–5), Popper reiterated his earlier claim that Freud's theory, as well as Adler's, is 'simply non-testable, irrefutable. There was no conceivable human behaviour which would contradict them' (Popper 1962: 37). Indeed, Popper emphasizes that 'psychoanalysis was immune [to falsification by any logically possible empirical findings] to start with, and remained so' (1974: 986). It is then a mere corollary of this thesis of non-testability that clinical data in particular cannot serve as a basis for genuine empirical tests.

(At the time that the writing of *Foundations* was completed, Popper's (1983) book, *Realism and the Aim of Science*, was not yet available in print

I could not take this later discussion of psychoanalysis into account, but I have the opportunity to do this as part of my Response to Critics in *Behavioral and Brain Sciences*, 9 (1986), 266–84.)

When Popper claims that his falsifiability criterion excludes psycho-analysis from the pantheon of the *bona fide* empirical sciences, his principal concern is not with Freudian theory as such, important though psycho-analysis is. In Popper's earlier works (1962: 156–7, 255–8) we find psycho-analysis playing a role not so much as itself the prime target of his charge of non-falsifiability, but rather as a centrepiece for his critique of inductivism as a method of scientific theory-validation or a criterion of demarcation between science and non-science. For, as I read Popper (1962: 33–8), inductivism does accept the claims of abundant empirical confirmation made by adherents of Freud's theory, as well as by proponents of Adler's revisionist version of psychoanalysis and by contemporary Marxists.

Indeed, Popper (1962: 35–7) seems to have become convinced of the unfalsifiability of psychoanalysis partly *because* he thought it was always confirmed inductively, come what may. Thus, by 1919 he had persuaded himself both that inductivism does not have the methodological resources to challenge the scientific status of psychoanalysis *and* that Freud's theory – as well as Adlerian revisionism and Marxism – was in fact empirically irrefutable. On this basis, Popper argued that the inductivist method of confirmation and its criterion of demarcation are unacceptably permissive.

Hence, the real philosophical villain of Popper's story was inductivism rather than psychoanalysis or Marxism as such, although he deplored the latter in their own right. Having found to his dismay in 1919 that inductivism still held sway as a criterion of demarcation, Popper used psychoanalysis – Freudian and Adlerian – as the *pièce de résistance* in his case against it. He therefore concluded: 'Thus there clearly was a need for a different criterion of demarcation' (1962: 256). In short, psychoanalysis has been and (at least as of 1974) remains Popper's prime illustration of the superiority of his falsifiability criterion. But if he were right that Freud's theory is untestable altogether, then it would clearly be pointless to inquire whether this theory has been or can be tested *clinically*. Popper's challenge must accordingly be dealt with from the outset. It turns out to be ironic that Popper should have chosen psychoanalytic theory as a prime illustration of his thesis that inductive confirmations can easily be found for nearly every theory if we look for them: it is precisely Freud's theory that furnishes compelling evidence against this caricature of the inductivist tradition (Grünbaum 1984: 280).

Popper is concerned to contrast the scientific status of modern physics with the non-scientific or pseudo-scientific character of psychoanalysis. He does so by claiming that the former is empirically falsifiable whereas the latter is not. But before he can say that potential negative findings can refute physical theories, Popper must make use of two important qualifications:

1 All reports of observations codifying contrary evidence in physics are fallible, if only because they themselves are already theory-laden; hence 'falsifications' are revokable.
2 'Disregarding the possibility of immunizing strategems' (Popper 1974, II: 1004), potential falsifying data do exist in physics. But because of this ever-present logical possibility of resorting to immunization, it would, in my view, have been preferable if Popper had used the term 'disconfirmability' rather than 'falsifiability' or 'refutability'. In discussing his views, I will use his locutions however.

It is important to note that, immediately after predicating the falsifiability of Newtonian physics upon 'disregarding' feasible immunizing strategies, Popper declares in the next sentence: 'And this is the heart of the matter, for my criticism of Freud's theory was that it simply does not have potential falsifiers' (1974, II: 1004). But what is sauce for the goose is, I submit, sauce for the gander. Accordingly, it is to be understood that when I claim that Freud's clinical theory *does* have potential falsifiers, I do so subject to the same two qualifications on which Popper relied in the case of physics.

Chapter 1 sets forth seven sets of grounds to refute Popper's charge that psychoanalytic theory is not falsifiable. This charge, I must emphasize, is logically independent of the sociological objection that Freudians are not responsive to criticism of their hypothesis. After all, a theory may well be invalidated by known evidence, even as its true believers refuse to acknowledge this refutation. That the recalcitrance of Freudians in the face of falsifying evidence, however scandalous, is not at all tantamount to the irrefutability of their theory should be especially evident from some of Popper's other doctrines. As he tells us, theories, on the one hand, and the intellectual conduct of their protagonists, on the other, 'belong to *two entirely different "worlds"*' (1974, I: 144; italics in original). Yet because Popper sometimes discusses them in the same breath, my response to his views on psychoanalysis takes both into account.

Foundations offers the following items in connection with the supposed unfalsifiability of Freudian theory: (1) examples of Freudian causal hypotheses that are demonstrably falsifiable and of predictions derivable from them that qualify as 'risky' by Popper's standards; (2) Popper's failure to furnish an actual proof of empirical irrefutability, with reliance instead on a contrived illustration of psychoanalytic explanation involving two men and a drowning child (1962: 35; 1974, II: 985); (3) Freud's own successive modifications of his evolving clinical theory (Fancher 1973; Sulloway 1979), conceptual changes that were neither immunizing manoeuvres nor capricious, but rather reactions to seemingly adverse findings; (4) Freud's explicit statement about the sort of evidence he would acknowledge as a refuting instance for his hypothesized aetiology of anxiety neurosis, as well as other documentation of sophisticated methodological tactics not vulnerable to Popper's wholesale criticism, even when Freud delayed for nearly a decade public acknowledgement of the 1897 collapse of his seduction theory of hysteria; (5) Popper's total neglect of Freud's 1937 'Constructions in Analysis' paper, which is addressed to the issue of evading clinical falsifications on the principle 'heads I win, tails you lose'.

Did Freud vindicate his method of clinical investigation?

Despite Freud's basic reliance on clinical testing, he did acknowledge the challenge that data from the couch may be unreliable, because they are influenced by patients' conformity to the doctor's self-fulfilling expectations. For example, the patient may obligingly produce a pseudo-memory that would lend spurious confirmation to the therapist's reconstruction of his patient's childhood. In this way, the doctor can regiment the 'memories' recovered by free association. Even friendly critics such as Wilhelm Fliess have charged that analysts induce their docile patients by suggestion to furnish the very responses needed to validate the psychoanalytic theory of personality (Freud 1954: 334–7). Freud himself deemed it necessary to counter decisively this serious charge of spurious clinical confirmation. For if the patient's responses are merely a result of brainwashing, then Freudian analysis might have beneficial emotional effects not because it allows the patient to acquire genuine self-knowledge, but because of suggestion operating as a placebo under the guise of non-directive therapy. (See also Rosenthal and Rubin 1978.)

Freud had actually provided fuel for such criticism. In order to overcome patients' fierce resistances to analysts' interpretations of their unconscious conflicts, he explained, analysts cannot rely on the patients' intellectual insight but must decisively enlist their need for their doctor's approval as a parental surrogate, the so-called positive 'transference' feelings (S.E. 1917, XVI: 445; 1919, XVII: 159). In fact, Freud himself points out that precisely this affectionate help-seeking subservience on the part of the patient 'clothes the doctor with authority and is transformed into belief in his communications and explanations' (S.E. 1971, XVI: 445). Thus, at the end of his 1917 lecture 'Transference', and much more fully in the crucial following one, 'Analytic Therapy', Freud squarely addressed the serious possibility that suggestion is the decisive agent in his therapy and, at the same time, the fatal flaw of the psychoanalytic method of investigation. As he put it there:

You asked me why we do not make use of direct suggestion in psychoanalytic therapy, when we admit that our influence rests essentially on transference [which amounts to the utilization of the patient's personal relationship to the analyst] – that is, on suggestion; and you added a doubt whether, in view of this predominance of suggestion, we are still able to claim that our psychological discoveries are objective [rather than self-fulfilling products of *unintentional* suggestion]. I promised I would give you a detailed reply.

(S.E. 1917, XVI: 448)

From the careful answer Freud goes on to give, I have teased out a central postulate on which he relies when it becomes one of the two premises of what I have dubbed his 'Tally Argument'. As I read this bold premise, it is a conjunction of the following two causally necessary conditions:

1 Only the psychoanalytic method of interpretation and treatment can yield or mediate for the patient correct insight into the unconscious causes of his neurosis.
2 The patient's correct insight into the conflictual cause of his condition and into the unconscious dynamics of his character is in turn causally necessary for the durable cure of his neurosis.

I refer to the conjunction of these two claims by Freud as his 'Necessary Condition Thesis' or, for brevity, 'NCT'. In view of its importance, I have also dubbed it 'Freud's Master Proposition' (Grünbaum 1983: 17). It is to be understood that Freud asserts it with respect to the 'psychoneuroses', as distinct from the so-called actual neuroses. A 'psychoneurosis' is a mental disorder caused by *repressed* infantile experiences, whereas the aetiologic factors in an 'actual' neurosis are external ones in an adult's current life situation.

Freud states his NCT more cryptically and immediately draws the corollary conclusion that the clinical data from successfully analysed patients are reliable after all:

After all, his conflicts will only be successfully solved and his resistances overcome if the anticipatory ideas [i.e. psychoanalytic interpretations] he is given tally with what is real in him. Whatever in the doctor's conjectures is inaccurate drops out in the course of the analysis [footnote omitted]; it has to be withdrawn and replaced by something more correct.

(S.E. 1917, XVI: 452)

More explicitly, if NCT is to be believed, the disclosure of the patient's hidden conflicts is indispensable to his cure and will occur only if incorrect analytic interpretations – spuriously confirmed by the patient's contaminated responses – have been discarded in favour of correct ones. Such interpretations will then presumably have derived from clinical data not distorted by the patient's compliance with his doctor's subtly communicated expectations. Though the data are initially contaminated by suggestion, they can be selectively sorted as they accumulate so as to discard the unreliable ones.

In short, Freud postulated his NCT, asserted that his therapy achieves genuine cures, and then went on to use these two risky claims to vouch for the trustworthiness (i.e. the reliability and validity) of clinical data from neurotic patients whose analyses had presumably been successful. In view of his use of the phrase 'tally with what is real', I have introduced the label 'Tally Argument' for the argument whose two premises I have just stated and whose conclusions I am developing. This designation has since been adopted by other writers.

Indeed, if one grants Freud the truth of his NCT, and the finding that there are successfully analysed ('cured') patients, then a whole series of major conclusions can be drawn. Each of these consequences, if true, contributes to answering the objection that suggestion contaminates clinical data and is the real cause of any therapeutic success.

These conclusions of the Tally Argument include:

1   If a patient has been cured, the causal interpretations his doctor gave him (at least in the later stages of the analysis) must have been correct or close to the mark. Hence the collective success of psychoanalytic treatment is evidence for the truth of the Freudian theory of personality, including the specific causes to which it attributes the psychoneuroses, and even its general hypotheses about psychosexual development. Furthermore Freudian analysis of the unconscious by means of free association is validated as an investigative method by its therapeutic success.

2   The clinical data furnished by successfully treated neurotics do not result from self-fulfilling predictions. The patient's assent to his analyst's interpretations is reliable and his own introspections can be believed, once his repressions no longer distort his outlook.

3   Only psychoanalytic treatment can produce genuine cures of

neuroses (S.E. 1917, XVI: 458), hence it can take credit for the recoveries of its patients without statistical comparisons with the results from untreated control groups or from controls treated by rival modalities (cf. S.E. 1917, XVI: 461–2).

Moreover, analytic therapy's successes are not placebo effects, for if NCT is to be believed, the working through of the patient's unconscious conflicts is the decisive therapeutic factor (although the analyst's role as a parent-surrogate serves as an icebreaker). Freud did recognize that the patient's so-called transference attachment to his doctor plays a catalytic role in the earlier stages of treatment (S.E. 1926, XX: 190). Yet he evidently singled out the patient's correct causal insight as the one quintessential ingredient 'which distinguishes [the therapeutic dynamics of] analytic treatment from any kind of treatment by suggestion' (S.E. 1914, XII: 155–6; cf. also 1917, XVI: 450–2).

As long as Freud believed in the validity of his NCT and the genuineness of his cures, he could have confidence in the three theses just formulated. The NCT, however, still requires successful treatment outcomes in order to be interpreted as a justification for making causal inferences on the basis of free associations. Thus, in Freud's Tally Argument, therapeutic success was needed to justify even those hypotheses that, by themselves, pertain neither to the dynamics (causal factors) nor to the outcome of psychoanalytic treatment.

Given that the empirical tenability of the NCT premise is the pivot on which the Tally Argument turns, what clues does Freud give us as to the evidence that prompted him to hold this premise until at least 1917? Apparently, he felt driven to postulate it to account for the observed patterns of failure and success in treatment. Before a decade had elapsed, however, even Freud's own evidence conflicted with the claim that the cure of a neurosis depends on the patient's correct insight into its causes. Thus, by 1926, he conceded that his type of treatment was not indispensable and merely expedited recoveries that were in the offing anyway (S.E. 1926, XX: 154). The possibility of such spontaneous remission contradicts NCT, which can then no longer be used to justify counting even spectacular therapeutic successes as support for causal inferences.

Then in 1937 Freud went on to report that a satisfactory psychoanalysis will not even prevent the recurrence of the problem for which the patient was treated, let alone immunize him against the outbreak of a different one (S.E. 1937, XXIII: 216–53). Thus, far from holding out hope for cures, Freud essentially confined the prospects of psychoanalysis to palliation.

Evidently, far from continuing to claim that there was empirical support for the two premises of his Tally Argument in his later years, Freud himself gradually renounced or significantly weakened both of them.

As if this were not enough, in recent decades, in comparative studies of treatment outcome from rival therapies, psychoanalytically orientated psychotherapy has not been found to be superior to any of the other therapies that exceed the spontaneous remission rate for untreated controls. Adequate comparative studies for long-term psychoanalysis still remain to be carried out, but it is not a promising sign that recent comparative investigations of psychotherapy do not find professional psychotherapy superior to treatments designed to be placebos (Prioleau, Murdock and Brody 1983). These results cast some further doubt on NCT, which implies that only analytic therapy can cause genuine cures of neuroses.

Yet if analytic treatment is not superior to its rivals in the pertinent diagnostic categories, it becomes quite reasonable – though not compelling – to interpret its therapeutic achievements as placebo effects. If so, any success of psychoanalysis is not produced by the patient's acquiring self-knowledge after all. In this vein, Jerome Frank (1973) has contended that both analysts and their rivals heal neurotics by being supportive, not by uncovering their repressions. Indeed Frank's hypothesis even allows rival therapies to have differential efficacy through different degrees of placebo effect. To be sure, it is still arguable that improvements after psychoanalytic treatment are not placebo effects. But because, as some noted analysts have conceded, 'all-pervading' improvements or even cures can be produced by rival treatments such as behaviour therapy, and also by extraclinical life events (Malan 1976: 172–3, 269, 147), Freud's NCT has become untenable.

The collapse of the NCT completely undercuts the pivotal therapeutic argument given by the mature Freud for the evidential value of the clinical data generated by the psychoanalytic method. As chapter 10 shows, without the Tally Argument, Freud's appeal to cross-corroboration by converging clinical findings fails, because each corroborating piece is secured by the free-association method whose validity is in question. Moreover, no empirically viable substitute for the NCT capable of supporting Freud's conclusions seems to be in sight. Without a substitute for the NCT there appears to be no way to free clinical data from the possibility of contamination by suggestion. Yet after Freud gave up the NCT, he seems to have forgotten that this left the evidential value of clinical data in serious doubt, and he continued to rest his case on clinical findings (S.E. 1926, XX: 254; 1917, XVI: 255).

The emphasis in Part I was on Freud's unsuccessful effort to neutralize doubts about the evidential value of clinical data. Part II shows that even if clinical evidence could be taken at face value, Freud's principal clinical arguments for his entire cornerstone theory of repression still turn out to be fundamentally flawed.

THE CORNERSTONE OF THE PSYCHOANALYTIC EDIFICE: IS THE FREUDIAN THEORY OF REPRESSION WELL-FOUNDED? (PART II)

In Part I, the focus was on Freud's appeal to therapeutic success as his evidence for claiming that his clinical method did not lead merely to self-fulfilling predications. Freud relied on therapeutic success, however, not only to validate (via the NCT) the data obtained by free association, but also as a basis for inferring the causal hypotheses of his theory of psychopathology in the first place. In 1926 he wrote that evidence of therapeutic gain was from the start intrinsic to the clinical validation of the psychoanalytic theory of the unconscious: 'In psycho-analysis there has existed from the very first an inseparable bond between cure and research' (S.E. 1926, XX: 256). Indeed, we shall now see that, in the cathartic method, the dependence of the causal inferences on treatment outcome was crucial: it was therapeutic success that enabled Breuer and Freud to conclude that repressed traumatic experience was necessary to cause hysteria.

Thus, psychoanalytic causal hypotheses that do not themselves pertain either to the dynamics or the outcome of analytic therapy (e.g. the trauma theory of hysteria) have none the less been parasitic on therapeutic results, since Freud used such results partly to validate making inferences from clinical data at all, and partly to guide and support the specific inferences themselves.

Appraisal of Freud's arguments for the repression aetiology of the psychoneuroses

The causal and explanatory significance of unconscious processes in psychoanalytic theory rests on two fundamental inductive inferences. These were made by Freud in collaboration with his senior mentor Josef Breuer. As we are told in their joint 'Preliminary Communication' of 1893 (S.E. 1893, II: 6–7), they began with an observation after having treated hysterical patients cathartically with hypnosis. In the course of the treatment it had turned out that, for each symptom, the victim had repressed the memory of a trauma that had closely preceded its onset and was somehow thematically connected to it (see 'thematic affinity fallacy' in the earlier section on Ricoeur). For example, Breuer's pioneering patient Anna O., who had a phobia for drinking liquids, had repressed the sight of a dog drinking water from a friend's glass, which had disgusted her. Besides repressing this traumatic memory, the patient had also suppressed the affect induced by the trauma. In the case of each symptom, our two therapists tried to lift the repression of the trauma and to release the pent-up affect. When their technique succeeded in both respects, they observed a dramatic (and apparently permanent) disappearance of the symptom.

Impressed by this outcome, Breuer and Freud formulated their first major causal hypothesis: the improvements observed after treatment were caused by the cathartic lifting of the repressions. But before the founders of psychoanalysis attributed the improvement to the lifting of the repression, they had considered the rival hypothesis that it was actually caused by the patient's expectations of relief from his symptom rather than by his achieving insight into his repression. In this perspective, the search for insight is only a treatment ritual serving to strengthen the patient's therapeutic expectations. Breuer and Freud believed they could rule out this rival hypothesis, which I call 'the hypothesis of *placebo effect*' (Grünbaum 1981; 1986).

Breuer and Freud pointed out that symptoms had been removed, one at a time, such that any one symptom disappeared only after the lifting of a particular repression (S.E. 1893, II: 7). I suggest, however, that even such separate symptom removals need not be caused by the lifting of repressions; instead, they may be placebo effects after all, generated by the patient's awareness that the therapist was trying to uncover an episode thematically connected to the symptom. Thus, it was presumably communicated to the patient that his doctor believed that recalling the episode might help to eliminate the symptom. Breuer and Freud do not tell us why the likelihood of a placebo effect is lower when several symptoms are wiped out than when only one symptom is involved. As evidence against the placebo hypothesis it would have been essential to compare treatment outcome with the results from a suitable control group whose repressions were not lifted. If that control group fared equally well therapeutically, treatment gains from psychoanalysis would then presumably be placebo effects, because they would not have been caused specifically by psychoanalytic insight. Hence there existed no adequate evidence that lifting repressions caused symptoms to disappear.

Yet Breuer and Freud did believe at the time that their therapeutic results had ruled out the placebo hypothesis and they accordingly attributed the gains made by their hysterics to the resurrection of buried painful memories. They also thought that this hypothesized process of producing therapeutic success was evidence that an original act of repression was necessary to cause the neurosis, and continuing repression was necessary to maintain it. It then followed that the removal of the repression would eliminate the neurosis.

Notice that the improvement itself was not what justified inferring that repression had caused the symptom: it was the causal attribution of the improvement to the lifting of the repression. Thus, without relying on what they assumed to be the causal dynamics that produced their therapeutic results, Breuer and Freud could never have interpreted these clinical data as evidence that repression was a cause of hysteria. Yet even if the therapeutic gains had been caused by lifting repressions, there would only be grounds for attributing the maintenance of the symptoms to those repressions, not their initial formation. Moreover, this conclusion still requires the qualification that either the cognitive repression or the affective suppression of a trauma is the required cause (Grünbaum 1984: 180–1).

Freud soon replaced Breuer's hypnotic technique by free association, believing that the new method retrieved repressed traumatic experiences, and concluding that free associations not only recover repressed memories, but can establish that the repression of the latter caused the neurosis in question. In this way, Freud elevated free association to the status of a specific causal litmus test: there was no other justification. In other words, the hypothesis that therapeutic success is caused by the removal of repressions is to this day the sole justification for assuming that free associations show repressions to be causes; hence there is nothing left when Freudians disclaim the therapeutic efficacy of their treatment.

Soon after Freud began to practise without Breuer, it became evident that they had been too hasty in rejecting the rival hypothesis of placebo effect. The remissions achieved by further patients Freud himself treated cathartically did not turn out to be durable. The pattern of relapses, additional treatment, temporary remissions and further relapses made it doubtful that removing the repressions of adult traumas was therapeutically effective. Freud began to be haunted by the triumph of the placebo hypothesis over his (and Breuer's) therapeutic hypothesis. As he recognized, the vicissitudes of his personal relations to the patient were highly correlated with the pattern of symptom relapses and intermittent remissions. In his own view, this correlation 'proved that the personal emotional relation between doctor and patient was after all stronger than the whole cathartic process' (S.E. 1925, XX: 27). But without the therapeutic support for the causal role of repression, the very cornerstone of psychoanalysis was completely undermined. Hence, at that point, the new clinical psychoanalytic structure tumbled down and lay in shambles. So also did free association as a method of establishing causation.

None the less, Freud was undaunted. He took courage, because he thought that, in a new sexual version, the aetiologic repression hypothesis could be rehabilitated on secure therapeutic foundations after all. The elimination of adult repressions had been a therapeutic failure. He conjectured, however, that uncovering much earlier childhood repressions with sexual content might eliminate hysteria, and he hypothesized that the patient's free associations would indicate an early sexual repression as the cause of hysteria (S.E. 1896, III: 194–9). As he reports, the very early repressions that then emerged had sexual themes.

Freud now rejected the placebo hypothesis by invoking NCT, as we saw. But, as the summary of chapter 2 made clear ('Did Freud vindicate his method of clinical investigation'), his attempt to provide therapeutic support for the new childhood sexual hypothesis in 1917 fared no better empirically than his and Breuer's original appeal to cathartic success in the mid-1890s. (Freud had disavowed Breuer's non-sexual aetiologic hypotheses as clinically dubious in 1896.) Nor has there been any other therapeutic validation.

Let me caution against a possible serious misunderstanding, however. Like Freud, the vast majority of his followers continue to maintain that free associations are crucial for the validation of both their aetiologic hypotheses about the causes of neuroses and the psychoanalytic theory of dreams and slips. These advocates cannot dispense with a therapeutic foundation. For my own part, however, I find it unwarranted to use free association to validate causal inferences. I therefore see no reason to assign any privileged role to therapeutic results among possible tests of psychoanalytic hypotheses. For example, Freud's 1915 theory of paranoia could be tested epidemiologically without any recourse to therapeutic data.

Freud did not limit his reliance on free association to research on the causes of neurotic symptoms. When he found that his patients reported their dreams while free associating to their neurotic symptoms, he concluded that 'manifest' dream contents are produced very much the way neurotic symptoms are (S.E. 1900, IV: 101). He saw such symptoms as vicarious gratifications and outlets, or 'compromises between the demands of a repressed impulse and the resistance of a censoring force in the ego' (S.E. 1925, XX: 45). Thus, he made the extrapolation that repression is causally necessary for both neurotic symptoms and dream production. He accordingly enlarged the scope of the free-association method from research on the causes of neurosis (aimed at therapy) to research on the unconscious causes of dreaming (S.E. 1900, IV: 101, V: 528).

The extrapolation was also extended, *mutatis mutandis*, to slips and bungled actions. Here too Freud used free association not merely heuristically, as a means of generating causal explanations of slips, but also as a basis for validating the explanatory hypotheses. For example, he conceived of a slip of the tongue as a compromise between a repressed motive that crops up in the form of a disturbance, on the one hand, and the conscious intention to make a certain utterance, on the other.

The theoretical extrapolation to dreams and slips of course inherited the problem of the original theory of neurotic symptoms, namely, the collapse of the therapeutic support. But even if that support had actually turned out to be empirically viable, the extrapolations would have been unjustified because they lacked any therapeutic base or other supporting evidence of their own. Freud provided no evidence that the permanent lifting of a repression to which he had attributed a slip would be 'therapeutic' in the sense of enabling the person to correct the slip or to avoid repeating it. Thus the two extrapolations had no independent support.

Chapter 3 concludes with an important caveat. Plainly, the very occurrence of repression – in the psychoanalytic sense of banishing a thought from consciousness or denying it entry (S.E. 1915, XIV: 147) – is a necessary condition for the causal role that Freud attributed to it. If repression does not even exist, it can hardly cause other phenomena. Yet it must not be overlooked that the mere existence of repression as a psychological phenomenon (which was conjectured before Freud by Herbart and Schopenhauer) is not sufficient to demonstrate that it causes neurotic symptoms, dreams, or slips.

Paul Kline (1981: 196, 208, 436), Seymour Fisher (1982: 680), as well as others (Erdelyi and Goldberg 1979), gloss over the large gap between merely showing that repression exists and providing evidence that it has the causal role that Freud attributed to it. These investigators use the phrase 'theory of repression' in a highly ambiguous way. It can denote either the hypothesis of bare existence or the far stronger assertion of a multiple causal role.

Examination of the psychoanalytic theory of slips – of memory, tongue, ear and pen

Freud referred to slips generically in German as *Fehlleistungen*, which means 'misbegotten performances' or 'bungled actions'. His translator James Strachey coined the neologism 'parapraxes' to render the German term. The category 'slips' does not include every failure of memory, speech or action, however. It is restricted to errors one does not make normally or habitually.

There are two necessary conditions that must be fulfilled by any slip if it is also to qualify as a Freudian slip in the technical, rather than the colloquial, sense. As Freud tells us: 'If we perceive the parapraxis at all, we must not be aware in ourselves of any motive for it. We must rather be tempted to explain it by "inattentiveness," or to put it down to "chance"' (S.E. 1901, VI: 239). A further necessary condition is that the slip be caused by a repression in the sense of being a compromise, resulting from the conflict between a repressed motive and a conscious intention. Typically, the repressed motive is one of so-called 'unpleasure' (Strachey's translation of *Unlust*) such as pain, distress, aversion or moral censorship. Thus, Freud's theory explains slips 'in which the parapraxis produces nothing that has any sense of its own' for either the subject who commits the slip or for others (S.E. 1916, XV: 41). Plainly, slips resulting from conscious or 'preconscious' motives are not Freudian, though Freud does give examples of them for the purpose of comparison (S.E. 1916, XV: 40–55).

The mere statement of what is meant by the term 'Freudian slip' does not entail that there do exist slips with the requisite property of being caused by a repressed motive and being laden with some negative affect. The burden of the psychoanalytic theory of parapraxes is to furnish evidence that there actually are such slips. My main aim here is to examine whether Freud's arguments were able to show this.

A certain memory lapse in the recitation of a Latin quotation is cited in the psychoanalytic literature as a typical example of a Freudian slip. A young man forgot the Latin word *aliquis* ('someone') in his recitation of a line from Virgil's *Aeneid*. The full line reads: 'Exoriare aliquis nostris ex ossibus ultor' ('Would that someone arise from our bones as an avenger'). The young man, an Austrian Jew – hereafter 'AJ' – used the passage to convey his resentment of religious discrimination against him. Freud supplied the missing word. Then AJ's association issuing from this word – interspersed with some of Freud's interjections – revealed, in due course, that he had harboured a repressed fear. He suspected that an Italian girlfriend had become pregnant by him. Freud then informed him that this repressed anxiety had 'undeniably' produced his *aliquis* lapse, whereas the subject was doubtful that his worry – though genuine – had had any causal bearing on his forgetting. Freud was convinced that AJ's repressed wish not to have any progeny from his sexual liaison had interfered with his Latin rendition of his desire to have descendants who would avenge the adversity suffered by the Jews.

In a detailed examination of the *aliquis* slip, I argue that far from furnishing evidence for the existence of *bona fide* Freudian slips, it serves to exhibit the weakness of the empirical basis of the psychoanalytic repression model of parapraxes. The grounds for this unfavourable conclusion include the following: there is no justification for drawing a *causal* connection between the fear of pregnancy and the memory lapse merely on the basis of the *thematic* connection between the content of the repressed wish and the desire expressed by the Latin phrase. As argued earlier, thematic affinity alone is not evidence for a causal connection; there is need for further evidence that a thematically connected repression actually caused the memory lapse. Moreover, in typical parapraxes, the thematic affinity is considerably more tenous than in the *aliquis* example. In fact, it is always possible to find *some* thematic thread, however far-fetched, connecting any given lapse to some repression or other. Thus, even if *strong* thematic affinity alone did implicate a repressed cause, it would not be present in typical parapraxes. The *aliquis* example is not representative.

Doubts about whether a given repression is really the cause of a slip cannot be countered by pointing, as Freud did (S.E. 1916, XV: 50), to the introspective confirmation of the subject who made the slip. Even if the person who 'slipped' were not under the suggestive, intimidating influence of the analyst, how could he possibly know any better than the rest of us that the unconscious fear in question had actually caused his slip? The case against Freud's appeal to introspective confirmation is well supported. There is substantial experimental evidence from cognitive psychology that subjects do not have knowledge of the causes of their own behaviour (Nisbett and Ross 1980).

The important conclusion is this: if any slips are actually caused by repressions, Freud gives us no good reason to think that his clinical methods could identify and empirically confirm their causes as such, no matter how interesting the elicited 'free' associations might otherwise be. This conclusion seems unavoidable, even if one were to grant that the analyst does not influence the subject's 'free' associations to the content of a slip. (The experimental psychologist Motley (1980) claims to have found experimental support for the psychoanalytic theory of speech errors. I argue that his ingenious experiments, valuable though they are, do not provide evidence for or against the Freudian theory of slips of the tongue.)

Thus far it has been granted, for argument's sake, that the analyst does not influence the patient's free associations, but in the remainder of this chapter, several sorts of questions are raised. Does free association indeed bring out repressed wishes, or anger, guilt, fear, and so on, without contamination by other influences? If unconscious thoughts surface, by what criteria does the analyst decide when, during the investigation of parapraxes and dreams, to call a halt to the flow of associations? Presumably if the intelligent and imaginative patient is permitted to free associate in this way long enough, his unfettered ruminations will in due course yield almost any kind of thematic content of which he had (at least recently) not been conscious: thoughts about death, God, and indeed cabbages and kings. But, if so, how does the analyst avoid a selection bias in the face of the thematic variety of the associations, particularly since imposing some limit on duration is unavoidable?

One of the answers is drawn from writings of the analyst Judd Marmor (1970), who summarizes experimental studies indicating how compliant patients are, even under free association, and how they thereby render clinical hypotheses self-fulfilling.

Chapter 4 concludes with a discussion of how some analysts coax their patients to fulfil prior theoretical expectations (e.g. penis envy in women), whereas other analysts deplore this practice without providing a recipe for successfully avoiding it.

Repressed infantile wishes as instigators of all dreams: critical scrutiny of the compromise model of manifest dream content

In 1895, Freud had a dream – the 'Irma Injection Dream' (S.E. 1950, I: 340–2) – which was destined to become *the* 'Specimen Dream' of his clinical theory (S.E. 1900, IV: ch. 2). It was his attempt to interpret the Irma dream which begat a 'eureka' experience yielding the 'secret' of all dream formation (Freud 1954: 322): The dream 'content was the fulfilment of a wish and its motive was a wish' (S.E. 1900, IV: 119; italics omitted).

In his 1895 'Project', Freud proposed a neurological rationale for the 'secret'. That neurobiological account, and its clinical notion of wish-fulfilment, have been challenged by Hobson and McCarley in two influential papers (Hobson and McCarley 1977, McCarley and Hobson 1977). As they point out, during the past 80 years various findings have undermined the concepts of neuronal function and of the energy economy of the brain out of which Freud's account was built. They conclude that recent neurophysiological findings have largely supplanted Freud's psychological theory of dreaming as wish-fulfilment by providing a better explanation of dream production. Yet they do not claim to have refuted the purely psychological aspect of the theory.

Chapter 5 critically analyses Freud's psychological theory of dreams with reference to his treatment of the Irma dream. His argument was that, in the case of Irma, free association yields wish motives that, from the viewpoint of commonsense psychology, have clearly given rise to that particular dream. Freud is then prepared to base his general theory of dreams as wish-fulfilments on the results from the method that he claims to have validated by his analysis of Irma (S.E. 1900, IV: 121). I argue, however, that Irma fails to validate Freud's method of dream interpretation or to support the hypothesis that repressed infantile wishes cause dreams.

Though touted as 'the dream specimen of psychoanalysis' (Erikson 1954), Irma no more qualifies as a paradigm for Freud's theory of dreams than the *aliquis* slip does for his theory of parapraxes. First, in this dream analysis, free association does not play the role it is claimed to play in revealing repressions. Moreover, Irma does not illustrate the causal role of a repressed wish (infantile or otherwise). At best, the Irma dream is a pedagogical preparation for psychoanalytic dream theory, rather than a representative specimen. At worst, it is a piece of salesmanship, offering a snare and a delusion to the unwary. Erikson's (1954) attempt to give Irma the infantile motivational underpinning required by orthodox doctrine does nothing to alter this verdict.

The chapter's main findings are that Freud's theory of dreams is at best ill-founded and that there are even two independent clinical arguments implying that it is false.

Appraisal of Freud's further arguments for the emergence of unadulterated repressions under 'free' association

The doubts that have been raised so far concerning the psychoanalytic accounts of slips and dreams include the failure of free association to ensure that repressed ideation emerges without contamination by suggestion. Always mindful of this problem, Freud kept offering further reasons for his belief that free association 'guarantees to a great extent that . . . nothing will be introduced into it by the expectations of the analyst' (S.E. 1925, XX: 41). In this vein, he assures us of the analyst's ability to distinguish the patient's *bona fide* memories from imagined ones: 'Any danger of falsifying the products of the patient's memory by suggestion can be avoided by prudent handling of the technique; but in general the arousing of resistances is a guarantee against the misleading effects of suggestive influence' (S.E. 1923, XVIII: 25). This is the myth that analytic interpretations are non-directive and that analysts are mere catalysts for the emergence of uncontaminated repressions.

There is empirical evidence against the view that psychoanalytic treatment is a valid means of gaining access to memories. Loftus (1980) has shown that (1) human memory is to a remarkable extent malleable (as illustrated by a pseudo-memory from Jean Piaget's early life); (2) there is considerable interpolation, reconstruction and distortion of memories by theoretical beliefs or expectations; and (3) under the influence of leading questions, there is a strong tendency to fill memory gaps with confabulated material.

Non-veridical memories seem to be most likely with just those responses that are supposed to lay bare repressions and disguised defences after resistances have been overcome. Yet Freud particularly emphasized such data in the validation of his theory of repression. To say that the contamination of clinical data cannot be eliminated without recourse to extraclinical findings is not, of course, to say that every analytic interpretation to which a patient agrees under the influence of the analyst is false. However, in the analytic setting one cannot identify which clinical data are valid.

Remarks on post-Freudian defences of the fundamental tenets of psychoanalysis

Is the present critique of the basic pillars of psychoanalysis anachronistic? Does it not focus on Freud's reasoning while disregarding the specific modifications and elaborations by those post-Freudians whose doctrines are recognizably psychoanalytic (in content rather than only in name)? The answer is that the unfavourable conclusions of Parts I and II are just as applicable to the currently fashionable revisionist versions of psychoanalysis that go under the names of Kohutian 'self-psychology' and of 'object relations theory'. Insofar as these post-Freudian theories are indeed psychoanalytic, they do subscribe to some version of the theory of repression. They also rely on free association to find the unconcious causes of behaviour, using the lifting of repressions as one means of therapy (Eagle 1983).

How, for example, can Kohut claim stronger clinical validation for his pre-Oedipal variety of unconscious cause than Freud can for the sexual ones? Eagle (1983; 1984) has argued that the causal and therapeutic claims of self-psychology and of object relations theory rest on even more dubious bases than do Freud's corresponding hypotheses. Hence the neorevisionist work does not answer the objections I have raised against orthodox psychoanalysis.

Can the repression aetiology of psychoneurosis be tested retrospectively?

As noted previously, Freud's clinical support for his causal inferences was ultimately predicated on therapeutic achievements. Hence one could by now ask impatiently: why could Freud not dispense with therapeutic arguments altogether and rely instead on other sorts of clinical evidence (see note 1) to provide support for his theory of psychopathology? Chapter 8 of *Foundations*, by considering Clark Glymour's account (1980) of testability on the couch, develops the reply that such attempts have been just as unsuccessful as therapeutic validation. I will summarize only one of several reasons given in *Foundations* for this conclusion.

Freud conjectured that the development of a neurosis N depends not only on an individual's exposure to pathogenic experiences P, but also on his hereditary vulnerability: P is necessary but not sufficient to cause N. One can hence retrodict that anyone afflicted with N has suffered P. It has been suggested that in Freud's Rat Man case, for example, clinical evidence would have supported this causal necessity hypothesis by confirming the occurrence of the retrodicted childhood experience P (Glymour 1980: 272).

Suppose for argument's sake that in his analysis the Rat Man had reported remembering the traumatic sexual event retrodicted by Freud. Assume further that one can trust so early a memory under the suggestive conditions of an analysis. It is then evident that confirming the prior occurrence of the trauma does not show that it was a cause of the Rat Man's obsessions. Surely the mere fact that an event is traumatic does not indicate a causal role in a neurosis. The human condition would be much worse than it already is if every psychic blow gave rise to a neurosis. Yet prominent psychoanalysts have reasoned that the causal relevance of P to N is supported by the mere fact that those who are beset by N and suffered P fit Freud's retrodiction (Waelder 1962: 625–6). Such an inference is no better than *post hoc ergo propter hoc*.

Two results emerge: firstly, the analytic setting appears unable to yield evidence to support the inference that the retrodicted P was a cause of N; and secondly its retrospective methods cannot even verify that P occurred.

To my knowledge, apart from the sorts of arguments I have examined, there is no other clinical support (either therapeutic or non-therapeutic) for Freud's theory of sexual repression as the cause of the neuroses. I conclude that the sexual version of Freud's theory of psychopathology has no more clinial support than Breuer's non-sexual version.

EPILOGUE (PART III)

The method of free association and the future appraisal of psychoanalysis

In chapter 9 I welcome the analyst Eissler's (1969) refreshing anticipation of the conclusion that the future validation or disconfirmation of Freudian theory will come largely from extraclinical findings. However, despite his suggestion that we expand the investigative horizons of Freud's theory well beyond the clinical setting, the lesson that Eissler derives from the limitations of clinical findings does not go nearly far enough. Accepting the validity of Freud's method of free association, he glosses over the serious problems of clinical testing set forth in my chapters 2–8.

Critique of Freud's final defence of the probative value of data from the couch: the pseudo-convergence of clinical findings

As noted at the end of the summary of chapter 1 (apropos of Popper), in a very late paper (S.E. 1937, XXIII: 257–69), Freud claims that psychoanalytic interpretations do not rely on 'heads I win, tails you lose' to evade falsification *nolens volens*. He argues that the analyst's response to the patient's assent and dissent does not invariable twist the patient's remarks into a confirmation (p. 262).

Freud appeals to converging evidence, contending that other clinical data can cross-validate a patient's acceptance or rejection of his analyst's interpretations. All clinical evidence, however, whether corroborative or not, is suspect, because it all depends on the method of free association with its potential suggestive effects.

Three major conclusions emerge from the appraisals I have given in *Foundations*:

1 Insofar as the evidence for the psychoanalytic corpus depends on data from the treatment setting, this support is remarkably weak.
2 In view of the methodological shortcomings of clinical psychoanalytic inquiry, a proper test of Freud's central hypotheses calls

for well-designed extraclinical studies, either epidemiologic or experimental (Eysenck and Wilson 1973; Kline 1981; Masling 1983). For the most part, such studies have yet to be performed.

3 Despite the poverty of the clinical support, it could still conceivably turn out that Freud's brilliant theoretical imagination was actually serendipitously right in some respects. But whereas psychoanalysis may thus be said to be scientifically alive, it is currently hardly well, at least insofar as its clinical foundations are concerned. Nor are the experimental findings I mention in chapter 3 (pp. 188–9), chapter 4 (pp. 202–5), chapter 5 (pp. 217–19), and chapter 9 (p. 270) favourable.

Coda on exegetical myth-making in Karl Popper's indictment of the clinical validation of psychoanalysis)

The inductivist methodology I used to assess Freud's causal hypotheses is the modern version of the centuries-old tradition going back to F. Bacon and J. S. Mill. On this basis, chapters 1–10 reached a rather negative conclusion about the clinical evidence for the theory of repression, and even about clinical testability in general. As is now clear, the clinical validation of psychoanalysis would be no more acceptable to a traditional inductivist (like Bacon or Mill) than to Popper (1962: 38, fn. 3). Hence, the specifically clinical support claimed by many Freudians, but rejected by inductivism, can no longer be used as a basis for Popper's charge that an inductivist criterion of demarcation between science and non-science is too permissive. Since psychoanalysis is in fact falsifiable, Popper cannot use Freud's theory to strengthen the case for his criterion of demarcation. Finally, his astonishing omission of Freud's reference to the Tally Argument from a key passage in his critique makes Popper's account of Freud rather unfair and misleading.

NOTE

1 Note that clinical arguments rest on data that are 'clinical' only in the following technical sense: clinical data are data obtained from the psychoanalytic treatment-setting through the analyst's observations of what the patient says and does. The results of research conducted outside psychoanalytic sessions – such as those of epidemiologic or experimental studies – are called extraclinical data.

REFERENCES

Brenner, C. 1982: *The Mind in Conflict*. International Universities Press.
Eagle, M. 1983: The epistemological status of recent developments in psychoanalytic theory, in R. S. Cohen and L. Laudan (eds), *Physics, Philosophy and Psychoanalysis*. Reidel.
Eagle, M. 1984: Psychoanalysis and modern psychodynamic theories, in N. S. Endler and J. McV. Hunt (eds), *Personality and the Behaviour Disorders*. Wiley.
Eissler, K. 1969: Irreverent remarks about the present and the future of psychoanalysis. *International Journal of Psycho Analysis*, 50, 461–71.
Erdelyi, M. H. and Goldberg, B. 1979: Let's not sweep repression under the rug: toward a cognitive psychology of repression, in J. J. Kihlstrom and F. J. Evans (eds), *Functional Disorders of Memory*. Erlbaum Associates.
Erikson, E. H. 1954: The dream specimen of psychoanalysis. *Journal of the American Psychoanalytic Association*, 2, 5–56.
Eysenck, H. 1963: *Uses and Abuses of Psychology*. Penguin.
Eysenck, H. and Wilson, G. D. 1973: *The Experimental Study of Freudian Theories*. Methuen.
Fancher, R. E. 1973: *Psychoanalytic Psychology*. W. W. Norton.
Fisher, S. 1982: The scientific vitality of Freud's theories. *Contemporary Psychology*, 27, 680–1.
Frank, J. 1973: *Persuasion and Healing*, rev. edn. Johns Hopkins University Press.
Freud, S. 1954: *The Origins of Psychoanalysis*. Basic Books.
Glymour, C. 1980: *Theory and Evidence*. Princeton University Press.
Grünbaum, A. 1981: The placebo concept. *Behaviour Research and Therapy*, 19, 157–67.
Grünbaum, A. 1983: Freud's theory: the perspective of a philosopher of science. 1982 Presidential Address to the American Philosophical Association (Eastern Division). *Proceedings and Addresses of the American Philosophical Association*, 57, 5–31.
Grünbaum, A. 1984: *The Foundations of Psychoanalysis: A Philosophical Critique*. University of California Press.
Grünbaum, A. 1986: The placebo concept in medicine and psychiatry. *Psychological Medicine*, 16, 19–38.
Habermas, J. 1970: *Zur Logik der Sozialwissenschaften*. Suhrkamp Verlag.
Habermas, J. 1971: *Knowledge and Human Interests*. Translated by J. J. Shapiro. Beacon Press.
Habermas, J. 1973: *Theory and Practice*. Beacon Press.
Hanson, N. R. 1958: *Patterns of Discovery*. Cambridge University Press.
Hobson, J. A. and McCarley, R. W. 1977: The brain as a dream state generator: an activation-synthesis hypothesis of the dream process. *American Journal of Psychiatry*, 134, 1335–48.

32 Adolf Grünbaum

Klein, G. S. 1976: *Psychoanalytic Theory*. International Universities Press.

Kline, P. 1972: *Fact and Fantasy in Freudian Theory*, 1st edn. Methuen.

Kline, P. 1981: *Fact and Fantasy in Freudian Theory*, 2nd edn. Methuen

Loftus, E. 1980: *Memory*. Addison-Wesley.

Malan, D. H. 1976: *Toward the Validation of Dynamic Psychotherapy*. Plenum Press.

Marmor, J. 1968: New directions in psychoanalytic theory and therapy, in J. Marmor (ed.), *Modern Psychoanalysis: New Directions and Perspectives*. Basic Books.

Marmor, J. 1970: Limitations of free association. *Archives of General Psychiatry*, 22, 160–5.

Masling, J. 1983: *Empirical Studies of Psychoanalytical Theories*, vol. 1. Analytic Press.

McCarley, R. W. and Hobson, J. A. 1977: The neurobiological origins of psychoanalytic dream theory. *American Journal of Psychiatry*, 134, 1211–21.

Motley, M. T. 1980: Verification of 'Freudian slips' and semantic prearticulatory editing via laboratory-induced spoonerisms, in V. A. Fromkin (ed.), *Errors in Linguistic Performance: Slips of the Tongue, Ear, Pen, and Hand*. Academic Press.

Nisbett, R. E. and Ross, L. 1980: *Human Inference: Strategies and Shortcomings of Social Judgment*. Prentice Hall.

Popper, K. 1959: *The Logic of Scientific Discovery*. Hutchinson.

Popper, K. 1962: *Conjectures and Refutations*, Basic Books.

Popper, K. 1974: Replies to my critics, in P. A. Schilpp (ed.), *The Philosophy of Karl Popper*, Books I and II. Open Court.

Popper, K. 1983: *Realism and the Aim of Science*, ed. W. W. Bartley, III. Rowman & Littlefield.

Prioleau, L., Murdock, M. and Brody, N. 1983: An analysis of psychotherapy versus placebo. *Behavioural and Brain Sciences*, 6, 275–85.

Ricoeur, P. 1970: *Freud and Philosophy*. Yale University Press.

Ricoeur, P. 1974: *The Conflict of Interpretation*, ed. D. Ihde. Northwestern University Press.

Ricoeur, P. 1981: *Hermeneutics and the Human Sciences*, ed. J. B. Thompson. Cambridge University Press.

Rosenthal, R. and Rubin, D. B. 1978: Interpersonal expectancy effects. *Behavioral and Brain Sciences*, 1, 3.

Schafer, R. 1976: *A New Language for Psychoanalysis*. Yale University Press.

Schafer, R. 1980: Narration in the psychoanalytic dialogue. *Critical Inquiry*, 12, 29–53.

Sellars, W. 1961: The language of theories, in H. Feigl and G. Maxwell (eds), *Current Issues in the Philosophy of Science*. Holt, Rinehart & Winston.

Sulloway, F. 1979: *Freud: Biologist of the Mind*. Basic Books.

Waelder, R. 1962: Review of *Psychoanalysis, Scientific Method and Philosophy*, ed. S. Hook. *Journal of the American Psychoanalytic Association*, 10, 617–37.

2

Epistemology and Depth Psychology: Critical Notes on *The Foundations of Psychoanalysis*

JIM HOPKINS

Adolf Grünbaum's recent work is widely acknowledged as a significant contribution to understanding and assessing Freud.[1] His argument – dense and complex, but logical and forceful – combines the methodological perspective and sophistication of a leading philosopher of science with intelligent and thorough attention to Freud's text and the related literature.

As well as recognition such work merits criticism, and I concentrate on this below. I hope this focus will not obscure my appreciation of the high standards of Grünbaum's argumentation, nor my admiration for his willingness and ability to engage the full range and complexity of Freud's thought with rigour and scholarship. In this field, as Grünbaum's own discussion of the literature points up, such qualities are rare.

I

Grünbaum seeks to assess the 'epistemologic' foundations (xi) of psychoanalysis, and uses certain methodological canons. In particular he holds that 'the establishment of a causal connection in psychoanalysis, no less than in "academic psychology" or medicine, has to rely on modes of inquiry that are refined from time-honored canons of causal interference pioneered by Francis Bacon and John Stuart Mill' (46). The canons fix 'demands for the validation of causal claims' (128), including 'the sort of controls that are needed to attest *causal relevance'* (185), as satisfied, for example, in 'experimental or epidemiological findings' (189).

Reference to these canons pervades Grünbaum's discussion, as emerges if we sketch how many sections of his argument can be related to them.

1   Roughly the first third of the book is a critique of hermeneutic treatments of psychoanalysis. A main point is that authors under discussion seek to evade inductivist assessment of psychoanalytic claims, either by holding that the claims are not causal, or again that they can be supported by means other than Grünbaum allows.

Here Grünbaum states his particular opposition to the idea that claims as to a causal connection between mental items can be cogently supported by a connection in content – a 'thematic affinity' – between them. He speaks of 'what might be dubbed "the thematic affinity fallacy"', and appears to reject the basing of causal claims on connection in content 'no matter how strong the *thematic affinity'*. For, he stresses, 'thematic affinity alone does not vouch for etiologic linkage in the absence of further evidence' (55). The evidence in point seems inductivist.

2   One of Grünbaum's noteworthy contributions is to have explicated Freud's 'Tally Argument'. Concerning the effect of suggestion or transference, Freud acknowleged that an analyst could make a patient 'a supporter of some particular theory and thus . . . share some possible error of his own'. Still, he held, 'this only affects [the patient's] intelligence, not his illness. After all, his conflicts will only be successfully solved and his resistances overcome if the anticipatory ideas [interpretations] he is given tally with what is real in him' (S.E. 1917, XVI: 452).

Grünbaum takes this to claim that psychoanalytic interpretation is causally indispensable for the cure of neurosis, which he dubs the necessary condition thesis, or NCT. This can be tested inductively, and would provide a significant justification for psychoanalytic theory and data.

A way of bringing this out – which may not reflect Grünbaum's thought – is as follows: psychoanalytic interpretation specifies causes of neurosis, in the context of a theory which describes how information about these causes may remove them. So if interpretation were the only means of relieving neurosis, the best explanation of this would surely be the accuracy of the interpretations and associated theory. (The idea of suggestion or placebo, for instance, would leave the differential efficacy of psychoanalytic interpretation unexplained.) Presumed accuracy, in turn, would certify both psychoanalytic data and inferences.

In light of his discussion Grünbaum urges that 'the epistemological considerations that prompted Freud to enunciate his Tally Argument make him a sophisticated scientific methodologist, far superior than is allowed' by either friendly or hostile critics (128). However, the success of therapies other than psychoanalysis makes it 'quite reasonable – though *not* compelling – to interpret [psychoanalytic] therapeutic successes as placebo effects' (161). And this and the fact of untreated remission now makes it reasonable to judge that the empirical claim (NCT) which forms the main premise of this argument has not been borne out.

Thus as matters stand the presumption that suggestion or transference distorts psychoanalytic inquiry and provides an alternative explanation of cure is not refuted. So, as Grünbaum summarizes matters, 'Freud unswervingly, brilliantly, but *unsuccessfully tackled* the contamination issues . . . though he failed pathetically for *empirical* reasons rather than for want of methodological sophistication' (284).

3 Popper has long argued against psychoanalysis and inductivism together, claiming the latter lends spurious credibility to the former. Grünbaum takes Popper to caricature both inductivism and psychoanalysis. He argues as 'one central thesis' that 'epistemic defects bedeviling the Freudian etiologies' are not exhibited by Popper's criterion of falsifiability, but rather by 'time-honored inductivist canons for the validation of causal claims' (125).

Grünbaum argues that psychoanalytic hypotheses are falsifiable, and hence, so far as Popper's criterion goes, scientific. He gives a number of examples, and points out that Popper has actually offered no argument of any weight to the contrary. (What Popper gives instead, as Grünbaum indicates, includes description of an imaginary case, 'deplorable neglect' of telling textual evidence as regards Freud's theory and practice (282), 'exegetical legerdemain', and truncated citation which 'borders on sheer travesty' (284).)

None the less, according to Grünbaum, psychoanalysis is methodologically defective, as 'Freud's theory is challenged by neo-Baconian inductivism to furnish a collation of positive instances from *both* experimental and control groups, if there are to be inductively *supportive* instances.' Psychoanalytic method, lacking appropriate controls, cannot do this. Hence 'to this day analysts have not furnished the kinds of instances from controlled inquiries that are *inductively required* to lend genuine support' (280). So if, as Popper says, he formulated his criterion of falsifiability to elucidate what was wrong with psychoanalysis, Grünbaum can reply that in this task in particular, Popper would have done better to attend to traditional inductivism.

Grünbaum's reasons for holding that psychoanalytic theory is as yet unsupported are consistent with the view, which he also takes, that Freud's explanations may in future be confirmed, and that, in any case, the psychoanalytic method is of distinct heuristic value. He stresses that he emphatically allows

for a weighty possibility: Future *extra*clinical evidence *may* turn out to reveal after all that Freud's brilliant intellectual imagination was quite serendipitous for psychopathology and other facets of human conduct. . . Neither I nor many of the other critics I know gainsay that psychoanalytic method equips its practitioners with a *heuristically* fecund basis for propounding hypotheses, especially in the hands of a soaring mind like Freud's.

(189)

4   Although Grünbaum rejects many methodological criticisms made against Freud, certain inductivist strictures flow naturally from his own account.

Freud and Breuer based their original conception of the causal role of the repressed on what they took to be the lasting removal of symptoms, in a process in which each symptom was removed separately by recovering (and reliving) memories, emotions, etc., associated with events which occasioned that symptom. Here the regular link between symptom, memory of occasioning trauma and therapeutic result can be regarded as providing inductive evidence bearing on their claims.

In his later work, however, Freud drew conclusions without this sort of evidential basis, and, according to Grünbaum, supported them defectively – by questionable causal reasoning and misextrapolation.

(a) Freud sought to trace repressed mental life beyond occasioning traumas – and hence to repressed sexual material of early origin – partly because his early therapeutic results were dependent on transference and not durable. For Grünbaum the early therapeutic results were the core of Freud's evidence for the causal role of the repressed. So he wonders why Freud kept to this. 'Why, I ask, did Freud adamantly retain the generic repression etiology instead of allowing that this etiology itself had simply become baseless?' (184). And he criticizes Freud for failing here to keep his causal claims in accord with his and Breuer's early inductive standards of evidence.

Grünbaum also seems to regard Freud's practice in determining whether material was causally linked to symptoms as both questionable and puzzling. He notes in particular an assumption that the causal role of psychic material in relation to symptoms is sometimes *directly identifiable*. As he says, Freud seemed to take it for granted that 'the concrete features of a repressed trauma can collectively vouch for its pathogenic potency, *independently* of any *therapeutic benefit* engendered by its mnemic restoration to the patient's consciousness.' Grünbaum notes that if this were so, the methodological points he stresses would be otiose: 'if such direct etiologic identifiability were indeed granted, then Freud could have spared himself the circuitous detour of trying to validate it via NCT' (152).

(b) Freud held that associations led to causes of symptoms, dreams and slips. Again sticking with the inductive evidence, Grünbaum urges that '*the attribution of therapeutic success to the removal of repressions not only was but remains to this day the sole epistemic underwriter of the purported ability of the patients' free associations to certify causes*' (185). Hence, he urges, 'it is unavailing to extol the method of clinical investigation by free association as a trustworthy resource of etiologic inquiry' (186) in the absence of further epistemic underpinning. Further, analysis does not cure dreams or slips, so there can be no 'counterpart to the *therapeutic* support . . . for the *investigative cogency* of lifting repressions via free associations to fathom the pathogens' (231). Since the claim that associations locate causes of dreams or slips lacks such inductive support, Grünbaum takes Freud to have misextrapolated from the case of symptoms in making it (194).

II

Grünbaum's use of neo-Baconian canons prompts an objection. In commonsense psychological practice we already establish causal connections (in particular concerning the role of motives) interpretively, in ways that are autonomous, cogent, and prior to such canons. So it seems wrong to hold generally that cogency in a psychology of motive must satisfy them; indeed, for motives, it is unclear how such canons could be used, or how inductive methods could replicate commonsense interpretation.

Further, psychoanalytic theory seems an extension of commonsense understanding of motives, by interpretive means internal to it. So psychoanalytic theory may also be cogent, but related to inductive methods no more closely than commonsense psychology itself. This is a natural view, and probably that of many advocates of psychoanalysis, but it gives a perspective very different from Grünbaum's.

Grünbaum himself stresses that we know motives to have a causal role, which he does not claim that we establish by neo-Baconian means: 'if an agent is actually moved to do A by having a certain reason or motive M . . .

the agent's having M qualified as being *causally relevant* to what he did, *regardless of whether M is conscious or repressed'* (72). Still he invokes this same notion, causal relevance, in claiming that a psychoanalytic view that repression is pathological 'lacks the sort of controls that are needed to establish *causal relevance'* (185). So the question arises as to why controls should be required for psychoanalytic but not commonsense judgements on the role of motives. If commonsense cogency as to causal relevance is in question, then surely, it seems, commonsense practices (or their extension) might suffice for it.

Since we interpret in commonsense terms naturally, and take the understanding so registered for granted, we have little explicit account of how the process works or what renders it cogent. Still, there are some things to be said about hypothesis and confirmation in commonsense psychology, and these seem to bear directly on psychoanalytic theory. As Freud's procedure was to interpret what people said and did, it is not surprising that commonsense and psychoanalytic interpretation and theory should fit in this way. The fit, however, gives some reason for holding that a mode of verification already regarded as cogent in one case has claim to weight in the other.[2]

Everyday psychological practice seems based, among other things, on our natural ability to take bodily movement as informed by intention, and to relate this to motive – belief, desire, emotion, and so on. Even a young child, for example, is able to discern patterns of intention in the consecutive movements of persons, and so to relate distinct movements to one another by relating them to a structure of motive. (Thus Augustine appropriately calls such movement 'as it were the natural language of all peoples'.)

Since we take the motives we discern in this way as causes of the movements, we can represent ourselves as making interpretive hypotheses as to causes (motives) on the basis of effects (sequences of apparently motivated movements). These hypotheses are based upon the apparent intentional content of the effects, and serve to specify this content more fully, in terms of that of the causes.

Thus by taking someone's moving a glass towards a tap as deriving from a desire so to move it, and this from a desire to get a drink and a belief that this is a way of doing so, we interpret him as intentionally moving the glass that way, and, deepening the account to cover more movements, intentionally getting a drink. The effect, thus explained, inherits the descriptions of the causes from which, if the explanation is correct, it derives. So the hypotheses are that the effects are derived from certain causes, so as to give them coincident content.

This illustrates how commonsense description of motives already displays their causal and explanatory role. Further, since the truth of interpretive hypotheses entails a coincidence in content between *explanans* and *explanadum*, or again between cause and effect, this is a field in which good explanation achieves a maximum of derivational descriptive fit, or connection in content, as between cause and effect. So quite generally, connection in psychological content is a mark of causal, and so potentially of explanatory, connection.

Our understanding relates movement to movement, and hence action to action and motive to motive, as interpretation proceeds. In effect we constantly integrate the explanation we are inclined to give for one action with that we are inclined to give for others, revising as we go. As we gain and apply further knowledge of motive, we relate our tentative understanding of each course of action with that of others more deeply and extensively. So, as the range of effects which we seek to bring into the pattern of coinciding content we have so far hypothetically understood broadens, we hypothesize further explanatory causes, which are deeper and therefore of wider explanatory scope.

So far as our efforts are successful, we will be able to employ a system of causes whose descriptions enjoy maximum derivational fit with those of the effects, and in which the integration of causes with one another will be shown in relations of psychological coherence. Relations of this kind hold among the desires and beliefs in the example above, as well as the further elements (e.g. beliefs about the behaviour of water, glasses, and so on) upon which the example implicitly draws. This again is a consequence of the way commonsense description shows causal role. Where explanation consists in assembling and relating elements (motives) whose explanatory and causal role is displayed in their contents, causal and explanatory connection is shown in connection of content, depth and scope of explanation in the range of such connection, and co-operation of causes in coherence of the content.

Beliefs and desires serve as reasons, and as reasons for reasons. Each reason must cohere with everything it serves to explain and everything which fits with it in explanation. We sometimes relate whole patterns of planning and action to a few sources of motive – deep desires, traits of character, and the like; and the ascription of beliefs and desires goes with that of concepts, and so further beliefs and desires, in co-determining patterns. The field of coherence, therefore, is dense, deep and extensive. In such a field commonsense understanding projects for each ascription a pattern of expectation and constraint, which further ascriptions will fit or fail to fit.[3]

This is a source of verification and cogency in commonsense psychology. Just as we can take ourselves to make hypotheses about motives, so we can take ourselves to confirm, disconfirm and modify these in light of the way our account for one action fits that for others. Roughly, as we proceed, an explanatory ascription of motive in one case is confirmed by coherence with those in others, and disconfirmed by dissonance or lack of expected coherence. So each intuitive ascription we register as we build up our picture of persons can be taken as answerable to, and as ultimately forming a cohering and mutually supporting network with, the many others with which it is integrated.

Now it seems that psychoanalysis is aimed at extending this kind of understanding, and in ways which use the sort of confirmation and disconfirmation that goes with it. This emerges clearly if we consider the key psychoanalytic claim that many dreams, slips and symptoms can be seen as wish-fulfilling.

The structure of this can be illustrated by reference to a simple dream reported by Freud. When he had eaten anchovies or other salted food, Freud noticed, he would frequently dream that he was drinking delicious cool water. Then he would wake up thirsty and get a drink. He took it that the thirst had caused a wish to drink, which in turn had caused the dream.

Here we have two elements which are related in content – the thirst which Freud felt on waking, and the dream, which was one of slaking thirst. These are connected in content as motive and satisfaction of motive. Thirst is a motive for drinking, and the dream is of drinking. In light of this connection of content, it seems, we are inclined to regard these elements as causally related. We take it, that is, that it is no coincidence that a person would have this sort of dream when he was thirsty, and so hold that the thirst caused the dream.

This ascription of a causal connection between two elements related in content, however, requires the introduction of a third. The dream occurred while Freud was asleep, and before he was aware of thirst on waking. So something related to the thirst must have acted while Freud was asleep. Freud takes this to have been a wish, caused by the thirst, to get a drink. Since the dream represents this wish as fulfilled, the dream can be regarded as a wish-fulfilment. The whole of the material, including that hypothesized, thus takes the pattern motive: wish: represented satisfaction.

Thus in even this simple and relatively transparent example, we find a certain inferential complexity. This can be indicated by saying that the operation of the wish to drink, which is supposed to have occurred in sleep and caused the dream, is not observed but rather purely hypothetical. We may take ourselves or Freud to have observed that he dreamt of drinking and was thirsty on waking. There is no such observable or introspectible contact with the operation of the wish, which is supposed to show solely in the occurrence of the dream itself.

In postulating this wish, Freud evidently introduces an element which coheres in content with both thirst and dream. There are two aspects of coherence – that of thirst to wish, and that of wish to dream. The wish to drink evidently coheres with the motive of thirst, as the kind of wish such a motive naturally causes. The link is simple here, but has much more complex instances. Secondly, as noted, the wish and the dream cohere as wish and representation of the fulfilment of the wish.

This second aspect of coherence thus imposes on the dream a further pattern already familiar from commonsense psychology. It is that of wishful thinking or imagining, in which someone thinks or imagines that something is the case simply because he wishes it were. In such cases wishes cause episodes of thinking or imagining that things are as wished. Freud is thirsty, and his dream represents things as a thirsty man would wish them. The situation is thus as it would be if the dream were a bit of wishful imagining. So it is natural to hypothesize the operation of a wish in sleep, and thereby to assimilate the dream to this familiar paradigm.

The explanatory inference here is thus one in which an interpretive hypothesis as to a cause is introduced, so that an effect (the dream) can be taken as derived from the cause in such a way as to have inherited content from it. The explanation is thus comparable to one in which a desire is hypothesized as a cause of action. There are, however, differences. In this case what is explained is not an apparent pattern in intentions and actions, but rather, first, an apparent pattern as between motive and dream, and secondly, the content of the dream itself. The patterns of derivation of content invoked here are also not those of rational action. In rational action motives produce willed intentions and real actions aimed at satisfaction. Here they produce wishes and mere representations of satisfaction, on the pattern of wishful imagining.

Let us now take some material from the example which Freud presented as a first specimen of his way of interpreting dreams, and which is also discussed by Grünbaum and Clark Glymour (1983). The content of part of Freud's dream was as follows:

I said to [Irma] 'If you still get pains it's really only your fault.' She replied 'If you only knew what pains I've got now in my throat and stomach and abdomen – it's choking me.' I was alarmed and looked at her. She looked pale and puffy. I thought to myself that after all I must be missing some organic trouble . . . Not long ago, when she was feeling unwell, my friend Otto had given her an injection

. . . injections of that sort ought not be made thoughtlessly . . . And probably the syringe had not been clean.

(S.E. 1900, IV: 107)

This content does not initially seem understandable on the pattern of the previous example. According to Freud, however, this is how it should be seen, in light of the background he is able to provide:

Irma was Freud's patient, and Otto a colleague. The day before the dream Otto has said to Freud that Irma was looking 'better, but not quite well'. On reflection, Freud was able to realize that he had felt some sort of reproof in this – as if Otto was saying that Freud had promised Irma too much. (This recollection evidently emerged clearly and fully only in the course of considering the dream: Freud says 'my disagreeable impression was not clear to me, and I gave no outward sign of it', whereas after the analysis he was enabled 'retrospectively to put this transient impression into words' (S.E. 1900, IV: 106, 120). He had, in fact, been writing out Irma's case history the night before, in order, as he realized, to justify himself against this imagined reproach.

Freud took it that wishes related to this desire to be justified – and for himself not to be at fault – showed in the dream and his associations to it, which he wrote down. In the case of his saying that if she still had pains, it was not his fault, he reflected that this showed that he seemed especially anxious not to be responsible for the pains she still had. The wish which he took to be operative in this part of the dream then emerged with the next association. (Freud italicizes the aspect of the dream linked with the association.)

I was alarmed at the idea that I had missed an organic illness. This, as may well be believed, is a perpetual source of anxiety to a specialist whose practice is almost limited to neurotic patients and who is in the habit of attributing to hysteria a great number of symptoms which other physicians treat as organic. On the other hand, a faint doubt crept into my mind – from where I could not tell – that my alarm was not entirely genuine. If Irma's pains had an organic basis, once again I could not be held responsible for curing them; my treatment only set out to get rid of *hysterical* pains. It occurred to me, in fact, that I was actually *wishing* that there had been a wrong diagnosis; for if so, the blame for my lack of success would have been got rid of.

(S.E. 1900, IV: 109)

The hypothesis that he had the wish which emerges here is, as Freud took it, strengthened by its coherence with the rest of the dream and what he could remember from the day before. For the dream goes on to reveal that the illness which Freud has misdiagnosed was also in fact Otto's fault.

So the reproach which Freud had felt as a fleeting and disagreeable impression on hearing Otto's remark was, in the dream, entirely deflected and put back onto Otto. As Freud puts it:

The dream fulfilled certain wishes which were started in me by the events of the previous day (the news given me by Otto and my writing out of the case history). The conclusion of the dream, that is to say, was that I was not responsible for the persistence of Irma's pains, but that Otto was. Otto had in fact annoyed me by his remarks about Irma's incomplete cure, and the dream gave me my revenge by throwing the reproach back on to him. The dream acquitted me of the responsibility for Irma's condition by showing that it was due to other factors – it produced a whole series of reasons. The dream presented a state of affairs as I should have wished it to be. *Thus its content was the fulfilment of a wish and its motive was a wish.*

(S.E. 1900, IV: 118–19)

The structure of this example is plainly that discerned in the last. Despite important differences, which we shall consider in a moment, it seems that there is good reason to take this dream too as a wish-fulfilment.

Although Grünbaum and Glymour do not discuss the particular association quoted, it would seem from their general description of the Irma dream that they would agree. Grünbaum emphasizes that this is a case where 'commonsense psychology regards a dream as patently wish fulfilling', and says that 'aggressive wishes which had remained unfulfilled by the end of the day in question are then patently acted out or realized in the manifest dream content' (221–2). Likewise Glymour says that 'the interpretation offered is enormously plausible largely because it is an almost literal reading of the contents of the dream, in which the blame for Irma's illness is placed with Otto, not Freud (1983: 63).

The reason for agreement is plain. As in the case of the dream of drinking, there is an apparent coincidence in content among motives and dream, in light of which we take them as causally connected. Grünbaum describes the coincidence as that of patent realization, while Glymour puts it as one content being 'an almost literal reading' of the other.

Despite its commonsense cogency, Freud's interpretation has a theoretical character, and one which goes beyond commonsense. This can partly be brought out by contrast with the previous example.

First, the dream of drinking seems plainly wishful, and would ordinarily be recognized as such. This is not so in the present example. It is not commonsense to suppose that a doctor's dreaming that he had made a kind of misdiagnosis that was a perpetual source of anxiety to him was in fact wishful, nor his dreaming that his patient was organically ill, nor that this had been caused by a colleague. Rather the wishful nature of these representations can seem clear only if we consider them together with a context of motive emerging in memories and association which Freud was able to remember, notice the relevance of, and report.

As before we have an apparent relation in content between motives and dream, which, together with the content of the dream, is explicable on the supposition of a wish operative in sleep. Previously the motive was thirst, and the wish – to drink – a nearly inevitable and commonsensically acknowledged accompaniment of this. Here the motive is Freud's desire to justify himself against a supposed reproach, etc., and his wish that he should have misdiagnosed the case and that his patient should have in fact been made ill by the author of the reproach. We readily understand such wishes as coherent with the motives in question, and so as derivative from them. But these are plainly *not* standard commonsense correlates of such motives. Rather, surely, it is surprising that the motive should have these effects.

The surprise is not just that a motive should cause wishes which might not have been predicted. Rather it is also that the wishes themselves, and the way of thinking shown in their production, are, by commonsense standards, quite extraordinary. They are not very rational. Convicting yourself of making a sort of diagnostic blunder about which you are perpetually anxious, for example, is hardly a sensible way of escaping reproach or anxiety about a patient's condition. The best that can be said for it, so to speak, is that it fits with things as represented in the rest of the dream. Again, in the way it reverses Otto's reproach, the dream seems like a transparently childish 'It's not *me* that's bad, it's *you*.'[4] This infantile quality of thought goes with something like ruthlessness, as Freud notes, for example, in saying 'I had a sense of awkwardness at having invented such a severe illness for Irma simply in order to clear myself. It looked so cruel . . .'

In an ordinary context we should find it strange that an adult who felt reproached should evince such irrational and ruthless wishes, or attempt a reversal which was so obviously baseless and silly. It may seem more natural that wishful thinking of such a character should occur during sleep. Still it is novel, and there is a discovery in noticing it.

The psychologically remarkable character of the wishes and thinking behind the dream is a direct product of the nature of Freud's theory together with the fact – which according to Glymour renders the interpretation 'enormously plausible' – that the wishes are, in part, read from the manifest content of the dream. This is theoretically determined: since the wishes are hypothesized as derivative from certain motives precisely in order to yield this content, the wishes must enjoy a certain coincidence with it. This, however, determines the ascription of wishes and ways of thinking that are otherwise unexpected.

In light of this it might seem that Freud should have introduced a special theoretical term – perhaps something like 'night-time motive derivative' – instead of the commonsense term 'wish'. Still, what Freud intuitively took himself to discover in the association quoted was a wish. Also it accords with commonsense to take wishes as derived from, and so to be connected in content with, motives like desire; but wishes are allowed greater detachment from reality and rationality. We do not expect someone's wishes to be entirely consistent with his actions, or, indeed, with one another. They are, so to speak, permitted as relatively unintegrated creatures of the mind of the moment. So the commonsense concept, in terms of which Freud's intuition about the dream comes, is one that admits of the extension which, in this case, it receives. Using the commonsense word, then, and accepting the implicit hypothesis in light of the context of memory and association Freud supplies, we find this surprising wishful thinking, as Grünbaum puts it, 'patently realized' in the manifest content of the dream.

Let us now take another example discussed by Grünbaum and Glymour. One of Freud's patients dreamt

I wanted to give a supper-party, but I had nothing in the house but a little smoked salmon. It thought I would go out and buy something, but remembered it was Sunday afternoon and all the shops would be shut. Next I tried to ring up some caterers, but the telephone was out of order. So I had to abandon my wish to give a supper-party.

The patient's first associations concerned, among other things, the fact that her husband had remarked

the day before that he was getting too stout and therefore intended to start on a course of weight-reduction. He proposed to rise early, do physical exercises, keep to a strict diet, and above all accept no more invitations to supper.

Although these associations seemed to indicate a link between going to supper-parties and being stout, they were not sufficient to interpret the dream. So Freud asked for more.

After a short pause, which would correspond to the overcoming of a resistance, she went on to tell me that the day before she had visited a woman friend of whom she confessed she felt jealous because her (my patient's) husband was constantly singing her praises. Fortunately this friend of hers is very skinny and thin and her husband admires a plumper figure. I asked what she had talked about to her thin friend. Naturally, she replied, of that lady's wish to grow a little stouter. Her friend had enquired, too: 'When are you going to ask us to another meal? You always feed one so well!'

(S.E. 1900, IV: 148)

This indicated an interpretation for the dream, parallel to that for the examples just considered. The dreamer's husband praised her friend, and the dreamer was jealous of her. The jealousy was mitigated by the fact that the friend was skinny. The friend had, however, just been saying that she wanted to get plumper, and that she wanted to be invited to supper to be well fed. So the dreamer had motives for wishing not to give a supper-party. This would be a wish represented in the dream.

Freud sought confirmation of this by asking about a further and as yet unconsidered detail of the dream. He says that what was now lacking

was some coincidence to confirm the solution. The smoked salmon in the dream had not yet been accounted for. 'How,' I asked, 'did you arrive at the salmon that came into your dream?' 'Oh,' she replied, 'smoked salmon is my friend's favourite dish.'

(S.E. 1900, IV: 147–8)

Freud's taking this as confirmation is readily understandable in terms of the common structure of this and the previous example. In each case the dreamer remembers events and motives from the day which are connected in content with the dream and so would seem to have played a role in bringing it about. This in turn gives reason to hyothesize something mediating the content of motives and dream, and a hypothesis which fits both contents is that a wish was derived from the motives and realized in the dream.

Since the reason for entertaining this hypothesis is connection in content between motives and the manifest content of the dream, the hypothesis is strengthened by further evidence of such connection. This is provided by the dreamer's acknowledgement that smoked salmon is her friend's favourite dish. Since this is something the dreamer knew, the information provides a further direct connection between motives and dream. Her jealousy was not just of a skinny friend, but of a skinny friend who particularly liked smoked salmon, and this latter content appears explicitly in the dream. Further, the way in which this content appears fits with the particular motive from which the content of the dream is hypothesized to derive. A jealous wish not to give a supper-party would serve to deprive the friend of an opportunity to get plumper and more attractive. That this is done while having some smoked salmon, however, adds something else which fits with jealousy. The dreamer herself has her friend's favourite food. The dream reverses the kind of deficit felt in jealousy, and represents the dreamer herself as having what the object of her jealousy would particularly like to have.

The hypothesized wish again is not commonsensical. We can no more assume that the dreamer would rationally think of treating her friend this way, than that Freud would so wish a misdiagnosis on himself, or illness on Irma. Also, the reversal of jealousy over food – which might, to stress the similarity, be put as 'It isn't *you* that will have what you want. It's *me*' – is as silly and infantile as Freud's more explicit treatment of Otto. None the less it seems that the ascription of such sub-reasonable wishes does affect our sense of the content and significance of the events and motives which gave rise to the dream. We see that Freud's feelings on hearing Otto's remark were connected with motives more important than their appearance to Freud in a mere fleeting impression might suggest, and these motives in turn may seem less reasonable and mature for their connection with the wishes that gave rise to the dream; again, we have reason to suppose that the lady's conversation with her friend roused her jealousy beyond her awareness, and that this had an element which found an unreasonable expression.

So we can see that these two examples present essentially the same elements. First, there are dream contents: misdiagnosis, inability to give supper. Secondly, there are associated memories of events from the day that are connected in content with the dream: Freud's of discussing Irma, the woman's of the conversation with her friend about coming to supper. Thirdly, these are connected with motives: Freud's sense of responsibility for Irma's condition and his resentment towards Otto, the woman's jealousy of her friend. Taking these into account, we see that the content of the dream can be regarded as representing the satisfaction of wishes derived from the motives, and so as related by derivative representation of satisfaction to the motives themselves. The material in these dreams, just as in the simple one with which we began, coheres in terms of derivation on the pattern motive: wish: satisfaction.

Discerning this pattern in the more complex cases gives a further gain in explanatory coherence. More elements, and elements which are more disparate in content, are brought under the pattern, and hence become explicable as instances of it. So the overall reason for accepting the hypothesis of wish-fulfilment here is that it provides, through relatively complex processes of inference, an explanatory account of the relations of varied apparently connected elements. This is the same as the reason for accepting explanations of elements of behaviour as action. There are different patterns, and different relations of coherence involved, but hypotheses, inferences, and relations of confirmation and disconfirmation are of broadly the same kind.

The wishes whose ascription is thus supported point beyond common sense, and in ways which require a certain effort of acknowledgement, and hence acceptance of an extended sense of self, on the dreamer's part. Freud has to admit, with a sense of awkwardness, that he entertains cruel-looking wishes; and the woman must feel that her jealousy of her friend, which she apparently finds a difficult topic, plays a certain further role in her mental life.

In both dreams this goes with something akin to self-ascriptions, in the associations, of the role of the motives in producing the dreams. Freud feels that his alarm is not quite sincere, and that he may be wishing a misdiagnosis on himself and (cruelly) illness on Irma. The woman says she arrives at the smoked salmon in the dream because it is the favourite food of her friend, and presumably thereby registers an alteration in her sense of her jealousy and its effects.

Grünbaum says of the Irma dream that 'commonsense psychology regards [it] as patently wish-fulfilling'. Still, it is the context including memory and association supplied by Freud, and not commonsense psychology alone, which yields this result.

It is possible that such contexts should be found for many other dreams, so that their interpretation would lead to the ascription of further wishes whose role and content is novel for commonsense psychology. Also the presence of many such unexpected elements might prompt further revisions – say, about the importance of such fragmentary and unintegrated mental items, the place of wishful thinking in life, or the role of what is egoistic or childish in the mind. But this is the possibility that Grünbaum does not countenance for psychoanalysis generally: that ordinary common-sense psychological inference, operating upon previously unnoticed or undiscovered material, should strongly support theoretical claims which go beyond psychological common sense.

There is of course far more to the psychoanalytic extension of commonsense psychology than figures in the examples considered so far. Nevertheless they begin to indicate something of the theoretical character of the extension, and also the sort of support it might enjoy. One of Freud's central claims was that what persons said and did in analysis – their associations, memories, transference of past feelings on to the analyst – provided a context in which many of their dreams, slips, symptoms and apparently irrational actions could be seen as wish-fulfilling. Wishes, or derivatives of motive, ascribed in this way, in turn, formed important elements of his theory. Thus Freud thought that ordinary memory provided evidence of childhood sexual desires; but that this could be supplemented by regarding certain seeming memories – e.g. of seductive behaviour on the part of a parent – as wish-fulfilling. His psychology is thus one in which commonsense ascription of content, and further ascription based on wish-fulfilment, go hand in hand.

Although utilizing distinct explanatory patterns, the finding of desires for actions and wishes for wish-fulfilments can both be regarded as parts of the project of relating motive to behaviour, by so ascribing motive as to provide for the derivation of the contents of behaviour from it. The importance of wishes, in turn, has two aspects. Since, according to Freud, these derivatives themselves power or structure much behaviour, interpretation in terms of wish-fulfilment has significance it its own right. Such interpretation, however, may cast further and distinct light on the nature of motive.

Wishes and actions both derive from motives like desire, and so can serve as the basis for hypotheses as to their contents. In action an agent's motives are constrained by his rationality and sense of reality, and the inferences we can make on the basis of action alone are correspondingly restricted. In wishlike derivatives, however, we see the content of motives as unleashed in the absence of such constraints. (Hence the irrationality, extremity, etc., of wishes; and the light knowledge of them, when we get it, casts.) Freudian wishes thus provide an intrinsically different perspective on motivation than rational intentions and one which is potentially informative.

The additional perspective gives further scope for the kind of modification and testing of hypotheses about motives described above. Interpretation of wish-fulfilment leads to new hypotheses about motive, which bear on both action and wish-fulfilment; and the interpretation of a given action or wish-fulfilment can be tested for coherence or dissonance with the results of interpretation of other actions and other wish-fulfilments. Thus the small extensions we have been considering in our examples could be carried further, as new hypotheses about motives entered the story, and were modified and confirmed in light of very many instances of coherence or dissonance as interpretation proceeded. Such an extension might be far-reaching, but supported at each step, and cogent over all. This is, at any rate, a possibility which a methodologist must take seriously.

III

The idea that psychoanalysis can be regarded (partly) as a sound extension of commonsense psychology leads to a number of criticisms of Grünbaum's argument.

First (see 1 above), it means that psychoanalytic accounts of motive have support which standard scientific methodology for assessing causal claims fails to register. This justifies a central contention of the hermeneutic writers Grünbaum criticizes, and indicates how causalist–hermeneutic disputation, Grünbaum's included, can rest on shared methodological error.

Schematically, Grünbaum and many he criticizes as 'hermeneuts' agree that causal claims generally cannot be supported other than in accord with scientific (e.g. inductivist) canons, and that much psychoanalytic evidence about motives is non-canonical. One party sees that psychoanalytic accounts of motive have non-canonical support and so ignores the causal role of motives, while the other keeps causality in clear view but ignores non-canonical suport. Neither draws the obvious conclusion from the fact of non-canonical evidence for the causal role of motives, namely that the canons leave evidence on certain causes – motives – out of account. This, I think, is because neither attends to the way commonsense understanding uses and displays causal information.

Grünbaum criticizes both analysts and 'hermeneuts' for using thematic affinity as a mark of causal connection. But commonsense psychology deals in causes which transmit content to effects, and so takes appropriate affinity as just such a mark. As fits this, we see in actual examples – the dream of drinking, or again that of Irma's injection or the smoked salmon – that connection in content between motives and dreams gives reason to hold that the former were causes of the latter.

In fact Grünbaum's own claim that certain wishes are 'patently realized in the manifest content' of the Irma dream is a causal claim established hermeneutically, since it turns on the thematic affinity he sees between contents of wishes and dream. So Grünbaum's natural and correct practice in inferring connection from affinity here rightly and effectively contradicts his own methodological strictures and accusations of fallacy.

Secondly, Grünbaum's account of the role of the Tally Argument (see 2 above) and his methodological criticisms of Freud (see the last of 3, and 4 above) require qualification. Freud's practices are at least partly justified by interpretative considerations, and these support claims which Grünbaum takes to rest solely on the Tally Argument. Hence the argument itself, and the therapeutic results on which it turns, should be taken as among the parts of an interlocking structure, rather than the foundation of the whole.

This is foreshadowed in Grünbaum's text. We saw above (4a) that he objected to Freud's assumption that 'the concrete features' of something repressed could 'vouch for its pathogenic potency' independently of therapeutic effect; and remarked that 'if such direct etiologic identifiability were indeed granted, then Freud could have spared himself the circuitous detour of trying to validate it via NCT'. Since pathogenic potency is causal role, the identification of causal role by content we have been discussing provides the direct etiologic identifiability in question; which, as Grünbaum acknowledges, can do part of the work he assigns to the NCT of the Tally Argument. Again, this is a possibility Grünbaum meant to rule out by his strictures on affinity; so naturally it returns if affinity is given a role.

Such identification comes to the fore, as we have seen, in Freud's use of wish-fulfilment. The examples we have considered instantiate a way of thinking – a process of interpretive hypothesis and testing – which locates psychological causes using the resources of commonsense psychology, and in a way which is methodologically quite distinct from the apparatus of 'collation of positive instances from *both* experimental and control groups' to which Grünbaum adheres. Hence Grünbaum's methodology and Freud's actual method partly pass one another by.

For an example of Freud's application of this way of thinking to symptoms, consider the following, from a consultation with an 'intelligent and unembarrassed-looking girl':

She was most surprisingly dressed. For though as a rule a woman's clothes are carefully considered down to the last detail, she was wearing one of her stockings hanging down and two of the buttons on her blouse were undone. She complained of having pains in her leg and, without being asked, exposed her calf. But what she principally complained of was, to use her own words, that she had a feeling in her body as though there was something 'stuck into it' which was 'moving backwards and forwards' and was 'shaking' her through and through. Sometimes it made her whole body feel 'stiff'. My medical colleague, who was present at the examination, looked at me; he found no difficulty in understanding the meaning of her complaint.

(S.E. 1900, V: 618)

Here a range of behaviour is explicable if taken as derived from sexual motives. There is, therefore, reason to hypothesize that these cause the behaviour, and the hypothesis could be supported by further information about their role in the girl's life and mind, which would be gained by further interpretation of her behaviour. Here the interpretation of action and wish-fulfilment, with their different patterns of derivation, go together. Intention presumably figures differently, for example, in her showing her calf and reporting her complaint. Since in the latter she is not engaging in intercourse but only (and unknowingly) representing herself as doing so, this part of her behaviour is to be seen as wish-fulfilling representation rather than action willed to real satisfaction.[5] Still, the overall process of ascribing motives whose content fits and further specifies that of the behaviour to be explained, and the testing such hypotheses by relation to others of the same kind, is the same in both cases.

Grünbaum's official methodology simply excludes such interpretive reasoning. Thus he says:

No matter how strong the *thematic affinity* between a conjectured repressed thought and a maladaptive, neurotic action, this 'meaning kinship' does not itself suffice to attest that the hypothesized repression is 'the hidden intentionality' behind the given behavior. For thematic affinity alone does not vouch for etiologic linkage, in the absense of further evidence that a thematically kindred repression actually *engendered* the behavior.

(55)

So he might have argued that the 'meaning kinship' between thirst and drinking does not vouch for causal connection in the dream of drinking. In the present example it is reasonable to take sexual motives as 'the hidden intentionality' behind the girl's leaving her blouse undone or showing her calf, or again behind her symptom; and further interpretive evidence, if needed, would be forthcoming. Since such interpretation – like all interpretation – turns on the thematic affinity of presumed causes and effects, we can see that the methodology which Grünbaum here uses against Freud would, if applied, render all everyday understanding groundless.

Grünbaum's ideal seems to be the case in which the right kind of correlational relationship is shown to hold between separately identified entities, e.g. a kind of pathogen on the one hand, and a neurosis or symptom on the other (see, for example, 253ff). Here correlations – repeated instantiations – are used to show that the coinstantiation of the items or properties in question is not coincidental, but causal. Applying this generally, he holds that establishing connection in any particular case requires two stages of inquiry. First, the existence of the purportedly causative entity must be established. Secondly, and separately, the entity must be shown to have the right kind of causal role. (This, apparently, is the 'further evidence' of causal role said to be required above.) This latter stage of neo-Baconian inquiry Grünbaum takes to require controls which must go beyond the clinical situation.

Commonsense psychological reasoning about action and wish-fulfilment, by contrast, does not seek to eliminate coincidence by repetition of instances of possible connection, but rather to explicate connection already grasped in a single instance by further causal hypothesis. Since the causes show only in their effects, they can be reached only by such hypotheses. Also, since commonsense specification of psychological entities already encodes causal information, a hypothesis as to the existence of an entity is at the same time one as to the discharge of a causal role, so that the two neo-Baconian stages are combined within interpretive (and so clinical) reasoning. Thus a hypothesis as to intention, desire or belief is introduced at a single step, as causal explanation of episodes (actions, thoughts, whatever) which can be seen as related to one another and to it in content; the case is the same for wish-fulfilment; and such hypotheses are confirmed or disconfirmed, as we have seen, by relation to others of the same type.

Commonsense reasoning thus suits the psychological properties of persons, which are rarely uniformly repeated but always pervasively and non-coincidentally related in content. The non-neo-Baconian nature of such reasoning enables it to establish connections cogently in a single instance or case, as in the Irma dream or any commonplace judgement of motivation, and so to go rapidly and accurately to the deeper judgements manifested in, and essential to, daily interaction. In the appropriate domain, therefore, such reasoning is more powerful than the neo-Baconian, and it is hard to envisage how the latter could function in its absence, or be brought to confirm its results fully or in detail. Intuitive and prescientific as commonsense reasoning is, it has countless indispensable and compelling instances, in which it appears as inference to the best explanation for the data it covers. It cannot be methodologically ignored.

Unsatisfactory and preliminary as these remarks about interpretive reasoning are, they enable us to see (4a) why Freud persevered with the hypothesis of repression despite the fragility of his early therapeutic results. It seems clear that he took himself to be following up connections in content which had derivational causal relevance, and he may have been right in doing so.

Since the kind of inference involved in wish-fulfilment has a degree of internal cogency, and connects the hypothesized causes of wish-fulfilments with the results of free association, Grünbaum errs (4a) in claiming that therapeutic success is the sole epistemic underwriter of the ability of associations to certify causes, and also in regarding the use of association and wish-fulfilment in explaining dreams and slips as mainly misextrapolation from the case of symptoms.

Grünbaum takes therapeutic success as the inductive touchstone of psychoanalysis. On the view here, by contrast, therapeutic success is to be seen in the context of the system of interpretive reasoning of which hypotheses regarding action and wish-fulfilment are part. This system can provide and to some degree confirm a hypothesis about the cause of a symptom, as in the example above. It also gives reason to think that awareness of the cause of a symptom may alleviate it, since it is part of commonsense psychology that motives and wishes can be modified by awareness and thought. Therapeutic success, and the manner of its occurrence, may therefore constitute further data explicable in terms of, and so supporting, the original hypothesis as to the cause.

This in turn provides reason – perhaps ultimately of the kind which Grünbaum associates with the Tally Argument – for holding that therapeutic success in psychoanalysis is not due to placebo effect. Therapeutic failure, however, does not refute the hypothesis or render it groundless, since the relevant motives and wishes may not be reached or modified by awareness, and there may be independent reason to think this. Success of alternative therapy may also accord with the hypothesis, since it is part of commonsense that things other than awareness can modify motives or wishes, and there may be independent reason to hold that this has happened.

The same reasoning also bears on the question of contamination, since this again involves hypotheses as to the causes of what persons in analysis say and do, which are relevantly tested by interpretation of their behaviour. The actual behaviour of persons in psychotherapy seems to me better explained by psychoanalytic motivational hypotheses than the vague alternatives provided by suggestion, etc., although of course this cannot be argued here.

Finally, the link with commonsense psychology renders the general differences between Grünbaum and Popper (see 3 above) less significant for psychoanalysis. In Grünbaum's hands his methodology yields a description of psychoanalysis which is far more comprehensive, subtle and convincing than Popper's few flawed remarks. Still, he agrees with Popper in simply ignoring interpretive relations of confirmation and disconfirmation. Since these are central to both commonsense psychology and psychoanalysis, this may be the most important point.

As Grünbaum urges, some aspects of Freudian theory can be tested apart from complex interpretive considerations. But it seems that many cannot, and as the above remarks about interpretation suggest, this may be intrinsic to psychoanalysis as to commonsense. If we grant evidential weight to some interpretive claims, then we can use inductive methods as well; but it seems unlikely that we will be able to escape reliance upon claims for which the main evidence is ineliminably interpretive.

Regarding these Grünbaum's position seems quite similar to Popper's: they are assigned to a sort of methodological limbo. (Popper speaks of claims which are metaphysical but contain truth and may become science; Grünbaum, of those with heuristic value.) Since we already take many of these claims to be true, and know that more have systematic commonsense and theoretical support, they deserve more selective treatment. The fault here is in methodology, not commonsense psychology or its psychoanalytic extension.

IV

Grünbaum opposes the sorts of conclusion drawn above. For example, he argues that 'the attempt to reconstruct psychoanalytic explanations of conduct hermeneutically . . . is basically undercut if important classes of psychoanalytic explanations simply defy assimilation to the practical syllogism' (75).

Since the commonsense paradigm for wish-fulfilment is not rational action but wishful imagining, this objection fails. Grünbaum does, however, argue separately against Freud's use of wish-fulfilment and free association.

Freud's discussions of the Irma and smoked salmon dreams were taken above as informative, connected and plausible examples of wish-fulfilment. Freud often presents examples in series in which the first is easiest, and each draws on the information in those before and adds new. The continuity between examples provides reason for accepting each in light of earlier ones, despite the new information and complexity involved. We saw this sort of progression in the Irma and salmon examples. In the first the dream is apparently merely unwishful, whereas in the second it seems counter to a wish; the associations in the first locate wishes which can be self-ascribed more or less directly, whereas those in the second lead, more slowly, to motives which are harder to acknowledge, in light of which wishes are more hypothetical; and so on.

Grünbaum and Clark Glymour do not see the examples this way. On their account Freud's interpretation of the Irma dream is plausible, but makes no informative use of free association and excavates no wishes. The interpretation of the smoked salmon dream, by contrast, lacks cogency, but claims spurious confirmation on the basis of fallacious reasoning about free association. This Grünbaum calls Freud's fallacy of 'reverse causal inference'. He says Freud embraces this fallacy generally, and 'argues fallaciously from the confluence of associations to a causal reversal in *explicitly generalized* form (S.E. 1900, V: 528)' (233–4).

This critique of association and wish-fulfilment has three parts, concerning the Irma dream, the salmon dream, and the explicitly generalized fallacy respectively. We shall take them in order.

First the Irma dream. Grünbaum argues that Freud's reported feelings from the day before already contain the wishes found in the interpretation. So interpretation and association here do no work: 'In sum, though the aggressive conscious wishes that Freud had on the day before the Irma dream were then patently fulfiled in its manifest content, free association played *no excavating role* in his recall of these wishes after the dream, for he had been avowedly conscious of them the evening before' (222).

Glymour agrees, saying that 'the Irma dream is one whose interpretation can be read almost on its face, and the elaborate "analysis" Freud offers us contributes virtually nothing'. Glymour says also that the thesis that dreams are wish-fulfilments in any case seems 'wholly implausible', since one thinks, for example, of 'dreams characterized by diffuse anxiety'. And he says Freud's distinction between manifest and latent contents of a dream, according to which anxiety belongs to the manifest content, while the wishes whose represented fulfilment causes anxiety belong to the latent content revealed by association and analysis, is 'a perfectly *ad hoc* hypothesis, that is, an hypothesis introduced for the purpose of reconciling a theory with apparent counter-evidence, and without sustaining evidence of its own' (Glymour 1983: 64, 66).

Grünbaum is wrong about the Irma dream, as examination of Freud's text makes clear. For example, it is not the case that a wish to have been wrong about Irma – to have misdiagnosed a severe organic illness as hysteria – is among 'the aggressive conscious wishes Freud had on the day before the Irma dream'. There is no evidence that Freud had such a conscious wish at any time, and his discussion indicates that it arose only during sleep. This wish emerged in Freud's associations. So these do play an excavating role, leading to a wish of which Freud was not aware until he entered into the process of association, and of which he would not otherwise have known. The excavation at this point is not deep, but this is a first example.[6]

Glymour misses this as well. Otherwise he could not say that Freud's interpretation is enormously plausible, but also that his distinction between manifest and latent content, as applied in the case of unpleasant affects like anxiety, is a perfectly *ad hoc* device. For the affect in the manifest content connected with Freud's wish to have misdiagnosed Irma was *alarm about a perpetual source of anxiety*: and the wish itself, as we have seen, was part of the latent content. So Freud's analysis showed clearly, among other things, how representation of the satisfaction of a latent wish could give rise to a manifest alarm, and how the connection between these could emerge in association. This is an instance of the point Freud later makes about anxiety. So it cannot be that this interpretation is enormously plausible but the hypothesis as to a distinction between manifest and latent content in such cases perfectly *ad hoc*. Since Freud's analysis contains information Glymour does not register, his claim as to its uninformativeness must be rejected.

Let us now take the claim that Freud's analysis of the smoked salmon dream instantiates a fallacy of 'causal reversal'. Here is how the fallacy is described.

Glymour (1983) has discussed the aborted dinner party dream as an illustration of Freud's device 'to confirm an interpretation by finding two or more elements of the dream which are independently associated with a key figure in the dream.' The dream illustrates such a device, because after Freud had inferred the aim to thwart the dreamer's rival as the dream motive he said: 'All that was now lacking was some coincidence to confirm the solution' . . . When his patient reported her rival's fondness for smoked salmon, he had seized on the role of this delicacy in the manifest dream content as the confirming coincidence.

Glymour challenges this claim of confirmation as spurious. As he points out, Freud's conclusion as to the motivational cause had asserted an order of cause and effect that is the *reverse* of the causal order exhibited by the free associations, for associations generated by two manifest dream elements (the dinner party and the salmon) had *each* prompted the patient to think of her rival. But Freud took this to be evidence that the affect bound to that rival was the motivational cause for the thematic occurrence of both a dinner party and salmon in the manifest dream content. Glymour objects that 'evidence for the first causal model is not necessarily evidence for the second,' a causal reversal he indicts as 'one of Freud's fallacies'. Hence Glymour . . . rejects Freud's invocation of the 'coincidence' that both a dinner party and salmon figured in the manifest dream content: 'the coincidence is manufactured: one associates, at Freud's direction, until one thinks of something which has connections with several elements in one's dream; the several elements cause the common thought, not vice-versa, and the coincidence requires no further explanation. The method of manufacture is all the explanation required.'

(233–4)

Again the criticism rests on misunderstanding. The coincidence with which Freud is concerned comes in the woman's saying, in answer to his asking how she arrived at the salmon in the dream, that smoked salmon is her friend's favourite dish. This confirms the interpretation because it is further evidence of the connection of the dream with the woman's motives (beliefs), and in particular evidence of derivation which fits the motive Freud thinks the cause of the dream, jealousy.

Freud had already pointed out that the dreamer's jealousy gave her reason for not giving her friend a supper-party which would make her plumper and more attractive to the dreamer's husband, and so would provide a motive for dreaming of not giving a supper-party. Now, and fitting with this, it could be seen that the food the dreamer represented herself as having in the dream was precisely what her friend would like. That is: the dreamer represented herself not only as not giving what the object of her jealousy would like to get, but also as having what the object of her jealousy would like to have.

This coincidence is confirming because it is explanatory, under the hypothesis already given. There has to be some derivation of the content of the dream from the dreamer's motives if Freud's hypothesis is to be correct, and the association not only provides a derivation of an as yet unexplained aspect of content, but one which coincides particularly with the motive in question. So the coincidence with which Freud is concerned is between the information provided by the new association and the already hypothesized latent content of the dream, and is significant precisely because it provides a derivation of a detail in the manifest content from this latent content, and in a way that coheres with it. This is why Freud says: 'All that was lacking was some coincidence to confirm the solution. The smoked salmon in the dream had not yet been accounted for.'

Grünbaum and Glymour do not seem to see that the coincidence concerns the derivation from hypothesized latent motives, for, as Grünbaum says, Glymour's target is the supposed coincidence that a dinner party and smoked salmon both figure in the manifest content, or again that two elements in the manifest content prompt 'a thought' of the rival. Since neither of these is the coincidence in question, the argument miscarries.

It is natural to take Grünbaum and Glymour to be saying that Freud's mistake in reasoning about this example consists in taking effects as causes – in supposing that thoughts which in fact arose after the dream were causes of it. This would be the literal meaning of the claim that the dream elements 'cause the common thought, not vice-versa', or again the idea that 'method of manufacture' can explain the connections in content among latent thoughts and dreams upon which Freud's reasoning turns. So it is worth pointing out that this cannot apply to any of the causes with which Freud is concerned. The dreamer's jealousy existed before the dream, as did her knowledge of her friend's unattractive skinniness, desire to gain weight, be fed well, be invited to supper, and so on. The same applies to the 'common thought' upon which Grünbaum and Glymour focus, that the friend's favourite dish was smoked salmon. Since the dreamer had this belief before the dream and associations, it cannot have been caused by them.

Having seen that there is no fallacy of 'causal reversal' in this dream, let us take the last part of Grünbaum's critique, the claim that Freud commits such a fallacy in explicitly generalized form. Grünbaum cites the following passage from *The Interpretation of Dreams*:

If in fact we were met by objections such as these we could defend ourselves by appealing to the impression made by our interpretations, to the surprising connections with other elements of the dream which emerge in the course of our pursuing any one of its ideas, and to the improbability that anything which gives such an exhaustive account of the content of the dream could have been arrived at, except by following up psychical connections which had already been laid down.

(S.E. 1900, V: 528)

We have already seen that associations serve to account for the content of a dream by leading to motives from which the content is explained as derived by wish-fulfilment. This, if the explanation is correct, means that the associations lead from effects to causes. In this, however, they are 'following up psychical connections which had already been laid down', that is, from causes to effects.

The case is the same for straightforward self-ascription. If someone considers his own action and gives a motive, the consideration leads from action to motive, whereas the causal order is from motive to action. This can be called 'reverse causal inference', but it is clearly not fallacious. Freud treats association as like self-ascription, in somehow drawing on information available to the agent, because of their partly parallel explanatory role.

Freud's claim about causality in this passage is therefore correct, and for the reason he states. It surely is improbable that associations should serve to explain the content of a dream, except by giving information about the causes and connections by which the content was actually formed or determined (derived). Likewise it is surely improbable that self-ascriptions could so far explain the content of actions, except by giving similar information, which of course they do more directly. Here, as in the salmon dream, we find no fallacy, but accurate reasoning on Freud's part.

So, finally, it appears that Grünbaum has made no case against the view informing this criticism of his book, that much of Freud's reasoning can be regarded as cogently extending commonsense psychology. If Grünbaum has missed something about connection in content and wish-fulfilment, and if what has been missed constitutes reason to accept Freudian claims, then his conclusions systematically understate the support for Freudian theory. The degree of support or underestimation would depend upon assessment of data we cannot here survey.

Grünbaum emphasizes that future research may prove Freud right, saying this would show that Freud's brilliant imagination was 'serendipitous'. This implies that Freud's unexpected discoveries would, although proved true, be so by accident. If he was extending commonsense psychology this will not be so. Whatever proves his inferences true will also show them well founded, and the correct judgement will be that he had good reason for his conclusions all along, which was not acknowledged until the last.

NOTES

1 As elsewhere in this book, references to Freud's works in English are given in parentheses with the abbreviation S.E. (see Preface, p. xiv). In this chapter references to Grünbaum 1984 are simply by parenthetic page number in the text.
2 I discuss some of the issues below in the Introduction to Wollheim and Hopkins 1982.
3 Essentially the same role for content will follow on views of commonsense psychology as a system of laws of propositional content (see, e.g., Churchland 1984: esp. 56–66).
4 G. S. Klein, one of the 'hermeneuts' Grünbaum criticizes, describes the pattern of active reversal of passive experience as one which is found pervasively in analytical material. See Klein 1976: ch. 8.
5 Further examples, and the role of intention, are discussed in Wollheim and Hopkins 1982: Introduction. In some cases, such as the Rat Man's representation of his father's death and torture, the associated motives can plausibly be traced back into childhood. The role of motives is traced back, with wish-fulfilment as with reasons, through repeated, and hence chain-like, derivations. Such structured derivation is discernible in the Irma dream, since the wish for misdiagnosis subserved others.
6 In fact Freud carried the analysis deeper and found unpublishable sexual wishes. See the letter to Abraham of 9 January 1903 (Freud and Abraham 1965).

REFERENCES

Churchland, P. 1984: *Matter and Consciousness*. MIT Press.
Freud, S. and Abraham, K. 1965: *A Psychoanalytic Dialogue*.
Glymour, C. 1983: The theory of your dreams, in R. S. Cohen and S. Laudan (eds), *Physics, Philosophy and Psychoanalysis*. Reidel.
Grünbaum, A. 1984: *The Foundations of Psychoanalysis: A Philosophical Critique*. University of California Press.
Klein, G. S. 1976: *Psychoanalytic Theory*. International Universities Press.
Wollheim, R. and Hopkins, J. (eds) 1982: *Philosophical Essays on Freud*. Cambridge University Press.

3

'Exegetical Myth-Making' in Grünbaum's Indictment of Popper and Exoneration of Freud

FRANK CIOFFI

Adolf Grünbaum believes himself to have shown that contrary to Popper's characterization of him as a dogmatist, Freud was 'hospitable to refutation', 'responsive to adverse findings', and 'alert to the need for safeguarding the falsifiability of [his] interpretations and/or reconstructions of the patient's past' (1984: 273). Popper was particularly guilty of 'exegetical myth-making' in charging Freud and his followers with evasiveness in dealing with the objection that the apparent confirmation of their theories was due to their own prepossessions in conjunction with the compliance of the patient (the Oedipus effect). In fact Freud 'carefully', 'brilliantly', 'squarely', 'unflaggingly', 'unswervingly' (though ultimately unsuccessfully) 'faced up' to the problem of suggestion.

I

In 'Is Freudian Psychoanalytic Theory Pseudo-Scientific by Karl Popper's Criterion of Demarcation?' (1979a) Grünbaum asserts that Freud's 'repeated modifications of his theories were (as a rule) clearly motivated by evidence'. He illustrates this claim by citing Freud's 'modification' of the seduction theory. Was the abandonment of the seduction theory and its replacement by infantile incestuous fantasies 'clearly motivated by evidence'? Let us take these questions separately.

Why did Freud abandon the seduction theory? This is *one* of Grünbaum's accounts:

The incidence of hysteria was unexpectedly high, but sexual molestation in childhood was causally quite insufficient to generate hysteria. Hence if actual childhood seductions were causally necessary for hysteria as Freud had hypothesized, then the required incidence of perverted acts against children was preposterously high, even in the face of the attempted concealment of these transgressions by the guilty adults. And this over-taxed Freud's own belief in his seduction etiology.

(1979a: 135)

Was the 'incidence of perverted acts against children' required by Freud's theory 'preposterously high'? In the first place the presence of adult seducers among Freud's cases was adventitious and not required by the seduction theory. In seven of Freud's first 13 cases the seducer was another child. If Freud's seduction theory were adequately glossed as sexual victimization by an adult paedophile then the required incidence might be plausibly maintained to be 'preposterously high'.

But though Grünbaum thinks of the seduction theory as a theory of child rape (perhaps influenced by Jeffrey's Masson's misrepresentations), he is wrong to do so (Cioffi 1984). Freud's seduction theory is not a theory of child rape, not even in the broadest sense of sexual relations between an adult and a child. Though adults figured in an unspecified number of his patients' seduction histories, this was not necessitated by Freud's account of the source of the pathogenic power of sexual arousal in childhood which lies quite simply in its precocity. The question is not 'What are the chances of getting through childhood without being at the receiving end of the attentions of an adult pervert?' but 'What are the chances of avoiding "doctor and nurse" games and kindred forms of sex play with other children?' If Grünbaum thinks that even so understood the incidence of acts required by the seduction theory was 'preposterously high' then either he is extrapolating from a particularly chaste and protected childhood milieu, or I lived in a particularly depraved one, for I can see nothing 'preposterous' about the asumption that such occurrences are common enough to account for the presumed incidence of hysteria.

Furthermore, Grünbaum's thesis that Freud discovered the acts required by the seduction theory to be 'preposterously high' contradicts the account Freud himself gives in *Three Essays on Sexuality* (his first public disavowal of the seduction theory), where he denies that he had exaggerated the frequency of seduction. The reason he then goes on to give, that he abandoned seductions because he discovered that healthy people may also have undergone experiences of infantile seduction, is both untrue and incoherent. Untrue in that he could not have *discovered* this since he explicitly alludes to it in the seduction papers themselves, and incoherent in that even had he discovered it it would have provided him with no grounds for abandoning his seduction aetiology since this only committed him to the necessary and not the sufficient condition of adult neuroses. In other words, for a case to overthrow Freud's seduction aetiology it would have had to consist of a neurotic who had *not* been seduced, and not just a non-neurotic who had. He repeats this spurious argument in 'My Views on the Role of Sexuality in the Neuroses' (1906a): 'Investigation into the mental life of normal persons yielded the unexpected discovery that their infantile history in regard to sexual matters was not necessarily different in essentials from that of the neurotic and that seduction in particular had played the same part in it' (Freud 1924: 279). How could the fact that non-neurotics may also have been seduced in infancy have been an 'unexpected discovery' when in one of the seduction papers themselves he went out of his way to insist on it? – 'We have heard and acknowledged that there are many people who have a very clear recollection of infantile sexual experiences and yet do not suffer from hysteria' (1924: 207). 'It is easy enough to find people who remember scenes of sexual seduction and abuse in their childhood but yet have never suffered from hysteria' (1924: 203).

But Grünbaum has an alternative account as to why Freud abandoned the seduction theory, one which does not depend on intuitive assessments of the incidence of seductions: he refers to 'adverse evidence [Freud] himself had uncovered', i.e. Freud simply came across a neurotic who had not been seduced in infancy. Freud himself gives countenance to this view in one of his belated accounts of the theory and its desertion when he speaks of 'contradiction in definitely ascertainable circumstances' (1924: 299). But a proper conception of Freud's seduction theory poses difficulties for this account as well. In 'Heredity and Aetiology' Freud describes the pathogenic agent in hysteria as a 'passive sexual experience undergone with indifference or with a slight degree of disgust or fright' (1924: 152) and this does raise the question of how he could be sure that an adult neurotic had not as a child had a 'passive sexual experience undergone with indifference'.

Grünbaum may have got the impression that seductions have a blatancy which makes Freud's claim to have discovered 'contradiction in definitely ascertainable circumstances' credible from Freud's reference to 'grave sexual injuries, some of them absolutely appalling' (1924: 157). But nothing in Freud's theory of the pathogenic effect of seduction commits him to brutal assaults such as we can easily credit might be discovered not to have taken place.

The 'grave sexual injuries' remark does, however, raise problems as to the credibility of Grünbaum's thesis that the alteration in Freud's views were 'clearly motivated by evidence' if it is construed to comprise Freud's seduction *reconstructions* and their later retraction. For it means that we are to imagine Freud, having originally decided that his patients had suffered grave sexual injuries, later deciding that this was a mistake. This raises doubts as to the empirical character of either the procedure which led him to assert the occurrence of 'grave sexual injuries' in the first place or to deny them in the second. We must distinguish between Freud's *aetiological* error and his *reconstructive* error when speaking of the 'seduction debacle'. There is a difference between failing to find any evidence of infantile seduction in new patients and deciding that many of his 18 patients whose seductions in infancy he was confident enough to have reported as confirmation of the seduction theory had not after all been seduced. Of Freud's ostensibly seduced patients how many did he change his mind about? He never gave a precise figure but he did say that the majority had not after all been seduced, which means at least ten errors. Now we can credit that with extraordinary luck and extraordinary pertinacity Freud might have confirmed his suspicions that he was mistaken in two or three cases; but in ten? Let me confide my nasty suspicions; we need not rack our brains to attempt to reconstruct how Freud could possibly discover that the reported brutal assaults of ten or more of his patients were 'contradicted under definitely ascertainable circumstances' because there may have been no such discoveries. Freud did not falsify his reconstructions. He merely withdrew from them. Why? Well, consider the alternative. Although there would have been no logical contradiction in Freud's maintaining both that the seduction theory was mistaken *and* that his own reconstructions were nevertheless sound, it would have strained their credulity excessively to ask his colleagues to believe that, *by chance* 100 per cent of his clientele had been seduced in early childhood.[1]

We can't be sure why Freud abandoned the seduction theory but only that his own account makes no sense. My own guess is that the major difference between 1896 and 1897 is not that in the interval Freud discovered the seductions had not always occurred but that he discovered how to do without them. To whatever theoretical reasons Freud had for clinging to infantile sexuality and therefore retreating to 'psychic reality' must be added the advantageous elusiveness and malleability of that 'psychic reality' itself.

In his book Grünbaum supplements his earlier account as to why Freud dropped the seduction theory with the suggestion (contained in the Fliess letter) that the disappointment of his therapeutic hopes may have caused Freud to doubt the correctness of his aetiology. That his therapeutic achievements were often incomplete was acknowledged by Freud in the seduction papers themselves and so need not have been felt by him to be inconsistent with the seduction aetiology. In any case he had never placed much weight on therapeutic success as the source of his aetiological conviction: 'Without wishing to lay special stress on the fact I will add that in a number of cases the therapeutic test also speaks for the genuine nature of the infantile scenes. . . . The aetiological pretensions of the infantile scenes rest . . . above all on the evidence of the associative and logical connections between these scenes and the hysterical symptoms' (1924: 206). Furthermore, though therapeutic failure might prompt Freud to suspect the pathogenic *influence* of seductions in childhood it could not, of itself bring their *historicity* into question.

Grünbaum is able to confer a semblance of plausibility on his thesis that the seduction episode illustrates Freud's hospitality to refutation by choosing a formulation which enables him to place the emphasis on what Freud abandoned rather than on what he retained.

Freud himself characterized his seduction phase in terms which permit us to pose more pointed questions about his transition from seduction to incestuous and polymorphous perversity than Grünbaum's. In his first extended account of the post-seduction aetiology Freud said: 'I consider it worth emphasizing that, in spite of all the changes in them, my views concerning the aetiology of the neuroses have never caused me to disavow or abandon two points of view: namely, the importance of sexuality and of infantilism' (1924: 280).

What grounds had Freud for not abandoning these more general views? He was able to retain both sexuality and infancy while abandoning seduction by persuading himself that the infantile seduction scenes he found in his 18 consecutive patients, when they were not authentic, were distorted recollections of infantile incestuous fantasizing. But it was not only a substantive thesis as to the infantile determinants of psychoneuroses that this manoeuvre enabled Freud to retain but also, and more essentially, the authenticity of his novel diagnostic and reconstructive methods. As Ernest Jones put it, 'In finding that these seductions had in most cases not taken place he could only conclude that his method was fallible or that there was some other explanation' (Jones 1957). The question Grünbaum does not address is what justification Freud had for not concluding 'that his method was fallible' rather than 'that there was some other explanation'.

Why should the belief that s/he had been sexually abused by a parent be less distressing to a patient than the memory of having sexually desired one? And why, since the fabricated memory of seduction was as unconscious as the genuine incestuous fantasy it replaced, was there any point to subjecting the latter to distortion in the first place?

There is reason to think that Freud himself came to find his account of adult seduction convictions as distortions of infantile incestuous fantasies unconvincing because twenty years after the desertion of the seduction theory he suggested that the seduction reminiscences were not illusory after all. Only they were authentic reminiscences of episodes in the life, not of the patient, but of a prehistoric ancestor at a time when paternal paedophile attacks on children were a reality ('in the pre-history of the human family' (Freud 1963: 323–4).) Ug-a-wug, it seems, was a *Kinderschander*. (Strange that Alley Oop never mentions it.) In any case, male cross-sex seduction memories require maternal paedophiles. Was this, too, a reality in the 'pre-history of the human family'? Did Mrs Ug-a-wug share her mate's kinks?

The alternative to the view that the seduction ideation Freud found to underlie his patients' symptoms was a self-protective distortion of their infantile incestuous fantasies is that Freud's *a priori* conviction that the neuroses had sexual sources led him both to influence his patients' productions and to place tendentious constructions upon them. Freud mentions the possibility only to dismiss it with the assurance that he had undertaken the treatment of the seduction patients without any such prepossessions.

In his autobiographical study Freud says of his discovery of the pathogenic influence of sexual life: 'I had begun my investigation of neurotics quite unsuspectingly' (1935: 41) and refers his readers to the book he had published with Breuer in 1895. 'It would have been difficult to guess from the *Studien über Hysterie* what an importance sexuality had in the aetiology of the neuroses' (1935: 39). Freud had issued the same reassurance in the lectures delivered in America in 1909, where he said of the development of his view that 'the predominant significance [in neurotic disorders] must be assigned to disturbances in erotic life'; that 'far from this position having been postulated theoretically, at the time of the publication of the *Studies on Hysteria* I had not yet adopted it' (Freud 1962: 69).

Would anyone have suspected from these utterances that what Freud had said of the pathogenic role of sexuality in the Preface to the *Studies on Hysteria* was that 'sexuality seems to play a principal part in the psychogenesis of hysteria' (Freud and Breuer 1966: xxx), or that in the body of the book he wrote, 'the determining causes which lead to the acquisition of neuroses . . . [are] to be looked for in sexual factors' and described himself as submitting his cases 'to a deliberate and searching investigation of their sexual foundations'? (1966: 305). Even earlier (at the beginning of 1894) he had expressed the view that 'the source of the incompatible ideas which are submitted to defence is solely and exclusively sexual life' (S.E. 1897, III: 225). Even if we construe Freud's disavowals of sexual expectations to refer specifically to infantile seductions rather than the general pathogenic influence of sexual life, they are untrue. In a letter to Fliess in 1895 he speaks of a patient 'giving me what I waited for, "infantile abuse"' (1985: 149). And in a draft sent to Fliess, dated 1892, he cites as one of the aetiological factors in neuroses 'sexual traumas dating back before the age of understanding' (1985: 33). And yet in his autobiography Freud says of the role of sexual factors in neuroses, 'I was not prepared for this conclusion and my expectations played no part in it' (1935: 41). Was it not Freud's memories rather than those of his patients that had undergone self-protective distortion?

So much for the state of Freud's convictions on the role of sexuality in the aetiology of the neuroses while he was treating the seduction patients. A related question rises. Did he tell his patients of these convictions? Did his patients' seduction material sometimes emerge only after Freud had told them of his suspicions? There are reasons for thinking so. In the *Studies on Hysteria* (1895) he dismissed the danger of suggestion: 'We need not be afraid of telling the patient what his next thought connection is going to be. It will do no harm' (Freud and Breuer 1966: 341). In the same work he says of a patient, 'I assured her that she would see something that was directly related to the causes of her condition in her childhood.' In one of the seduction papers themselves Freud says of his patients' response to the seduction scene, 'They are generally indignant if we tell them something of the sort is now coming to light' (1924: 199); and in another, 'The mental image of the premature sexual experience is recalled only when most energetic pressure is exerted by the analytic procedure against strong resistance' (1924: 150).

Even if Grünbaum was unfamiliar with these pronouncements of Freud he ought not to have accepted Freud's account of the seduction error since it is apparent from the seduction papers themselves, without any familiarity with Freud's other statements on the subject, that his denial that his expectations of a seduction aetiology anticipated his patients' confirmation of it is quite impossible. For example, how had Freud so cleverly managed to synchronize his treatment of the first 13 seduction patients as not to permit the conclusion he had arrived at concerning any one of them to affect his anticipations with respect to any of the others? Furthermore, we know that Freud followed up his report on these 13 in which he had committed himself to the indispensability of infantile seduction with a report on five more. Could he have approached them too without anticipation, as he claims?

There are still other considerations internal to the seduction papers themselves that are inconsistent with Freud's denials that his conviction that his patients had undergone infantile seductions anticipated their own. In the last of them, 'The Aetiology of Hysteria', Freud argued that it was not sufficient that an occurrence be found which had been repressed and had coincided with the beginning of the illness. In order to be a satisfactory explanation the trauma must meet two other requirements. First, it must have traumatic force. Thus, an occasion on which a patient had bitten into a rotten apple would not be a satisfactory explanation of his nausea even if he had repressed it and his neurosis had dated from it, for it was not severe enough for the neurosis to be attributed to it.

Freud's second requirement of an adequate trauma was that it have what he called 'determining quality'. Even though the patient's memory efforts terminated in the recovery of an experience which did have traumatic force, like a railway accident, this too was unsatisfactory as an explanation since it did not explain why the patient was suffering from nausea rather than an hysterical paralysis, say. The railway accident lacked 'determining quality'.

Let me quote Freud's own words: 'When the scene first revealed does not satisfy our requirements, we say to the patient that his experience does not explain anything, but that there must be hidden behind it an earlier and more significant experience' (1924: 189).

Now Freud tells us that a common presenting complaint of his hysterical patients was painful genital sensations. But if you begin with a patient among whose presenting symptoms are painful sensations in the region of the genitals, painful sensations while defecating, say, and you further insist that the originating trauma must have determining quality, how can it be a matter for astonishment that the infantile trauma turns out to involve penetration of the rectal area? In any case Freud is explicit that before arriving at the infantile seduction he had already invariably uncovered a pubescent sexual trauma (1924: 194). He construed this to mean either that hysterics were so constituted as to respond pathologically to sexual life or that they had suffered a still earlier trauma related associatively to the pubescent one and capable of supplying its explanatory deficiencies.

Once Freud laid down the determining requirement, the sexual character of the traumas was a foregone conclusion, and Freud must have known this; so he couldn't have been surprised at the character of these traumas. Why then does he insist that he was? Because, I suggest, of his need to undercut the objection that the patient's production of seduction material was due to Freud's own anticipations of it.

A particularly deplorable instance of Grünbaum's 'exegetical myth-making' is his claim that 'the prima facie confirmations of the postulated seduction episodes had been furnished by the seemingly vivid and presumably repressed memories that Freud had been able to elicit from his hysterical patients in the course of analysis'. Grünbaum goes on to refer to 'the subjective certainty felt by his adult patients in the reality of purported memories going back to childhood'. I have given my reasons elsewhere for doubting that Freud's patients generally had seduction memories of which they were subjectively certain (Cioffi 1975: 172–4). ('Patients assure me emphatically of their unbelief'; 'They have no feeling of recollecting these scenes' (Freud 1924: 199).) But Grünbaum's more important error is in claiming that it was his patient's 'subjective certainty' that formed Freud's grounds for his belief in the reality of the seductions. Though this is Freud's later account, in the seduction papers themselves he is adamant that this is not the case ('I would charge myself with blameworthy credulity if I did not offer more convincing proof'). Nor is this 'more convincing proof' Grünbaum's highly touted Tally Argument. It is what Grünbaum himself describes as 'the consilience of extra-clinical inductions'.

It was to such 'consilience' that Freud appealed in the seduction papers. In the last of them he wrote: 'Just as when putting together children's puzzles we finally, after many attempts, become absolutely certain which piece belongs to the gap not yet filled . . . so the content of the infantile scenes proves to be an inevitable completion of the associative logical structure of the neuroses' (1924: 200–1). What Grünbaum's account mischievously obscures is that it was this very mode of reasoning, or at least Freud's uncritical confidence in it, which led to what he refers to as the 'seduction debacle'. And yet a quarter of a century later Freud was still at it. In 'Remarks on the Theory and Practice of Dream Interpretation' (1923) he wrote: 'What makes [the analyst] certain in the end is precisely the complication of the problem before him, which is like the solution of a jigsaw puzzle' (1950: 142).

Freud made a tendentiously inadequate response to his realization that many of his reconstructions of the patient's infantile sexual life were erroneous. His dealings with the possibility that this was due to a combination of the contaminating effect of his own prior convictions and the looseness of his criteria for determining the correctness of his reconstructions was uncandid. His failure to modify these accordingly meant that his grounds for assigning his patients a history of polymorphous, perverse and incestuous fantasizing were as dubious as his grounds for assigning them histories of infantile seductions had been. Grünbaum's laudatory account of Freud's response to the seduction error performs a serious disservice in allowing this point to be lost. Contrary to Grünbaum's assertions the abandonment of the seduction theory is equivocal evidence that Freud was 'clearly motivated by evidence'. His replacement of it with the incestuous fantasy theory is unequivocal evidence that he was not.

II

Grünbaum holds that one of the 'episodes of significant theory modification that eloquently attests to Freud's responsiveness to *adverse* clinical and even extra-clinical findings' is 'the lesson that Freud learned from the failure of the Rat Man case to bear out his etiological retrodiction' (Grünbaum 1984: 281). What Grünbaum means by Freud's 'etiological retrodiction' is that Freud said that the Rat Man had been beaten by his father for masturbating but it turned out that he hadn't. The 'significant theory modification' (the 'lesson') is Freud's supposed consequent supplementation of public events like beatings with private events like fantasies in the aetiology of the neuroses. Grünbaum misdescribes Freud's post-seduction aetiology and misdescribes the Rat Man case itself but, even had he done neither, the supplementation of public events by fantasies would not constitute evidence of a creditable reponsiveness to 'adverse findings'.

Clark Glymour (on whose papers Grünbaum draws) says of Freud's speculation that the Rat Man had been beaten for sexual misbehaviour, 'Freud makes it sound as though the construction was but a conjecture peculiar to this case and not required required by psychoanalytic theory. But that is not correct' (Glymour 1974: 299). It *is* correct and nothing Glymour goes on to say shows otherwise. Grünbaum follows Glymour in confounding a particular reconstruction with a generic aetiology. What Grünbaum calls Freud's aetiological retrodiction in the case of the Rat Man was not 'based on' his 'specific etiology for obsessions'. He had none. Freud's claim to have anticipated that the Rat Man was beaten in childhood is contradicted by the account given in the Original Record of the case (Cioffi 1985).[2] The fact that the Rat Man had not been beaten for a sexual offence could not in any case have had any adverse bearing on Freud's post-seduction aetiology. Grünbaum writes: 'Freud had postulated that premature sexual activity, such as excessive masturbation, subject to severe repression is the specific cause of obsessional neurosis' (1984: 281). Not so. This is Grünbaum's account of the concept of specific causation:

'by claiming that P is a specific pathogen of N, he was asserting not only that P is causally necessary for N but also that P is never, or hardly ever, on etiological factor in pathogenesis of any other pathologically distinct syndrome'. And yet, whereas Grünbaum tells us that Freud's post-seduction theory held excessive masturbation to be the specific cause of obsessional neuroses, Glymour, whom he invokes in support, takes it to be the specific cause of hystria (1974: 302). It cannot have been the specific cause of both. In fact it was the specific cause of neither. In his first extended account of his post-seduction aetiology Freud writes, 'A specific aetiology in the form of particular infantile experiences is not forthcoming' (1924: 281).

The proffering of premature sexual activity as a specific cause of the obsessional neuroses occurs for the first time in the Rat Man case itself and is contradicted by the cases of Dora and of Little Hans, both of whom are said by Freud to have been sexually precocious, as well as by the statement in the *Three Essays on Sexuality* that sexual precocity is a characteristic of neuroses generally (section in the 'Summary' headed 'Precocity').

Freud had no independent criteria for either 'premature sexual activity such as excessive masturbation' nor for 'severe repression'. The fact that someone had fallen ill as an adult was adequate grounds for the retrospective attribution of either. What was excessive for one child might be tolerable for another, and what was optimal for one child might be pathogenic for another. In the 1905 edition of the *Three Essays on Sexuality* Freud wrote: 'It was not possible to say what amount of sexual activity can occur in childhood without it being described as abnormal or detrimental to later development' (1965: 139).

Thus the case of the Rat Man could not have refuted Freud's post-seduction aetiology because even if his childhood had been without abnormal sexual traumas this was fully consistent with the role allotted in Freud's theory to the constitutional factor which was capable of rendering traumas otiose. (This is not to say that Freud's post-seduction theory was without empirical content but only that it was not testable by single case studies but only by large-scale epidemiological inquiry. Freud was committed to there being a lesser incidence of sexual intimidation, such as castration threats, among non-neurotics but he was not committed, as Grünbaum thinks, to any particular neurotic, e.g. the Rat Man, having been sexually intimidated.)

Furthermore, in implying that Freud's discovery that the Rat Man had not been beaten for a sexual offence would have left him bereft of eligible pathogens, thus forcing him to fall back on fantasies, Grünbaum is misrepresenting the contents of the Rat Man case itself, which is replete with eligible pathogens. How could the 'lesson' that infantile sexual fantasies would do as well as infantile sexual experience as a pathogenic agent be learned from a case history which in fact records infantile sexual experiences?[3]

Let us suppose that Freud *had* held that sexual intimidation in early childhood was a necessary condition of adult neuroses and that the only eligible candidate for such intimidation in the Rat Man's childhood had been his father beating him. Why should Freud's response to the discovery that the beating was not an instance of sexual intimidation by supplementing sexual intimidation with fears of sexual intimidation as factors in the aetiology of the neuroses be held to illustrate responsiveness to adverse evidence? Ought we not to reserve that expression for the admission that the Rat Man's neurotic disposition may have been brought about by castigation which was *not* construed as sexually intimidating? There is something disingenous in Grünbaum's invoking as 'telling evidence' of Popper's 'exegetical oversight' an account of Freud's procedure which makes it illustrative of just those practices that Popper was concerned to reprobate.

The introduction of infantile fantasies as pathogenic factors meant that though Freud's reconstructions might still be imperilled by independent inquiry if they contained allusions to public states of affairs, his aetiology was, nevertheless, proof against refutation since the child's propensity to pathogenic fantasizing was freed from environing circumstance.

One of Grünbaum's more original discoveries is that Freud was a good falsificationist, always 'alert to the need for safeguarding the falsifiability of the analyst's reconstructions of the patient's past' (1984: 237). This is both false and misleading. Misleading because, whatever the formal position with respect to extraclinical events, it was Freud's practice to validate his reconstructions of the patient's past intraclinically. False, because when Freud does deal with external evidence he often manifests no alertness to safeguarding anything but his own reconstructive pretensions.

In *The Psychoanalytic Movement* Ernest Gellner writes: 'Freud rather revealingly repudiated the relevance of historical reconstructions of the public event on the ground that by invoking independent witnesses it imposed an external judge on the process of analysis' (1985: 183). The passage that Gellner had in mind occurs in a footnote to the second chapter of the case history of the Wolf Man: 'It may be tempting to take the easy course of filling up the gaps in a patient's memory by making inquiries from the older members of his family; but I cannot advise too strongly against such a technique. Any stories that may be told by relatives in reply to inquiries and requests are at the mercy of every critical misgiving that can come into play. One invariably regrets having made oneself dependent upon such information . . . confidence in the analysis is shaken and a court of appeal is set up over it' (Freud 1925: 482).

I put the same construction as Gellner on these remarks in 'Freud and the Idea of a Pseudo-Science' (Cioffi 1970). Grünbaum argued that any implication of evasiveness is neutralized by a sentence I 'tendentiously omitted' – 'Information of this kind may as a rule be employed as absolutely authentic material.' Since the information Freud is referring to in this sentence is 'stories about his childhood which the patient was told' *before* the analysis and these were just those external facts from which Freud had least to fear as he could ascertain them before he advanced his reconstructions, I do not think the self-protective interpretation of Freud's remark is necessarily undermined. However, Grünbaum has another argument:

But does Freud here reject all use of independent external evidence as to the historical veracity of his clinical reconstructions of a patient's infancy after the completion of the analysis? It would seem not. What Freud does renounce here is the questioning of senior relatives, conducted by the analyst, to fill up the gaps in the patient's memory as a procedural technique for making progress in the analysis. This renunciation does not preclude his willingness to test his clinical reconstructions by means of independent external evidence once the analysis has been completed. Indeed he displayed this kind of willingness in his retrospective external evaluation of his clinical findings in the Rat Man case.

(1979b: 86)

Grünbaum then goes on to cite Freud's withdrawal of his original conjecture as to why the Rat Man was beaten.

There are times when Grünbaum goes through Freud's text like a sleepwalker. For of course it is not the case that Freud waited until after the analysis was completed before making inquiries as to the circumstances under which the Rat Man was beaten. He even wove the information provided by the patient's mother (that he had bitten someone) into his solution of 'the great obsessive fear'. So Freud had no hesitation in using information from the very sources he condemns in his Wolf Man remarks. Doesn't this entitle us to suspect a degree of opportunism in the advice he there gives?

In the case history of the Rat Man Freud has no scruples about inciting the patient to make 'pointed enquiries' of his mother as to the beating episode and of incorporating the reply (that it was for biting someone) into his interpretations, using it to bolster his view that the Rat Man identified himself with rats since he and they both bit and both were persecuted for it. 'It is seldom that we are in the fortunate position of being able, as in the present instance, to establish the facts upon which these tales of the individual's prehistoric past are based, by recourse to the unimpeachable testimony of a grown-up person' (Freud 1925: 344). What had happened to transform 'the unimpeachable testimony of a grown-up person' of 1909 into 'stories that . . . are at the mercy of every critical misgiving' of 1915? Until Grünbaum can bring himself to address such questions he ought to attempt to control his compulsion to issue ill-considered testimonials to Freud's 'responsiveness to adverse evidence'.

III

Grünbaum calls Popper's observation that suggestibility 'seems to have failed to attract the attention of analysts, perhaps not accidentally', 'incredibly uninformed and grossly unfair' (1984: 282). Grünbaum insists on glossing Popper's remark to mean that Freud and his followers never raised and discussed the problem of suggestion. This would be 'incredibly uninformed' and for that very reason it is incredible. I know of no one who has ever taken Popper to mean anything other than that Freud and his followers never took proper account of the influence of suggestion on their patients' productions, however infelicitously he may have put it.

Fortunately, Grünbaum advances arguments which do not depend on his pedantic construal of Popper's remark. He argues that Freud did more than merely discuss the problem of suggestion. He 'brilliantly', 'unswervingly' faced up to it even if he failed to resolve it. How did Freud, on Grünbaum's view, 'face up' to suggestibility? Via the Tally Argument. 'Freud's 1917 Tally Argument was a brilliant effort to come to grips with the full dimensions of the challenge of epistemic contamination by adulterated clinical response' (1984: 283). What is the Tally Argument? Grünbaum derives the expression from the Standard Edition translation of a sentence in Introductory Lecture 28: '[the neurotic's] conflicts will only be successfully solved and his resistances overcome if the anticipatory ideas he is given tally with what is real in him' (S.E. 1917, XVI: 452). Grünbaum makes three errors in his dealing with Freud's Tally Argument: he gratuitously concedes Freud's entitlement to therapeutic superiority; he gives therapeutic superiority justificatory powers it does not possess; and he overstates Freud's dependence on and commitment to its justificatory status.

Grünbaum has not sufficiently emancipated himself from the bad historiographic habits of psychoanalytic commentators. He speaks of Freud's having dealt 'brilliantly' with objections to his theories but shows no knowledge of these objections except through Freud's account of them. For example he denies that Freud's reply to the charge of suggestibility was a mere *ipse dixit*. While it may not have been so with respect to the question Freud set himself, it was with respect to the question he was asked. The objection Freud had to meet (from Aschaffenburg, Kraeplin and Janet among others) was that he could not use therapeutic efficacy to support his infantile sexual aetiology since other therapists had treated neuroses as successfully without holding such an aetiology. What Grünbaum calls Freud's necessary condition thesis (NCT) amounts to the claim 'Only my therapy really works, your results are either ephemeral or superficial'. (In 1904 he wrote: 'The analytic method of psychotherapy is the one that penetrates most deeply and carries farthest' (1924: 252).) What grounds had Freud for the assumption that his therapy refreshed the parts Aschaffenburg, Ziehen, Prince, Sidis, Janet et al. could not reach?

The question Freud set himself in Lecture 28 was how to distinguish the rationale of psychoanalytic therapy from that of suggestion therapies since both exploit the physician's ascendancy over the patient. That is, Freud assumes a critic who concedes the efficacy of his methods but objects that they amount to disguised versions of suggestive therapy. Having assumed both the efficacy of his therapeutic efforts and their superiority to those of rival practitioners, Freud addresses himself to the question of how, given the admitted role that the physician's relation to the patients plays in the treatment, he can be sure that either his acquiescence in Freud's aetiological and dynamic proposals, or his production of material apparently confirmatory of them is not due to his compliance rather than the truth of Freud's interpretations and/or reconstructions. Freud's reply is an account of how the rationale and procedure of psychoanalysis differ from those of suggestive therapies and an assertion that the efficacy of psychoanalytic therapy depends on the veridicality of the account of himself that the patient comes to accept. Grünbaum thinks that Freud was entitled to advance this argument until sometime in the mid-twenties when he was compelled to acknowledge the reality of spontaneous remission and so lost his grounds for maintaining that psychoanalytic treatment was a *sine qua non* of recovery from neurosis. But Freud had never been in a position to claim that psychoanalytic treatment (i.e. treatment in which an essential component was the anamnesis of the content of Freud's infantile sexual aetiology of the neuroses) was a *sine qua non* of therapeutic efficacy and even less that veridical anamnesis was.

The question Grünbaum evades is how Freud could *ever* have employed the Tally Agument with any credibility or conviction when it commited him to an assertion that it was manifest he was in no position to make, viz., that he had examined the outcomes of other therapeutic methods and found them inferior to his own.

It is likely that the ephemerality of the results of hypnotic suggestion was a familiar fact. In any case there was nothing implausible about Freud's claim to have employed suggestion with generally disappointing results. What Freud could not plausibly claim was that he had had patients who had anamnesed or abreacted, e.g. Adlerian pathogenic episodes, and had shown only short-term remission of their illness in consequence. But the situation is worse for Grünbaum's thesis than even these considerations bring out. Not only could Freud have no grounds for believing his NCT true; he had reason for believing it false.

For the Tally Argument to have any force Freud would not only have had to accompany it with reasons for doubting the efficacy of rival therapies but also with a retraction of his own claims to therapeutic achievements before adopting the 'Oedipal' view of neurotic difficulties. He would have had to explain away the 'countless successes' remark of the 1898 paper 'Sexuality in the Aetiology of the Neuroses' (Freud 1924: 244). The least that such a claim would imply is that Freud was able to compare the post-analytic condition of his 'seduction' patients with that of his 'Oedipal' patients and found that the condition of the latter was much more satisfactory. But Freud never made such a claim and if he had would have raised some awkward questions as to what opportunity he had to make the comparison and how he went about it.

Grünbaum says of Freud's seduction patients: 'Clearly the NCT would have been strongly disconfirmed if there had been cases of patients who had been genuinely cured after being given pseudo-insight by their analyses into episodes of sexual abuse that had presumably never occurred in their childhood' (1984: 159). This remark indicates some degree of confusion on Grünbaum's part. The NCT is meant 'to constitute cogent evidence for the specific etiologies of the psychoneuroses'. But since the core of Freud's 'specific etiologies of the psychoneuroses' was the Oedipus complex, i.e. the repression of incestuous longings for the cross-sex parent, the fact that the episodes of sexual abuse had not occurred is completely irrelevant to the disconfirmatory status of genuine cure among the patients of the 1896 papers. For even those who *had* been sexually abused and thus had been given *veridical* insight would, nevertheless, not have anamnesed/abreacted their incestuous desires and castratory fears and thus would have attained their neuroses-free status without benefit of the theory on whose behalf the NCT was advanced. That is, if any single one of Freud's 18 'seduction' patients had been genuinely relieved of their neuroses then Freud would have had reason to doubt that his therapeutic efficacy could be enlisted in support of his Oedipal aetiology.

But even if the assumption of differential therapeutic efficacy was granted Freud, this could still not meet scepticism as to his aetiological claims. The differential therapeutic efficacy of psychoanalysis might have been due to a feature not present in other therapies and yet not related to the veridicality of Freud's theory of pathogenesis. As the psychoanalyst J. C. Flügel conceded in 1924, the argument over the relevance of therapeutic efficacy ended in deadlock because it could not be shown that even if psychoanalysis was more effective this was not because 'psychoanalytic suggestion was more effective than suggestion of a simple and more direct kind' (Flügel 1924: 51).

In 1959 Ernst Nagel wrote: 'The changes in various symptoms which the patient exhibits as the interview progresses do not constitute evidence for an interpretation unless it can be shown that such changes are not produced by some combination of factors for which the whole interview is responsible' (Nagel 1959: 51–2). These considerations were as available to Freud in 1917 as to Nagel forty years later. How then could Freud have believed that with the Tally Argument he had rendered suggestion 'epistemically innocuous'? Stuart Sutherland's accusation, which Grünbaum quotes (1984: 172), that Freud was 'taking for granted the very point he is trying to prove' is perfectly just and Grünbaum's exposition leaves us perplexed as to why he thinks otherwise.

So infatuated is Grünbaum with the notion that he has discovered in the Tally Argument something momentous and hitherto overlooked that the most obvious objections escape him. If we state Freud's NCT as 'No one can recover from a neurosis who doesn't anamnese the content of my infantile aetiology' then every time Freud makes a change in this aetiology he either has falsified his NCT anew or has to revise his notion of what constitutes recovery from neurosis; neither a very persuasive proceeding.

The arguments I have hitherto advanced for the feebleness of the Tally Argument are also to a lesser extent reasons for denying that Freud depended on it. But Freud's behaviour in relation to contamination objections provides more direct evidence for thinking that he had little confidence in the Tally Argument.

Grünbaum attributes to Freud 'a sovereign patronizing serenity' (1984: 170) towards sceptical arguments based on suggestibility, and he attributes this serenity to Freud's conviction that the distinctive therapeutic efficacy of psychoanalysis rendered suggestibility 'epistemically innocuous'. But the evidence is that the suggestibility argument, rather than meeting with a 'patronizing serenity' goaded Freud into lying. He more often met the suggestibility objection by unveracious accounts of psychoanalytic procedure than by invoking his therapeutic results, which indicates that he did not have much confidence in the Tally Argument. This is what he said in 'The Question of Lay Analysis': 'The analyst never entices his patient on to the ground of sex. He does not say to him in advance: "We shall be dealing with the intimacies of your sexual life!" He allows him to begin what he has to say wherever he pleases, and quietly awaits until the patient himself touches on sexual things. I used always to warn my pupils: "Our opponents have told us that we come upon cases in which the factor of sex plays no part. Let us be careful not to introduce it into our analyses and so spoil our chance of finding such a case"' (1962: 118–19). This is what he said in the 1898 paper 'Sexuality and the Aetiology of the Neurosis' (the one in which he should have announced his desertion on the seduction aetiology but did not): 'an experienced physician does not meet his patients unprepared, and as a rule asks of them not elucidation but merely confirmation of his surmises . . . in the very description of their symptoms, which they volunteer too readily, they will usually have acquainted him with the sexual factors hidden behind' (1924: 224). On the same page: 'It would be a great advantage if patients could know the extent to which physicians will henceforth be able to interpret their neurotic ailments with certainty, and to infer from them the sexual aetiology at work.' I think it fair to infer from these remarks that Freud had no inhibitions about informing his patients of the importance he attached to their sexual lives.

The paper whose solution to the problem of patient compliance Grünbaum charges Popper with misrepresenting ('gross unfairness') is 'Remarks on The Theory and Practice of Dream-Interpretation' (S.E. 1923, XIX). This is how Freud deals in it with the suggestibility problem:

Is it possible, then that confirmatory dreams are really the result of suggestion, that they are compliant dreams? . . . I recall a discussion which I was led into with a patient (who asked) whether his narcissistic wish to be cured might not have caused him to produce these dreams, since, after all, I had held out to him a prospect of recovery if he were able to accept my constructions. I could only reply that I had not yet come across any such mechanism of dream-formation.

(Freud 1950: 143–4)

But Freud had come across such a mechanism. As early as 1897 he had invoked it to account for a dream of erotic play with his nine-year-old daughter which he attributed to his wish to produce evidence supporting the theory of paternal seduction. And had he forgotten 'counter-wish' dreams'? If a patient was capable of producing a dream in order that it might appear to contradict Freud's theories, why should not another patient produce one in order to confirm them?

In this same paper this is the account Freud gives of how he met a patient's objections that his dreams may have been influenced in a manner which deprived them of evidential value: 'He recollected some dreams which he had had before starting analysis and indeed before he had known anything about it; and the analysis of these dreams, which were free from all suspicion of suggestion, led to the same interpretations as the later ones' (1950: 144). But since dream interpretation depends on the patient's associations to his dream, how can the 'analysis of these dreams' have been 'free from all suspicion of suggestion'? Do not the lengths to which Freud is willing to go to undermine suggestibility objections suggest that 'sovereign patronizing serenity' is not the *mot juste*? In the same 1923 paper, Freud says: 'On the mechanism of dream formation itself, on the dream-work in the strict sense of the word, one can never exercise any influence; of that one may be quite sure' (Freud 1950: 142). Ten years earlier, in 'Dream Interpretation in Psychoanalysis' (1912) he said 'The more the patient has learnt of the method of dream interpretation the more obscure do his later dreams become . . . All the acquired knowledge serves as a warning to the dream-work' (1924: 310).

Even if Freud was as scrupulous about not prompting his patients to produce theoretically congenial material as he maintained, this would not have met the compliance argument. As early as 1906 Aschaffenburg explained the apparent confirmation Freud was receiving from his patients as due to their prior familiarity with his views (1906: 1796). Freud never addresses this obvious objection but instead merely issues repeated (and untruthful) denials that his views anticipated his patients' confirmation of them. A reminiscence from Freud himself supports Aschaffenburg's conjecture. As an illustration of the misrepresentation from which he suffered early in his career he once recalled an occasion at the turn of the century when it was reported to him that a young girl suffering from hysteria, when asked why she didn't consult Freud, remarked, 'What for? He will only ask me if I have ever wanted to sleep with my father' (S.E. 1895, II: 236). Freud denies indignantly that he ever asked patients anything of the kind. But the interesting and relevant point is that as early as 1900 it was a matter of common knowledge in the circles from which Freud drew his patients that he believed the source of neurotic difficulties to lie in incestuous wishes. Another illustration of the justice of Aschaffenburg's conjecture and of Freud's unwillingness or inability to graps its pertinence is to be found in the Rat Man case history. The Rat Man, Paul Lorenz, volunteers a sexual revelation and Freud comments: 'I then got him to agree that I had not led him to the subject either of his childhood or of sex, but that he had raised them both of his own free will' (1925: 320). Yet some pages earlier, in his account of the first session, which Paul began by retailing his masturbatory history, Freud says: 'When I asked him what it was that made him lay such stress upon his telling me of his sex life, he replied that that was what he knew about my theories' (1925: 297). In such circumstances Freud's repeated assurances that he did not himself introduce the topic of sexuality into the analysis were, at best, disingenuous.

At the period during which Grünbaum holds that Freud believed himself in possession of an absolute reply to sceptics by reason of his unmatched therapeutic achievements Freud shows many signs of believing neither in the cogency of the Tally Argument nor in his dependence on it. The most the Tally Argument could do is to justify, for a time at least, Freud's non-capitulation to the argument from comparable therapeutic efficacy by insisting on subtle though as yet undemonstrated differences between his therapeutic outcomes and that of his rivals; it could not justify Freud's claims to have repeatedly confirmed his aetiological and dynamic theses. But there were arguments that could and Freud availed himself of them. One was the extraclinical validation of *a priori* implausible claims about childhood initially based on analytic experience.

Grünbaum says at one point that if challenged as to the grounds for this theory of infantile sexuality Freud 'would' have appealed to his Tally Argument. Not so. We know what he 'would' appeal to because we know what he did appeal to: direct observation.

This is how he dealt with the issue in 'The Question of Lay Analysis':

'Now tell me, though, what certainty can you offer for your analytic findings on the sexual life of children? Is your conviction based solely on points of agreement with mythology and history?'

Oh, by no means. It is based on *direct observation*. What happened was this. We had begun by inferring the content of sexual childhood from the analysis of adults – that is to say, some twenty or forty years later. Afterwards, we undertook *analysis on children themselves* and it was no small triumph when we were thus able to confirm in them everything that we had been able to divine, in spite of the extent to which it had been overlaid and distorted in the interval . . . we have become quite generally convinced from the direct analytic examination of children that we were right in our interpretation of what adults told us about their childhood.

(Freud 1962: 127)

Freud used the same argument from direct observation in the 1910 edition of the *Three Essays on Sexuality*, in 'The History of the

Psychoanalytic Movement' (1914) and in the *Autobiographical Study*, to stop before the date at which Grünbaum says Freud abandoned the appeal to therepeutic superiority, after which such remarks could be explained as Grünbaum (mistakenly) explains the appeals to consilience after 1926, as a fall-back position.

The most succinct statement of the principal grounds for Freud's conviction as to the veridicality of his aetiological and dynamic theses occurs in 'The History of the Psychoanalytic Movement' (1914) where Freud says that the test of the correctness of his hypotheses is that a 'neurosis must become intelligible'.

He responded to Adler's objection that 'the nervous character was the cause of the neurosis rather than its result' not by invoking his therepeutic achievements but by declaring that if Adler abandoned sexuality he would not be 'in a position to account for a single detail of symptom formation or a single dream' (1963: 331).

The single most crucial inference in Freud's career was made without the benefit of the Tally Argument. This was his response to the charge that the apparent confirmation his '1896' patients provided for the seduction aetiology was due to the operation of suggestibility by assigning them infantile incestuous fantasies whose subjection to self-protective distortion led to their emergence as 'memories' of seduction, and thus misled him. Freud was precluded from invoking the Tally Argument in these cases since where the analysis was successful it was so in spite of the falsity of Freud's reconstructions, and where it was not there was nothing to appeal to.

It escapes Grünbaum's comment if not his notice that in the very lecture from which he extracts the Tally Argument it is advanced along with others which render it, if not entirely otiose, at least merely supplementary.

a great many of the detailed findings of analysis, which would otherwise be suspected of being produced by suggestion, are confirmed from other, irreproachable sources. We have unimpeachable witnesses on these points, namely dements and paranoiacs, who are of course quite above any suspicion of being influenced by suggestion. All that these patients relate in the way of phantasies and translations of symbols, which have penetrated through into their consciousness, corresponds faithfully with the results of our investigations into the unconscious of transference neurotics, thus confirming the objective truth of the interpretations made by us which are so often doubted.

(Freud 1963: 394)

In 'The History of Psychoanalytic Movement' (1914) Freud devotes a paragraph to 'the most irrefragable proof that the source of the propelling forces of neurosis lies in the sexual life'; it is an argument that 'has never received anything approaching the attention it merits, for if it had there would have been no choice but acceptance. In my own conviction of the truth it remains beside and above the more specific results of analytic work the decisive factor (1924: 293). If Freud were here referring to the Tally Argument then Grünbaum would have a formidable case. But he wasn't; he was talking about the transference. Another indication that Freud did not think of therapeutic effectiveness as his guarantor of veridicality is a rather cold-blooded remark in a letter to Jung concerning a patient who was reluctant to continue her analysis with Freud: 'Of course she is right. Because she is beyond any possibility of therapy, but it is still her duty to sacrifice herself to science' (1974: 473–4).

Another reason for holding that Freud did not rely on therapeutic effects (the Tally Argument) is that he professes himself ignorant of things he would on this assumption be expected to know, and professes to know things of which dependence on the Tally Argument would leave him ignorant. An example of the first of these is the psychology of women. The editors of the Standard Edition bring together Freud's various pronouncements on the limits of his knowledge of feminine psychology and comment:

From early days Freud made complaints of the obscurity enveloping the sexual life of women. Thus, near the beginning of his *Three Essays on the Theory of Sexuality* (1905d), he wrote that the sexual life of men 'alone has become accessible to research. That of women . . . is still veiled in an impenatrable obscurity.' (Standard Ed., VII, 151) Similarly, in his discussion of the sexual theories of children (1908c), he wrote: 'In consequence of unfavourable circumstances, both of an external and an internal nature, the following observations apply chiefly to the sexual development of one sex only – that is, of males.' (Ibid., 9, 211) Again, very much later, in his pamphlet on lay analysis (1926e): 'We know less about the sexual life of little girls than of boys. But we need not feel ashamed of this distinction; after all, the sexual life of adult women is a "dark continent" for psychology.' (Ibid., 20, 212)

(S.E. 1925, XIX: 241)

Why did Freud feel that feminine psychology was a 'dark continent' to the analyst? Grünbaum's reply would have to be that he had had less therapeutic success with women. But there is no reason for thinking so and Grünbaum offers none. A plethora of illustrations that Freud's confidence in the correctness of his interpretations and reconstructions was independent of their therapeutic effects is to be found in the case histories. Freud often expresses confidence as to the correctness of an interpretation where there is no question of therapeutic effect, e.g. Dora's playing with her reticule, her pseudo-appendicitis, her limp, etc. Such examples seem more typical than those where it is therapeutic effectiveness to which he appeals. (It is arguable that even in these cases Freud's conviction that his interpretations were therapeutically effective was based on their thematic affinity with the symptom content which remitted.) Freud's allusions to the Wolf Man case after it became apparent that he was once more deranged are untouched by any trace of uncertainty or tentativeness as to the correctness of his original account.

One is curious as to how Grünbaum will deal with Freud's complacency once his therapeutic pessimism precluded his appealing to the Tally Argument. He cites a consilience argument put forward in 1937 and explains that, since Freud no longer felt he could fall back on the Tally Argument, he now had to resort to considerations of consilience. But considerations of consilience had been, since the jigsaw puzzle analogy of 1896, the principal basis adduced by Freud in support of his reconstructions. In 'An Infantile Neurosis' (the Wolf Man) Freud once again advances considerations of coherence and circumstantiality as the justification for his aetiological conviction. He says of the charge that the theoretically congenial sexual episodes of infancy were the products of the patient's compliance:

An analyst who hears this reproach will comfort himself by recalling how gradually the construction which he is supposed to have originated came about and when all is said and done how independently of the physician's incentive many points in its development proceed; how after a certain phase in the treatment everything seemed to converge upon it, and how later, in the synthesis, the most various and remarkable results radiated from it; how not only the large problems but the smallest peculiarities in the history of the case were cleared up by this single assumption. And he will disclaim the possession of the amount of ingenuity necessary for the concoction of an occurrence which can fulfill these demands. But even this plea will be without effect upon an adversary who has not experienced the analysis himself. On the one side there will be a charge of refined self-deception, and on the other obtuseness of judgement; it will be impossible to arrive at a decision.

(1925: 525)

How can it be 'impossible to arrive at a decision' if Freud has the Tally Argument at his disposal?

Grünbaum says at one point that NCT is meant to 'constitute cogent evidence for [Freud's] general theory of psychosexual development'. But so conceived the Tally Argument is particularly feeble. Freud can hardly have thought it a reasonable reply to sceptics as to the generality of his putative discoveries that unless neurotics came to accept them they remained ill. An argument which could only salvage Freud's psychopathology would have been of little polemical use to Freud and, in fact, reliance on it would have actively weakened his claims for his general psychology because it would have displayed doubt as to the cogency of non-therapeutic considerations. Since one of the standard objections to Freud was that he was wantonly extrapolating from the mental functioning of neurotics to that of humanity at large, he must show no doubts, such as excessive reliance on theapeutic success would indicate, as to the cogency of arguments not confined to psychopathology. But even within psycho-pathology therapeutic outcome did not play the role Grünbaum assigns it. Does Grünbaum think that Freud intended the Tally Argument as a vindication of his own interpretations/reconstructions exclusively or was it meant to extend to his followers as well? It is natural to assume that Freud would not intend the entire edifice of psychoanalytic psychopathology to rest on *his* therapeutic achievements alone. We would thus expect to find that Freudians other than himself appealed to therapeutic superiority to undermine suggestibility and contamination doubts, for example, Jones, Pfister, Brill, Schwab, Putnam, Hitschmann, Eder, Forsyth, Mitchell, Frink, James Glover, Flügel, to confine the list to those who have left us records of their replies to objections to psychoanalytic claims before the date Grünbaum sets for abandonment of the Tally Argument. Did they meet scepticism by an appeal to their therapeutic achievements? Grünbaum doesn't say and appears neither to know nor to know that he needs to know.

CONCLUSION

At one point Grünbaum raises the question of Freud's 'intellectual hospitality to refutation by others' and resolves it in Freud's favour on the basis of a phrase in a letter to Fliess: 'refutations . . . will be welcomed' (Grünbaum 1984: 188). Popper is once again chastised for exegetical malpractice in overlooking it. But the following remark of 1914 from a public source, i.e. one available to Grünbaum for a much longer period than the Fliess letters have been available to Popper, needs to be put alongside Grünbaum's *trouvaille* before a conclusion can be drawn:

Many a one is tormented by the need to account for the lack of sympathy or the repudiation expressed by his contemporaries and feels their attitude painfully as a contradiction of his own secure conviction. There was no need for me to feel so; for psychoanalytical principles enable me to understand this attitude in my contemporaries and to see it as a necessary consequence of fundamental analytic premises. If it was true that the associated connections I had discovered were kept from the knowledge of patients by inward resistances of an affective kind, then these resistances would be bound to appear in the healthy also, as soon as, from some external source, they became confronted with what is repressed. It was not surprising that they should be able to justify on intellectual grounds this rejection of my ideas though it was actually affective in nature. The same thing happened just as often in patients . . . the only difference was that with patients one was in a position to bring pressure to bear on them.

(1924: 306)

Either Grünbaum has once again been sleepwalking his way through Freud's text or he thinks these remarks consistent with 'intellectual hospitality to refutation by others'.

When one considers the extent to which Grünbaum leans on Popper's Oedipus effect to undermine Freud's claims, the emphasis he places on Popper's deficiences begins to look like an instance of the narcissism of small differences. His real objection to Popper amounts to one of anachronism. Popper's accusation of evasiveness with respect to the suggestibility objection only applies to Freud after 1926. In fact it is Grünbaum who is guilty of anachronism. The Tally Argument was not killed by Freud's discovery of spontaneous remission between 1923 and 1926. It was stillborn.

Citizen Kane in the Orson Welles film responded to refutation in what we would all concur was a non-exemplary fashion. On the eve of the election in which he is running for governor he prepares two headlines, 'Kane Elected' and 'Fraud at the Polls'. Grünbaum thinks it libellous to suggest that Freud characteristically behaved in this fashion. I think it pusillanimous to deny that he did. In attempting a demonstration of his claim that Freud was 'clearly motivated by evidence' and 'alert to the need for safeguarding the falsifiability of his reconstructions and interpretations', and that he dealt 'brilliantly' and 'unswervingly' with the contamination issue, Grünbaum has only succeeded in illustrating how prophetic were Wittgenstein's words of almost half a century ago: 'It will be a long time before we lose our subservience' (Cioffi 1973: 76).

NOTES

1   I would like to correct a mistaken argument on this point employed in a previous paper (Cioffi 1985). I there argued that seductions are so blatantly observable that the acknowledgement of counter-instances was not evidence of any notable degree of 'hospitality to refutation'. Whereas I still think that capitulation to counter-instances is equivocal evidence of an investigator's probity where the phenomena are blatant or easily replicable, I was wrong to

think seductions an example of this. I only thought so because I confused the event, seduction, with the indirect evidence for the event, testimony and memory. I confused the relative ease with which someone witnessing a putative seduction could discriminate it from mere horseplay (what one might call its intrinsic observability) with the trouble he would have in determining whether an act of unconscious incestuous fantasizing was taking place. But of course this is a gross *non sequitur* since what is at issue is the relative accessibility of the evidence for these and not their intrinsic observability.

2   This is what Freud says in the published case history: 'Starting from these indications and from other data of a similar kind I ventured to put forward a construction to the effect that when he was a child of under six he had been guilty of some sexual misdemeanour connected with onanism and had been soundly castigated for it by his father' (S.E. 1909, X: 342). This is what he says in the notes he made at the time: 'I could not restrain myself here from constructing the material at our disposal into an event: how before the age of six he had been in the habit of masturbating and how his father had forbidden it, using as a threat the phrase, "It would be the death of you" and perhaps also threatening to cut off his penis' (S.E. 1909, X: 263).

3   To complicate matters further Freud forgot that the Rat Man had been beaten on another occasion, and for bedwetting, which Freud held to be a substitute for nocturnal emissions. So the Rat Man was after all beaten for a sexual offence, the same one Freud himself had been berated for (see the dream of Count Thun in the *Interpretation of Dreams*). This extenuates Freud's error but not Grünbaum's (unless he has similarly poignant revelations to make).

REFERENCES

Aschaffenburg, G. 1906: Die Beziehungen des sexuellen Leben zur Entstehung von Nerven- und Geisteskrankenheit. *Münchener medizinische Wochenschrift*, LIII, 1793–8.

Cioffi, F. 1970: Freud and the idea of a pseudo-science, in R. Borger and F. Cioffi (eds), *Explanation in the Behavioural Sciences*. Cambridge University Press.

Cioffi, F. (ed.) 1973: *Freud: Modern Judgements*. Macmillan.

Cioffi, F. 1975: Was Freud a liar? *The Listener*, 7 February: 172–4. Repr. *Journal of Orthomolecular Psychiatry*, 5 (1975), 275–80.

Cioffi, F. 1984: Review of Masson 1984. *Times Literary Supplement*, 6 July 1984. (Masson's letter of protest appeared 16 November 1984 and Cioffi's reply 14 December 1984.)

Cioffi, F. 1985: Psycho-analysis, pseudo-science and testability, in G. Currie and A. Musgrave (eds) *Popper and the Human Sciences*. Martinus Nijhoff.

Flügel J. C. 1924: Critical Discussion. *British Journal of Medical Psychology*, 51.

Freud, S. 1924: *Collected Papers*, vol. 1. Hogarth Press.

Freud, S. 1925: *Collected Papers*, vol. 3. Hogarth Press.

Freud, S. 1935: *An Autobiographical Study*. Hogarth Press.

Freud, S. 1950: *Collected Papers*, vol. 5. Hogarth Press.
Freud, S. 1962: *Two Short Accounts of Psychoanalysis*. Penguin.
Freud, S. 1963: *A General Introduction to Psychoanalysis*. Simon & Schuster.
Freud, S. 1965: *Three Essays on the Theory of Sexuality*. Avon Books.
Freud, S. 1974: *The Freud–Jung Letters*, ed. William McGuire. Hogarth Press and Routledge & Kegan Paul.
Freud, S. 1985: *The Complete Letters of Sigmund Freud to Wilhelm Fliess*. The Belknap Press of Harvard University Press.
Freud, S. and Breuer, J. 1966: *Studies on Hysteria*. Avon Books.
Gellner, E. 1985: *The Psychoanalytic Movement*. Paladin Books.
Glymour, C. 1974: Freud, Kepler and clinical evidence, in R. Wollheim (ed.), *Freud: A Collection of Critical Essays*. Anchor Books.
Grünbaum, A. 1979a: Is Freudian psychoanalytic theory pseudo-scientific by Karl Popper's criterion of demarcation? *American Philosophical Quarterly*, 16, 131–41.
Grünbaum, A. 1979b: The role of psychological explanations of the rejection or acceptance of scientific theories. *Transactions of the New York Academy of Science*, vol. 37.
Grünbaum, A. 1984: *The Foundations of Psychoanalysis: A Philosophical Critique*. University of California Press.
Jones, E. 1957: *Sigmund Freud: Life and Work*, vol. 3. Hogarth Press.
Masson, J. M. 1984: *The Assault on Truth: Freud's Suppression of the Seduction Theory*. Faber.
Nagel, E. 1959: Methodological Issues in Freudian Theory, in S. Hook (ed.), *Psycho-Analysis, Scientific Method and Philosophy*. New York University Press.

PART TWO

Psychoanalysis and Consciousness

4

Psychoanalysis and the Personal

MORRIS EAGLE

Philosophical interest in psychoanalysis has tended mainly and consistently to focus on the concept of the unconscious and on issues of unconscious mentation, consciousness and unconsciousness, awareness and unawareness. This is so, in part at least, because the psychoanalytic idea of unconscious mental processes challenged the long-cherished equation, associated with, among others, John Locke, between the mental and the conscious.[1]

Recently, philosophical interest in the concept of unconscious mental processes has also been stimulated by the growth of artificial intelligence, cognitive science and cognitive psychology. These fields are replete with references to cognitive structures and processes that are not in awareness and not directly represented in conscious experience – for example, the hypothetical 'deep structures' that permit us to generate an indefinitely large number of coherent and grammatically correct sentences without our necessarily being able to state explicitly the 'rules' according to which we generate these sentences (Chomsky 1957; 1966). This interest in unconscious mental processes on the part of cognitive psychologists is consistent with information processing, with computational and modularity models of the mind and with a focus on so-called cognitive structures which do not require any direct reference to a conscious person or agent. Information processing and computations not requiring awareness are precisely those properties shared by minds and machines.

OWNERSHIP AND DISOWNERSHIP OF MENTAL CONTENTS
(EGO AND ID)

Although philosophical interest in psychoanalysis has focused on unconscious
mental processes, I want to present the view that at least as significant an
issue raised by psychoanalysis – particularly, by the concepts of repression
and the so-called 'dynamic unconscious' – is the question of personal
ownership versus disownership of thoughts, wishes and desires. Another
way of putting this is to say that while the processing of information is a
key function of mind, a central function of mind highlighted by
psychoanalytic concepts is the rendering personal of such information and
making it one's own. I will try to show that these questions of ownership
and disownership, avowal and disavowal are core considerations in
Freud's thought, considerations that are overlooked when one interprets
Freud's formulations solely in terms of awareness and unawareness
(conscious and unconscious) and from the perspective of information
processing and computational models of mind.

The claim that mental contents isolated from one's dominant personality
organization have pathological effects is not distinctively psychoanalytic.
The basic idea had already been stated by Charcot, Binet and Janet. Janet,
for example, writes in 1889 that 'one should go through the entire field of
mental diseases to show that mental and bodily disturbances result from
the banishment of a thought from personal consciousness' (quoted in
Ellenberger 1970: 436). What is distinctively psychoanalytic was Freud's
claim that certain mental contents remained unintegrated within the
personality, not because of constitutional weakness or because they were
experienced in hypnoid states, but because they were purposively
disowned and extruded from consiousness and from one's dominant ego
organization.

While in his earlier work, *The Interpretation of Dreams*, for example,
Freud focused on the so-called topographical model of mind in which
unconscious–conscious is the predominant dimension, in his later work,
The Ego and the Id, for example, the topographical model is replaced by
the so-called structural model of the mind – that is, structures of the id,
ego and super-ego. Freud writes that 'we shall have to substitute for this
antithesis [that is, between conscious and unconscious] another, taken
from our insight into the structural conditions of the mind – the antithesis
between the coherent ego and *the repressed one which is split off from it*'
(S.E. 1923, XIX: 7, my italics). This change of emphasis is sharply
reflected in the shift of the stated goal of psychoanalysis from making the

unconscious conscious to 'where id was, there should ego be'. A major significance of this shift is that it betokens a decreased preoccupation with whether or not a mental content is conscious or unconscious, in awareness or outside of awareness, and an increased concern instead with the dimension of avowal versus disavowal.

That a shift to the structural model betokens a concern with avowal and disavowal is obscured by the dominant way in which the terms id and ego have come to be understood in contemporary psychoanalysis. Particularly under the influence of ego psychology and reflecting an interpretation of Freudian theory primarily in terms of an impulse-control model, id is defined in terms of instinctual impulses and ego in terms of controlling and mediating (including reality-testing) functions. Consider afresh however, the German 'das Es' and 'das Ich' and rather than the latinized version of id and ego the more direct English translation of 'the it' and 'the I'. The English clearly conveys, respectively, that which in the personality is impersonal (and, as I will try to show, disavowed) in contrast to that which is personal, owned, and experienced as part of oneself (see Brandt 1962; and Bettelheim 1983 for a further discussion of the translation of Freud's works).[2] It will also be noted in the passage quoted earlier that Freud contrasts 'the coherent ego', not with instinctual drive, but with 'the repressed [ego] which is split off from' the coherent ego. In other words, here Freud is not contrasting biological drive with controlling structure, but two cognitive-affective ego structures dissociated from each other.

I have argued elsewhere (Eagle 1984) that Freud confuses levels of discourse by attributing the 'it' status of instincts and instinctual impulses to their links to the somatic. He writes in *An Outline of Psycho-Analysis* that instincts 'originate in the somatic organization and . . . find their first mental expression in the id in forms unknown to us' (S.E. 1940, XXIII: 14). He also writes in 'Instincts and their Vicissitudes', that 'an instinct can never become an object of consciousness – only the idea [*Vorstellung*] that represents the instinct can' (S.E. 1915, XIV, 177). But, as I have tried to show, this is no different in form from saying that neuronal firing and other neurophysiological processes can never become objects of consciousness – only the percept or thought (corresponding to the neurophysiological processes) can. Or that hormonal secretions and, say, hypothalamic excitation, can never become the object of consciousness – only sexual desires and fantasies can. In short, Freud appears to confuse levels of discourse and what he says about instincts and objects of consciousness is *generally* true of the relationship between the biological and the psychological.

Thus, the definition of id involves a conflation of meanings: id as impersonal through disavowal and id as instinct and therefore *inherently* alien ('it') and impersonal. If one rejects this conflation, it becomes clear that the legitimate core idea contained in the id–ego model lies in the early distinction between unacceptable disavowed mental contents experienced as impersonal and alien to oneself and owned mental contents experienced as personal, as 'mine'.[3]

The conscious–unconscious dimension is subsidiary and somewhat orthogonal to the more superordinate id–ego structural model in the sense that rendering a mental content unconscious is only *one* possible means (albeit the most frequently employed means) of rejecting and disowning an unacceptable mental content. And from the fact that a mental content is consciously experienced it does not necessarily follow that it will be owned and experienced as part of oneself. For example, a mental content that is fully conscious and yet quintessentially disowned and ego-alien is a troubling obsessive thought. When someone has an unbidden obsessive thought it is often described as 'it keeps occurring to me' rather than 'I think'. The very grammatical structure reflects the fact that the thought has an 'it', ego-alien status rather than being experienced as an owned part of oneself. And yet, the thought is fully conscious – indeed, it obtrusively occupies conscious experience. That is why we call it obsessive.

If the above interpretation of Freud is reasonable, it follows that in examining the implications of psychoanalysis for a theory of mind we would consider not only, or perhaps not even primarily, the question of unconscious mental processes, but the issue of owned versus disowned, the rendering personal and impersonal of mental contents. I would like to spell out below some implications of and some questions raised by a focus on the issue of owned versus disowned, ego-syntonic versus ego-alien.

TWO MENTAL FUNCTIONS: INFORMATION PROCESSING AND LINKING INFORMATION TO ONESELF

One implication of the above rendering of Freud's id–ego model is that in addition to the broad mental function of information processing, another basic function of mind, in human beings at least, is the linking of information processed to one's self-structure. And, indeed, there is a good deal of evidence from different sources that supports this basic distinction. Most broadly, the evidence indicates that one can distinguish between, on the one hand, the registration, processing, storage and utilization of information and, on the other, experiencing and storing that information in an autobiographical and spatio-temporal context. In the literature on the experimental psychology of human memory, the general distinction has been drawn by Tulving (1983) between *semantic* versus *episodic* memory. (Recently, Tulving (1984) has also included the category of *procedural* memory, but that is not directly relevant here.) According to Tulving, episodic memory is characterized by organization and storage of events or episodes in a spatio-temporal context involving the rememberer either as actor or observer.[4] It is episodic memory that is implicitly referred to when one discusses the role of memory in personal identity. By contrast with episodic memory, the basic units for semantic memory are facts, ideas, concepts and propositions, rather than events or episodes. Temporal organization is not an aspect of semantic memory and 'the knowledge recorded in the semantic system has no necessary connection to the knower's personal identity' (Tulving 1983: 39).

The most striking evidence for the episodic–semantic distinction is taken from work with amnesic and Korsakoff syndrome patients. There is consistent evidence that while Korsakoff patients can register, process, store and utilize information presented to them, they show marked defects in storing and remembering that information autobiographically and personally.

In 1911 Claparède reported the following incident with a woman suffering from Korsakoff syndrome. A few minutes after Claparède pricked her hand with a pin hidden between his fingers, the patient no longer remembered the event. However, when Claparède reached out for her hand, she pulled it back. When asked why she did this, she responded, 'Doesn't one have the right to withdraw her hand?' And when Claparède pressed her, she said, 'Is there perhaps a pin hidden in your hand?' Further, when Claparède asked her why she suspected him of hiding a pin in his hand, she replied, 'That was an idea that went through my mind', adding, 'Sometimes pins are hidden in people's hands' (Claparède 1911: 69–70). Claparède also reports that despite the fact that when this woman was told a story or read items of a newspaper she remembered nothing, not even the fact that someone had read to her, one could nevertheless elicit, with questioning, some of the details of what was told or read to her. However, she would not experience these details as memories, but as 'something that went through my mind' or simply an idea she had 'without knowing why'. Since Claparède, similar phenomena involving dissociation between episodic and semantic memory have been reported by many different investigators. Williams and Smith (1954; as reported in Tulving 1983) report the case of an amnesic man who, prior to his illness, had taken a clerk's training course in the army. When he was shown a group photograph of those in the course, he reported the name of every man in the photograph, but could remember nothing about the specific occasion on which the photograph was taken nor how he knew the names of the men.

After obtaining successful eye-blink conditioning (using an air puff as the unconditioned stimulus and a compound auditory and visual signal as the conditioned stimulus) in two amnesic patients, Weiskrantz and Warrington (1979) found that they had no memory for the first conditioning sessions in which the air puff was paired with the auditory and visual signal. One patient claimed that he 'had a weak right eye because someone had once blown some air into it (p. 192). As a final example, Schachter, Wang, Tulving and Freedman (1982) report that although an amnesic patient could acquire little-known facts (e.g. 'who holds the world record for shaking hands?'), he was unable to state accurately where, when or how he acquired these facts. Instead, he would typically say that he 'read about it somewhere', 'heard some people talking about it just recently', or 'my sister once told me about it'.

As has long been recognized (e.g. James 1890; Claparède 1911; Koffka 1935), the above kinds of phenomena provide strong evidence that the processing, storage and utilization of information and the autobiographical linking of such information to one's self-organization are separable – clearly physiologically based – mental functions.

In both the Korsakoff patient who cannot process and store incoming information autobiographically and the neurotic individual who disowns and represses certain ideas and wishes, there is a disjunction between, so to speak, the mere existence and operation of mental contents and the linking of such mental contents to one's self-organization. However, a critical difference between the Korsakoff patient and the neurotic individual – and it is to this difference that we now turn – is that the latter does not suffer from a general organic impairment of the 'self-linking' function, as does the Korsakoff patient, but rather *selectively* consigns only certain mental contents to an 'it' status – mental contents that are at sharp variance with one's sense of who one is. In short, the neurotic *represses* certain mental contents. However, as we shall see, the very concept of repression warrants examination in the light of the foregoing interpretation of Freud's basic id–ego model.

REPRESSION

It should be clear from the earlier discussion that in saying that the neurotic represses certain mental contents, I am not defining repression in the traditional sense in which the focus is primarily on unawareness and the unconscious status of mental contents. Rather, in accord with my interpretation of the id–ego model, the essence of repression is held to be the motivated disownership of mental contents, the consignment of certain mental contents to an 'it' rather than an 'I' status for the purpose, in G. S. Klein's words, of preserving self-continuity and integrity through dissociating certain contents from the self (1976).

DISJUNCTION BETWEEN MIND AND SELF

Just as the traditional definition of repression implies a disjunction between mind and consciousness, a disjunction now eminently acceptable to cognitive psychologists and to the current philosophical mood, my re-definition of repression suggests that mind and self are not co-extensive. The Korsakoff patient, as noted, *is* processing and utilizing information, but he has no sense that *he* as person has experienced events containing this information. The neurotic woman who has the obsessive thought 'I will harm my baby' is, after all, having that thought, but she has no sense that *she* is *thinking* the thought. If mind and self are not co-extensive, it follows that a mental content (a thought, wish or desire) can be *mine* in some sense and *not mine* in another sense. It seems to me that a recognition of this simple distinction beween mind and self does much to resolve at least some controversies and apparent paradoxes in this area.

ARE UNACCEPTABLE DESIRES PART OF ONESELF?

Consider the controversy between Frankfurt and Penelhum regarding the question of ownership of unacceptable desires. Penelhum (1971) takes the position that to represent a desire with which one does not identify as not one's own is 'moral trickery' and that 'that part of us from which we wish to dissociate ourselves is as much a part of us as that with which we wish to identify' (1971: 671). Frankfurt disputes Penelhum's claim and argues that 'a person is no more to be identified with everything that goes on in his mind . . . than he is to be identified with everything that goes on in his body' (1976: 242). When we disapprove of certain desires and want not to have them, they are, Frankfurt tells us, external to us.

Of course, it is true, as Penelhum and Frankfurt seem to agree, that a desire I disown is mine in some sense. As Penelhum notes, it certainly is not someone else's. I would suggest that it is mine in the sense of being an element in the totality of my mental activity or a constituent part of my total personality. However, if 'mine' is defined in terms of my self-system, my sense of who I am, then a disowned desire is not mine. This, I have been arguing, is precisely the basic point made in Freud's distinction between 'das Es' and 'das Ich' – namely, that disowned mental contents, including disowned ideas, wishes and desires, have an 'it', ego-alien quality. Consider once again the obsessive thought described above. By saying it is not mine, I am saying that I reject and disown the thought, that it is sharply at variance with my sense of who I am and what I want to think, and that it is unbidden, peremptory, and independent of my volition and intentions – in short, it has an 'it', ego-alien quality. Of course, the obsessive thought is mine in the sense that it is going on in my mind and in the sense that, however disturbing the idea may be, it possibly reflects important, even if rejected, aspects of my personality. However, this latter sense in which the obsessive thought is mine in no way contradicts the former sense in which it is not mine – indeed, the two are quite consistent with each other.

Penelhum is concerned that allowing 'a person to *decide* what is to count as part of his past or present' (1971: 675) too easily permits 'moral trickery'. However, Penelhum's exclusive focus on 'moral trickery' and inauthentic responses runs the risk of converting clinical phenomena and issues into exclusively moral ones, a position that places him squarely on the side of Sartre (1956), with his emphasis on 'bad faith', and Szasz (1961) with his replacement of mental illness language with moral language. For Penelhum self-alienation is primarily a matter of someone yielding 'regularly to desires he does not want to give way to' (1971: 669). It is largely a matter of weakness of will. The kinds of phenomena ignored by Penelhum and with which psychoanalysis is concerned are far more complex than yielding to desires one does not want to give way to. Desires that one wants to resist but does not do not necessarily have 'it' status. Or, to state it in Sullivan's (1953) language, yielding to desires one does not want to give way to may generate 'bad me' experiences but not necessarily 'not me' experiences. The kinds of phenomena Penelhum overlooks and that are of central concern to psychoanalysis and to the psychoanalyst are the largely pathological *transformations of disowned desire such that they no longer appear in consciousness as desire but rather as obsessive thoughts, compulsive rituals, phobias and other symptomatic expressions*. It is such phenomena that give concrete meaning to the concepts of id and ego. A desire one wants to resist can nevertheless be experienced as 'I desire'. But a desire that is expressed in an obsessive thought, compulsive ritual or phobic fear no longer has the form of 'I desire' but rather of an 'it happens'. If Freud is correct in his linking of such symptoms to repressed desires and wishes, then one could say that in an important sense these desires are no longer part of oneself.

The same issue arises in regard to slips and dreams which, according to Freud, are minineurotic symptoms of everyday life. In Freudian theory, slips and dreams are held to express and to be caused by repressed desires and wishes. It has been tempting to argue, therefore, that one is responsible for one's slips and dreams (see Schafer 1976; Freud himself so argued). After all, they are one's own slips and dreams and express, even if in disguised form, one's own wishes and desires. Therefore, to make a slip or have a dream with disguised contents can perhaps be seen as a piece of 'moral trickery' or 'bad faith'. For in that slip or dream, one is expressing a desire from which one wants to dissociate oneself, but which is nevertheless one's own desire, as if it were not one's own desire. However, this way of looking at slips and dreams would mistakenly assimilate them to actions or quasi-actions carried out by an agent rather than something happening to an agent.

As Shope (1970) points out, a careful reading of Freud (and, I would add, a careful conceptual analysis) indicates that while he thought of slips and dreams as expressing and caused by unconscious intentions and desires, he did not believe that they were themselves intentional. And he was correct. A dream or a slip is not an intentional action in the sense of following the practical syllogism in which one has a particular desire (or goal or intention), a belief that a particular set of actions will fulfil that desire, and then carries out one of those actions in order to fulfil that desire. While a slip or dream may express a wish or desire, it is not an action or quasi-action through which that desire is satisfied. Nor does the agent believe that making a slip or having a dream of a particular content will satisfy the desire. For example, a slip in which one announces the closing rather than the opening of a meeting may express a desire to end the meeting quickly or not hold the meeting at all. The slip, however, is not a means by which the meeting is, in fact, ended, shortened or avoided altogether. Nor does the person believe that the slip constitutes such a means (see Grünbaum 1984; Moore 1984; and Shope 1970 for further discussion of this issue).[5]

At least as far as psychoanalytic theory is concerned, there is little room for 'moral trickery' with regard to repression. For while in his earlier work (1893–5), Freud thought that repression was a conscious process, he came to conceptualize repression as itself an unconscious automatic mechanism that operates according to the pleasure principle. And within psychoanalytic theory, that is the way it has come to be understood. Hence, the step of disowning and repressing a mental content is itself an involuntary 'act' for which one cannot rightly be held responsible and which does not easily lend itself to description in terms of 'moral trickery'. Indeed, if one accepts Rubinstein's (1977) argument regarding unconscious mental processes, properly speaking, repression is not something a *person* engages in. While there may be no harm in describing repression (and other unconscious processes) *as if* it were carried out by a person, it is essentially a subpersonal process whereby certain mental contents are 'automatically' disowned and banished from conscious experience. Philosophers and others may want to adapt Freud's concept of repression to the language and ideas of 'moral trickery', 'bad faith' and self-deception; but as far as I can see, an accurate and precise rendering leaves little room for such an adaptation. There may be instances of 'moral trickery', 'bad faith' or self-deception which, in certain general respects, are *similar* to repression. But, unless I am mistaken, they are not what Freud had in mind when he wrote about repression. There may be on the one hand many serious questions as to the degree of empirical support for the existence of repression and on the other very little doubt regarding the existence of 'moral trickery', 'bad faith' and self-deception, but, of course, it would not follow from this that these phenomena are therefore instances of repression.

Even from a commonsense point of view, Penelhum's account of inner conflict as a lack of harmony between first-order and second-order desires and volitions seems lacking. Consider someone who is having a sexual affair and feels guilty and anxious about his sexual desires and behaviour. Imagine that this man is given the opportunity to be rid of his sexual desires toward the other woman. Would he necessarily avail himself of this opportunity? I think we can agree that he would not necessarily take the opportunity to rid himself of the 'forbidden' sexual desires. For one thing, he might not want to forgo the pleasure that, in addition to the guilt and anxiety, is part of his sexual encounter. If, however, inner conflict were simply a matter of yielding to a desire one wants to be rid of, why would our hypothetical person not necessarily and unequivocally rid himself of the unwanted desire? The point I am making with this hypothetical and yet, undoubtedly, very real example is that inner conflict does not necessarily consist simply in having a desire that one wishes one did not have, but in having a desire on the one hand and experiencing guilt and anxiety on the other. One might more likely want to be rid of, not the desire, but the guilt and anxiety accompanying it. And, as I have tried to show, the more pathological form of inner conflict may consist in having a desire that is no longer experienced as a desire, but is transformed into symptomatic expressions of various sorts.

DOES A DISOWNED WISH OR DESIRE HAVE AN AGENT?

Implicit in Penelhum's position is the idea that every desire or wish (or thought) must, so to speak, have an agent who is doing the desiring or wishing (or thinking). As we have seen, Penelhum's rhetorical question and answer are: 'Whose desire is it if not A's? Surely not someone else's.' Frankfurt's reply, to the effect that a dissociated desire belongs to *no one*, raises an interesting and important issue, the issue of desires without agents, desires that belong to *no* person. It seems to me precisely the issue raised by Freud in his notion of unconscious desires and wishes. However, while Frankfurt refers to normally experienced first-order desires that are in conflict with second-order desires, Freud has in mind desires so alienated from oneself that they are not directly represented as desires but rather, as we have seen, *as* 'it' experiences such as obsessive thought, compulsive rituals, hysterical conversions, phobic fears and so on. In such cases, it is not a matter of *my* desires of which I disapprove or from which I wish to dissociate myself, but of having no experience of 'I desire'. In Sullivan's (1953) terms, as noted earlier, it is the difference between 'bad me' (desires of which I disapprove) and 'not me' experiences (desires not experienced as part of myself or even as desires).

It seems to me that, properly speaking, a repressed desire does not belong to a person but is rather a subpersonal phenomenon (Dennett 1978). Or, to put it in the language employed by Rubinstein (1977), a repressed desire or wish belongs to the world (and language) of organisms rather than of persons. I agree with Rubinstein that to speak of unconscious repressed desires is to speak in an 'as if' metaphorical manner which does no harm as long as one is aware that one is speaking metaphorically and as long as one is aware that terms such as unconscious or repressed desires are extensions of and derived from (perhaps degenerate forms of) ordinary desires. Essentially, an unconscious or repressed desire is, as Rubinstein suggests, a neurophysiological phenomenon that influences conscious experience and behaviour. Because we know next to nothing about unconscious or repressed desires on the neurophysiological level and because there are, as Freud expressed it in 'The Unconscious', enough 'points of contact' between ordinary desires and unconscious repressed desires (S.E. 1915, XIV: 159–216), we speak in a metaphorical and functional language regarding the latter.[6]

When unconscious repressed desires are thought of in Rubinstein's sense, it becomes clear that Freud's dictum 'where id was, there should ego be' can be partly understood as where neurophysiology only was, there should psychology also be. That is, a transformation of id into ego is, in some sense, a movement from neurophysiology into psychology. From another perspective, it is also a movement from purely subpersonal processes to the level of personal processes, from 'desire occurs' to 'I desire'. In short, while unconscious desires have no agent (although they 'belong' to a person), they can be transformed into personal desires.

A question I want to turn to briefly is the function of consciousness in Freudian theory.

ADAPTIVE FUNCTIONS OF CONSCIOUS EXPERIENCE

Self-reflective functions

If, as Freud argues, the major part of mental life goes on outside awareness and if, as we know from research in cognitive psychology, much adaptive functioning takes place on a subpersonal level, why has conscious experience been selected out and refined in the course of evolution? One classic answer to the above question is that conscious experience makes possible the self-reflective functions of delay, planning and self-criticism. By contrast, tacit knowledge acquired and the tacit processing carried out through subpersonal processes is, in Polanyi and Prosch's (1975) words, 'not subject to damage by adverse evidence'. One can, for example, demonstrate that certain experienced perceptual illusions are irresistible and not especially alterable even when explicit contradictory information is provided. The perceptual experience is not subject to damage by adverse evidence. However, while the perceptual illusion may be the result of genetically 'wired in' mechanisms and therefore relatively fixed and unalterable, because it is consciously experienced rather than simply acted on, one can reflect upon the experience and explicitly know that it is an illusion. While such reflection and criticism may not alter the compellingness of the immediate perceptual experience, it can influence judgement, planning and action.

Freud's justification of his early therapeutic goal of making the unconscious conscious and his description of thought as the exploration of alternative courses of action and their consequences mentally rather than in actual behaviour entail an emphasis on the importance of a self-reflective function and the judgement, planning and delay it permits.

Consciousness and self-organization

Implicit in Freud's id–ego model is a strong link between consciousness and one's self-organization. Normally, what enters consciousness is experienced ego-syntonically, as part of oneself, and mental contents sharply at variance with one's self-organization are, as we have discussed, either kept from conscious experience or experienced in an 'it' manner, as not part of oneself.[7] This suggests that a second major adaptive function of consciousness, or at least of the selective and defensive processes that shape consciousness, is the preservation of the unity and integrity of one's self-organization. That is, by excluding that which is alien to oneself and therefore threatening to one's self-structure and by including only that which is generally congruent with one's self-organization, consciousness serves to preserve the integrity of the existing self-structure. This is the point that Sullivan (1953) makes when he suggests that the self-system is the guardian of conscious experience, permitting the congruent and excluding the radically incongruent.[8]

One can speculate – and it seems to me that this is implicit in Freud's id–ego model – that when consciousness is functioning optimally, relatively free of defence and distortion, conscious experience is the single most comprehensive guide to one's overall welfare and interest. However, conscious experience is an adaptive 'tool' only to the extent that the self-organization it 'represents' is truly and adequately representative of one's overall personality and organismic needs. If one's self-organization is unduly restrictive and denies entry to consciousness of information vital to one's personality and organismic needs, conscious experience is carrying out its adaptive function poorly.

By contrast, the more representative of one's overall needs is one's self-organization, the wider is the range of one's conscious experience and, hence, the more adequately it carries out its adaptive function. In the language of Freud's id and ego (at least as it is understood here), the wider the realm of the personal, of the owned and the ego-syntonic, the greater the degree of representation and integration of one's overall needs in the personal, that is, in conscious experience. Along with this there is less likelihood of unrepresented or poorly represented vital organismic needs and less likelihood of 'islands' or 'pockets' of semi-autonomous subpersonal cognitive-effective structures which remain unintegrated into a superordinate self-structure and which gain entry into conscious experience mainly in the form of 'eruptions', of ego-alien 'not me' experiences and symptoms. When such 'eruptions' occur the normal unity of conscious experience is disturbed and one experiences mental contents in an 'it' manner, as not mine; or in a depersonalized form in which mental contents are experienced 'as emanating from outside one's person' (Lichtenstein 1977: 356).

REPRESSION AND UNITY OF CONSCIOUSNESS AND OF SELF

The unity of consciousness and of self is, then, neither a necessary fact nor a given, but a developmental integrative *achievement*. It reflects the fact that one has evolved a self-organization in which cognitive and affective structures and other subpersonal processes are either represented personally and ego-syntonically ('I experience'; 'I want'; 'I desire') or, if unrepresented or poorly represented, do not erupt into consciousness in an ego-alien manner, but instead are successfully repressed. That is to say, when mental contents are sharply at variance with one's self-organization, generally speaking, the alternatives are either successful repression of them or, when repression fails, eruption of these mental contents into consciousness in an ego-alien manner. The third alternative – the ideally healthy one – implied in the above discussion, is the growth and enlargement of the self so that what was formerly ego-alien and unintegratable can now be assimilated by the new self-organization. However, this is not always possible. And when this is not possible, repression, and even denial, are more adaptive alternatives to the eruption of this material into consciousness, with resulting severe anxiety and threat to the integrity of one's self-structure. It seems to me that the central theme of Eugene O'Neill's (1946) *The Iceman Cometh* is the destructiveness of forcing utterly unpalatable and unacceptable truths upon the consciousness of desperate men who live and are sustained only by illusions, by what O'Neill calls 'pipe-dreams'. Such truths, O'Neill tells us through the character of Hickey, the Iceman, can be soul-destroying and death-dealing.

What O'Neill is telling us and what is implied in the concept of repression is that for many of us certain information and certain mental contents cannot be integrated into self-organization if the latter is to preserve its integrity.[9] *This*, rather than consciousness or unconsciousness, is the central logic of the concept of repression. In other words, in certain circumstances, repression of certain mental contents may be necessary in order to preserve the subjective experience of unity of consciousness and of self. Both ego-alien symptoms and the development of multiple personalities represent threats to the unity of consciousness and of self (in the former, one has 'non-self' or 'not me' experiences at a given time; in the latter, there is no stable self-organization over time) and both reflect the deleterious effects of unintegrated and fragmented mental contents upon such unity.[10]

In coming to the end of this chapter, I want to note again that the idea of mental contents that are unintegrated and fragmented off from one's self-organization is the single most dominant and important idea linking pre-psychoanalytic to psychoanalytic thinking. It is obviously the central motivation for Freud's dictum 'where id was, there should ego be'. For what is essential in this dictum is the idea of integrating what was formerly an ego-alien 'it' into a personal 'I'. This is possible only if the realm of the personal is enlarged and expanded to include formerly unintegrated fragments of mental contents. Also implied is the claim that the essence of effective psychoanalytic treatment consists not simply, or perhaps not even primarily, in recollection and knowledge, but in avowal, self-acceptance and integration. If Freud believed that knowledge and intellectual insight were sufficient for therapeutic change and growth, he would have remained with the therapeutic goal of making the unconscious conscious. In adopting the goal of 'where id was, there should ego be' Freud made clear his belief that real therapeutic change consisted in an enlargement of the personal so that one could now integrate into 'the coherent ego' what had been ego-alien and split off from it.

If I am correct in my assessment of what constitutes the central idea of psychoanalysis, then it follows that an exclusive focus on computation and information-processing functions of mind will not do justice to psychoanalytic formulation and insights. One will need to focus on the important mental functions that are involved in rendering information personal or impersonal, ego-syntonic or ego-alien, owned or disowned. One will need to consider the central questions of the nature of the representational and transformational processes through which mental contents are rendered personal or impersonal; of how mental contents become or fail to become *my* mental contents; and of how and in what form the subpersonal, including the biological, gets to be represented in personal experience.

NOTES

1   Locke (1924: 50) writes, for example, 'it cannot be less than revelation, that discovers to another, thought in my mind, when I can find none there myself: and they must needs have a penetrating sight who can certainly see that I think, when I cannot perceive it myself, and when I declare that I do not'.
2   My citing of Bettelheim's book should not be interpreted to mean that I agree with his central claim.

3   Also implicit in Freud's thinking of instinctual drive as the disowned 'it' part of one's personality is the idea that even if one denies instinctual drive derivatives access to conscious experience, their effects cannot be eradicated altogether, insofar as they are biologically rooted. They make their presence and 'demands' felt, albeit indirectly, even when they are disowned and denied access to consciousness. Freud makes this point in the context of contrasting external with internal stimulation and excitation. Although one can, he notes, physically escape from noxious external stimulation, one cannot physically flee from the internal stimulation of instinctual drives (at best, one can attempt to escape psychologically through repression and other defences). The latter kind of stimulation and the attendant neural excitation, Freud tells us, one cannot fully escape from because it is constant (or at least cyclical) in nature and rooted in our biological make-up. Hence, in contrast to other mental contents (or even other, more neutral and less biologically rooted wishes and desires), which will dissipate if disowned, contents linked to instinctual drives will continue to exert an influence on the personality even when disowned. Given the fact that instinctual drives (which, in psychoanalytic theory, are primarily sex and aggression) are also taboo areas, subject to prohibition and denied free expression by society, it becomes exceedingly likely that the disowned components of one's personality will consist primarily of mental contents (ideas, wishes, desires) linked to instinctual drives.

The above is, I believe, an important aspect of the logic that led Freud to conceptualize id *both* in terms of instinctual drive and disowned mental contents. One can accept the point that in our society sexual and aggressive wishes and impulses are especially likely to be disowned without accepting Freud's conceptual and definitional conflation of id as both instinctual drive and disowned mental contents. That is, one can accept the empirical or contingent fact that sex and aggression are, under specifiable conditions, especially subject to disownership without accepting the claim that that which is disowned is *necessarily* equated with sexual and aggressive wishes and impulses. Rejection of the latter claim permits one to recognize that needs, wishes, desires and other mental contents beside those linked to sex and aggression can also be both disowned and continue to exert an influence on one's overall personality functioning. For example, attachment needs and wishes (Bowlby 1969), other object relational needs and wishes (Fairbairn 1952), and so-called narcissistic needs and wishes linked to self-esteem (Kohut 1971; 1977) may also be both disowned and continue to exert an influence on behaviour and experience. Also there is at least the clinical claim that certain beliefs and representations (e.g. of parents) both exert important influence on one's behaviour and feelings and are denied and disowned (Bowlby 1979; Eagle 1985; Weiss 1982).

4   As James (1890: 650) puts it: 'Memory requires more than mere dating of a fact in the past. It must be dated in *my* past.' Here, James is obviously referring to what Tulving would call episodic memory.

5   While slips, dreams and some symptoms clearly do not conform to the practical syllogism, I am not at all certain that this is true of *all* symptoms. Consider first a symptom that does *not* conform to the practical syllogism. Let us assume that Freud's theory regarding the relationship between the syndrome of paranoia and repressed homosexual wishes is correct. Clearly, paranoid symptoms are not based on an unconscious desire to ward off homosexual wishes and a conscious or unconscious belief that such symptoms are the means by which this can be accomplished. However, other symptoms do appear to conform, generally at least, to the practical syllogism. To take one example, I treated a patient who experienced obsessive homosexual thoughts whenever he got too emotionally close to his girlfriend and whenever she put pressure on him for an emotional commitment. The evidence for the relationship between homosexual thought and emotional closeness and commitment was overwhelming. There was also evidence that he experienced emotional closeness and commitment, as expressed in one of his dreams, as 'being smothered' and 'slipping into black nothingness'. It seemed clear to me that my patient's symptom of obsessive homosexual thoughts were self-protective in the sense that they 'protected' him against 'being smothered' and 'slipping into black nothingness'. In effect, through his symptom, he expressed both to himself and to his girlfriend the following 'message': 'Don't expect heterosexual emotional closeness or commitment from me – after all, I'm homosexual.' In what way does the above symptom conform to the practical syllogism? The whole symptom pattern can be understood to express the unconscious wish or desire to avoid the anticipated engulfment and 'black nothingness' associated with emotional closeness and commitment; the unconscious belief that being homosexual represents a means to fulfil the above wish; and 'implementing' the means by developing obsessive homosexual thoughts. The question of the processes by which one develops symptoms that fulfil unconscious desires and are based on unconscious beliefs – that is, *how* one develops symptoms that appear to 'resolve' conflicts and satisfy unconscious wishes and desires – is, of course, a complete mystery and, as Freud recognized, has always been a mystery.

Consider as another example an agoraphobic woman I treated. She became agoraphobic after a difficult pregnancy and birth and she, her husband and new baby were forced to move in with her parents. It is important to include in this brief description the facts that my patient's mother had used a kidney dialysis machine for many years and that my patient had, from the beginning, changed her mother's filters. At one point in treatment, my patient decided on her own that she would no longer change the dialysis filters. Following shortly upon her informing her mother of her decision, the mother went off on a trip and had to return precipitately because she had not taken a sufficient number of filters with her. When my patient recounted this story, she suddenly exclaimed with intense emotion: 'My God! No wonder I had to move back home. This way I can oversee both Jack [her new baby] *and* my mother.'

From this point on, my patient improved dramatically and eventually moved, with her husband and baby, into their own apartment. Assume the validity of my patient's dramatic insight to the effect that her agoraphobic symptom served the purpose of satisfying her unconscious desire to oversee both her baby and her mother. It is clear that seen this way the symptom can be understood to represent the unconscious desire to oversee *both* her baby and mother; unconscious belief (1) that leaving mother was equivalent to leaving her to die; and unconscious belief (2) that moving back home would permit her to take care of both mother and baby (and thereby prevent the former's death). Implementation of the desired goal was achieved through the agoraphobic symptom.

It appears, then, that some symptoms can be understood as quasi-actions 'designed' to fulfil certain disowned and unconscious desires and wishes. Does this mean, however, that 'moral trickery' and 'bad faith' are at work here? Can one argue legitimately that insofar as one disowns desires that are, in fact, one's own desires and insofar as one attempts to satisfy these desires in a manner (i.e. symptomatically) that itself entails the avoidance of responsibility and falsely suggests that these desires are not one's one desires, one is engaged in 'moral trickery'? I think that this argument is invalid. For while some symptoms may be best understood as quasi-actions 'designed' to fulfil certain disowned desires in a disguised way, the fact is that one does not produce even these symptoms wilfully and voluntarily. As noted earlier, *how* one develops symptoms that appear to resolve conflicts and satisfy unconscious desires is a complete mystery. What is clear, however, is that one does not bring that about voluntarily; rather, they just happen. Hence, symptoms are, in one sense, intentional and yet involuntary, a combination that, as Flew (1949) has pointed out, violates our commonsense way of ordering behaviour. In the present context, the important point to reiterate is that even symptoms that appear to follow the practical syllogism, and hence can be thought of a quasi-actions do not appear to lend themselves to notions of 'moral trickery' and 'bad faith'.

6   One can think of unconscious desires, as Moore (1984) does, as 'functional states' which occupy 'a kind of middle ground between body and mind' and as provisionally independent from neurophysiology. However, as Moore notes, 'ultimately some kind of physical structures must realize such functional states' (p. 278).

7   As Claparède (1911: 67) put it, 'The propensity of states of consciousness to cluster around a me which persists and remains the same in the course of time, is a postulate of psychology, as space is a postulate of geometry.' And Williams James (1890: 206) put it, 'The Universal fact [of consciousness experience] is not "feelings exist" and "thoughts exist" but "I think" and "I feel".'

8   If it is true that normally only that which is consistent with one's self-organization is permitted to enter consciousness, it follows that ego structure is essentially a *conservative* force, an implication noted by others (e.g.

Greenwald 1980; Sullivan 1953). Mental contents radically discrepant from one's self-organization are not as likely to be given direct representation in conscious experience. And if, in turn, one's self-organization is in large part shaped by social forces, then it follows that mental contents radically discrepant from the prevailing and predominant social ideologies will not be likely to receive direct representation in conscious experience. This is, of course, what Marx and Engels (1848) had in mind when they observed that class membership shapes the very form of one's consciousness.

Recognition of the essential conservativeness of the self is seen in a number of other, subtle ways. For example, we often think of (and experience) creativity and originality as emanating, not from the self, but from mysterious unconscious sources. We speak of creativity in terms of *receiving* inspiration from these mysterious sources external to the self. It is interesting that both pathological phenomena, such as obsessive thoughts, and creative inspirations are often experienced as 'it' phenomena not belonging to the self. The same for the more ordinary phenomenon of intuition, which is often experienced and described as a thought 'popping into one's mind'. And, of course, a basic rationale for free association in psychoanalysis is that in permitting thoughts to simply emerge, to 'pop into mind' rather than to engage in 'I think', one will more likely by-pass the conversative and censoring ego and thereby increase the likelihood that material discrepant from the ego – id material – will be given more direct representation.

9   There are occasions when even denial is not pathological but adaptive. One sees subtle and non-pathological expressions of denial in response to confrontation with devastating information such as the death of a loved one. As Bowlby (1980) points out, a not uncommon initial response to loss is a 'numbed' reaction in which the traumatic event seems unreal and in which one experiences only numbed and dulled affect. However, in this and related cases of denial – e.g. denial of serious life-threatening illness – what is denied is the full significance of the information received rather than the perceptual information itself.

10 According to Bahnson (1984), who has studied multiple personalities over a long period of time, the multiple personality disorder is more likely to occur when the individual experiences conflicting demands as so different from each other and of such an intensive emotional character 'that they could not be integrated centrally' (p. 5). He compares the more primitive personality in multiple personalities to neurotic (and psychotic) ego-alien dreams and symptoms and notes that 'the multiple personality has no capacity for repression of dangerous emotions of impulses *other than* through the shift from one personality nucleus to another' (p. 6). According to Bahnson, 'The individual must either succumb to the experience of alarm and overwhelming affect of traumatic dimensions carried by one nucleus and its attendant emotions, or shift the location of consciousness to another nucleus' (pp. 6–7).

REFERENCES

Bahnson, C. B. 1984: Integration and disintegration of personality: multiple personality and altered ego states. Paper given at Annual Convention of American Psychological Association, Toronto, 24–8 August 1984.
Bettelheim, B. 1983: *Freud and Man's Soul*. New York: Knopf.
Bowlby, J. 1969: *Attachment and Loss. Vol. I: Attachment*. London: Hogarth Press.
Bowlby, J. 1979: On knowing what you are not supposed to know and feeling what you are not supposed to feel. *Canadian Journal of Psychiatry*, 24, 403–8.
Bowlby, J. 1980: *Attachment and Loss. Vol. III: Loss*. New York: Basic Books.
Brandt, L. W. 1962: Process or structure? *Psychoanalytic Review*, 53, 50–4.
Chomsky, N. 1957: *Syntactic Structures*. The Hague: Mouton.
Chomsky, N. 1966: *Cartesian Linguistics*. New York: Harper & Row.
Claparède, E. 1911: Recognition and 'me-ness', in D. Rapaport (ed.), *Organization and Pathology of Thought*. New York: Columbia University Press, 1951: 58–75.
Dennett, D. C. 1978: *Brainstorms*. Montgomery, Vermont: Bradford Books.
Eagle, M. 1984: *Recent Developments in Psychoanalysis: A Critical Evaluation*. New York: McGraw Hill.
Eagle, M. 1985: The psychoanalytic and the cognitive unconscious. Colloquium given in Departments of Logic & Metaphysics and of Psychology, University of St Andrews, Fife, Scotland.
Ellenberger, H. 1970: *The Discovery of the Unconscious*. New York: Basic Books.
Fairbairn, W. R. D. 1952: *Psychoanalytic Studies of the Personality*. London: Tavistock/Routledge & Kegan Paul.
Flew, A. 1949: Psychoanalytic explanation. *Analysis*, 10, 8–15.
Frankfurt, H. G. 1976: Identification and externality, in A. Rovey (ed.): *The Identities of Persons*. Berkeley and Los Angeles: University of California Press.
Greenwald, A. G. 1980: The totalitarian ego: fabrication and revision of personal history. *American Psychologist*, 35, 603–18.
Grünbaum, A. 1984: *The Foundations of Psychoanalysis: A Philosophical Critique*. Berkeley: University of California Press.
James, W. 1890: *The Principles of Psychology*, vols. I and II. New York: Holt.
Klein, G. S. 1976: *Psychoanalytic Theory: An Explanation of Essentials*. New York: International Universities Press.
Koffka, K. 1935: *Principles of Gestalt Psychology*. New York: Harcourt, Brace.
Kohut, H. 1971: *Analysis of the Self*. New York: International Universities Press.
Kohut, H. 1977: *The Restoration of the Self*. New York: International Universities Press.
Lichtenstein, H. 1977: *The Dilemma of Human Identity*. New York: Jason Aronson.
Locke, J. 1924: *An Essay Concerning Human Understanding*, ed. A. S. Pringle-Pattison. Oxford: Clarendon Press.

Marx, K. and Engels, F. 1848: Manifesto of the Communist Party, in *Selected Works*. New York: International Press, 1951: 31–63.

Moore, M. S. 1984: *Law and Psychiatry: Rethinking the Relationship*. Cambridge: Cambridge University Press.

O'Neill, E. G. 1946: *The Iceman Cometh*. New York: Random House.

Penelhum, T. 1971: The importance of self-identity. *Journal of Philosophy*, 68, 667–78.

Polanyi, M. and Prosch, H. 1975: *Meaning*. Chicago: University of Chicago Press.

Rubinstein, B. B. 1977: On the concept of a person and of an organism, in R. Stern, L. S. Horowitz and J. Lynes (eds), *Science and Psychotherapy*. New York: Haven Publishing.

Sartre, J.-P. 1956: *Being and Nothingness*, trans. Hazel Barnes. New York: Philosophical Library.

Schachter, D. L. and Tulving, E. 1982: Memory, amnesia, and the episodic/semantic distinction, in L. Isaacson and N. E. Spear (eds), *Expressions of Knowledge*. New York: Plenum Press.

Schachter, D. L., Wang, J., Tulving, E., and Freedman, M. 1982: Functional retrograde amnesia: a quantitative case study. *Neuropsychologia*, 20, 523–32.

Schafer, R. 1976: *A New Language for Psychoanalysis*. New Haven: Yale University Press.

Shope, R. 1970: Freud on conscious and unconscious intentions. *Inquiry*, 13, 149–59.

Sullivan, H. S. 1953: *The Interpersonal Theory of Psychiatry*. New York: W. W. Norton.

Szasz, T. 1961: *The Myth of Mental Illness*. New York: Harper & Row.

Tulving, E. 1983: *Elements of Episodic Memory*. New York: Oxford University Press.

Tulving, E. 1984: Memory and consciousness. *Canadian Psychology*, 26, 1–12.

Weiskrantz, L. and Warrington, E. K. 1979: Conditioning in amnesic patients. *Neuropsychologia*, 17, 187–94.

Weiss, J. 1982: Psychotherapy research: theory and findings, theoretical introduction. The Psychotherapy Research Group. Department of Psychiatry, Mount Zion Hospital and Medical Center, Bulletin no. 5.

Williams, M. and Smith, H. V. 1954: Mental disturbances in tuberculous meningitis. *Journal of Neurology, Neurosurgery and Psychiatry*, 17, 173–82.

5

Psychoanalysis, Cognitive Psychology and Self-Consciousness

JOHN HALDANE

> Nobody knows that he is knowing save in knowing something else, and consequently the knowledge of an intelligible object precedes intellectual self-consciousness.
>
> St Thomas Aquinas, *Super Boethium De Trinitate* i, 3[1]

1 INTENTIONALITY AND THE OWNERSHIP OF THOUGHTS

Wittgenstein asks the question: What makes my image of him into an image of him? (1976, II: 3) and so sets the problem of intentionality and mental reference. If we shift the emphasis from 'him' to 'my' and read the question in a different way, the problem presented is that of the ownership of mental contents: What makes my thought *my* thought?

This question, understood in yet another fashion, characterizes the central concern of Professor Eagle's illuminating chapter. For he argues that the issue of the avowal and disavowal of ownership of thoughts is no less important in Freudian theory than the distinction between conscious and unconscious mental states, events and processes. Accordingly any theory of mind that aims to accommodate the phenomena disclosed by psychoanalysis must give account of both unconscious cognitive activity and the acceptance and rejection of contents manifest in consciousness. The invitation from psychoanalytic theory, therefore, is for philosophers to construct a model of the mind incorporating these two features together with other familiar elements. Interestingly, this project partially coincides with that set by the two earlier intepretations of Wittgenstein's question and I shall be concerned with features of this coincidence among other matters.

2   SELF-CONSCIOUSNESS

Several of the themes developed in Professor Eagle's chapter merit detailed consideration but space is limited and I have chosen to proceed in this discussion towards the issue which I believe to be of prime importance, viz. *self-consciousness*. This phenomenon combines the psychological features mentioned earlier and collects around it the various other problems he presents. My thoughts are thus ultimately directed towards aspects of it: its nature, its place in human psychology and the adequacy of currently fashionable theories of mind to give account of it.

'Self-consciousness' suggests: consciousness of a *self* and this of course was Descartes' view:

> From [reflection] I knew that I was a substance the whole essence or nature of which is to think, and that for its existence . . . [it does not] depend on any material thing; so that this 'me', that is to say, the soul by which I am what I am, is entirely distinct from body, and is even more easy to know than the latter.
>
> (Descartes 1970, IV: 101)

Most of us, however, are not Cartesians, and Professor Eagle adds to the stock of familiar philosophical objections further reasons derived from Freud's work for rejecting Cartesianism. Freud was a physicalist and so allows no place for an immaterial subject, but features of his mental taxonomy including the unconscious and ego-alien mental contents are equally damaging to the theory. For Descartes, the mental is essentially conscious and mind is wholly transparent to itself: 'Nothing can exist in the mind, in so far as it is a thinking thing, of which it is not conscious' (Descartes 1970, IV: 115). What Freud's topographical and structural models claims however, is that the self is a construction out of elements in the psychological domain other parts and contents of which may never be disclosed to it or accepted by it.

3   REDUCTIONISM AND HOMUNCULARISM IN FREUDIAN THEORY

The invitation to fit these claims into a coherent account of mind naturally leads one to wonder what Freud himself made of them. The answer seems to be: not much, or else: too little that is self-consistent. In his writings he describes psychological structures and processes by means of analogies drawn from, on the one hand, such sciences as mechanics, chemistry, biology and pathology; and on the other, various humane disciplines including politics, economics and assorted social studies. Yet nowhere is there a final, clear, trouble-free statement of how id, ego and super-ego are related, or of which if any is to be identified with the enduring subject of consciousness – if indeed such exists. Unlike some other contributors to this volume I am not here concerned either to praise Freud or to bury him. Rather, I wish to extract from his evident difficulty in articulating a stable conception of mind an acute tension between two basic accounts of the mental in terms of one or other of which the various analogies may be interpreted: the mechanistic and the anthropomorphic.

Assuming the former conception, the constituent parts of mind are conceived of as internal organs periodically ingesting, transforming and secreting material from and into the environment but not as being possessed of the psychological properties attributed to the person to whom they belong; and sometimes these attributions are regarded as in principle eliminable in favour of non-intentionalistic, organic descriptions. In the famous passage in which Freud characterizes the id, the mechanistic conception is clearly dominant:

> We approach the id with analogies: we call it a chaos, a cauldron full of seething excitations . . . It is filled with energy reaching it from the instincts but it has no organisation, produces no collective will, but only a striving to bring about the satisfaction of the instinctual needs subject to the observance of the pleasure principle. The logical laws of thought do not apply to the id . . . Contrary impulses exist side by side, without cancelling each other out or diminishing each other: at most they may converge to form compromises under the dominating economic pressure towards the discharge of energy.
>
> (S.E. 1932, XXII: 73–4)

When anthropomorphic accounts are proposed, however, the prospects fade for the kind of eliminative materialism advocated in the 'Project for a Scientific Psychology' in which psychological predicates are replaced by organic ones, which in turn may be reduced to those of brain chemistry, or even physics. Whatever is the supposed relationship between subpersonal, inner goings-on and the conscious life of an individual; intentionalistic descriptions (attributing beliefs, desires and purposes, etc.) must be treated realistically at least at one of these levels. Thus, if the characterization of unconscious processes in terms of social relationships between intelligent agents is analogical, it presumably applies forms of description that are literally appropriate with respect to whole persons.

Neither Freud (so far as I can discover) nor many of his followers who seek to combine the original reductionist programme of the 'Project' with the anthropomorphic conception of the mental recognize this implication of the latter and its contradiction of the former. Generally there is a strong pull towards reductionism: firstly, because it characterizes the methodology of the physical sciences, which are generally assumed to be the paradigm of theoretical inquiry; and secondly, because it promises to explain all phenomena by means of the ontological resources of naturalism. Accordingly, when confronted with the contradiction derived above, latter-day 'scientific psychologists' will no doubt simply abandon anthropomorphism entirely, or else regard it instrumentally, as a convenient though ultimately dischargeable tool for describing higher- and lower-level functions physically realized in the neurophysiology of the brain.

In section 9 I consider whether a naturalistic account of the psychological such as science aspires to could ever be provided. For the moment, however, I want to point out that the other option, i.e. the rejection of reductionism and the affirmation of psychological realism, has two variants. One could claim that mental properties are features of persons and that the characterization of subpersonal components and activities by intentionalistic vocabulary is a form of courtesy attribution justified by the roles these things occupy in supporting the mental life of a normal human being. Alternatively, the order of priority could be reversed. It might then be argued that the proper bearers of mental attributes are entities contained within the human frame, and that what we ordinarily think of as basic psychological units are in reality communities of subjects. On this view a man or woman is a society of selves and it is only by analogy, made apt by the fact that he or she contains mental subjects and is the vehicle of their transactions with the world, that we may speak of human beings in personal terms.

This second version of the anti-reductionist option may seem bizarre but has appeal to those who believe there are psychological facts and also find reasons to postulate mentally active, subhuman components within us. As we shall see, a certain tradition in cognitive psychology subscribes to a view of this sort and, notwithstanding his early commitment to reductionism and employment of mechanistic analogies, it seems that Freud sometimes intends his anthropomorphic characterizations to be understood literally, thereby representing the 'mind' as in effect an inner realm inhabited by homunculi. In explaining hysteria he writes:

everything points to one solution: the patient is in a special state of mind in which all his impressions or his recollections . . . are no longer held together by an associative chain . . . it is possible for a recollection to express its effect by means of somatic phenomena without the group of the other mental processes, the ego, knowing about it or being able to intervene to prevent it.

(S.E. 1893, III: 20)

Similarly, he concludes that to account for dreaming it is necessary to postulate multiple agency within the psyche:

The fact that the phenomena of censorship and of dream distortion correspond down to their smallest details justifies us in presuming that they are similarly determined. We may therefore suppose that dreams are given their shape in individual human beings by the operation of two psychical forces . . . and that one of these forces constructs the wish which is expressed by the dream, while the other exercises a censorship upon this dream wish.

(S.E. 1900, IV: 143–4)

4 PSYCHOANALYSIS AND COGNITIVE PSYCHOLOGY

The tension between Freud's mechanistic and anthropomorphic accounts of psychological phenomena remains unresolved (as it must), and the adoption of a homuncular version of the latter simply fails to provide the required explanations. To give account of human psychology by reference to that of lesser entities out of which we are composed is unacceptably regressive. The interest of these problems in the present context, however, emerges when one returns to the issue of the accommodation of Freudian insights within current philosophies of mind.

Professor Eagle remarks that the conscious/unconscious dimension of psychoanalytic explanation is indirectly supported by cognitive psychology. Clearly we discriminate features of the environment below the level of consciousness. Our linguistic practices depend upon subconscious recognition of syntactical structures, and most external actions involve processing information about the location of objects and the disposition of one's limbs, etc., of which one remains largely, if not entirely, unaware.

Recognition of such capacities and of their role in action, together with the demise of behaviourism and the development of Artificial Intelligence (AI) research, have encouraged widespread adoption of an account of the mind as an abstractly specified, information-processing system. To date, philosophical interest in this area has been motivated by two concerns. First, by the wish to restore the old idea that cognitive states intervene between sensation and behaviour, thereby warranting our rationalization of the latter by either direct reference or allusion to beliefs and appetitive attitudes. Second, by the thesis that the semantic power of language is not intrinsic to it and derives from some content-conferring source. On both counts computational psychology seems to deliver what is required. For it makes the following three, related claims:

1   that purposeful behaviour including linguistic activity is to be explained by reference to causally effective, inner mental episodes and dispositions;
2   that these latter are productive of action in virtue of their informational content;
3   that their possession of content results from operations of engagement with (internal) symbolic representations.

Assuming the coherence of these claims, a theory advancing them should have no difficulty accommodating the idea of unconscious thought and could include, as explanation of part of this, the dynamics of repression. When Professor Eagle describes the psychological phenomenon of rendering personal (and impersonal) mental contents he observes that this is likely to be overlooked if one approaches Freud from the perspective of AI-inspired theories. If this is so it is due to the fact that interest in computational psychology generally derives from a desire to understand the nature of human cognition and deliberative processes rather than from an interest in the affective aspects of personal psychology.

There is no *a priori* reason why an AI theorist of the relevant sort should not incorporate the Freudian unconscious and content-acceptance/rejection phenomena within his scheme of things. Indeed, Professor Eagle notes that cognitive science already postulates mental structures and processes not given in consciousness and does not suggest that this second function cannot be accommodated within such accounts. Moreover, he casts descriptions of it in terms reminiscent of modular, computational theories. Consequently I assume him to be at least agnostic, if not actually to give an affirmative answer, with respect to the question: Can theories of this kind admit and (in principle) explain the phenomena of repression and self-organization as he describes them? I, by contrast, have serious doubts which I elaborate below connected with general scepticism about the very coherence of such theories.

5   CONSCIOUSNESS AND COMPUTATION

The tension identified in section 3 between mechanistic and anthropomorphic accounts of the subpersonal as Freud envisages it already has a counterpart in current attempts to answer Wittgenstein's question about intentionality and mental reference: What makes this *a thought of him*? There is a clear division among philosophers committed to their own 'project for a scientific (cognitive) psychology' between those like Fodor who ascribe intentional properties to internal, subpersonal states, and thereby recognize as genuinely cognitive the implicated computational procedures and representations over which they are defined;[2] and others such as Dennett who regard the postulation of psychological entities as confusion and thus favour some form of reductionism.

Both parties see the implications of treating intentional-content ascription realistically within the context of computational psychology, viz. commitment to mental representations and subpersonal assignments of semantic value. But while Dennett regards this as a *reductio* on the realist assumption and therefore retreats to a type of instrumentalism (the 'intentional stance') which regards the attribution of psychological states as warranted only by its predictive power, Fodor simply detaches the consequent and returns with the counter: 'No representations, no computations. No computations, no model' (1975: 31; see also 'Three Cheers for Propositional Attitudes' in Fodor 1981).

The prospects for achieving an understanding of thought and intentional reference and more generally of developing a philosophical account of human psychology depend in large part upon the resolution of this dispute. Before attempting this, however, it will be as well if I consider briefly how the different advocates of computational psychology will respond to those phenomena which are of importance in Freudian theory.

It is reasonable to suppose that when presented with the ownership issue proponents of the two tendencies – to anthropomorphic and mechanistic accounts of subpersonal computation – will simply insert additional executive functions overseeing information processing and selecting from among its output acceptable contents (the conscious manifestation of which is the avowal of ownership) and rejecting others. Ego-alien representations subsequently surfacing in awareness will then be explained in terms of limitations or failures of these procedures.

Here it is unnecessary to consider how such functions might operate, since for present purposes the important point is that such an accommodation will be viewed both by Professor Eagle and by the philosophers in question as an extension of a programme that has already given account of intentionality, to cover the further phenomena of content integration and self-awareness.

So viewed the main problems facing this extension are firstly, one specific to the instrumentalist: to admit higher-order functions, including self-consciousness, operating on lower-level computations while resisting Fodor's modern mentalism, or more generally, psychological realism; and secondly, one facing all theories, reductionist or otherwise, including the psychoanalytic view: to explain *why* there are these higher functions and in particular why *consciousness* of the reflective sort presupposed in the phenomenon of avowal and disavowal of ownership of mental contents should exist at all.

Professor Eagle sketches an answer to this puzzle in terms of the adaptive utility, and hence survival value, to a creature of its capacity to survey and critically assess its responses to the environment, and one can see how in principle this form of explanation might be developed to show the utility of the various complex procedures involved in evaluation, deliberation and repression, etc., all of which consciousness makes possible. By contrast, a creature equipped to register the presence of certain features in its environment yet unable to examine its responses, check for consistency and relate them to stored information and instinctive drives, has greater liability to error and consequently is more vulnerable. Awareness permits supervision, correction and reorientation and thus contributes to an agent's welfare. Where the subject is psychologically complex these higher-level functions may combine to promote the integration of various contents and to eliminate, or failing this to repress, harmful elements. In short, consciousness provides conditions for the genesis and preservation of 'self'-organization, and when the latter psychological structure is subject to inspection and assessment we have the phenomenon of self-consciousness – but without a Cartesian *self*.

Interestingly, Fodor cautiously entertains a similar reply to those who note that contemporary cognitive psychology postulates large-scale information processing below the level of subjects' awareness and who therefore ask: Why consciousness?

the question of selectional advantage is extremely obscure. It may be that what you get out of introspectability is the possibility of conscious correction . . . [But] unlike Freud's situation, ours in respect to this problem is a bit embarrassed. We don't have a clear aetiological explanation in terms of say selectional advantage or something of that kind, of why those things that are conscious are conscious and why the rest of them aren't. It is also possible that there isn't going to be such a story.[3]

For reasons which I expound in section 9, the last remark is deeply ironical. At this point, however, it could be thought that his embarrassment is unnecessary since an explanation by reference to adaptive utility seems appropriate, even if the details remain obscure. Certainly Dennett believes that such an account is both possible and appealing and sets out what he takes to be a coherent version of it:

[Proceeding] through several iterations of the basic Darwinian motif . . . out of an inorganic world came not only replicators (living things) but also the reasons their striving after replication created.
  Out of tropistic and unlearning creatures . . . arose conditionable . . . creatures, who could redesign themselves in the direction of an even closer sensitivity to their reasons, especially enhanced by their emerging ability to react to patterns in their own reactions to the patterns in nature. Out of the crude protolinguistic practices of some of these creatures emerged, by opportunistic mutation, an even more powerful reflexive activity: the representation of some of these activities, and the use of these representations in self-monitoring and self-evaluation . . .
  [So begins] the process by which we becomes selves.

(Dennett 1984b: 43–4, 81)

As I remarked, I have worries about the coherence of any such story. Prior to elaborating these, however, I wish to suggest that the two problems corresponding to Wittgenstein's question are not in fact distinct but that intentionality and mental reference are in part functions of self-consciousness and cannot, as has so far been assumed, be explained independently of it. My argument has negative and positive aspects. I first outline the case against *both* Fodorian realism and Dennettian instrumentalism about intentionality and then sketch an alternative view in which the connection with self-consciousness is indicated. At that point I return to the question: *Why consciousness?* I then proceed to my main conclusion, which is that while the mental is a constituent feature of reality there cannot be a naturalistic account of it: no 'project for a scientific psychology' can succeed.

6 REDUCTIONISM AND REALISM IN PHILOSOPHICAL PSYCHOLOGY

One possible reason for supposing that there can be no natural science of psychology is the thought that there is no psychological reality. Such a thought, however, is self-defeating. Were there no psychological reality, this truth could not be thought. To entertain the proposition is thus to have conclusive evidence for its falsity and this point cannot be met by casting doubt on whether one really is thinking this proposition, or merely seeming to and hence perhaps not thinking at all. To doubt that one is thinking *this* is to be thinking, and *ipso facto* implies the truth of the proposition in question. Thus one cannot coherently doubt that there is a psychological reality.

This important conclusion must be the starting point for all theories of mind, be they scientific, philosophical or informal. They then are led on to consider the scope and nature of the psychological. While the argument of the previous paragraph showed that one cannot simply assert that there is nothing to explain, it seems there is still room for reductionist theories which allow that psychological claims may be true in virtue of reality but maintain that what they characterize is not something over and above the behaviour which is otherwise taken to result from logically prior mental dispositions and episodes.

The belief that the earlier conclusion is compatible with behaviourism and various forms of instrumentalism is widely held and is even shared by many non-reductive realists (henceforth termed intentionalists), who therefore assume that quite independent argument is required to show the falsity of reductionism. Against this I contend that if one reflects upon the thought that there is a psychological reality one can both show it to be true *and* demonstrate that the only coherent account of it is an intentionalist one.

Earlier, I identified two reasons why philosophers have moved towards theories of an AI-type, functionalist sort: the concern to explain the relationalization of action, and the need to give account of linguistic meaning. These interests can be brought together in relation to one kind of action, viz. intentional, referential utterances, of any of which one may ask: *Why* was it performed? and also: *How* can it have semantic significance? Standardly, we take ourselves to have explained a speech act (S) of this sort by adverting to beliefs and communicative intentions of its utterer including his belief that 'S' means that p. (In section 7 I consider the second question about how the latter, semantic fact is possible.) The problems for behaviourism in giving account of these matters are familiar enough to justify a fairly brisk presentation of relevant points.

The folk-psychological explanation of the speaker's behaviour refers to operative cognitive states but behaviourism construes these as dispositions to engage in certain routines. To ascribe to the utterer the belief: that 'S' means that p, is on this view to attribute a propensity to behave in certain ways including uttering 'S'. If this disposition is not then grounded in some actual structural aspect of the subject two problems arise: first, the theory denies what we believe, viz. that the explanation of action involves reference to independent sources; and second, it assumes what is at least contentious (and arguably incoherent), that there can be unsupported dispositions.

Further to these worries is the thought that the theory even lacks the resources to give content to the notion of purposeful behaviour. For the individuation of these types is psychologistic. There is no coherent way of distinguishing patterns of *action* in terms that can be made sense of in the explanation of what an individual is about other than by reference to the types of psychological attitudes such behaviour expresses or embodies. Purposeful behaviour is engaged in for *reasons*, on the basis of beliefs and desires; hence reference to purposeful behaviour presupposes effective mental states. Moreover, these states are productive of action in virtue of their interactions one with another, typically through practical reasoning to which we advert in giving psychological explanations. Behaviourism can give no principled account of the distinction between action and mere movement since it denies the reality of features other than behaviour in terms of which this distinction can be drawn.

Action words type-individuate behaviour under intentional descriptions. Accordingly the identification of a set of movements as an action is only apt – the movements only are an *action* – if the set exhibits intentional properties, i.e. if it issues from a structure of beliefs and desires, etc. Thus, if there are actions behaviourism is false; and the behaviourist is hardly able to save his thesis by contraposition, since he is committed to applying action concepts in characterizing the phenomena to be explained and in specifying (some of) the relevant behavioural dispositions. Moreover, his own avowal of the thesis is an action partly rationalized by the beliefs supporting it. In fine, behaviourism presupposes the applicability of some action concepts; all true applications of action concepts entail the reality of the intentional; and the existence of intentional properties implies the falsity of behaviourism.

This conclusion is compatible with two claims often employed by behaviourists and others with one foot in their camp,[4] viz. that some psychological states are dispositional; and that not all actions (and in particular not all speech acts) are preceded by mental episodes of judgement, decision etc., as mentalists seem to suppose. No doubt some realists have claimed that all mental phenomena are episodic, though with no good reason, save perhaps the Cartesian assumption quoted in section 2: that 'nothing can exist in the mind . . . of which it is not conscious'. There are, however, compelling reasons to reject Cartesian psychology. As psychoanalysis and ordinary experience imply, not all thought is conscious; and as the philosophical analysis of propositional attitude ascription easily shows, not all contents implicated in a judgement are currently entertained, and the most plausible explanation of many of these and other elements of a subject's psychology is that they consist in cognitive and affective dispositions.

None the less, the anti-behaviourist conclusion stands on grounds already given and for a related reason. The performance of an action presupposes the existence of intentional properties. This fact damned behaviourism, since it relies on action concepts in identifying the phenomena to be explained and in characterizing the dispositions of which they are taken to be realizations. Yet there remains the point that not all intelligent behaviour is immediately preceded by mental judgements or rehearsals. When I say: 'There is a psychological reality', this may not follow upon any interior utterance of that proposition; and its absence suggests to reductionists that to appeal to it in other contexts is therefore gratuitous.

These considerations imply the following 'antimony of action': The performance of an action is not based upon prior intentions, for if it were we would know of them; and: The performance of an action is based upon prior intentions, for if it were not it would be mere behaviour – for action presupposes intentionality. One might suggest that the epistemological assumption of the first proposition is false but this is neither plausible nor necessary. The correct resolution of the antinomy grants that there may be no prior rehearsal and traces the tension to a fallacy of equivocation. Action presupposes intentionality, thus thought is logically prior to the behaviour it informs. But it does not follow that every purposeful act is preceded by a mental statement of its purpose; that every utterance of 'S' follows upon the entertainment of its content.[5] Behaviour is not action without thought but sometimes thought is embodied in behaviour. My utterance of 'S' may be my thinking of it.

The foregoing shows how intentionalist realism is able to accommodate the two claims which have often been taken to provide support for behaviourist and neo-behaviourist theories. In addition, analysis of the notion of action shows that *only* intentionalism can make sense of it. Beliefs and desires enter into the genesis and constitution of intentional behaviour and, while some of the psychological determinants of action may be dispositional, psychological reality cannot be composed of nothing but overt behaviour and related propensities. This impossibility is not due solely to the metaphysical requirement that dispositions have a categorical grounding in structural properties of their bearers, but has an independent foundation in the fact that the behaviour in which psychological dispositions of the relevant sort issues depends upon other mental states. Of course, some of these may also be dispositional but they cannot all be. Necessarily some mental acts, e.g. of judgement and decision, are implicated.

Consider again the utterance of the sentence: 'There is a psychological reality.' Suppose one is interested in why someone (me, say) uttered this on a given occasion. The explanation presented is that I am disposed to do so in certain circumstances; for example, when I have been reading about scepticism in the philosophy of mind, or when asked to give my opinion about the reality of the psychological. However, if this behaviour is a purposeful response and not just a mechanical blind reaction then it depends upon the occurrence of appropriate mental events. I shall only respond to reading the text by uttering 'S' if I *recognize* that the thesis described is a sceptical one; and shall only reply in like vein if I *believe* I have been asked for my opinion; and shall not use these words unless I *intend* to communicate my view and *believe* that the inquirer understands English; nor shall I reply if I *wish* to be unhelpful or *desire* to cause puzzlement. In short, the realization of the relevant behavioural dispositions standardly depends upon occurrent intentional states.

It is now possible to justify the earlier conclusion that reflection upon the proposition that there is a psychological reality can establish both its truth and the failure of any non-intentionalist account of this truth. The argument for the first claim is that with which this section began. The argument for the second can be presented in the form of a dilemma for the reductionist posed by asking the question: What does entertaining this proposition consist in? One reply is that it is having the thought that p, where this is construed non-reductively in familiar mentalist fashion. The other possibility is that it consists in uttering or inscribing 'S', or in some other form of overt behaviour. But none of these possible replies will be performances of the speech act S, or actions with p as their semantic content, unless they express or embody appropriate intentional states. That is to say, unless they issue from communicative or performative *intentions* and *beliefs* about the content and truth of p. The first reply makes direct appeal to non-dispositional, non-overt behavioural intentional states while the second makes reference to items presupposing them. Either way the intentionalist account of psychological reality is vindicated.

7 MEANING AND MENTAL REPRESENTATION

I remarked that one may view an intentional, referential utterance as raising two questions: *Why* was it performed? and *How* does it have meaning? I related the pursuit of these issues to the rise of AI-type functionalism (AIF) as a theory of mind. It should be clear how consideration of the first question leads to views acknowledging the existence of internal springs of action but it is necessary to recall other aspects of recent philosophical inquiry to complete the set of conditions widely judged to be sufficient for this view.

The failure of behaviourism calls for an account of the psychological that recognizes its reality and causal role. Central state materialism meets the latter condition and satisfies the former by identifying thoughts with states of the cerebrum and central nervous system, but it entails an absurd ontological imperialism: it implies that no state lacking a constitution correctly describable in terms of human neurophysiology could be psychological. Thus, the move is made to a weaker physicalist theory – token identity.

This is compatible with the possibility of different material realizations of the psychological. Internal interaction is presupposed by reference to reasoning in the explanation of action. Together these suggest the following 'theory specification':

Wanted: An account of mind that

1   permits abstraction from particular physiology;
2   connects psychological states to (a) sensation, (b) behaviour and (c) one another;
3   allows the various subject/world transactions to correspond systematically to the informational content of the internal states.

This has generally been taken to require the appointment of a theory conjoining functionalism with what by itself it fails to provide, viz. an account of content. That is, of those characteristics of internal states in virtue of which they effect transitions from sensation to appropriate behaviour. Such an account seems to be available from AI research. Thus, to be (occurrently) in a particular psychological state of an attitudinal sort (to believe that S means that p, say) is on the appointed theory to be in a functional state involving a relation with some internal item possessed of information in virtue of its syntactical or formal properties.

To this point agreement is widespread but beyond it lies a battleground and the fight is quickly joined when one considers the second question about a speech act: How does it have meaning? I argued that its performance presupposes intentions and beliefs, including the belief that S means that p. AIF theory proposes that this thought is the belief it is because of the character of an inner object which partly constitutes it. The central problem in philosophical cognitive psychology is the interpretation and evaluation of this claim, and it is with respect to the accounts given of it by Dennett, Fodor et al. that it is now apt to recall the difficulties encountered when reviewing Freud's attempt to characterize the mind by means of mechanistic and anthropomorphic models.

Adoption of computer analogies such as AIF endorses may seem equivalent to a mechanistic account. However, this is not how both parties view it. Fodor argues that the computer analogy provides a way of restating the essence of anthropomorphic or homuncular theories of mind, viz. the claim that purposeful behaviour is to be explained in terms of the intentional properties of entities located within our heads. Dennett, by contrast, does assume that the computer metaphor is reductionist and welcomes it as a way of exorcizing these ghosts of Descartes' ghost; a fruitful way of 'discharging the homunculi'.

The relative strengths and weaknesses of these opposing views are best displayed in regard to the problem of meaning. Wittgenstein (1976: I, 432) presents the following observation and puzzle: 'Every sign *by itself* seems dead. *What* gives it life? – In use it is *alive*. Is life breathed into it there? – Or is the *use* its life?'

Consideration of this problem dates from antiquity, as does an initially compelling solution to it. Expounding the latter Aquinas writes (my italics): 'Since the exterior word [an utterance] is sensible it is better known to us than the inteior word [a thought] and hence the vocal word is called a "word" before the interior word, although *the interior word is prior in nature being the efficient and final cause of the exterior word*' (*De Veritate*, q4, a1).

Clearly speech acts have meaning, but their media are not in themselves significant. There is nothing about the set of marks – *This page is white* – which gives it sense and reference. Yet, its conventional usage to convey information presupposes possession of semantic value. How is this possible? Ancient wisdom has it that we invest marks with meaning by using them to express the intentional content of thoughts. *Conventional* linguistic representation is possible, therefore, because *natural* mental representation already exists. The former came into being as a solution to the need to communicate thought through observable media but such behaviour only has significance in virtue of the content of speakers' intentional states: signs have meaning because ideas have sense.

Given this account it is clear why Aquinas speaks of the basic constituent of thought as both *conceptus* and *verbum mentis* and refers to the articulation of concepts in mental judgements as speech (*dicere*).[6] Fodor follows the same route and, assuming that thought must have structural and intentional properties equivalent to the basic syntax and semantics of the linguistic behaviour which expresses it, is led to postulate a 'language of thought'.

For Fodor this is a paticularization to the case of language use of the general thesis that what lies behind and explains intelligent behaviour is a system of information processing involving computations defined over a range of types of representations. Such a view has the attractions of the old and familiar theory of ideas of which it is simply a modern version. But it also suffers from the same difficulties, chief of which in the present context is that it is regressive.[7] The problem of linguistic meaning has been transferred to that of which it is the public manifestation. Indeed, it is not even a transfer from one *kind* of phenomenon to another. For Aquinas the description of thought in linguistic terms is no more than an analogy warranted by its (efficient and final) causal efficacy in respect of speech; yet Fodor supposes that mental representation quite literally consists in the manipulation of symbols.[8] But since syntax only has significance under an interpretation (this was the original problem) it follows that representation entails the assignment of content; and given that all (or most?) mental representation is taken to be subpersonal the theory is committed to interpretation at this level also. Thus, the AIF account, so construed, is nothing other than homuncularism and is thereby a near relative of Freud's anthropomorphic model of mind.

Dennett's appeal to modular information processing as a way of understanding the character of the internal causes of linguistic and other intelligent behaviour aims to avoid the regress flowing from Fodor's theory by showing how it is possible to explain meaning and other intentional phenomena by distributing features constitutive of them throughout a network of subpersonal computational systems of increasing simplicity. Instead of reproducing the puzzling phenomena within the total system Dennett offers a strategy for reducing them to philosophically unproblematic, syntactically defined processes. On this account what AIF presents is not a regressively anthropomorphic, but a mechanistic philosophy of mind:

[You] replace the little man in the brain with a committee [whose members] are stupider than the whole; they are less intelligent and 'know' less. The subsystems don't individually reproduce all of the talents of the whole. That would lead you to an infinite regress. Instead you have each subsystem doing a part, so that each homuncular subsystem is less intelligent, knows less, believes less. *The representations are themselves, as it were, less representational*, so you don't need an inner eye to observe them; you can get away with some sort of an inner process which 'accesses' them in some attenuated sense . . . put together . . . a whole system of these stupid elements can exhibit behaviour which looks distinctly intelligent, distinctly human.'

(Miller 1983: 78; my italics)[9]

Unfortunately this theory is fatally flawed and once its weakness is indicated its claims can only be represented in one or other of two unacceptable ways: either as a version of behaviourism, or as equivalent to

Fodor's regressive mentalism. Its defect is that it rests upon a fallacy of equivocation committed in the sentence italicized in the quotation. Certainly the powers of the subsystems are less than those of the whole but in the important sense the former are not *less* powerful since their capacities are of the same type. Representations may be less representational in virtue of representing less (carrying less information) but they are not on that account any less representations. Indeed, as regards the point at issue the poorest representation possible is as powerful as the most richly endowed. The philosophical problem of meaning and intentionality is not that of showing how things can have so *much* of them but rather one of explaining how they can have them *at all*.

Two options are available to the AIF theorist in the light of this objection. First, he could follow Fodor and allow that the springs of language and action are themselves intentional in character – if less 'intelligent' than the form of life to which they contribute. Second, recognizing that this offers no philosophical explanation of the mental, he could retain the assumption that we are simply information-processing systems of a mechanical, non-semantic sort and embrace the reductionist implication of this view: that human beings do not in reality possess psychological properties. At times Dennett indicates his implicit acceptance of this conclusion, as when he writes of the merely instrumental value of regarding ourselves as properly the bearers of mental attributes (Dennett 1979: ch. 1).

Whichever option is chosen, AI functionalism meets damning objections. Anthropomorphic homuncularism does justice to the reality of the intentional but by reintroducing it in the *explanans* in a wholly regressive way. Reductive mechanism avoids this only by denying the reality of the *explanandum* in a manner analogous to the earlier forms of behaviourism from which it descends and whose liability to refutation by the sorts of arguments presented in section 6 it inherits. In sum, computational cognitive psychology cannot accommodate the Freudian insights for the same reason that Freudian psychology cannot: they both present incoherent theories of mind.

8 INTENTIONALITY AND CONSCIOUSNESS

The position thus arrived at may seem somewhat confusing. I began with the suggestion that the two interpretations of Wittgenstein's question are connected one with another and with Professor Eagle's psychoanalytic concerns. I next allowed that the phenomena identified by Freud add to the case against Cartesianism. Prior to taking up the suggestion that an appropriately extended version of computational cognitive psychology *might* provide the required theory, I reviewed Freud's own attempts to structure a model of mind and found those efforts to be unsuccessful. One response to repeated failure is to conclude that the task is misconceived and that in effect is the claim made by the various forms of reductionism. In opposition to this I elaborated an argument for the existence of irreducibly intentional phenomena and thereby returned the discussion to Wittgenstein's original puzzle about content, now recast in the form of the question: How can words have meaning? At this point Professor Eagle's proposal is of interest since attempts to explain the possibility of representation – whether semantic or intentional – have focused on AI theories of information processing, and it is in this direction that he suggests we might look for the basis of a philosophical psychology equipped to explain avowal, disavowal and content-integration. Sad to say this convergence does not herald arrival at the desired destination: an adequate and correct theory of mind. For modular, computational psychology follows the pattern of Freud's investigations and emerges either as a version of anti-realist mechanism or else incoherent anthropomorphism.

Thus far my conclusions have been largely negative. The efforts of Descartes, Freud, Dennett and Fodor have all been judged failures. And in the final section I suggest that it is impossible to succeed in the project of providing a naturalistic explanation of intentional phenomena. Notwithstanding all of this I hold fast to the earlier conclusion that intentionalism, or non-reductive realism, is inescapable. Its denial is not logically contradictory: it could have been the case that there did not exist creatures such as ourselves, possessed of mental properties. However, our capacity to entertain the original claim or its negation is decisive evidence of its truth.

Given these conclusions it behoves me to provide some indication of an alternative philosophy of mind equipped to give account of the phenomena so far mentioned (and of various others besides). Here I can do no more than identify essential elements in such a theory, suggest how they relate to ideas already discussed and show the prime importance of self-consciousness.

One reason why philosophers have been drawn to computational psychology is that much of our behaviour seems best explained by postulating information processing in essence no different to the operations of machines. Recognizing this, Dennett fallaciously infers that everything we do is explicable in terms of non-intentional 'information' processing; that we are driven by purely *syntactic* engines – brains. Fodor, by contrast, interprets the notion of 'information' intentionally, i.e. as essentially involving symbolic representations, and so posits subpersonal *semantics* – provided by intra-cranial interpreters. Thus, he conjoins the intentionalist insight: that only what has sense can bestow it, with the AI evidence that complex discrimination/response behaviour can be produced in appropriately programmed computers, to derive the erroneous and regressive conclusion that all of *our* behaviour issues from semantically characterized computations.

The truth of the matter lies between these 'all or nothing' positions. Many of our responses are neither intentional nor presuppose intentionality; but equally not all of what we do can be explained without invoking beliefs, desires and other conceptually contentful states. The latter responses resist the attempted reduction of mind to mechanism.[10] The former on the other hand are unproblematically mechanical.

Having distinguished two phenomena corresponding to the intentional and non-intentional concepts of 'information', I need next to suggest an account of their connection in human psychology. Some first-order states of ours are simply exercises or products of innate sensitivities (to features of the environment) of kinds also possessed by other animals and by machines. Such states often have behavioural effects, usually through interactions with others of similar or different sense – modalities. One may choose to describe an entity having only discriminative powers of this kind as 'conscious', but if so this is a non-psychological attribute since there is neither need nor warrant for attributing intentionality to such sensory states. While they are isomorphic with their environmental causes they are no more 'about' them than is the impression on a pillow 'about' the head that previously rested there. Moreover, states of this sort do not have a subjective quality or phenomenological aspect. There is nothing it feels like to have mere environmental sensitivity. Accordingly, as the idea of consciousness is usually taken to include at least the latter feature and sometimes the former also, the use of the term in this context is not well chosen and risks confusion.

Informational states, as I shall term them, may however, be *transformed* into properly conscious states possessed of either (or both) phenomenological character and intentional content; as when there is a transition from a mere register of reflected light from an object to a perceptual thought of it, i.e. a conceptually informed perception. The question arises: What effects this transition? The obvious answer is: Consciousness – in the familiar full-blooded sense. Broadly this is correct but more needs to be said about the character of consciousness and of how it is related to the puzzling phenomena of *qualia*, intentionality and mental ownership.

Given a complex network of informational states initiating and modifying behaviour in accord with a programme, it is tempting to lapse into the mental idiom when describing them. As was seen, however, complexity is not to the point in explaining the syntax/semantics gap; nor can consciousness be explained in the terms favoured by AIF theorists discussed in section 5. Their proposal is to treat it in Cartesian fashion as introspection directed upon mental contents, but to give a *mechanistic* account of this operation as a higher-order computational function defined over the output of first-order information processing.

There are two objections to this proposal. The first is simply that increasing the quantity of machinery cannot close the gap. The second is directed at Cartesianism generally and is that consciousness and relatedly self-consciousness are not reducible simply to introspection, i.e. to mental states whose *sole* objects are other mental states. One reason for resisting this account is the prospect of a regress of introspecting subjects. Another is that there is a quite different psychological phenomenon which contributes largely to the puzzling features of mind and *ipso facto* to their philosophical explanation. This is the phenomenon of mental reflexivity indirectly adverted to by Aquinas in the passage which prefaces this chapter. Elsewhere he writes:

since the intellect reflects upon itself, by such reflection [*reflexionem*] it is aware of its own activity.[11]

Just as we know, through itself, that the soul exists, in so far as we perceive its activity . . . so also do we know of the things within [it], such as abilities and dispositions, [both] *that* they exist, by virtue of perceiving their acts [and] *what* they are, from the qualitative character of their acts.[12]

Reflexive consciousness is distinct from introspective reflection which also exists but is posterior to it. The former (unlike the latter) is not an activity additional to first-order operations but is a feature of a class of these characterized by awareness of their occurrence. Consider for example the situation in which there is a distant sound to which one is non-consciously (i.e. informationally) sensitive and in time with which one's foot is tapping. Suddenly, however, one becomes aware both of what one is doing and of the cause of it. But the primary object of this new state is not its predecessor; rather it is the complex of sound and foot-tapping. There are not two states – one directed upon the other (as in internal scanning); instead one kind of phenomenon (amenable to a mechanist explanation) has been replaced by another (which resists it). In reflexive consciousness sensory states are conceptualized as the subject brings input under a description and the transformation wrought by this phenomenon includes the dawning of the qualitative aspect of sentience. What was formerly the cause of an informational state is now perceived as an object of experience. In the same act one is simultaneously aware of the object and of one's awareness of it.[13]

The experiential content of this emergent state might be the following: *a faraway, steady, mellow beat to which I am keeping time.* This exhibits the three puzzling properties of intentionality, phenomenological character and self-consciousness. The new state has *content, quality* and *personal ownership.* It is important to see how reflexivity enters into the explanation of these features as this also contributes to the argument against a scientific psychology. The pre-reflexive sensitivity is an entirely causal phenomenon and can be described in non-psychological terms. Once awareness is included, however, descriptions of states involving it must indicate both to what aspects of the environment the individual is related *and* how this relationship presents itself to him or her. Content ascriptions must be sensitive to the modes of representation through which the world is experienced. Where previously there existed a wholly extensional relation there now exists mental reference mediated by a conceptual content, sometimes accompanied by a phenomenological aspect; and when these features are taken into account the resulting content specifications are patently non-extensional. Substitution of co-extensive predicates and co-referring expressions for those occurring within the scope of psychological verbs reporting the mode of reflexive awareness cannot be sure to preserve the truth of an original content specification for the simple reason that they may fail to capture the character of the subject's state (and, of course, existential inference out of such contexts is likewise fallible as nothing in the world may answer to the content of an experience).

Reflexivity is no less important in explaining mental ownership and the genesis of the concept of the *self.* At the outset I rejected the Cartesian account of self-consciousness as awareness of an entity distinct from the living human being. In the course of the discussion arguments have been directed against psychological reductionism and in favour of intentionalism. Together these support an account of persons as members of a distinct class of primary substances possessed of both physical and psychological properties. This indeed is my view[14] but it not obvious that to postulate the existence of irreducibly psychophysical entities is yet to have explained the nature of selfhood. The latter appears underdetermined by personhood since it seems logically possible that one could know of a group of persons and of their physical and psychological properties but not know with which if any of them one is identical.

The concept of introspection, whether in original Cartesian or AIF variants, fails to provide the means of determining one's identity. The former is excluded on special ontological grounds, but both share a common epistemological defect inasmuch as they regard self-consciousness as constituted by introspection and construe this simply as a second-order function directed upon first-order states. In the envisaged circumstances this can hardly help for there I have access to the content of the first-order states of *every* member of the group. Given the rejection of an immaterial subject it might be suggested that I am the person with whose body these thoughts are associated (see Kenny 1979: 3–13). The question now becomes, since these thoughts are associated with *every* body: Which body is that? My body is the one it is by virtue of being the body of the person I am. Consequently the identity of persons is prior to that of their bodies and so the problem remains – until one returns to the phenomenon of reflexive consciousness.

There are many ways in which I learn about myself: by inference from what I say, do and make; by recognizing how others regard me; by discovering general truths about human nature; by reflection upon my motives and beliefs, etc.; and, presupposed in all self-knowledge, by direct acquaintance with my mental states. This last depends ultimately upon reflexivity. Unlike second-order consciousness which takes intentional acts (both my own and others) as *objects* of thought, reflexive awareness is a unique form of access to psychological states in which they are presented as the *content* of the awareness. In the terms of the earlier example, there is an important difference between the following:

1 being sensitive to a distant sound;
2 being aware of a state of sensitivity to a distant sound; and
3 being aware of being sensitive to a distant sound.

The last of these provides direct, non-inferential establishment of ownership and thereby secures the foundation upon which the various processes of self-organization discussed by Professor Eagle may build. But the subject of reflexive consciousness and of the other forms of self-knowledge listed above is neither a Cartesian Ego, a Humean bundle of perceptions nor a machine. It is nothing other than the person one is.

9 CONSCIOUSNESS, EVOLUTION AND THE POSSIBILITY OF
    A SCIENTIFIC PSYCHOLOGY

In conclusion I turn briefly to the statement of doubts noted earlier about the possibility of scientific psychology and about explanations of consciousness which view it as an evolutionary product having selectional advantages. These doubts are connected and can best be presented in order of increasing strength.

First, while there are obvious benefits to be derived from having the capacity to scrutinize first-order informational states, make corrections to them and involve them in higher-level calculations, it is not at all clear that consciousness is required for these functions. Dennett in particular should be unhappy about resorting to this kind of explanation. If life on the ground floor can (and must on his account) proceed without real psychological properties then non-intentional executive functions should be sufficient. In any event no others are available to him.

Second, even if selectional advantage does attach to consciousness, something far less than we possess seems both adequate and indeed preferable from the perspective of adaptive utility. Human thought answers to reason and affection, and thereby may propose ends of action independent of any concern to promote the survival of an individual, group or species, and sometimes at odds with their continuing existence. One reply to this objection is to suggest that it absurdly assumes a *principle of evolutionary economy*: that when an adaptive feature emerges it does not extend in quantity or degree beyond that sufficient to serve the interests of the species. I do not assume this, however, but only what the advocate of the evolutionary explanation himself assumes, viz. that the development of species extends over time and that just as features having adaptive utility will tend to be selected for, others having inutility will tend to be selected against. Evolution is economical in this sense, therefore: that over time a feature which in abundance is a handicap to survival will tend to be reduced to a level of 'maximin' equilibrium. If the objection is now put that this may not tell against an evolutionary explanation of consciousness since we do not know if what we possess is useful or dangerous, the reply is clear: such ignorance indicates that the assumption of an evolutionary explanation is unwarranted.

My third, final and greatest doubt derives from an implication of consciousness. The project of scientific naturalism is to develop a complete account of reality sufficient to explain the occurrence of all events. Given as premises a statement of the initial conditions of the universe and the set of laws of nature, a description of any phenomenon requiring explanation should, in principle, be logically deducible. The theory assumes a wholly extensional language. As was seen in section 8, however, some part of the total psychological description of people must be sensitive to the modes of their experience, to the concepts under which they bring aspects of the world and to the phenomenology of their perception. Such descriptions are thus irreducibly intensional. No extensional statement entails any intensional one and accordingly there can be no deductive explanation of the emergence of intentional states or of the evolution of what they presuppose, i.e. reflexive consciousness. In short, although it assumes that the psychological is a causal consequence of prior physical conditions, naturalism is logically incapable of explaining emergence of intentional phenomena.

Let me anticipate and indicate replies to likely objections. First, it may be supposed that I wrongly assume intensionality is the distinguishing mark of the mental when it is neither necessary nor sufficient for it. In fact I do not believe that all psychological phenomena are inten*t*ional (sensations lack this feature). Furthermore, I do not assume that all inten*t*ional state descriptions prohibit existential inference and substitution *salva veritate*. However, if content ascription generally is to be faithful to the content of subjects' psychological states (as it must be if it is to rationalize their actions) then intensionality is unavoidable.

A second objection might be that scientific naturalism is already committed to intensionalistic descriptions independently of characterizing the psychological, and hence there is no logical gap between statements describing reality minus consciousness and those descriptive of the present state of affairs. Against this response I contend that intensionality is not an ineliminable feature of non-intentional descriptions. First, scientific laws may not require alethic modality since their capacity to sustain counterfactuals may be explicable in the manner proposed by Ramsey and Lewis (as being consquences of those propositions which we should take as axioms if we knew all there is to know and organized it into a deductive system). Second, in any case modal realism does not generate intensionality as the necessity is *de re* and this is extensional. *De dicto* modality by contrast does present a problem for the scientific naturalist but only because it is a special case of the intensionality of the psychological: it is a feature arising out of our conceptual characterization of states of affairs; out of our ways of thinking and speaking of them. Relatedly, such intensionality as may be exhibited by non-modal decriptions of natural phenomena is a shadow cast by human thought as it shapes explanations in forms relative to the interest of inquirers.

We can have no natural explanation of the emergence of self-consciousness and of its attendant mental features. Intentionalistic psychology is not simply a special case of lower-level empirical sciences. Moreover, what distinguishes it is not merely that it contains specialized concepts which do not appear in substanding theories, as is true of ecology with respect to biology, of biology with regard to chemistry, and of the latter in relation to physics. Rather, the radical discontinuity between psychology and the natural sciences is marked by the non-extensionality of the former. The existence of self-consciousness is, as Professor Eagle shows, an important fact. I have taken up the invitation to accommodate it within a general philosophy of mind and have been led to conclude that while there is a coherent account available of the structure of mind there can be no natural explanation of its origin – the project for a scientific psychology is misconceived. Two possibilities now suggest themselves: *panpsychism* and *emergent mentalism*. I am inclined to adopt the latter; not as a solution but as a characterization of this problematic phenomenon.[15]

NOTES

1 Elsewhere (*Summa Theologiae*, Ia, q87, a1) Aquinas writes: 'Therefore our intellect knows itself, not by its own essence, but by means of its activity . . . as when Socrates or Plato perceives himself to have an intellectual soul from the fact that he perceives himself to be actually acting.'

2 See Fodor 1981 for a clear statement of the representational theory of mind and studies of its implications; and also Field 1978.

3 From a discussion with Jonathan Miller in Miller 1983.

4 For example Ryle 1979: 73–93, where he opposes his view to those of 'Reductionists' and 'Duplicationists' (*sic*). Here, as elsewhere, he assumes that the non-reductive realist is committed to claiming that intelligent behaviour is always accompanied by a parallel flow of thoughts. As I argue, the intentionalist is not thus committed.

Ryle's own account of the difference between 'mere behaviour' and 'action' involves reference to contextual features. Thus A and B may be behaviourally indistinguishable movements yet have different associated intentions, involve different (cognitive) skills and occur in different institutional surroundings (pp. 81–4). What Ryle fails to recognize is that the appropriate aspects of context directly involve, or presuppose, intentional states. Significantly, he adverts to the number and complexity of relevant conditions, for his project is the familiar reductionist one of trying to extract a *qualitative* difference out of a *quantitative* one. Equivalently, he attempts to eliminate the intentional by spreading it far and wide throughout the surrounding environment. Dennett's programme for discharging the homunculi posited by cognitive psychology differs from this only in the direction of spread: *inwards* rather than *outwards* (see section 7 on 'Meaning and Mental Representation').

5 A similar fallacy is committed by the anti-abstractionist argument which claims that concepts cannot be acquired through experience as they are presupposed in it. In Haldane 1984, I argue that the acquisition and first

exercise of a concept may be simultaneous, notwithstanding that the latter logically presupposes the former.

6   *De Veritate*, q4, a2: 'intelligere est dicere'; see also Aquinas, *De Potentia*, q8, a1.

7   This implication of the language of thought thesis has long been the target of objections. In his *Philosophical Orations*, Reid writes: 'suppose that ideas represent things as signs . . . in the manner of a book . . . this will not solve the problem however, for who will interpret the book for us . . . Signs without an interpretation signify nothing.' I explore the connections between medieval, modern and contemporary views of mental representation in Haldane 1988.

8   It might be supposed that Aquinas's view must generate a similar regress. I believe it does not and try to show why in *Intentionality and Epistemological Realism* (University of London: Ph.D. thesis, 1983); but there is not the space to discuss this here. For a hint of how the explanation proceeds, see Haldane 1983a; esp. pp. 237–9.

9   See also Dennett 1984a: 220–1.

10   Equivalently: semantic understanding cannot be reduced to syntactic competence. In his *Orations*, Reid (following the scholastics) develops this point by way of denying the possibility or deriving meaning from uninterpreted syntax. For a recent version of this argument for intentionalism, see Searle 1980.

11   *Summa Theologiae*, Ia, q85, a2.

12   *Summa Contra Gentiles*, III, 46.

13   This claim does not entail a regress of conscious subjects of mental acts. See Haldane 1983b for a parallel case.

14   A further (small) part of the argument for which is given in Haldane 1985.

15   The anti-evolutionary arguments of this section require fuller elaboration and are only briefly stated here owing to shortage of space. In particular, more needs to be said about the general character of the project of scientific naturalism and its relation to ineliminably non-extensional descriptions. I hope to have the opportunity to return to these issues at a later date.

REFERENCES

Aquinas, St Thomas: *De Potentia*.
Aquinas, St Thomas: *De Veritate*.
Aquinas, St Thomas: *Summa Contra Gentiles*.
Aquinas, St Thomas: *Summa Theologiae*.
Aquinas, St Thomas: *Super Boethium de Trinitate*.
Dennett, D. C. 1979: *Brainstorms*. Sussex: Harvester.
Dennett, D. C. 1984a: Styles of mental representation. *Proceedings of the Aristotelian Society*, 83, 213–26.
Dennett, D. C. 1984b: *Elbow Room*. Oxford: Oxford University Press.

Descartes, R. 1970: *Discourse on Method*, in *The Philosophical Works of Descartes*, vol. I, trans. Haldane and Ross. Cambridge: Cambridge University Press.

Field, H. 1978: Mental representation. *Erkenntnis*, 13, 9–61.

Fodor, J. 1975: *The Language of Thought*. New York: Crowell.

Fodor, J. 1981: *Representations*. Sussex: Harvester.

Haldane, J. J. 1983a: Aquinas on sense-perception. *Philosophical Review*, 92, 233–9.

Haldane, J. J. 1983b: A benign regress. *Analysis*, 43, 115–16.

Haldane, J. J. 1984: Concept-formation and value education. *Educational Philosophy and Theory*, 16, 22–8.

Haldane, J. J. 1985: Individuals and the theory of justice. *Ratio*, 27, 178–84.

Haldane, J. J. 1988: Reid, Scholasticism and current philosophy of mind, in M. Dalgarno and E. Matthews (eds), *The Philosophy of Thomas Reid*. Dordrecht: Reidel.

Kenny, A. 1979: The first person, in C. Diamond and J. Teichman (eds), *Intention and Intentionality*. Sussex: Harvester.

Miller, J. 1983: *States of Mind*. London: BBC Publications.

Reid, T. 1937: *Philosophical Orations*. Aberdeen: Aberdeen University Press.

Ryle, G. 1979: Thinking and saying, in *On Thinking*. Oxford: Blackwell.

Searle, J. 1980: Minds, brains and programs. *Behavioral and Brain Sciences*, 3, 417–24.

Wittgenstein, L. 1976: *Philosophical Investigations*. Oxford: Blackwell.

6

Mind, Brain and Unconscious

MICHAEL MOORE

INTRODUCTION

My specific topic is the notion of the unconscious as it is and should be
conceived in psychoanalytic theory. I say this is my *specific* topic because I
have a more general topic in mind for which the unconscious will only be a
convenient example. This more general topic is the status of the
metapsychological theories of Freud. The concept of the unconscious,
standing as it does with one foot in the clinical theory and the other foot
solidly planted in the metapsychologies, should serve to illustrate some
general points about Freud's metapsychological undertakings.

The argument will proceed in the following way. First, I shall
distinguish what I call the pre-theoretical conception of the unconscious
from what I shall call the theory-laden sense of the word. I shall also show
how these two conceptions of the unconscious naturally track into a
distinction, current amongst many psychoanalytic theorists, between two
kinds of theory in psychoanalysis, the clinical and the metapsychological
theories.

The rest of the chapter deals with two mistaken treatments of this
distinction: the body of the paper deals with the mistake of taking the
distinction too seriously, so that one writes off the metapsychological
theory as a kind of logically absurd attempt to bridge the supposedly
unbridgeable gap between body and mind. In the conclusion I suggest that
there is an opposite mistake, that of not taking the distinction seriously
enough, so that the important boundaries of self and responsibility are

ignored in the rush to integrate the concept of the unconscious into contemporary psychological theory.

THE TWO CONCEPTIONS OF THE UNCONSCIOUS

Although Freud often distinguished three senses of 'unconscious' as he used the word in his theory, these three senses of Freud's can be parsed into two conceptions (Moore 1984: 126–37). The first is what I have called the pre-theoretical notion of the unconscious. The claims made with this conception are: (1) the existential claim that persons are possessed not only of mental states that are not the subject of present attention (preconscious), but also of states that are not subject to recall even if attention is directed toward them; (2) the relational claim that such mental states may influence behaviour as a cause or as a reason without awareness of their influence by the subject; (3) the epistemic claim that such states are accessible to the extended memory of the subject, who in principle can come to know that he had a mental state that was unconscious in the same way as he can come to know of any other contents of his mind, namely, by non-inferential recall; and (4) the content claim, according to which the objects of such mental states are (ultimately) sexual or aggressive in content. None of these claims are dependent upon Freud's metapsychology being true. The concept of the unconscious used in such claims is 'pre-theoretical' because of this independence; such claims are of course theoretical in the same sense as is commonsense psychology, of which such claims are an extension.

The second conception of the unconscious is Freud's theory-laden conception. Here one conceives of the unconscious as an aggregation of mental states that not only share the phenomenal property of being unconscious but also share a functional role (and perhaps some common structure) in the conflict-ridden and tension-reducing mechanisms that human beings are posited to be by the metapsychological theory. Mental states that are unconscious in this theory-laden sense could be aggregated into a 'System Ucs.' because of their systematic role within the mind, namely, as one pole of a set of basic conflicts all persons are supposed to possess. As Freud noted in his discussion of the concept in 1912, the 'index-value' of a state being unconscious was the important thing in his theory, not the phenomenal property of importance to the clinical theory. (Freud 1959a: 29).

These two conceptions of the unconscious are matched by dual conceptions of other concepts used in psychoanalytic theory. Thus, for example, George Klein wrote of Freud having implicitly two theories of sexuality. The clinical theory of sexuality, as Klein called it, 'emphasizes the cognitive matrix – the meaning – of sexuality' (Klein 1976a: 36). In studying the significance of sensual experience to persons, such a clinical theory would focus initially on the mental experience of infants regarding sensual pleasure, chart the 'conceptual affiliates' that develop as the child develops patterns of sensual stimulation and regulation, chart the pattern of conflict that can develop about human sexuality, chart the ties between sensual activity and the development of a self-conception and self-esteem. The 'drive-discharge' theory of sexuality, by way of contrast, would talk not of mental experience, meaning, conflict and self, but rather of energic forces seeking discharge.

These kinds of attempts to distinguish two accounts among the various of Freud's concepts should be seen as instances of a more general divorce between clinical psychoanalysis and the metapsychological theories of psychoanalysis. What is in fact meant by this general distinction is not always clear. My own reading of the recent literature suggests several possibilities that the distinction is *not* about. For one thing, it is not the distinction between theory and therapy, for clinical psychoanalysis is itself a theory and not merely a therapy (which would then be part of the data for a genuinely explanatory theory). Secondly, the distinction is not that between broader and narrower subject matters for theory. That is, clinical theory does not aim only at explaining the success/failure rate of psycho-analytic therapy or the aetiology of the neuroses to which such therapy is applied; rather, clinical theory at least purports to be part of a general psychology that explains all human behaviour, healthy as well as neurotic. Thirdly, the distinction is not one between an object language and a metalanguage, because the metapsychology is not about statements in the clinical theory but, rather, is about the very same actions, states and entities as is the clinical theory (Holt 1981).

Perhaps the best way to get at the clinical theory/metapsychology distinction is that suggested by Morris Eagle:

An examination of the writings of advocates of the clinical-theory-only approach [Klein, Gill, Rycroft, Schafer] indicates that essentially what they mean by clinical formulations or clinical theory is an explanatory account in which a person's behavior or symptoms are explained by reference to his conscious or unconscious aims, wishes and goals.

(Eagle 1984: 148)

The reason such writers focus on 'aims, wishes and goals' in order to draw their distinction is because of some general views about how such mental states differ from the events and states that figure in the explanations of natural science. The clinical theory is concerned with actions rather than with bodily motions, with reasons and not mere causes, with Intentionally characterized states rather than with the object-less states of physical science, with 'experience-near' rather than 'experience-distant' concepts, with empathetic understanding rather than ordinary explanation. In all such ways, psychoanalysts have attempted to portray the clinical theory as conceived in the vocabulary of *persons* and the metapsychology as conceived in the vocabulary of mechanistic causation.

The pre-theoretical unconscious, being a phenomenal property of the mental states of persons, readily fits the clinical theory side of the distinction. The only reason one might think otherwise would be because one accepted various scepticisms about whether states can have the characteristics that make them *mental* states, and yet be unconscious. B. Rubinstein, for example, has argued that unconscious mental states cannot be a *person's* mental states, cannot be part of one's sense of self, because such states are not discovered through any first-person experience. This shows, both Rubinstein and Eagle conclude, that there can be no conception of the unconscious that is part of the clinical theory only; further, that unconscious wishes, emotions, etc., must be conceived in terms of brain states and thus must be part of the metapsychology (Rubinstein 1976: 245, 253–4; Eagle 1984: 150).

This view ignores Freud's extraordinary insight about extended memory. When a patient comes to see that he was unconsciously angry at some time in the past, he has done more than learn a bit of neurophysiology (indirectly he may have done that as well – see below). He has recovered the non-observational knowledge that he was angry, known that the anger was part of him, in the same way as he acknowledges his conscious anger as his. His unconscious anger is part of his self (Moore 1980, 1984; Hampshire 1963; Wiggins 1976).

One might think that such insight is a kind of performance by the patient whereby he makes the anger part of himself just by 'avowing it' to be his (Eagle 1982). Yet this is not the way he sees it. He sees himself recapturing an experience that he was having even though he was unaware of it at the time. We should not restrict ourselves to a physiological conceptualization of unconscious wishes, beliefs, emotions, etc., on grounds of no privileged access when the clinical theory asserts that there is such access, only deferred. (See Moore 1984: 17, 135–6, 254–65.) Hence, there is no justification for denying a place to the pre-theoretical unconscious within the clinical theory just because of a temporary absence of privileged access.

The theory-laden unconscious is a conception belonging to the metapsychological theory. Freud's theoretical explanation for why some mental states are very hard to recapture (i.e., are unconscious) is cast in terms of the conflict between instinct and control that Freud meant to conceptualize with his topographical and structural metapsychologies. Hence, the 'System Ucs.' plainly belongs in the metapsychology. How much of what Freud called his dynamic unconscious goes into the metapsychological theory is a more difficult question. As I have argued elsewhere (Moore 1984: 131–2), Freud made two claims with his dynamic sense of the word. His descriptive claim – about there being states that are not only latent (preconscious) but also very hard to recapture – is part of the clinical theory. Contrary to Grünbaum (1984) and others (W. D. Hart 1982), however, I think the explanatory claim in Freud's dynamic usage – explaining why some mental states are so hard to recapture in terms of repression – is properly part of the metapsychological theory, not the clinical theory.

Seeing how this issue is resolved clarifies the distinction between the two kinds of theories. If one thinks of repression in the way I would think of resistance, as an unconscious action a person engages in for various unconscious reasons, then one will classify repression as part of the clinical theory. For although unconscious, the repressing in such a case is an activity carried on by the self and recapturable by one's extended memory. Alternatively, however, one might think of repression as a kind of internal process that no person performs as an action, not even as an unconscious action, because the activity is beyond recapture by extended memory. The seeming intelligence of repression, the sense that repression makes in avoiding painful thoughts, is just the function it serves in keeping us healthy. Such a process should not be analogized to resistance, but rather to processes like those in the dream-work. The dream-work processes of secondary revision, displacement and condensation are also not actions a person performs, even unconsciously; they are functionally defined processes that must take place if dreams are to have the form they have and yet be caused by the kind of unconscious wishes Freud envisioned (Moore 1984: 306–8).

In a cogent recent paper Harvey Mullane (1983) argues that repression should be construed in the latter way. Mullane distinguishes the material that is repressed from the repressing activity itself. The repressed material is part of the pre-theoretical unconscious and of the clinical theory, but the repressing activity itself, being beyond the self-boundaries of extended memory, is part of the theory-laden unconscious of Freud's metapsychological story.

TAKING THE DISTINCTION TOO SERIOUSLY: THE ALLEGED
CHASM BETWEEN BODY AND MIND

A presently popular way to take the distinction too seriously is to use it for the twofold purpose of insulating the clinical theory from scientific criticism; and writing off the metapsychology as an impossible enterprise. The general strategy of theorists like George Klein (1976b), Merton Gill (1976), Roy Schafer (1976), W. W. Meissner (1981), Paul Ricoeur (1970), Robert Steele (1979), and H. J. Home (1966), goes like this: one takes the distinction between clinical theory and metapsychology to be a distinction between two different 'logical planes' (Klein 1976a) or two different 'types of discourse' (Gill 1976). The language of the clinical theory is the language of mind, meaning and the humanities, whereas the language of the metapsychology is the language of physical events, mechanisms and natural science. Further, 'the logic and method of the humanities is radically different from that of science . . .' (Home 1966: 43). Accordingly, the two theories have nothing to do with each other but are descriptions (cum interpretations cum explanations) sufficient unto themselves in their respective realms of discourse.

This *Geistwissenschaften* view is then used to say, first, that the clinical theory is exempt from the rigours of scientific validation because it is not science – it is hermeneutics. Secondly, this view renders illegitimate any attempt to create something like the metapsychology, which purports to explain the clinical theory. The entire metapsychology can be written off, on this view, not by a painstaking comparison of its tenets with adequate standards of scientific theory construction and validation, but by the discovery of one big, underlying mistake, the kind philosophers used to call a category mistake. Since the clinical theory and the metapsychology operate in different 'universes of discourse', it must be a mistake about the category in which such theories operate to conjoin the concepts of the clinical theory with those of the metapsychology into one overarching theory. Psychoanalysis, on this view, can only be the clinical theory. The other stuff, the metapsychology, is just that – other stuff, the concern of some other discipline, presumably biology, but not of a true science of mind.

To understand how this sort of view is arrived at from more general views in the philosophy of mind and the philosophy of language, see the work of Ilham Dilman (1959, 1972, 1983, 1984) and Roy Schafer (1976). Dilman has concluded that the pre-theoretical unconscious cannot also be construed as a theoretical term in Freud's general metapsychological theories of human behaviour. Dilman's argument is based on the epistemic claim of deferred privileged access that is part of Freud's clinical theory. Freud's clinical ideal of 'making the unconscious conscious' is only attained by the recapture *through memory* (rather than by an inference from evidence) of what was previously unconscious. Dilman bases two arguments on this clinical ideal. The first is that it is a kind of category mistake to think that one could have such privileged access to a theoretical entity, as one would if the pre-theoretical unconscious were also the System Ucs. of Freud's topographical theory. As Dilman puts it:

One cannot talk of seeing an electron (not even as a possibility one might wish to speculate about) without sinning against logic; for if the concept of an electron is theoretical . . . then seeing cannot have a place in statements in which the concept of an electron has a place . . . While we can talk of observing the effects of electrons, the expression 'seeing an electron' is at best a misleading locution. The same would be the case of 'making the unconscious conscious' if the concept of the unconscious were a theoretical concept.

(Dilman 1959: 455)

Dilman's second argument is also based on the privileged access we each have to the contents of our own pre-theoretical unconscious. Such privileged access gives rise to an asymmetry in the modes of verification of first- and third-person statements about our mental states, unconscious included. Dilman's argument is that treating the unconscious as a theoretical entity would do away with this asymmetry for unconscious mental states, because then even first-person statements would be verified only by inference from a theory, and not directly from awareness:

My main objection to the view that the unconscious is a theoretical construct has been that it does not recognize the difference between a person's recognition of his own unconscious feelings and desires and another person's recognition of them. It hinders a proper appreciation of what is involved in what is unconscious becoming conscious.

(Dilman 1972: 339)

This kind of argument can be constructed no matter what one takes to be the touchstone of mind. Roy Schafer (1976) fastens upon those aspects of language characteristic of our talk about personal agency as such a touchstone of mind. For Schafer too there can be no metapsychological theory about neurotic symptoms because these symptoms are accurately conceptualized as the actions persons perform for reasons. Because of this 'action language' conceptualization of neurotic symptoms, the metapsychology becomes an illegitimate enterprise for Schafer no matter how it is construed. If framed in terms of the non-action vocabulary of the economic metapsychology – forces, energies and drives – then the theory is not a theory of mind because it has left the only vocabulary in terms of which mind can be discussed, what Schafer calls the 'action' vocabulary. If framed in terms of little people performing little actions for little reasons, Schafer's complaint is that such vocabulary is only appropriate for *whole* persons.

In short, for Schafer as for Dilman, Freud's metapsychology and its theoretical unconscious is caught in a dilemma: the mentalistic vocabulary of persons in terms of which clinicians prompt patients to recapture unconscious wishes and so on is not a vocabulary in which it makes sense to construct a deep theory such as the metapsychology purports to be. But it also is true that any theory constructed in a non-action vocabulary (or one without asymmetry in its modes of verification) cannot be a theory about the *mind*, for these features – agency and privileged access – constitute what is mental.

It should be apparent that what we have encountered is the doctrine of category differences between the extensional, non-Intentional, observation-dependent, mechanistic, causal vocabulary appropriate to explain movements of bodies (including human bodies), on the one hand; and the intensional, Intentional, non-observational, purposive, reason-giving vocabulary appropriate to explain human actions, on the other. Which aspect of this apparent categorical divide is seized upon by sceptics about the theory-laden unconscious does vary. Dilman, as we have seen, seizes upon privileged access whereas Schafer picks semantic features of the action vocabulary. Other psychoanalytic theorists latch onto the fuzzier hermeneutic notion of meaning (Home 1966; Ricoeur 1970; Gill 1976; Klein 1976a, 1976b; Steele 1979). But the general dilemma for the metapsychology that each of them poses is wholly the same: no theory can be constructed 'on the mental side', and although theories are perfectly appropriate 'on the physical side', they cannot be theories of mind. The unconscious, on such a view, is something about which one can generalize in the clinical theory; it is not something one can develop a theory about in the metapsychology. Metapsychological concepts of the unconscious are simply the results of category mistakes, the mistaking of brain theory for a theory of mind.[1]

This cannot possibly be right. The philosophical doctrine of category mistakes has unfortunately got in the way of theory construction in psychiatry, truncating the idea of what the unconscious is and what a theory about it should be. To see this in any convincing detail would require that we re-examine the doctrine of categorical differences that dominated the philosophy of mind between Gilbert Ryle's *Concept of Mind* in 1949 and (roughly) 1965. Rather than engaging in what many philosophers would regard as an exercise of arguments now difficult to motivate, I shall only examine Roy Schafer's argument to exemplify the philosophical mistake common to all forms of the position.

Schafer essentially deploys two linguistic arguments in reaching his conclusion that a non-action language cannot be about mind. Firstly, he argues that the normal matrix of discourse in which we use words that truly refer to things is inappropriate to mental words. About 'anger', Schafer asks (in a close paraphrase of Ryle):

The vocabulary of anger . . . depends on the legitimacy of assuming or referring to an inside and an outside – but, I ask again, inside or outside of what? Where? Is anger anywhere? . . . The questions are unanswerable, of course, because they cannot be asked in a logical inquiry. *Anger is not the kind of word about which such questions may be asked.*

(1976: 165)

From this feature of usage Schafer concludes that 'anger,' and 'the unconscious' do not refer to anything, and that we must regard the unconscious not as a thing, but only as a property of actions.

Second, Schafer argues that from usage it is possible to tell what the reference is of his preferred way of speaking (i.e., where actions are performed *angrily* or *unconsciously*). 'Angrily' or 'unconsciously' cannot refer to anything unknown to the speakers of these words; for what it is that guides the usage of these words from competent speakers is what the words mean. Schafer blatently makes Ryle's ordinary language philosophy assumption that the rules of correct usage can fix the reference of the words used, so that, if speakers don't know the deep theory of the emotions or of the unconscious, then the things such theories postulate *cannot* be referred to by 'angrily' or 'unconsciously'.

Yet there is no reason to think that the patterns of usage to which Ryle or Schafer (or Dilman) advert can place any *a priori* limit on what it is that is referred to by mental words, 'unconscious' included. As Roderick Anscombe (1981) concludes in his generally perceptive review of Schafer's work, 'questions about how best to conceptualize the unconscious have more to do with fact than with language' (1981: 233; see also Spiro 1979: 278–9).

What Anscombe means can be got at through a *Gedanken*-experiment. Suppose we place ourselves back in ancient Babylon at just the time the Babylonian astronomers were discovering that the star that appeared in the morning (the 'Morning Star') and the star that appeared in the evening (the 'Evening Star') were one and the same thing, namely, the planet Venus. One can imagine a Babylonian ordinary language philosopher 'disproving' the astronomer's claim in the following way: that he (the philosopher) has not been looking at stars, but at language use; that he has observed the phrases 'Evening Star' and 'Morning Star' in all of their ordinary uses, and that from such observation it is clear that the phrases appear in different categories of discourse (evening talk and morning talk); that, accordingly, the phrases cannot refer to the same thing, or else (by Leibniz's Law) the expressions would be equivalent, which their differing use shows that they manifestly are not; indeed, that it is absurd – a category mistake – to even speak of the Evening Star and the Morning Star existing in the same sense of 'exist' (cf. Ryle 1949: ch. 1).

The problem with this view of meaning, and with its accompanying doctrine of categorical differences, is that systematic connections in the ordinary usage of certain concepts are allowed to suspend questions of reference and identity in a way that is very counterintuitive. Why should the fact that ordinary people built up a set of systematic usages for the phrase 'Evening Star', and another set of usages for the phrase 'Morning Star', have anything to do with the questions of whether those phrases refer to something and whether the things to which they refer are in reality one and the same thing? To be sure, if there were something in the patterns of usage that showed us that the phrases did not refer, all well and good; yet none of the arguments ever deployed to show this have succeeded.[2]

The upshot is that we must reject the idea that there is some categorical divide that prevents one from asking about the *things* to which mental terms refer. The doctrines of categorical difference cannot justify the foreclosing of the question of whether the phrase 'pre-theoretical unconscious' ultimately refers, not only to the mental states recapturable by extended memory, but also to the primary process of Freud's metapsychological theory and ultimately, perhaps, to neurophysiology. No argument from ordinary usage can show it to be a category mistake to seek the answer to such a question by research and refinement of theory.

There are of course routes to showing the impossibility of the metapsychology that are alternative to the 'linguistic dualism' (Landesman 1965; Bernstein 1971) of Rylean ordinary language philosophy. One such is metaphysical dualism. Yet such a metaphysical dualism is implausible for all the reasons Ryle so elegantly presented, as most psychoanalytic theorists seem to sense in their avoidance of it (Rubinstein 1965: 45). Metaphysical dualism leads to the blind alleys of mysterious relations, to *ad hoc* exceptions to laws like that of the conservation of mass and energy, and in general to dead-endings of inquiry. It thus seems preferable to keep it as one's last-ditch position, a strategy to be adopted only when all else fails. Better to take seriously Intentionality, agency and immediate, subjective experience as important attributes of mind yet try to integrate states with those characteristics into one's view of the natural world. The currently fashionable strategy for doing this is functionalism, usually conjoined with a kind of physical identity theory. Exploring such a strategy will allow us to see how the metapsychological enterprise should be construed in light of a more contemporary philosophy of mind.

To understand functionalism we need to distinguish two kinds of it in the contemporary philosophy of mind. There is first of all the view which Ned Block (1980) has called metaphysical functionalism. Metaphysical functionalism is the view that mental terms such as 'pain' refer to functional states of the human body (more specifically, brain and central nervous system). A functional state is a state whose nature is given by its role (function) in explanations of behaviour. Pain, for example, is the state that plays the role of the cause of certain reflex reactions, as the cause of certain learning abilities, and plays the role of the effect of certain physical stimuli (see generally Block 1978, 1980).

Metaphysical functionalism by itself is not committed to there being any physical realization of the functional states so defined. Still, the motives for becoming a functionalist usually include the desire for there to be one world, so that one urges that those functional states that are states of persons' minds are physically realized. Instances of such states, in other words, are (identical with) certain physical states. Pain states, for example, may in human beings be C-fibre stimulation in the cortex of the brain. That doesn't mean that pain as such *is* (identical with) such C-fibre stimulation. On the functionalist theory pain is the state that plays certain causal roles; such functional states could be realized differently in different physical systems, and still be pain states.

A second kind of functionalism is what Block (1980) calls functional analysis. This kind of functionalism is a research strategy, not a metaphysical position. This research strategy is part of the general research programme of relating mind to brain, psychology to neurophysiology. Within this general research programme there are two research strategies (see, e.g. Arbib 1972). A 'bottom–up' strategy is to study the physical structures of the brain and try to discover how they function; eventually one hopes to work upwards from very particular functions of discrete physical structures to explain the molar behaviour and mental states of the whole person. A 'top–down' strategy, by way of contrast, starts with the behaviour and mental states experienced by the person and asks, 'What kind of subroutines might a system go through in order to arrive at such experience and such behaviour?' One might, for example, start with a person's perceptual beliefs about what he sees, and ask what steps he must have gone through in order to have begun with the visual stimulus with which he began and ended with the perceptual belief that he did.

It is the second of these strategies that is called functional analysis. It is sometimes called 'homuncular functionalism' because its functionally defined subdivisions of a single person often are made to look like several smaller persons, or 'homunculi'. As described by William Lycan:

> The homuncular functionalist sees a human being or other sentient creature as an integrated collection of component subsystems or agencies which communicate with each other and cooperate to produce their host creature's overall behavioral responses to stimuli. A psychologist who adopts the homuncular format and applies it to humans will describe a person by means of a flow-chart that portrays the person's immediately subpersonal agencies and their various routes of communicative access to each other. Each of these agencies, represented by a 'black box' on the original flow-chart, will in turn be described by a flow-chart which breaks *it* down into further, more specialized sub-subsystems which corporately produce *its* behavior, and so on; and each of the subsystems, sub-subsystems and sub- . . . subsystems will be characterized in terms of its job or function within the corporate hierarchy . . . at some point the psychologist would have to burn biologist, then chemist, and finally physicist in order to bring this explanatory process to completion.
>
> (1982: 16)

These two strategies are of course complementary, not antagonistic. One ultimately has to pursue both strategies, hoping in the end that workers pursuing each will meet. This means that the homuncular functionalist cannot claim any *ultimate* freedom from neurophysiology. If one is devising functional subroutines for subdividing mental operations in order to find connections of mind to brain, one would do well not to include subroutines that the physical equipment (the brain) just could not perform. There are many possible functional subdivisions of any mental operation. A homuncular functionalist is looking for that *one* organization that is in fact realized in the brain of his subject. Hence, the functionally defined states or processes this strategy posits should be thought of as hypotheses that more information about the structure of the brain may falsify; they should not be thought of as states or processes existing in their own 'realm of being', different from physical states; nor are the disciplines that define such states (linguistics, artificial intelligence, systems theory, or cognitive psychology) ultimately autonomous from the physical sciences. The top–down strategy is just a way of putting your trousers on one leg at a time.

Metaphysical functionalism can be thought of as a way of motivating the research programme of the homuncular functionalist, for it assures him that what he will find with his increasingly finely individuated functional states is the essence of the mind. By taking the position that it does on the reference of mental state terms, metaphysical functionalism tells the researcher that the best theory he can devise, e.g. about the condensation, displacement, etc., of the dream-work will be *about* dreaming.

Consider as a more familiar example the state of pain. Phenomenal descriptions of painful feelings will be about pain. Connecting such feelings of pain to their behavioural inputs (pain-causing stimuli) and outputs (pain-expressing behaviour) will be a theory about pain. So will a theory that connects various subpersonal routines that go on (reflex arcs, formation of pain-thresholds, and the like) together. So will a theory that correlates C-fibre stimulation with pain-experience, pain behaviour, and the subroutines of pain. All of these approaches will be progressively deeper theories about the nature of pain. Denied is any attempt to say that any of these scientific theories is not about pain, or that they use different concepts of pain. 'Pain' names a natural kind whose essential nature it is the business of science to reveal (Putnam 1975; Platts 1979; compare Block 1978).

The same is true for those mental states that make up the pre-theoretical unconscious. The metapsychological story about them, in terms of repression, other mechanisms of defence, the dream-work and the System Ucs., is a theory about those very same mental states and why they are unconscious. The 'System Ucs.' is not another sense of the word 'unconscious' just because it is part of a deeper story most ordinary users of the word 'unconscious' do not know; rather, the reference of both terms is to that same collection of states. In much the same way 'H$_2$O' is part of a deeper story about water that most ordinary users of 'water' at one time did not know; but that does not mean that 'water'and 'H$_2$O' referred to different things. Thus, on this Putnamesque version of metaphysical functionalism (compare the different versions of Block 1978 and Shoemaker 1982), we have but one unconscious even if one have progressively deeper layers of theory about it.

It is fairly clear that Freud viewed his metapsychology as justified by its ability to relate mind to brain. From the unpublished 'Project' of 1895 (S.E. 1895, I: 281–93) to the *Outline* (S.E. 1940, XXIII), he first and last saw his task as building a theory to relate brain to mind. As he put it in the *Outline* (S.E. 1940, XXIII: 144):

We know two things concerning what we call our psyche or mental life: firstly, its bodily organ and scene of action, the brain (or nervous system), and secondly, our acts of consciousness, which are immediate data and cannot be more fully explained by any kind of description. Everything that lies between these two terminal points is unknown to us.

The metapsychology is Freud's attempt to make known to us what it is that lies 'in between' brain and mind.

Less clear is how much of Freud's metapsychology is fairly construed as an exercise in homuncular functionalism (the top–down strategy) and how much of it should be seen as pursuit of a bottom–up strategy. The 'Project', it seems to me, does represent Freud's attempt at a bottom–up strategy, but he was wise enough to see that he didn't know enough about the structure of the brain to get very far. Abandoning the 'Project' was a significant shift for Freud. Although not giving up his hope of relating mind to brain, Freud did shift to the other strategy that was available to him, working from the top down.[3] The difference in the two strategies (again) is not that they ultimately aim at something different, but that they attack the same problem in different ways.

Unlike the 'Project' (S.E. 1895, I), the metapsychology itself should be seen as an exercise in homuncular functionalism. Consider that aspect of the theory-laden unconscious Freud called 'primary process' thinking. The unconscious, Freud thought, has no idea of time; it replaces external with internal reality; terms and concepts have multiple reference, that is, ideas are 'condensed'; notions of identity are loosened because the affects attached to one object are 'displaced' onto another (which is to say that in the unconscious they are identified as one and the same object); contradiction is acceptable in the unconscious; and negation is unknown there.

These characteristics are not part of our pre-theoretical notions of the unconscious. They are not experienced, nor are they recapturable by any extended memory, as *thoughts* a person has. States with these relations and characteristics are 'subpersonal' states (Dennett 1969) hypothesized to exist as states underlying ordinary thinking in the same way that the subpersonal states of information pre-processing are hypothesized by cognitive psychologists to underlie conscious perception.

The homuncular functionalist should regard these six characteristics of primary process thinking as forming a system. Matte-Blanco (1975) has attempted to weld these six characteristics together into a kind of logic, what he calls a 'symmetrical' logic quite different from the 'asymmetrical' logic of Frege–Russell–Quine. Such characteristics form a *logic* in the sense that they state the general principles of 'valid' inference in the unconscious. The thesis is that even irrationality may draw inferences systematically, that what is irrational need not be chaotic.

Such a systematization of unconscious inference drawing is a theory that seeks to explain ordinary thinking and the mental states that *persons* possess. Ordinary thinking is not perfectly rational; although we are all fairly good intuitive logicians – in the ordinary sense of 'logic' – we are not ideally rational inference drawers. One way of seeking to explain this fact is to see ordinary thinking (the 'secondary process') as an output of two subsystems. There is, Eric Rayner hypothesizes, an

interweaving of symmetrical and asymmetrical logics in the individual's emotional and intellectual life. In extreme emotions infinite experiences and symmetry probably hold sway. But mild, deep, or quiet emotionality is likely to contain thinking which compounds the two logics. In normal states the two logics seem to be in harmony while in pathology they are in discord.

(Rayner 1981: 409)

There is no guarantee that this is a fruitful organization to give to the subroutines underlying ordinary thinking. There is no guarantee that there are two subsystems in conflict, or that, if there are, the opposition of ordinary to symmetrical logic is the way to define them. But some sort of states underlie ordinary thinking, and the primary process represents Freud's hypothesis about what sort of states they are. Such a hypothesis is not unverifiable. It must fit not only the (personal) characteristics of ordinary thought, but ultimately it must fit as well the physiology of the brain. There is thus no 'queer stuff' or 'unverifiability' objections to be lodged against this kind of theorizing (cf. Nagel 1959).

Consider as a second example the id/ego split posited by the structural metapsychology. If (contrary to Freud's express warnings) we take this to be directly about the brain, then we should look in the brain for corresponding subdivisions. Such subdivisions might be in gross anatomical terms – ego in the left hemisphere, id in the right, for example – or in more subtle electrochemical terms. In either case, since 'at present there is no indication that id, ego, and superego may one day be definable in strictly neuroanatomical terms' (Rubinstein 1965: 47), one might well discard the structural metapsychology on the same ground as is often used to get rid of the economic metapsychology of pscyhic energy: such theories seem simply false if taken to provide straightforward, physiological descriptions.

Homuncular functionalism, in contrast to this bottom–up interpretation, is the strategy of restraint in looking right away for neurophysiological structures. As characterized by Dan Dennett (1978: 80–1), it is only when the continued subdivision of functionally defined homunculi reaches the level 'where the homunculi are not more than adders and subtractors, by the time they need only the intelligence to pick the larger of two numbers when directed to, [will] they have been reduced to functionaries who can be replaced by a machine.' It is only at this point that 'a mechanistic view of the proceedings becomes workable and comprehensible'.

Ego, id and super-ego are Freud's highest level of the subdivisions of self. The multiple functions assigned to each need to be separated and themselves broken down into subsystems of subsystems of . . . subsystems, before one should expect direct structural correlates. Ego, id and super-ego may only be very high-level organizational principles; but once their role in a top–down strategy is understood, they may be no worse for that.

To construe the metapsychology as an exercise in homuncular functionalism provides a plausible enough insulation of the theory from any metaphysical embarrassment.[4] This is not of course to say that Freud succeeded in devising a *fruitful* functional subdivision of mind. In fact, there are three serious reservations to make about the metapsychology, even when viewed in this charitable light.

One is the lack of depth of many of the Freudian subdivisions. To have any chance of succeeding at connecting mind to brain, a top–down strategy must have great depth in the sense that there must be subdivisions of subdivisions of . . . subdivisions. One needs what Dennett calls an army of pretty stupid homunculi with which to replace the intelligent (whole) person; this, because to make structure/function correlations likely, one needs each homunculus to be so stupid that he need only flip a two-valued switch.

The subdivisions of most of the metapsychology does not have depth in this sense. Consider the id/ego subdivision. Freud conceived of the id as 'instinctual cathexes seeking discharge – that . . . is all there is in the id' (Freud 1965: 74). The ego, on the other hand, was assigned the functions of consciousness, sense perception, the perception and expression of affect, thought, control of motor action, memory, language, defence mechanisms, control of instinctual energy, the interpretive and harmonizing function, reality testing, and the capacity to suspend any of these ego functions and to regress to a primitive level of functioning (Arlow and Brenner 1964: 39).

Without further subdivisions, the structural metapsychology takes us no further than Plato's like subdividing of the soul between rational reason and irrational appetite. Such subdivisions by Freud and Plato are much too large to be, by themselves, fruitful exercises in homuncular functionalism. The functions assigned to the ego in particular make it almost like a whole mind, with a full panoply of functions. This is no 'army of less clever homunculi', but one much too clever general. Needed are layers upon layers of further subdivisions if the structural metapsychology is to have a chance of succeeding as a top–down strategy.

A second problem with the metapsychology is that Freud could not bring himself to the kind of patience about seeking ties to physiology that marks a well-executed top–down strategy. Such impatience is particularly pronounced in the economic metapsychology. It has long been noticed that the *psychological* (functionalist) account of chapter VII B of *The Interpretation of Dreams* is patterned on the *physiological* speculation of Freud's unpublished 'Project' of 1895. Such functionally defined states, processes and systems were not derived from a continued subdivision of the conflict Freud thought to exist between a person's mental states during dreaming. Freud did not arrive at these divisions by looking at the preconscious wish to sleep and an unconscious wish from childhood jointly producing through their conflict the manifest content of a dream. Rather, Freud brought the economic metapsychology to his account of dreaming from his physiological speculations. This is not homuncular functionalism so much as bad bottom–up speculation about a physiology that Freud knew he did not know enough about. (Contrast this kind of illegitimate homuncular functionalism with the genuine article Freud also produced in the dream theory, namely, the dream-work subdivisions.)

A subtler instance of Freud's impatience is to be found in the structural and topographical metapsychologies. Seen as part of Freud's concern with conflict, the System Csc./System Ucs. and ego/id splits are the beginning of a functional subdivision of self based on hints from the phenomenology of conflict. But these splits are also conceived by Freud in terms of 'distance' from physiology on the one hand and consciousness on the other. The id for Freud is tied to physiology and does all the moving of us to action and thought, whereas the ego consists of all the functions that mediate between the demands of the id (the instincts) and reality. One might label these two different id/ego splits as the horizontal split (of experienced conflict) and the vertical split (between physiology and consciousness).

Freud force-fits this vertical conception of the split onto his horizontal one because he thought he had to reach to physiology all at once. A pure top–down strategy would be more patient. One reward for such patience in this instance would have been much less confusion about what the split is. A second reward for patience here would also be less need to gerrymander the conflicts persons *must* experience (e.g., about sex) in order for the id that is 'not-me' to match in content the id of the instincts (Moore 1982, 1984; Eagle 1982, 1984). Freed of the necessity to find such a match, Freud could have listened to his patients' conflicts without preconceptions about what *must* have been their conflicts. (This I take to be one of the central insights of Fairbairn (1954) and the object relations theorists (see Eagle 1984), rejecting as they do this vertical reading of the ego/id split and focusing instead on what I call the horizontal reading. Although such object relations theorists see themselves as eschewing Freud's goal of relating mind to brain, they may unwittingly be furthering Freud's goal by forcing the theory into the patience about function/structure correlations that marks a top–down strategy.)

A third reward would be a set of subdivisions with a chance of succeeding as part of a programme connecting mind to brain. In a properly executed top–down strategy, the ego is as close to physiology as is the id. Even if we continue to conceive of the initial subdivision as one between the passions and that which controls them, the ultimate (and very finely) subdivided functions of control will correlate with physiological structure as much as will those subdivisions of the passions. One would not be 'closer' to physiology than the other, nor would one (ego) be correlated to physiology only *through* the other (id).

Actually, my own suspicion is that once one frees the structural and topographical metapsychologies from any need to reach immediately to physiology via one pole of their posited conflicts, we would not see ego and id as control and passions. Rather, if psychoanalysts are faithful to the phenomenology of conflict, we may see a rich variety of different conflicts being proposed as the initial subdivisions of self. A glance at the literature of the object relations theorists indeed shows this, for they have increasingly abandoned Freud's old subdivisions in their search for a more accurate description of the conflicts persons experience (Eagle 1984).

The third problem for the metapsychologies as an exercise in homuncular functionalism is the most serious of all. Why should we think that the conflict experienced by neurotics is a way of beginning those functional subdivisions of self that will prove fruitful in developing the relations between mind and brain? How, in other words, could one expect to develop the general psychology that the metapsychology purports to be, from such narrow beginnings?

A Freudian, I should think, would seek to avoid this question by refusing its presupposition. He would deny that the 'data of conflict' are limited to the experiences of conflict-ridden neurotics. He should say, with Freud himself, that slips and dreams also are compromise formations arising out of the conflicts between mental states in different systems; further, that normal adults as well as neurotics are conflict-ridden in all of their actions and experiences of everyday life, not just in their dreams, parapraxes and occasional neurotic symptoms.

The main problem with this response is that it does not seem to be true. Reconsider the example of normal inference-drawing. What is the evidence for there being conflict between two subsystems, each with its own logic, the output of which is the good but not perfect inference-drawing capacities of normal adults? I don't think anyone has experiential clues that would suggest such a subdivision of normal inference-drawing. The conflict is rather a *posited* one by those already steeped in Freudian theory.

Consider a like claim that a Freudian could make about the acquisition of perceptual belief. All macro-seeing, he might say, is a compromise formation between conflicting subsystems; mistakes in perception would be seen as due to dominance of one subsystem by another, accurate vision being a blend of just the right proportions. This is a possible way to subdivide perception for a homuncular functionalist. But why would it ever occur to one to proceed with these kinds of subdivisions (rather than, say, ones that deal with co-operating subsystems with feedback loops to correct themselves)? Surely not any phenomenology of conflict about perceptual beliefs, no matter how lengthy or intense the psychoanalysis.

One can raise like charges even about some of the classic data of psychoanalysis, such as dreams. It looks very much as if Freud simply invented a wish to sleep that is supposed to be part of the double motivation of a dream in order to maintain a thesis that dreams, like symptoms, were compromise formations between the conflicting mental states belonging to different topographical systems (see Moore 1980, 1984). Certainly Freud never recaptured – nor made any effort to recapture – the preconscious wish to sleep, as he did the unconscious wishes from childhood that also produce dreams. Conflict is not an obvious feature of dreaming as it arguably is for slips and symptoms.

If conflict is not the fundamental feature of our minds as we experience them, then it is unlikely that the functionally defined subdivisions of self that will prove fruitful in relating mind to brain will be found by beginning with the divisions experienced by conflict-ridden neurotics. That does not mean that there is no role for a metapsychology of some kind – even though in content it need resemble Freud's actual theory only slightly and even though it could not claim for itself the mantle of 'general psychology'.

Such a less ambitious metapsychology might proceed in the following way about the specific topic of this chapter, the pre-theoretical unconscious. Suppose that we began to attempt a top–down explanation of two claims of the clinical theory about the pre-theoretical unconscious: (1) that it exists, and (2) that it influences behaviour. We might explain the clinical fact that there are mental states that a person has a very hard time recapturing with the metapsychological theory that there is a process of repression that keeps such states from awareness. This process is beyond extended memory, and so must not be thought of as an action a person does (even unconsciously); rather, it is a process hypothesized to exist that has as its function the keeping of certain contents from consciousness. It might further be hypothesized that this keeping from awareness itself serves a function, namely the maintenance of some minimum level of coherence in a person's total set of his conscious/preconscious mental states such that he can have a sense of self-identity.

One might arrive at these hypotheses because of the content of the unconscious mental states that are either recaptured by patients in therapy, or for whose existence the analyst has good evidence despite the failure of the patient to avow them as his. If such mental states predominantly conflict with the patient's conscious/preconscious mental states, that is a reason to think that some process must be operating that sorts mental states in this systematic way.

Analogously, one might seek to explain why such unconscious mental states manifest themselves in behaviour in such peculiar ways. Why don't symptoms, parapraxes and dreams directly express the unconscious wishes that cause them in the way conscious wishes are expressed in the actions they cause? Again, one might explain this clinical fact with a bit of metapsychological theory: certain processes occur that distort the wish in a way that makes it unrecognizable in the behaviour that it produces. The names for these functionally defined processes are the processes of the dream-work (for dreams) and the mechanisms of defence (for symptoms and parapraxes). If one were to explain why such processes of distortion occur, again one might hypothesize that the distortion that they cause has as its function the maintenance of a minimal level of coherence in the total set of a person's conscious-preconscious mental states, which in turn serves the function of allowing the person a sense of self-identity.

A houmuncular functionalist might continue this line in the following way. First, he might seek to find a function for such a sense of self-identity, a function such a sense serves in enhancing the chances of survival. This would give him an evolutionary reason to expect there to be such a sense in persons and thus to expect them to have some such processes as repression for achieving and maintaining such a sense (Eagle 1984). Secondly, the functionalist would subdivide the processes of distortion in the dream-work, for example, between those that distort by condensing multiple aspects of an unconscious mental state into one, and those that distort by displacing the affect normally felt towards one object onto another where such affect is normally inappropriate. He might then further subdivide each of these modes of distortion into submodes of condensation or of displacement. At some point, his hope would be to reach such simple operations that an on/off switch could perform them. For at that level a digital computer, or a brain, could be shown to realize the functionally defined subroutines.

In some such way psychoanalysts would seek to relate the mental phenomena with which they deal – neurotic symptoms, dreams, parapraxes – to brain processes via the metapsychological concepts of repression, condensation, displacement and the like. As part of this task, they would here be explaining the existence (and influence on behaviour) of the pre-theoretical unconscious by reference to a metapsychological unconscious.

I think that this is just the sort of research programme in which psychoanalysis should be engaged. When conflict is a salient fact in an area of phenomenology or behaviour – as it arguably is for neurotic symptoms and parapraxes – then it makes sense to use the facets of experienced conflict as clues to underlying processes and structures. Even when conflict is not in the picture, if patients persistently experience dreams that e.g., have images in them that call to mind diverse references or inappropriate affect, a functionalist might well utilize these phenomenal facts in positing subroutines of dream construction such as the processes of condensation and displacement.

CONCLUSION

There is nothing impossible or absurd about explaining the existence and influence of (pre-theoretical) unconscious mental states in persons by the existence of subpersonal processes and states that have only functional definitions and that are beyond recapture by a person's consciousness (the theoretical unconscious). Secondly, more generally, there is nothing impossible or absurd about a metapsychological theory that explains all the facts (of conflict and otherwise) with which a clinical theory deals, even though the terms of such a metapsychology are not cast in the personal vocabulary of the clinical theory. Thirdly, the particular metapsychological theories we have inherited from Freud – built as they are on a posited universal conflict and on a too hasty flight into physiology, shallow as they are in the degree of their subdivisions – are unlikely candidates for a true metapsychological theory.

To these three conclusions we need to add a fourth. This is a reminder that, no matter how successful the research programme outlined above might be in relating mind to brain via the subpersonal states of the metapsychology, we cannot afford to ignore the distinction between clinical theory and metapsychology, pre-theoretical unconscious and theory-laden unconscious, as do some cognitive psychologists and systems theorists (see Bowers and Meichenbaum 1984; Peterfreund 1971; Winson 1984.) There is an important difference between *my* goals, conscious or unconscious, and the goals of repression, of the dream-work, and the like. My goals are part of me, my character structure. I am *held* resonsible for them in law, morals and everyday life, and I *take* responsibility for deciding what they should be, both in therapy and out. None of these things is true about, e.g., the goal of the dream-work, which is to distort the true meaning of the dream. That is not *my* goal, not even unconsciously. It is not accordingly, part of self.

I would urge that this line between the mental states a person has and those subpersonal states posited by homuncular functionalism should be drawn in terms of consciousness. That of which we are aware (conscious), can easily become aware (preconscious), or can potentially become aware through extensive procedures (unconscious), are all part of our selves.[5] The subpersonal states are not, and that is a fact worth marking in therapy, in everyday life, and in the construction of adequate explanations in psychology.

NOTES

1   For the general form of this dilemma, see Dennett 1969: 90–6.

2   Typical arguments were those that confused speech-act analyses (pragmatics) with analyses of meaning (semantics). Thus, action words were said not to refer because used to ascribe responsibility (H. L. A. Hart 1949); words describing reasons for action were non-referential because they gave justificatory warrants rather than descriptions (Louch 1966); words of sensation did not refer because used to express (but not describe) sensations (Wittgenstein 1958). Cf. Dennett (1969, ch. 1), for an alternative kind of argument from usage (since abandoned) for the non-referential use of mental terms.

3   There are important alternative interpretations of what Freud's abandonment of the 'Project' represents in terms of his underlying metaphysics:

    1   He can be seen as never really giving up his physiological speculations, so that the later metapsychology is just as straightforward a physicalism as was the 'Project' of 1895.

    2   He can be seen as returning to the dualism of Brentano, thinking that 'the mental' could be studied as a subject in its own right and by its own method, independently of any connection to physical science.

3 It was once fashionable to interpret Freud as adopting a behaviourist position. There are two variants here: the 'shallow' behaviourist interpretation of the metapsychology as a set of behavioural constructs (Ellis 1956; Miles 1966), and the 'deep' behaviourist interpretation that make the System Ucs. a theoretical entity in the neo-positivist sense of the later Carnap (Rapaport 1960).

4 At least, no embarrassments greater than those suffered by functionalism as a philosophy of mind generally. For problems in accommodating Intentionality and subjective qualia into a functionalist view of mind, see Shoemaker 1975, Block 1978, Churchland and Churchland 1982, and Richardson 1982.

5 Even though the mechanisms of defence serve the function of maintaining self-cohesion by keeping certain states out of our sense of ourselves, such states are still part of our selves. Our sense of our self does not include such states when they are unconscious or experienced as ego-alien; but our true self does include such states. That is why *we* can be said to be conflicted when we have conflicting mental states even though one-half of the conflict is unconscious or otherwise rejected.

REFERENCES

Abrams, Samuel 1971: The psychoanalytic unconscious, in M. Kanzel (ed.), *The Unconscious Today*. New York: International Universities Press.

Anscombe, Roderick 1981: Referring to the unconscious: a philosophical critique of Schafer's action language. *International Journal of Psycho-Analysis*, 62, 225–41.

Arbib, M. 1972: *The Metaphorical Brain*. New York: Wiley.

Arlow, Jacob and Brenner, Charles 1964: *Psychoanalytic Concepts and the Structural Theory*. New York: International Universities Press.

Bernstein, Richard 1971: *Praxis and Action*.

Block, Ned 1978: Troubles with functionalism, in C. W. Savage (ed.), *Perception and Cognition*. Minnesota Studies in the Philosophy of Science, vol. 9. Minneapolis: University of Minnesota Press.

Block, Ned 1980: Introduction: What is functionalism? in N. Block (ed.), *Readings in Philosophy of Psychology*, vol. 1. Cambridge, Mass.: Harvard University Press.

Bowers, K. and Meichenbaum, P. (eds) 1984: *The Unconscious Reconsidered*. New York: Wiley.

Churchland, P. and Churchland, P. 1982: Functionalism, qualia, and intentionality, in J. Biro and R. Shahan (eds), *Mind, Brain and Function*. Norman, Okla.: University of Oklahoma Press.

Dennett, Daniel 1969: *Content and Consciousness*. London: Routledge & Kegan Paul.

Dennett, Daniel 1978: *Brainstorms*. Montgomery, Vt.: Bradford Books.

Dilman, İlham 1959: The unconscious. *Mind*, 68, 446–73.

Dilman, İlham 1972: Is the unconscious a theoretical construct? *Monist*, 46, 313–42.
Dilman, İlham 1983: *Freud and Human Nature*. Oxford: Blackwell.
Dilman, İlham 1984: *Freud and the Mind*. Oxford: Blackwell.
Eagle, Morris 1982: Anatomy of the self in psychoanalytic theory, in M. Ruse (ed.), *Nature Animated*, vol. 2. Dordrecht: Reidel.
Eagle, Morris 1984: *Recent Developments in Psychoanalysis*. New York: McGraw-Hill.
Ellis, Albert 1956: An operational reformulation of some of the basic principles of psychoanalysis, in H. Feigl and M. Scriven (eds), *The Foundations of Science and the Concepts of Psychology and Psychoanalysis*. Minnesota Studies in the Philosophy of Science, vol. 1. Minneapolis: University of Minnesota Press.
Fairbairn, W. Ronald D. 1954: *An Object-Relations Theory of the Personality*. New York: Basic Books.
Freud, Sigmund 1959a: A note on the unconscious in psychoanalysis. *Collected Papers*, vol. 4. London: Hogarth Press.
Freud, Sigmund 1959b: Repression. *Collected Papers*, vol. 4. London: Hogarth Press.
Freud, Sigmund 1959c: The unconscious. *Collected Papers*, vol. 4. London: Hogarth Press.
Freud, Sigmund 1959d: Instincts and their vicissitudes. *Collected Papers*, vol. 4. London: Hogarth Press.
Freud, Sigmund 1960: *The Ego and the Id*. New York: Norton. (First published in 1923.)
Freud, Sigmund 1965: *New Introductory Lectures on Psychoanalysis*. New York: Norton. (First published in 1933.)
Gill, Merton 1976: Metapsychology is not psychology, in M. Gill and P. Holzman (eds), *Psychology versus Metapsychology*. Psychological Issues Monograph 36. New York: International Universities Press.
Grünbaum, Adolf 1984: *The Foundations of Psychoanalysis: A Philosophical Critique*. Berkeley: University of California Press.
Hampshire, Stuart 1963: Disposition and memory. *International Journal of Psycho-Analysis*, 42, 59–68. Repr. in S. Hampshire, *Freedom of Mind*. Princeton: Princeton University Press, 1971.
Hart, H. L. A. 1949: The ascription of responsibility and rights. *Proceedings of the Aristotelian Society*, 49, 171–94.
Hart, W. D. 1982: Models of repression, in R. Wollheim and J. Hopkins (eds), *Philosophical Essays on Freud*. Cambridge: Cambridge University Press.
Holt, Robert 1981: The death and the transfiguration of the metapsychology. *International Review of Psychoanalysis*, 8, 129–43.
Home, H. J. 1966: The concept of mind. *International Journal of Psychoanalysis*, 47, 42–9.
Klein, George 1976a: Freud's two theories of sexuality, in M. Gill and P. Holzman (eds), *Psychology versus Metapsychology*. Psychological Issues Monograph 36. New York: International Universities Press.

Klein, George 1976b: Two theories or one? in *Psychoanalytic Theory*. New York: International Universities Press.

Landesman, C. 1965: The new dualism in the philosophy of mind. *Review of Metaphysics*, 19, 329–45.

Louch, A. R. 1966: *Explanation and Human Action*. Berkeley: University of California Press.

Lycan, William 1982: Psychological laws, in J. Biro and R. Shahan (eds), *Mind, Brain and Function*. Norman, Okla.: University of Oklahoma Press.

MacIntyre, Alasdair 1958: *The Unconscious*. London: Routledge & Kegan Paul.

Matte-Blanco, I. 1975: *The Unconscious as Infinite Sets*. London: Duckworth.

Meissner, W. W. 1981: Metapsychology – who needs it? *Journal of the American Psychoanalytic Association*, 29, 921–38.

Miles, T. R. 1966: *Eliminating the Unconscious*. Oxford: Pergamon Press.

Moore, Michael 1980: The nature of psychoanalytic explanation. *Psychoanalysis and Contemporary Thought*, 3, 459–543. Also in L. Laudan (ed.), *Mind and Medicine: Problems of Explanation and Evaluation in Psychiatry and the Biomedical Sciences*. Berkeley: University of California Press, 1983.

Moore, Michael 1982: The unity of the self, in M. Ruse (ed.), *Nature Animated*. Dordrecht: Reidel.

Moore, Michael 1984: *Law and Psychiatry: Rethinking the Relationship*. Cambridge: Cambridge University Press.

Mullane, Harvey 1983: Defense, dreams and rationality. *Synthese*, 57, 187–204.

Nagel, Ernst 1959: Methodological issues in psychoanalytic theory, in S. Hook (ed.), *Psychoanalysis, Scientific Method, and Philosophy*. New York: New York University Press.

Peterfreund, Emanuel 1971: *Information, Systems and Psychoanalysis*. New York: International Universities Press.

Platts, Mark 1979: *Ways of Meaning*. London: Routledge & Kegan Paul.

Putnam, Hilary 1975: *Mind, Language and Reality*. Cambridge: Cambridge University Press.

Rapaport, David 1960: On the psychoanalytic theory of motivation, in 1960 *Nebraska Symposium on Motivation*. Lincoln: University of Nebraska Press.

Rayner, Eric 1981: Infinite experiences, affects and the characteristics of the unconscious. *International Journal of Psycho-Analysis*, 62, 403–12.

Richardson, R. C. 1982: Internal representations: prologue to a theory of intentionality, in J. Biro and R. Shahan (eds), *Mind, Brain and Function*. Norman, Okla.: University of Oklahoma Press.

Ricoeur, P. (1970). *Freud and Philosophy*. New Haven, Conn.: Yale University Press.

Rubinstein B. 1965: Psychoanalytic theory and the mind–body problem, in N. Greenfield and W. Lewis (eds), *Psychoanalysis and Current Biological Thought*. Madison: University of Wisconsin Press.

Rubinstein B. 1976: On the possibility of a strictly clinical theory: an essay on the philosophy of psychoanalysis, in M. Gill and P. Holzman (eds), *Psychology versus Metapsychology*. Psychological Issues Monograph 36. New York: International Universities Press.

Ryle, Gilbert 1949: *The Concept of Mind*. London: Hutchinson.

Schafer, Roy 1976: *A New Language for Psychoanalysis*. New Haven, Conn.: Yale University Press.

Sherwood, Michael 1969: *The Logic of Explanation in Psychoanalysis*. New York: Academic Press.

Shoemaker, Sidney 1975: Functionalism and qualia. *Philosophical Studies*, 27, 291–315.

Shoemaker, Sidney 1982: Some varieties of functionalism, in J. Biro and R. Shahan (eds), *Mind, Brain and Function*. Norman, Okla.: University of Oklahoma Press.

Spiro, A. 1979: A philosophical appraisal of Roy Schafer's *A New Language for Psychoanalysis*. *Psychoanalysis and Contemporary Thought*, 2, 253–91.

Steele, Robert 1979: Psychoanalysis and hermeneutics. *International Review of Psycho-Analysis*, 6, 389–411.

Wiggins, David 1976: Locke, Butler and the stream of consciousness: and men as natural kind, in A. Rorty (ed.), *The Identities of Persons*. Berkeley: University of California Press.

Winson, Jonathan 1984: *Brain and Psyche: The Biology of the Unconscious*. New York: Doubleday/Anchor.

Wittgenstein, Ludwig 1958: *Philosophical Investigations*, 2nd edn. Oxford: Blackwell.

PART THREE

Psychoanalysis and Commonsense Psychology

7

Intentions and the Unconscious

İLHAM DİLMAN

FEELING AND CONSCIOUSNESS

Philosophers have raised difficulties about 'unconscious mentality' in general and 'unconscious intentions' in particular. I should like to comment on the general difficulty first and then turn to the question of unconscious intentions.

We all know that people can be in a particular state of mind, be depressed, irritable and angry, for instance, or continue to resent the way someone is treating them, while remaining unaware of this. Yet when we think about it, it may seem that this is impossible and that what is in question needs to be redescribed: How can a person be in a state of mind (we may ask ourselves) and yet lack the consciousness which constitutes it? Behind this difficulty is the assumption, articulated by Descartes, that the mind is identical with consciousness. Freud called this assumption 'the first shibboleth of psycho-analysis'.

Descartes modelled his conception of what is mental on the logic of sensations, and it is of course true that if it *seems* to a person that he feels pain, physical pain, then he must *be* in pain, whether or not he has an injury or something physically wrong with him. Its *seeming* to him that he is in pain is, as Descartes would call it, a 'mode of consciousness', and it constitutes his *being* in pain, the very reality of the pain he feels. Take that away and you have taken away his pain.

Now if fear, for instance, were a sensation, if it were a mental state constituted by the here and now of consciousness, as Descartes thought, then indeed a person could not be afraid and not know that he was, nor could he think he was afraid when he was not. But what makes it true that a person is afraid are not his sensations of the moment, the sensations that characterize his consciousness severed from the before and the after. Fear characterizes a person's consciousness in an altogether different way. The consciousness that it characterizes is the person's consciousness of what it is that he is responding to in fear. If, for instance, he really fears an imminent confrontation, then his fear is the form which his consciousness or anticipation of that confrontation takes, the terms in which he thinks of it, his affective response to it. The state of consciousness which takes this form is directed to the object of his thoughts and response, namely the dreaded confrontation. What gives it the particular character it has, the one we designate as 'fear', is not a matter of what goes on in him at the time. At least this is relevant only in the light of the significance it assumes in its relation to what took place before it and what will come after. It is his relation to the imminent confrontation, together with the circumstances that surround his present thoughts, sensations and inclinations, that constitute his fear, characterize his state of mind – his consciousness of the imminent confrontation. If he is afraid he must not only see that confrontation in a certain way, think of it in certain terms, but this vision and these thoughts must enter his responses, affect his behaviour in a certain way. In certain cases it must affect the very rhythm of his physical life.

This, namely how he is related to the imminent confrontation, what he makes of it, how he responds to it, is *itself* a possible object of reflection, and the way *it* figures in his consciousness may be quite different from the way he anticipates the confrontation in reality. The content of his consciousness and what he really feels need not coincide. It may seem to him that he is confident and without fear when in fact the opposite is the case. He may say to himself that his adversary is a coward, as one whistles in the dark, while he continues to think of him as possessing devastating powers. Alternatively, the fear which the thought of the confrontation seems to evoke in him may be part of the way he misrepresents to himself his response to it. In reality the object of his trepidation may be his own aggressiveness, the fear which the confrontation evokes in him may not be, as he thinks, a fear of what his adversary may do to him, but a fear of what he might do to his adversary. The qualities to which he responds in his adversary in the fear he feels, whether or not he recognizes this, may be a mirror image of his own unacknowledged fantasies and inclinations.

I am suggesting that it is both the idea of consciousness and that of what is mental that we misapprehend, as Descartes did, when we identify the two and think of an unconscious emotion or inclination as a contradiction in terms. Consciousness is not the stuff that constitutes what is mental; rather it is the person's apprehension of what concerns or affects him. It may be explicit in his thoughts or implicit in his responses – in his distress at what has happened, for instance, his guilt about what he has done or is inclined to do, his pleasures at or fear of what he anticipates, the attraction he feels for someone, his interest in something. These are forms of consciousness of things.

Equally, and in the same way, a person's own responses, his emotions and inclinations, can be the object of his consciousness. Here too his consciousness of them may be unreflective. He may apprehend them correctly, without ever spelling this out for himself, or he may misapprehend them. In the latter case they take a distorted form in his consciousness, they take on an appearance there which is different from what they are. Where the discrepancy between appearance and reality is great in such cases we could rightly say that the person has no consciousness or awareness, for instance, of the way he feels. In other words, his feelings do not figure in his consciousness, or what figures there has little to do with what he really feels. He actively avoids taking cognizance of what he feels. This is where Freud speaks of the feelings and emotions in questions as unconscious.

So much on the side of consciousness. As for its object, the feelings and emotions in question, their reality or existence is, as I said, a matter of the person's relation to their objects, the significance these have for him, the way they touch or affect him. The latter embraces his thoughts, actions and responses, the actions he takes, the reponses he controls or contains, and also the bodily, somatic reactions or reflexes which he experiences as sensations and bodily feelings. It is these things, taken as a whole, which John Wisdom once referred to as 'patterns in time'. Obviously what patterns they constitute depend on the particular circumstances of the person's life which surround them. These patterns may be hard to take in at a glance and so offer scope for error and misapprehension from which the person himself is not immune. Indeed it may suit him to avoid recognizing them for what they are and he may actively pursue such self-deceit.

BECOMING CONSCIOUS OF WHAT IS UNCONSCIOUS

One further question I would like to touch on before considering the possibility of unconscious intentions is this: Given that a person can feel angry, anxious, afraid or depressed without being conscious of it, what does his becoming conscious of what he feels amount to or involve? One might think that it involves the dawning of a new aspect, an aspect perhaps that was being resisted. In other words, the change is a change in aspect. While this is true, it is only part of the truth, for the change in aspect is only one aspect of the change in question. I referred to Wisdom's remark that what we have here are 'patterns in time that are hard to take in at a glance'. The patterns are the aspects or 'gestalts' which our actions and reactions, together with what these are directed to, constitute in our apprehension or consciousness. Indeed, the particular aspect *is* our consciousness of what is in question.

But, in our examples, what constitutes this or that pattern for a particular person is what he himself feels. He is not related to it *externally*, as a third person might be. It is *he* who feels the fear, *he* who responds to what he anticipates with fear. That in which this fear finds expression, that in which he is or becomes conscious of it, are his own actions and reactions, his own movements, gestures, quivers and heart beats. And some of these at any rate are subject to his will. It is *he* who gives in to the fear, *he* who gives expression to it, contains or controls it. In the latter case, when he comes to be aware of what he feels he *also* gives up this control, he enters into what he feels, even allows himself to be taken over by it, instead of fighting it. And that means that his very way of responding to what inspires fear or anxiety in him *changes*, but without losing the continuity in identity it has with his original mode of response. He does not *become* afraid, for he *was* afraid before this change. No, he now gives *more direct expression* to the fear he continues to feel. He no longer hides it from himself, no longer disguises it from his own consciousness.

Let me use the analogy of a piece of music played on the piano. This could be recorded so that the different playings of the record are identical. Yet the way one hears it may change. This is a change in aspect, the aspect under which one hears the music, the particular performance. Suppose now that someone plays it on the piano and changes the emphasis he gives to the different notes. He may thus play it more expressively, for instance, bring to life something which the composer put into the music and meant to be there. Here, in this second rendering, one still hears the same melody; but it now contains or expresses something which was absent in the first performance. Not only is it the case that a new aspect dawns on the listener, but what he hears differently is also played differently. Now roll the player and the listener into one and you have *some* analogy to what takes place when someone, perhaps in the course of a psychoanalysis, becomes conscious of something in himself which he has so far resisted recognizing. The player gives expression to something he discovers in the music: it was previously in the melody without being in his rendering of it. Now he gives expression to it in the way he plays the melody – except, of course, that what was in the melody exists independently of him, whereas this is not true of a person's unconscious feelings. This is the respect in which the analogy breaks down.

What is important from the therapeutic point of view is that when the patient's unconscious feelings become conscious they become accessible to his critical appraisal in a way which they were not previously. He thus gains the ability to do something about them so that he is no longer ruled by them as before. He has at least relinquished some of the defensive behaviour to which he was anxiously committed without realizing it. He has now more of himself to put into what he does, and he doesn't have to go on in a way which up to now it seemed he could not avoid. As for the feelings that have surfaced into his consciousness, what inspires them may itself change aspect in the light of his present orientation, his adult consciousness may cut them down to size. Or at least in allowing them to take over he may find the opportunity to live them out; what has been smouldering in his affective life, unknown to him, may now find the opportunity to spend itself out, like an ember that has been exposed to the air. Or, in a different case, what he now faces in his feelings may call for an affective reorientation: he may give up his grudges, forgive those he holds responsible in his feelings for real or imaginary injuries. Until he knew he was sulking, for instance, he could not stop doing so; until he became aware of the grudge he was nursing he could not give it up; and until he faced his feelings of guilt he could not make amends. There are different cases here and different possibilities of inner change. This kind of inner change is itself made possible by, but is not identical with, that change in the analysand which constitutes what is unconscious in him becoming conscious.

CONSCIOUSNESS AND INTENTION

A person's emotions, we have seen, characterize his consciousness in a very different way to what Descartes imagined. Descartes thought a man's present state of consciousness to consist of private shadows that pass before his inner gaze which at once lights them up and gives them being. When these shadows lose their luminosity they cease to exist and are replaced by new ones. Inevitably the shadows show themselves to the person whose present state of consciousness they constitute since what makes them visible to him is what gives them substance – their luminosity is the only substance they have. As such these shadows are the furniture of his mental life – his feelings, his thoughts, his perceptions, his intentions, etc. Iris Murdoch described this as the 'magic lantern' view of consciousness.

I suggested (and this idea is to be found in both Sartre and Wittgenstein, both of whom criticized Descartes) that consciousness is not something internal and distinct from the human body. It is originally something external and as such visible to other people. For its only expressions in the first place are the person's responses to what goes on around him. Only when the possibility of reflection brings these responses under his voluntary control does his consciousness acquire the possibility of existing apart from these outward responses and can become something internal, that is something he can keep to himself if he so chooses. Secondly, consciousness is in the first place directed outwards. It does not reflect itself, as Descartes imagined, it reflects what lies outside it. Only when the person is able to articulate the aspects under which he responds to things does his consciousness become an object of thought itself, and as such its own object. But primarily it is *not* something the person knows in himself, or cannot help knowing. It is primarily what he lives in his responses to things; his responses are forms of his apprehension of them. Thus the example of fear which I considered earlier. In the fear a person feels he may be said to be conscious of danger, or something that threatens him, in whatever it is that he fears, even when he does not spell this out to himself or take explicit cognizance of it.

In a similar way to have an intention is to envisage doing something in the future. Thus in having an intention I have the future action in my thought – which is not to say that I am thinking of it all the time. I make up my mind to do something, form an intention, say 'That is settled', and I may not think about it again until the time comes to carry it out. I have the future action in my thought in the sense that the declaration of an intention has the form: 'I will do so-and-so' – which is not a prediction, as it would be in the third person. I do not have inductive grounds for what I say, and I do not wait to see whether it will come true. I proceed to make it come true, I act in conformity with the intention I have announced, or at any rate I try.

If I am to be able to try I must know how to do or bring about certain things, I must have the ability to perform certain actions. If I intend to play chess, for instance, I must know how to play chess, and this is obviously something I have learned. In playing chess I put this knowledge into practice, I utilize or exercise it. It is this knowledge that enables me to have the future action in my thought now, in the special way I have it there, when I have the intention to do it. There is no way of identifying the intention without mentioning the intended action. The intention, we could say, represents the intended action – or, as Wittgenstein at one time said, 'pictures' it. In other words, the intention is itself *a form of consciousness*, namely of what I am going to do – much in the way that my fear is a form of consciousness of what I fear as something dangerous, or threatening, or hair-raising.

An intention may lie in an action, as when we do things with intention, or it may be formed in advance and so precede the action. In the former case it is not something over and above the action, a mental accompaniment of outward movements. The intention with which, for instance, I may dig potatoes into the ground, the intention to grow potatoes, is not something additional to the digging I do. It resides in the way I follow up the digging, the way I go on with what I am doing. This is not something arbitrary. I go on with what I have started in accordance with what I have learned to do. My way of going on belongs with certain farming practices which embody beliefs and expectations about the environment in which I act. What I bring into the first step, the digging, the direction I bestow on it, comes from my practical knowledge. It is this which enables me to stand in this kind of relation to the future, the relation which constitutes my intention.

There is a lot that a man must have learned before he can have intentions in advance of acting, before he can have intentions which he can abandon without translating them into action. Certainly he has to have learned to do certain things on request and also not to do them when asked not to. He has to have learned to describe actions and to understand their descriptions. These go together. When he does such an action at will the intention lies *in* the action we see him doing, it has no existence independent of the action. Such an intention acquires a separate existence in the life of an individual only after he has learned, as a child, to consider whether or not to do certain things, when he is able to think about future situations and future developments in his present situation which may call for action now. Where an intention can thus exist apart from the action it envisages it is still true that unless the agent knows how to perform the action he cannot intend to do so. Furthermore to speak of such an intention is still to refer to the pattern the man would realize in performing the action. An unexecuted or half-executed intention makes sense only in relation to executed ones, that is in relation to the completed action which constitutes its fulfilment. For that is what the agent envisages in forming the intention.

We see that a man who acts intentionally anticipates what he is going to do next, but not in the way that an observer does. What he is going to do next is already in his thoughts, it is part of the pattern which constitutes the action he is engaged in or envisages. His knowledge of this pattern, of what constitutes its realization as well as how to realize it, is the practical knowledge which enables him to have in mind what he is going to do next before doing it. Possessing this knowledge and being committed for the future by what he embarks on, or by his intentions, are the two sides of the same coin. To intend to do something is thus to think that one will do it, and doing it intentionally, or with intention as we might say, entails knowing what one is doing. What that is cannot be identified independently of the agent's thoughts. That is why he can normally say what he is doing without reflection.

UNCONSCIOUS INTENTION

It is this knowledge I have as an agent of my own future actions that Professor Stuart Hampshire (1963) has in mind when he says that an intention cannot be unconscious: '"Intention" [he writes in his paper 'Disposition and Memory'] is the one concept that ought to be preserved free from any taint of the less-than-conscious. Its function, across the whole range of its applications, is to mark that kind of knowledge of what one is doing, and of what one is inclined to do, that is fully conscious and explicit.' In his book *Thought and Action* he says that 'consciousness [is] inseparable from action, or attempted action, in the sense that we are always able to answer the question – "What are you doing now?"' (1959: 119). When he speaks of 'consciousness' he means this knowledge and the beliefs presupposed by it – beliefs about one's surroundings. In fact, in ordinary language, 'intentionally' is opposed to 'accidentally' and 'inadvertently', and it means 'with knowledge' (1959: 145). Thus Hampshire speaks of intention as a 'form of knowledge', the peculiar knowledge which an agent has of his own future actions by virtue of his intentions: 'My own conscious intentions are, before all other things, present to me as a form of knowledge and constitute the centre of my consciousness at any particular moment' (p. 133). When he then goes on to list some features of the concept of intention, he writes: 'The subject cannot be ignorant of his intention, although he may make a variety of mistakes in stating it, in putting it into words' (p. 134).

He says: 'If my intentions are . . . unknown to me, then I have no fixed and formed intentions' (p. 103). Indeed, if someone says that he doesn't know what he is going to do or what he intends to do, we take this to mean that he has not yet made up his mind, formed an intention. It isn't that there is something he is going to do which he does not know. If this were the case, he would be surprised by what he does, which means that he was not acting intentionally. In that case, what he doesn't know is what he is going to find himself doing. So it is not a case of not knowing what one's intention is, or that one has a particular intention – an intention one has formed oneself. But is that really impossible?

A man is considering an invitation the acceptance of which involves his leaving home and so his family for a period of time. He is greatly attracted, but he wants to bring his wife's views and wishes into the equation which he is trying to resolve. He starts with an open mind, without any formed intentions. But as the dialogue with his wife continues over a certain period, he begins to move towards making up his mind. When his wife points this out to him, he protests. Yet the terms in which he considers the question now give her the impression not merely that he would like to go, but that he has made up his mind to do so and is merely seeking her endorsement. Various things he does confirm this impression: he makes inquiries about the journey, clears up his papers, thinks about what he would take with him. But when any of this is brought to his attention he is always ready with a plausible justification. He feels guilty and uneasy about not thinking enough about his family. Eventually, he chooses the grounds on which 'to make up his mind' to go, those that are the least damaging to his idea of himself as a caring husband and head of the family, doing so a little too ostentatiously.

Can we not say that his mind was already made up before then? Hampshire would say that if he had formed an intention to accept the invitation, he must have *known* he would be going. I do not dispute this, but I claim that a person may know something and still not recognize that he knows it. Certainly when he is able to say to himself, 'I will go', this is a change in him, and without this change he could not go in the way he does – without having to give excuses, as someone who is fully behind what he is doing and prepared to take the consequences. For there is, indeed, a difference between acting as 'an intentional agent in the full sense' and acting with an unconscious intention.

Certainly the kind of commitment for the future we have in an intention or intentional action involves the agent's knowledge and thoughts in the sense explained. If the agent has an intention then what he intends to do must be in his thoughts and so he must know what he intends to do. The relation between an intention and what would fulfil it is, as we have seen, an *internal* one, so that if someone acts intentionally he necessarily *knows* what he is up to. Thus the husband in the example I have just given.

It is true that normally the agent's words, when we are satisfied that he is speaking frankly, constitute an important criterion of what he knows and so of what his intentions are. But it is not our only criterion, and in some cases it can be overruled. Normally, when there is a conflict between what the agent says and what certain features of his words and behaviour suggest, once we are satisfied that he is not lying, we go by what he says. But there are exceptions to this rule. In some circumstances where there is such a conflict it is not unreasonable to attach little weight to what in other cases weighs heavily. There is no absurdity in this, and I see no contradiction in speaking of a person as knowing something which he won't admit to himself. If so, we can attribute to him the knowledge necessary to his having a particular intention but not a consciousness of the intention.

POST-HYPNOTIC ACTION AND THE PARADOX OF UNCONSCIOUS INTENTION

Take the case of post-hypnotic action: can it be characterized as intentional? We know that the subject was ordered to do something under hypnosis. We know that the hypnotist talked to him in a language he understands, and also that he is capable of doing what he was asked. We have seen some expressions of his willingness to comply. It is true that at the time of the action he has no recollection of the hypnotist's words, and he does not think of himself as obeying anyone. Yet the fact remains that his deeds match the words he heard, understood and showed a willingness to obey. What is more, if put under hypnosis, he recalls the words and admits that he was following instructions. When on this basis we claim that he was obeying an order we attribute to him the intention to do what he was told. We also attribute to him the knowledge and memory which finds expression in what he does, although it is not accessible to him in the normal way.

So there is a strong analogy between the post-hypnotic subject and a man obeying an order or an actor following stage directions, although there is, of course, also a strong disanalogy. If we use words which emphasize both the analogy and the disanalogy this seems to involve us in a contradiction: 'He is obeying an order but he has no idea that he is, and he is unable to do otherwise.' There are two features here which seem fatally to go against saying that the subject is obeying an order. The first is that he doesn't know he is obeying an order, he doesn't remember the order. The second is that he is unable to do otherwise. Try as he may he cannot stand on his feet or move them. Or, he feels he must do what he does, he becomes anxious if anyone tries to prevent him.

Let me consider these two features in turn. Can a man be said to be obeying an order when he has no recollection of the order? My wife asks me to bring her the scissors from the bedroom. I go to fetch them. But I am thinking of something else and open the drawer absent-mindedly. I ask myself, 'What did I come here for?' and cannot answer. Would one say that I am looking for the scissors, that I intend to take them to my wife?

Let me alter the example slightly. I do not ask myself what I am doing but I continue to rummage about in the drawer while absorbed in thought. I then sight the scissors, pick them up and take them to my wife. Before I sighted the scissors I did not know what I was doing in the sense that had I been asked I would not have been able to answer. But was I not looking for the scissors all the same? Do not the circumstances give us good reason for saying that I was?

Besides, what does my lack of knowledge, my failure to remember, consist in? It consists in the fact that I am unable to answer certain questions at the time. This does give us reason for saying that I did not remember what I went to the bedroom for, that I did not know what I was doing. But have we got no reason for saying that I had not forgotten, that I knew what I was doing?

To see that there is, contrast with the following example. Again my wife asks me for the scissors. I say that I shall fetch them as soon as I come to the end of the page I am reading. I finish the page, but I continue to read on. After ten minutes she says: 'What about the scissors?' 'Oh,' I say, 'I am sorry, I have completely forgotten. I shall bring them straight away.' What I do not remember here, I still remember in the first example. There, when asked what I am doing I cannot answer; but I have left my place, I have opened the right drawer, and when I sight the scissors I pick them up.

The use of the words 'I know', 'He knows', 'I remember', 'He remembers' is governed by several criteria which on a particular occasion may give us conflicting reasons for wanting to use them. At first we were inclined to say, 'If a man doesn't remember, he cannot be said to obey an order.' We now see that insofar as we have some independent reason for saying that he is obeying an order, we also have some reason for saying that he does remember, that he hasn't forgotten the order. There is, of course, a tie between the concepts of obeying an order, remembering it, and knowing what one is doing. But the use of these concepts is not governed by rigid criteria and is wider than we think at first, going by the most familiar cases. These criteria are complex and it is not necessary for all of them to be satisfied in a particular case for the concept to be applicable.

All the same, what the man himself is able to tell us, or tell himself, is an extremely important criterion for saying that he knows and remembers. Hence when it is not satisfied, however much reason we may have for saying that he knows or remembers, there will be some reason for saying that he does not. And this will give us reason for saying that he is not obeying an order. Such a conflict of reasons is inevitable in the cases we are considering. So when asked whether the post-hynotic subject is obeying an order, the answer is: 'Well, he is and he isn't.'

Yet there is nothing provisional about these words. Nothing further can come to light to make us modify our answer into 'He seems to be obeying an order, but he isn't really', or 'He is really obeying an order and only pretends not to know anything about it.' For otherwise this would not be a case of someone *unconsciously* obeying an order. Hence the final answer to our question is paradoxical, though there is nothing pernicious in this. For what makes our paradoxical statement true are those respects in which the subject is both like and unlike men whose actions constitute central and familiar instances of obeying an order. If only we could bring these respects vividly before our minds we would see how they may co-exist in a particular case and appreciate the sort of picture to which they add up. We would then stop being troubled by 'the incompatibility of the predicates' used to present them.

I now turn to the second feature of post-hypnotic actions which I singled out earlier as seeming to go fatally against their intentional character, namely their 'somnambulistic' aspect well illustrated in such extreme examples as sleepwalking and automatic writing. In these examples the subject is unable to help doing what he does, or at any rate the actions in question do not seem to engage his will. They seem to happen to him; he seems to be on the receiving end. Certainly the post-hypnotic subject is not doing what he wills. There is no part of him that endorses the action except under the aspect of what he was ordered to do. Let us imagine that he was ordered to stab someone; he picks up a knife and stabs the man in question. Presumably he is fully awake and at the sight of the man he is overcome by an impulse to stab him, on which he acts. If he is acting on impulse does it not follow that his action cannot be characterized as intentional? Not necessarily.

Imagine two different cases. A man is walking on the cliffs and he has a sudden impulse to push his companion off the cliffs. He does so. When questioned he can say nothing more than that he had a very strong urge which he could not resist, but that he had otherwise no reason at all for what he did – a veritable brainstorm. He did not hate his companion, he had no reason for wanting him dead. He was not responding to anything in his companion, however transitory, which filled him with repugnance. We have here an action which comes from a sudden, strong urge which has got detached from an otherwise sane and responsible person's nexus of reasons for doing things. The connections broken make it at least tempting to deny that we have an intentional action here.

In the second case a man has a good and well-paid job. He is bored with it from time to time, but he has never considered giving it up. One day he suddenly has the thought: 'Is it worth slaving for money or security in this way? Wouldn't it be nice to chuck it all in and do something I would really like to do?' He does not pause to consider what it is he would like to do and whether or not he has the means; he goes and hands in his resignation. The thought is sudden and he may have acted irresponsibly, but the action is clearly intentional. He intended to resign his job at the time and he knew what he was doing.

What we describe as 'impulsive action' or 'acting on impulse' has a certain range. It shades and changes into fully intentional action at its upper limit, and it includes irresistible impulse at its lower limit, where a person's action becomes an 'aberration', bearing no relation to the reasons that normally weigh with him. At this extreme we say that he didn't know what he was doing. Where a person has such knowledge he can, normally, say 'I am doing so-and-so.' But this is neither necessary nor sufficient. What is crucial is how he goes on with what he is doing at present.

What would make us say that the man who pushed his companion off the cliff didn't know what he was doing? Such things as the lightness with which he does so, his immediate response to it. He says, 'I felt like pushing him', but seems oblivious to what is involved in doing this – the consequences for his companion, his family, himself. If he later 'comes to his senses', as we say, he may be overwhelmed with remorse at the gravity of his action. He may say, 'He was my friend. He was the father of two children.' Had he simply forgotten about these things at the time or had he stopped caring about them? There is little difference. The point is that at the time these facts or their significance are blotted out of his consciousness. Were they nevertheless in his thoughts unconsciously? I have imagined not. At this extreme 'intention', 'knowledge of what one is doing' and 'having reasons for it' disappear – more or less together.

We see that the fact that a person can be properly described as having acted on impulse does not as such disqualify his action from being characterized as intentional. We also see that a distinction has to be made between a 'brainstorm' and 'unconscious determination'. In the former what a person knows and cares for is temporarily lost to him. In the latter what is not accessible to him consciously is nevertheless in his thoughts and enters into what he does and how he behaves. The post-hypnotic subject obeys an order which he remembers unconsciously, and he obeys simply because he was told to do it. Yet how is this compatible with his acting on impulse?

Imagine that it is important for me to get to a place to keep an appointment. I am half-way there when I have an accident and suffer a concussion. One possibility is that I am found on the scene of the accident wandering aimlessly all over the place. Another possibility is that I only recall that I have to get to a certain place, not remembering what for. When questioned all I can say is: 'I must get there, but I don't know why.' I will, in all probability, do my utmost to get there. You may try to dissuade me: 'You are not in a fit state to go. You need medical attention. The roads are treacherous.' But you will not succeed, unless perhaps you can frighten me out of what I am intent on doing. You will not succeed because I cannot weigh the reasons you give me against the reasons I have. Not being able to recall them I cannot say to myself: 'I am only going to meet a friend for a meal; it is not a matter of life and death.' Not subject to scrutiny, my reason acquires an absolute character: I only know I must get there, come what may.

The case of the post-hypnotic subject is the same. He only knows he must do whatever it is he was told to do, and any reason he may have for not doing it cannot get him to change his mind. At least this is one aspect of what is in question. His original willingness to comply, his uncritical agreement, has to do with another aspect, namely the regressive character of the position into which hypnosis puts him. This makes him open to suggestion, or brings his suggestibility into play. But his sticking to the original intention, after he has woken up, is at least partly the result of his mind remaining closed in the way I have suggested, insulated from considerations relating to the time of action and encompassing future consequences. He has no choice; he is prevented from exercising judgement. So we cannot hold him responsible for what he does. Yet if he were ordered to do a degrading thing, this would degrade him. Thus Mario in Thomas Mann's story 'Mario and the Magician'.

An unconscious intention, then, is one which a person cannot give up in the normal way. The agent has no choice but to pursue it. I asked whether in that case we can speak of an intention. I argued that we can. But if we can speak of an intention in the absence of choice, can we speak of autonomy? I have already suggested that we cannot. This means that an unconscious intention is an intention in an attenuated sense.

UNCONSCIOUS INTENTION AND AUTONOMY

The man executing an unconscious intention is at once agent and victim; he cannot be said to be acting on his own behalf. This is certainly the case with the post-hypnotic subject, but not simply because he is doing what he was told to do; for a man may act in obedience to an order and still act on his own behalf. The question is: In what sort of relation does he stand to the order?

We do sometimes act in obedience to inner voices which we have not made our own and which are not, therefore, an expression of our will. While we may then be considered responsible for the outcome of what we do, it remains the case that we have not acted as an autonomous agent. We have not exercised judgement and we have yielded to the demand of these voices. We have no one to blame but ourselves, yet we were not completely behind what we did. For instance, we keep hurting someone, meaning to hurt him, but we think that this is only a regrettable outcome of what we do for his good. Presumably what we do here is acceptable to us only under this description. But this description or redescription is (I am imagining) what Freud calls a 'rationalization'.

The autonomous agent, in contrast, considers himself responsible not in the sense that he may blame himself afterwards, but in the sense that he is willing *now* to pay for the consequences of what he undertakes to do; he is prepared to do so while he acts. He has thought about the possible consequences and has weighed them in the light of what he values and cherishes. Having done so he wants to do it and appreciates the risks involved. The action he envisages has thus his full endorsement: he is wholehearted in what he does and he can be trusted not to go back on himself. But what does it mean to say that he is fully behind his action? We can only answer this question by giving an open-ended list of the ways he does not act: he is not acting in order to please or appease anyone. And if he is doing what is in question to please someone then this is what he wants and he has no ulterior motives. He is not doing what he does to justify himself before an accuser, whether it be a real person or the inner voice of his conscience. He is not doing so out of fear, acting out of cowardice. He is not doing so rashly, unable to take the time to think. Nor is he doing so at the call of a desire that has made him too eager to act, unable to heed considerations that do normally weigh with him. Of course, an autonomous agent need not reflect each time before he acts. The point is that he is prepared to do so if necessary. He is not rushed into action. His desires are not fragmented or locked in conflict. The present or the immediate future does not have a greater claim on his attention than any other time. He is in touch with what goes on around him; he is not so absorbed by his present purposes as to forget about other aspects of the matter which normally count for him.

This is not true of the man who executes an unconscious intention or pursues an unconscious policy. He is so taken up by his present purposes that there isn't enough of him left to mind the considerations that do weigh with him. Yet he differs from a 'single-minded' person in that what he is doing or pursuing does not have his full backing. It is unwelcome to the rest of him, or at least not endorsed by part of him; and the price at which it is to be achieved is not something he has thought about and accepted. What he is seeking remains segregated from the rest of his concerns, sentiments and interests. The rest of him is simply dragged into the action. It submits or at best remains an observer and suffers the infringement of its interests, the violation of its convictions, or at least the degradation of being by-passed. Even then, what he does here he intends or means to do. It is not an accident, nor yet the result of yielding to an impulse of the moment. But he does not do it willingly.

If he knew what he was doing in the sense of being able to spell it out, if he were acting as 'an intentional agent in the full sense', that is with autonomy, then what he does would have to have been accepted by the rest of him. So for him to do it with conscious intention he would have to face the question whether he should do it, whether it is really what he wants to do. If there are many occasions on which what we do does not face us with such a question that is because it does not present us with any problem, because it does not go against the grain of our interests and convictions, or at any rate we are not aware that it does. This, however, is not the case with the person who acts with an unconscious intention. For him to do what he does with conscious intention he would have to be different in himself – lose some conviction that he has, acquire a new one, develop new sentiments. Thus if, being who he is, he came to face what he is up to he would have to choose between giving it up or paying the price for it.

This, I believe, is what Freud had in mind when in his *Introductory Lectures on Psycho-Analysis* he said that the sole task of psychoanalytic treatment is to make the patient's inner conflict accessible to decision: 'the conflict [in a neurotic] can never have a final outcome one way or the other, the antagonists meet each other as little as the whale and the polar bear in the well-known story. An effective decision can be reached only when they confront each other on the same ground. And, in my opinion, to accomplish this is the sole task of the treatment' (1965: 362). 'By extending the unconscious into consciousness,' he said, 'the pathogenic conflict [is] exchanged for a normal one which must be decided one way or the other. We do nothing for our patients but enable this one mental change to take place in them' (p. 363). In lifting the repression, Freud wrote, we bring issues decided in the past up for revision in changed circumstances (p. 366). This enables the patient to act with greater autonomy, to become a more autonomous person.

I had pointed out earlier that when an unconscious feeling becomes conscious more is involved than a person grasping what the indirect expressions of this feeling in his behaviour amounts to. He finds the courage to give it more direct expression and he grasps the identity between what he previously tried to hide and what he now expresses openly. But he still has the problem of what to do about the way he feels. Analysis helps him to find his own solution. It does so by enabling him to bring more of himself to bear on his problems and by pointing out to him where he deceives himself in the solutions he seeks.

We now see that similarly when an unconscious intention becomes conscious more is involved than a change in the person's understanding of what he does and what he is seeking. He finds, for the first time, the opportunity to assess critically his reasons for wanting to pursue the course of action intended and either to pursue it and take responsibility for it or to give it up. With an unconscious intention a person lacks this opportunity and he is, therefore, not an agent in the full sense: he is both agent and victim at the same time. Thus in many cases where a patient in analysis complains of being in a rut or trapped in a pattern of behaviour which he wishes to shake off, it turns out that he is at once the gaoler and the gaoled. That is why analysis cannot advance without the patient's active participation.

REFERENCES

Freud, S. 1965: *Introductory Lectures on Psycho-Analysis*. New York: Norton.
Hampshire, S, 1959: *Thought and Action*. London: Chatto and Windus.
Hampshire, S. 1963: Disposition and memory. *International Journal of Psycho-analysis*, 42, 59–68.

8

Mirrors, Lamps, Organisms and Texts

ROBERT SHARPE

> I always thought that starting it from the beginning was yet another chance of stopping the ending happening.
>
> David Hughes, *The Pork Butcher*

I

Few contributors to this volume have had much to say about the humanist or hermeneutic approach to Freud. Considering the attention which has been given to it elsewhere, the omission is certainly surprising. Professor Dilman is, to some extent, the exception, though he tends to collapse Freudian claims into commonsense, or what are sometimes called folk-psychological claims about the unconscious. The reduction is not unproblematic. I shall raise and answer some questions about hermeneutic theory ending with a somewhat modified form of interpretative theory.

For this account of Freudian procedure differs from Freud's own account. Freud, I believe, brought to the study of the mind a certain model of what a suitably scientific explanation would be. The model is that of the explanation of visible phenomena through a concealed mechanism. We may call it the 'hidden mechanism' model, the 'essentialist' model or the 'systemic' approach. The 'essentialist' label refers us to Locke's doctrine of 'real essences', one of the earliest and certainly a seminal formulation of the model. 'System' reminds us of the formal properties of the type of explanation; post-Freudians like Heinz Hartmann and Kohut use 'system' or 'structure' to characterize the complex structure of the mind, for example the distinction between ego, super-ego and id (Hartmann 1958: 11; Kohut 1981: esp. 47–8, 51, 183–4, 187, 198). David Pears's recent book *Motivated Irrationality* (1984: esp. 20, 40), which, without being an explicit defence of Freud, is one of the most sophisticated available philosophical accounts of the mind as a complex structure, also refers to 'system'. In brief, the idea is that the observable disturbances of the neurotic can be explained by occurrences at a deeper level. Like the classical instance of the Brownian motion, the surface changes prove to be caused by processes beneath the level of observation and the causation is what we might call 'vertical'. Confirmation of such events in the physical world often requires the development of new observational techniques or new instruments like the microscope or the electron microscope or the cloud chamber. It is not hard to see that the various models of the mind that Freud developed match this paradigm in one way or another. Like his determinism, it is one of the legacies of nineteenth-century science in his thought. The visible behaviour of a person is seen as the product of warring agents within him. Thus the method of free association has been compared variously with the microscope, the telescope and, when speaking of psychoanalysis generally, Freud often compares it with archaeology in the uncovering of hidden layers. There is a further aspect worth stressing and that is the extent to which the model was biological; Frank Sulloway aptly speaks of Freud's biologization of the mind (1980: 3–5).

Those writers who favour treating Freudian explanations as forms of interpretation rather than as explanatory in the scientific manner assume that the understanding of the behaviour of a person, like the interpretation of a work of art or of a historical source, is a very different matter from the explanation of an event in the natural world. In general, advocates of the hermeneutic approach have in their sights the idea, false in their view, that human behaviour is law-governed and can be explained in terms of causal ·generalizations. It is possible to hold that human behaviour is law-governed without subscribing to an essentialist model, though the converse is presumably impossible. To the question which of the two had priority for Freud it is my contention that the essentialist model had a very much more important role to play in the development of his theory: it is here that his scientism has a formative role. Although not all scientific explanations are essentialist in their form, if all psychoanalytic elucidations are interpretative, essentialist-type explanations are excluded *a fortiori*. Now, of the main branches of human activity where we speak of interpretation, the interpretation of art shows hermeneutics at its most sophisticated; in the course of this century, we have become more subtle in our delineation of its methodology. I propose then to take the interpretation of art as a model for psychoanalytic interpretation in order to see what features they have in common. I believe, though I shall not defend it here, that 'interpretation' is pretty well a paradigm of a Wittgensteinian family resemblance notion and that, in art and psychoanalysis, interpretation takes different forms.

I have implied that I think that Freud's practice was interpretative. What are the criteria for counting a theory as interpretative rather than descriptive? I take it that the two are somehow opposed. Interpretations we think of as somehow going beyond the facts in a way which descriptions do not. Usage seems to require that interpretations be plausible or implausible, inventive or boring, whilst descriptions are merely true or false. Interpretations display the gift of the interpreter for seeing connections and forming a synoptic view of the object being considered. The interpreter places his mark on his interpretations; they reflect his idiosyncrasies. If this is correct, then writers such as P. D. Juhl, E. D. Hirsch and M. C. Beardsley who, whatever their other differences, insist that interpretations are either right or wrong, true or false, collapse the distinction between descriptions and interpretations.

Roy Schafer is perhaps the most prominent advocate of a hermeneutic approach amongst psychoanalytic theoreticians and he takes the view that any analytic situation can be matched by a multiplicity of interpretations of which no single one is true (Schafer 1980a: 80–3).[1] The interpretation is underdetermined. We can draw a parallel with the performing arts. There are many ways of playing a Beethoven sonata, many of which will be of equal validity. The notation underdetermines the performance; it does not tell us how fast allegro con brio is, just how long a pause is, or precisely how many decibels a fortissimo should register. Equally, the analytic history of a patient can be told in various ways depending on which episodes we take to be significant. A Kleinian and a Jungian might disagree about which experiences in the analysand's earlier life were of the greatest importance. But, it may be objected, is this indeterminacy of interpretation not also to be found in natural science? After all, there are, at any time, unsettled disputes within science where rival theories may seem equally plausible. The difference is, of course, that truth is a goal of science; we seek to resolve a dispute between rival theories by improved experimentation, improved theory or both. The existence of rival theories is a matter for regret rather than a testimony to the richness of the object. Admittedly, there may be propositions within a science to which no 'facts' correspond; the choice of a space geometry may always be a matter of convenience, for example, and there may be no way of choosing on the basis of the falsification of one rival. But we are speaking of broad analogies and disanalogies here and at this level the point holds.

For Freud, judgements about the mind are always determinate. He was a Realist. With the scientific model came the conviction that such judgements were either true or false regardless of our capacity to discover the facts. From what we have said about the multiplicity of possible interpretations, it is clear that any thinker who believes that the mind is the object of interpretation rather than of explanation finds himself pushed towards a non-Realist indeterminacy in this area.

The indeterminacy of the mental is a highly fashionable doctrine which can be taken in a number of ways, not all of which exclude one another: the best known relates it to Davidsonian holism (Davidson 1984: esp. 154); here the attribution of any mental predicate to a person is internally related to a whole galaxy of desires, intentions, responses and beliefs; the upshot is that it is never conclusively established where our commitments stop once we ascribe a mental state. Now in most cases the criteria for the attribution are clearly satisfiable; but in a minority of cases it may not be clear whether this is a case of one mental state rather than another.

At this point it is necessary to distinguish two cases. On the one hand there is the case which allows that there is a right answer though we may be never able to tell what it is. This form of realism is familiar in hermeneutics in the writings of literary theorists like Hirsch and Juhl. Indeterminacy proper, however, takes the view that no truth as to the matter exists independently of what we have available to us and this seems close to Dilman's position and agrees with the ideas of Schafer on the subject.

As I have said already, I do not think Freud could have conceded such indeterminacy, for he must claim that there is a lower level of mental structure causally connected with behaviour such that it either is or is not true that the neurotic condition is created by certain concurrent wishes in the unconscious to which the agent was not privy. The analogy he draws between the practice of psychoanalysis and the solution of a jigsaw puzzle emphasizes the uniqueness of the solution he expected (see S.E. 1937, XXIII: 257–69). Now, commonsense cases of unconsciously motivated behaviour do not need metapsychological assumptions about the structure of mental life. Imagine a woman, for instance, who smashes a vase 'by accident', a vase that was a present from her husband whom she has just discovered in adultery. If she eyed it with some chagrin before and if she is usually careful we have most of what we needed to conclude that the smashing was motivated, albeit unconsciously. We do not need the apparatus of ego, super-ego and id to draw this conclusion; this is an example of what is sometimes called the pre-theoretical unconscious. Folk-psychology is full of such cases. Now if the signs are less clearcut than in our example, if she did not think about the vase beforehand, for instance, then it is reasonable to conclude that there is no answer as to whether the accident was or was not motivated. Such cases, like cases of self-deception, are not 'about' anything more than the sheer complex of human behaviour and judgements of these cases may be indeterminate in either way. They will certainly be indeterminate, on this theory, in the sense that there is no underlying pattern of mental events with which their judgement corresponds or fails to correspond and they may be indeterminate in the sense that no correct answer exists to a question about their truth.

This brings us to a second mark of interpretation, the matter of selective emphasis. So far we have noted that interpretations are not fully controlled by the facts. Equally they rely on picking out salient elements in the patient's recollections of his past (what the psychoanalyst Joseph Sandler calls 'hot spots'). On these the analyst constructs his own pictured history of the patient's difficulties. We speak of a narrative here; Schafer insists that the analyst's job is to construct narratives which rival and will replace the patient's narrative. Patient and analyst offer rival histories. However, since the analyst is reliant upon what the patient tells him, his narrative stands in a relationship at once dependent and critical to the narrative given by the analysand. As I have argued elsewhere, the analyst may not only give a different significance to what the patient says; he may actually rearrange the priorities; what the patient passed over as of little importance in his story may be given great prominence in the analyst's and vice versa. There is what structuralists would call a change in foregrounding and Freudians a correction of displacement.

But how is this selection different from that of the scientist? He chooses a field of study. One scientist may account for the location of certain rocks whilst another examines their molecular structure. We might say that the two theories select different aspects of the facts for consideration. But for this precise reason they cease to be rivals whereas two accounts of a play, one of which sees it as a parable and a second as a defence of scepticism, remain rival accounts even though the two interpretations originate from different selective emphases. One takes certain speeches or a certain part of the plot as salient, the other another, and each might claim that they have picked out the most important features of the play.

On my account, the analyst is much like a historiographer. He examines an existing attempt to interpret the past by the patient. We can find, as we see, analogies in the arts. I may misunderstand a novel. A more acute critic helps me to understand either by showing me the real significance of events in the work whose point I have failed to grasp or by drawing attention to episodes I have simply missed. Whilst writing this chapter I went to see the *Sleeping Beauty* ballet for the first time. Perhaps because I saw it in a Freudian frame of mind, I took the ballet as being about sexual awakening, about the attempts of the King and Queen (Father and Mother, naturally) to prevent the Princess growing up, and I understood the pricking of the finger as the first menstruation. Ripe for sexual experience, she sleeps until awakened by the Prince's kiss. This is all very obvious, of course. My point is that even here a selection of elements which the interpreter takes to be of significance is the first step. We will not reach such an interpretation if we think that the climax of the ballet is the arrival of Puss-in-Boots.

There are two further defining marks of interpretation. Firstly, the objects of interpretation are single; secondly, the phenomena in question are the products of intentional action. These claims are not without controversy but are not, I think, central to the present argument, so I will be brief.

Objects of interpretation are singular. Of course, an interpretation that is both valid and illuminating, which both encapsulates all the foregrounded elements and which enhances our experience of the work, may still illuminate another and quite distinct work, but this is, at best, a lucky accident. Objects of interpretation, whether they be persons, works of art, cultures or historical periods, do not fall into classes which can be interpreted in a standard way for all members of the class. In an attempt to counter the claim that the objects of a hermeneutic inquiry are unlike those of natural science in being unique, Grünbaum (1984: 35) instances an earthquake.[2] This is a single event. Nothing just like it may have occurred before or since; the precise geological structure which led to it and in virtue of which it has the causal consequences it does may be unique. What we can say, however, is that the closer another earthquake is to it in precise configuration, the more likely its cause will have the same character. Like cause, like effect. This does not apply in cases of interpretation. From the fact that two different cultures have the same apparent phenomenon it does not follow that they must be explained and interpreted in the same way. Amongst the Indians of North-West America prestige may be acquired by the deliberate destruction of property; Mauss describes it as destroying in order to give the impression that one has no desire to receive anything back. But when a neighbour of my father-in-law deliberately smashed the windows of his bungalow in frustration at the repossession of a houshold item by bailiffs, he did not acquire prestige nor did he seek to. Gloucestershire does not have potlatch ceremonies.

Although superficially the action was very similar, its sense or meaning was quite different. He merely displayed an irrational lack of self-control. Again, the *Mona Lisa* and its very many copies and parodies are as similar as works of art may be; yet what the art historian says about them will be very different.

Finally, the objects of interpretation are the products of intentional action. This holds even though the features which may be of particular interest in any one interpretation are themselves unforeseen and unintended consequences of an action. It is merely required that the initial action be intentional. So the task of the interpreter of a work of art may include bringing to light all sorts of features of a work which the author was not even aware of having produced. Manifestly this holds for psychoanalysis; indeed, one of Schafer's theses is that the task of the analyst is so to enlarge the scope of agency that what was previously thought not to be a matter of agency is shown to be. Perhaps the most telling point here is that if an object or an event were not the product of intentional action the physical explanation would remain the same. We could still cite the various muscular movements and nervous stimuli. But it would not remain a candidate for interpretation.

My aim is to raise two problems for an interpretative or, to follow Roy Schafer's usage, a 'narrative' approach to psychoanalysis (Schafer 1980b). First of all, how can we reconcile this approach with the causal form which analyses commonly take? Analyses, after all, also give an account of the course of an illness; they give its aetiology. The problem is that a causal story seems to invite the very scientific paradigm which we have rejected. The second problem derives especially from Roy Schafer's presentation of analysis as the construction of narratives. Now, Schafer sees the analyst as presenting an alternative to the analysand's own narrative of the course of his life. Furthermore, in keeping with what many writers say about interpretation, he believes that many interpretations are possible of any particular case history. The problem is that many patients quite character-istically feel a sense of unfreedom; they cannot help doing the things they do; the neurotic rituals are compulsive. Now, how can the conquering of such compulsive rituals simply depend upon the mere exchange of one story for another, particularly if the choice between many of these stories is arbitrary? Once again a reasonable account of what is going on seems to require that there is a causal determination of the actions of the neurotic which can only be changed by altering the causal origins of his behaviour. If this is true, must not there be a single correct narrative which recapitulates these causal connections? Neurotic rituals are the most dramatic of these unfree actions. Take the Rat Man's famous nocturnal ritual for example. If we are free to form what narratives we like, then we ought to be able to choose freely between a narrative which, on the one hand, exhibits these actions and omissions as unfree, behaviour which the agents cannot really control, and a second narrative which presents them as a freely chosen response to pressures upon him. If there is no correct answer and if the narrative does not match the way the world is, then the impression of compulsion is an illusion. There is no reason why he should not take up his bed and walk. For whether or not he is free is narrative-relative and by choosing another narrative he can view his actions as free. Otherwise therapy cannot be effective.

II

So far then we have some idea of the competing merits and demerits of the scientistic and hermeneutic approaches. To some extent I have already disclosed my hand; in this section I shall say more about the reasons for rejecting Freudian essentialism.

What possible objections can be given for rejecting an essentialist ontology of subprocesses? First of all, such an ontology raises problems of identity and individuation. For example, weakness of will is on this theory naturally explained in terms of two competing agencies within the person. But such a move too easily collapses akrasia into something much more like conflict between rival agencies or homunculi and conflict is not weakness of will. Parallel considerations apply to the closely related problem of self-deception. What was, originally, a claim about the deceiving of a person by that same person becomes a form of deception of others. I do not want to overstress the probative force of these objections as I have stated them here. It is rather that I think there are serious difficulties about how certain familiar and characteristic features of human beings can be described in terms of this theory. A second problem is the problem of multiplication of entities; just how many entities have we within us? Why should we stop at three? Why not specify an agent for each desire? The advocate of an essentialist metapsychology needs to give some reasons why we need precisely the number of subagents we have. So far as I know, no reason has been given. A third objection is that there is no call to multiply entities when a straightforward account can be given of the phenomena without such recourse. The deeper question is why our concept of mind is not spatial. Why is there this fact of grammar? Why cannot we say that one thought is above, below or to the right of another? Why is it that my memory of Vienna is not spatially related to my memory of London? We could, after all, make changes in the concept of imagining and remembering so that spatial predicates could be applied to thoughts in a way similar to physical objects. Wollheim (1974), in fact, thinks that this is already so, but this is, no doubt, connected with his Freudianism. He believes that our mental concepts are 'tinged with spatiality'. The first two objections, as I conceded, are not conclusive. The problems of identity can be circumvented by distinguishing elements within an individual as opposed to the macroscopic forms of identity of the person, and the charge of arbitrariness in identifying subagents is not a telling objection. But the model of spatiality is more problematic.

The deeper reason for rejecting the systematic model is one which philosophers have not much articulated. It is the requirement that our ontology match our form of understanding. I shall suggest in the next section that our form of understanding of the person is paratactic and sequential. Our mode of understanding is based on temporally succeeding states, whereas the mode of explanation of why physical objects react one with another in the way they do is based on the idea that they have a generating internal physical constitution. This latter idea as to the norm of explanation may be recent but it certainly dominates and equally certainly was Freud's model. He probably could not think of understanding in other terms.

The idea of real essences matches a form of inquiry where we literally look into things. What goes on under the skin or under the surface quite literally determines what happens on the surface. But this is not an intelligible model of how we understand mental life. It seems that we understand people, to use John Wisdom's phrase which Dilman quotes, in terms of 'patterns in time'. The same form of objection must apply to other theories about the mental such as Fodor's theory of mental representation, if it is to match the manner of our understanding persons.

Earlier I concurred with Schafer's description of psychoanalysis as the construction of a narrative by the analyst which replaces the patient's own narrative. The analyst also has to persuade the patient to accept the new analysis. If analysis ever has any therapeutic force, then this seems to depend upon the analysis being correct and this surely flies in the face of what has been said about the indeterminacy of the mental and about the indeterminacy of interpretation. Our thesis was that no sense can be attached to which out of a range of alternatives is true, though we did not preclude interpretations being shown to be false. But is it necessary for an interpretation to be true for it to be effective in therapy? The problem of the effectiveness of therapy is one of the most familiar of philosophical incursions into psychoanalysis. But Grünbaum (1984) and Farrell (1981) regard what effectiveness it has as a matter of the placebo effect. So in solving the second of the two unanswered questions left at the end of the last section, I shall try to give a rationale for the placebo effect. What I propose here is an account of why it is successful when it is; one way of putting it is to say that I try to give an explanation for the placebo effect, arguing that analysts ought not to be worried about conceding the truth of the charge. With some trepidation I shall try to sketch an account which shows how the patient accepts the analysis and how the illusion of determinacy is created.

There is, after all, no special reason to suppose that an ideological or religious conversion that enables a man to make sense of his life, that recognizes as important what he feels to be important, which only demands of him those things which he can achieve, which gives him the moderate self-esteem and the mutual support of people he admires, is of necessity a conversion to a set of true doctrines. That there is balm in Gilead does not have to be true any more than we should think that a plausible interpretation of a fiction is true. There are two aspects of this which need to be drawn out. Firstly, at a rather banal level, there is an assumption common in psychodynamics and that is that the past influences the present. In the terminology of Grünbaum, we do assume that 'pathogens' exist. Successful therapy, however, does not, on this story, require that the pathogens are identified with any degree of precision.[3] It is merely required that the narrative which replaces the original redresses the emphases placed upon the pathogen and it can do this simply by relegating to comparative insignificance a sector of the analysand's past which contains that experience.

The second is that a sharp distinction between folk-psychological or pre-theoretical notions of the unconscious and the more theoretical understanding becomes untenable. By our account of their pasts we can change people's conception of themselves and this may involve a degree of theory. The picture of man as an economic animal whose prime motivation is economic self-interest has undoubtedly changed human behaviour. To say that it is false is not to say that there are no instances but rather to say that such a picture of man does not answer to his possibilities and to what makes for a satisfying life. Similarly, when somebody is offered a Freudian narrative of his life, by changing his picture of himself we may also change his behaviour so that we create an identity in the course of trying to describe it.

If somebody accepts the proffered narrative it now becomes the case that what he views as significant about his past changes. He may be right or wrong about its causal role in bringing about the trauma which caused him to seek help in the first place, but if the new significance which a previously displaced memory creates also brings with it its own network of causal interconnections then there is no gap between his estimate of significance and the actual significance of these events. We deny space to the Realist contrast between surface and reality. The superficies are all there are.

Another way of making the point is to point out that, when the patient accepts a narrative, he immediately embarks on a convergence between that narrative and the course of his life. The pictures we have of our life and the ranking of memories go in part to make up that life. Just as displacement is a feature of his attention, so is its correction. So there is a sense, after all, in which interpretations may converge on determinacy and that is through the acceptance of the patient. The claim of various theorists from Freud to Fenichel that the criterion of truth in analysis is the patient's acceptance of that analysis has often been criticized; there is no doubt that many analysts are dominating individuals who reinforce any signs of agreement by the patient. But from this hermeneutic perspective the criterion of acceptance can be seen rather as an oblique way of making the point that no gap need occur between the accuracy of an analysis and its acceptance by the patient. The subsidiary lesson is that one parallel between art and mind disappears. For we can have nothing very close to the contrived determinacy of interpretation in the case of art. The parallel would have to require that the work of art somehow reformed to mirror the selective emphasis given by the interpreter. Of course, the view of the work taken by the victims of the persuasive interpreter might well change but that does not give us the analogy at the level we require.

III

In a famous book, M. H. Abrams (1953: 57ff) contrasted two views of the mind, the mind as mirror and the mind as lamp: he took the former to exemplify the eighteenth-century view of the mind and the latter, the Romantic. Both of these use models of the mind drawn from perception, light and the visual world; sometimes the mind is seen as an internal theatre. Naturally scholars immediately set about pointing out the numbers of Romantic writers who speak of mirrors and the pre-Romantics who use the metaphor of the lamp. For mirror and lamp Freud substituted the model of an organism with a functional relationship between its parts and with homeostatic properties. Now, through Lacan, Ricoeur and others, the Freudian model has itself been superseded by the image of the mind as text.

This model, of course, invites the hermeneutic approach. But at the forefront of my mind in this chapter has been a stronger form of interpretation than that involved in merely understanding the meaning of behaviour, intentions, desires and thoughts. The emphasis I have placed on selection and foregrounding connects with a view of interpretation as paratactic. According to Cullers (1983: 43) whilst Barthes was in a sanatorium recovering from TB he amused himself by cutting up a text of Michelet into little segments which he then rearranged so as to reveal 'themes'.[4] Nothing better exemplifies the initial procedure of the interpreter. Before he can identify themes in a play or a novel he must select and this act of foregrounding, as the Prague structuralists called it, is the prolegomena to a new act of metalinguistic redescription which incorporates these 'lexia' in a new and coherent whole. Parataxis is followed by syntaxis.

So let us return to the analyst. He listens to what the patient says and, from the narrative the patient offers, he selects. What strikes him as salient may be what the patient regards as salient or it may not. Either way he may give it a significance of which the patient was himself unaware. The paratactic organization involves, as I have hinted, the interpretation of an existing interpretation, namely the patient's own view of his past. Schafer thinks of this as something uniquely characterizing psychoanalysis. This is not so. The historian, too, uses sources which are already narratives. Indeed Freud himself was aware of the analogy. Of the early history of a nation he writes 'many things had been dropped from the nation's memory, while others were distorted and some remains of the past were given a wrong interpretation in order to fit in with contemporary ideas' (Freud 1963: 119). Recent theoretical work on fiction, for example Wayne Booth's *The Rhetoric of Fiction*, shows that the situation with respect to fiction is not so different. We do not necessarily think of the narrator as an all-seeing eye and, if we do feel that this is part of the convention of a particular fiction, we are still aware of alternatives. The narrator may be jaundiced, ironic or even deceived. The narrator Erich in Marguerite Yourcenar's superb novella *Coup de Grace* may be, as the author says in her foreword, self-deceived. Ostensibly, this is the story of a man, the narrator, who is loved passionately by a woman to whom he is indifferent and upon whom she eventually avenges herself. The narrator is surely more jealous of her rather sordid liaisons than he appears to be; vanity occludes his own narrative. Might we say that the possible world of the fiction is different from the way it is portrayed? The point is that the interpreter handles a narrative which is already an account, a narrative of a fictional world by the narrator, much as the analyst handles an existing narrative, the analysand's view of his past.

The moral of this is that those thinkers who have found the model of the text a more persuasive model of the mind than the fashions of bygone years have not really grasped the full implications. The appropriate form of interpretation is what we can call 'deep' interpretation and this is not merely a matter of applying the categories of 'meaning' and 'significance'; it involves a much more complex work of attention and analysis in parataxis and reformatory syntaxis.

IV

Armed with these reflections I now return to the problems I set myself earlier. First of all the causal question: Can we square a narrative view of psychoanalysis with the recognition that it describes causal connections within the life of the person? Now the point about a trauma is that it has its causal force because the person who suffers it describes the occurrence in a certain way. The mode of individuation here is essential. We may compare it with what holds in ordinary commonplace action. For an opportunity to be an opportunity for me to do something in particular I have to recognize it as an opportunity and this means that I describe the event to myself in certain terms. Now to do this makes the causal force dependent on a particular form of individuation. Equally the analysand has to see his own past in a certain way if it is to be causally efficacious.[5] By the same token, if the analyst is to change the present behaviour of his patient he must reveal the possibility of so describing the original event that it loses its causal force. To understand *may* help us to control. This connects with my second problem, the question of the unfreedom of the neurotic.

The neurotic may have a range of compulsive actions which he cannot help. Not only is there a puzzle about redescription here but it is not clear how redescription can empower the agent to refrain from some neurotic ritual which previously he could not avoid. Tics, grimaces, etc. are merely the relatively harmless end of this particular spectrum. There are some extraordinarily complicated rituals in the literature. My remarks on this are sketchy. I am inclined to think that the necessity is relative to a particular mode of narrative. A neurotic cannot see that other accounts of his behaviour are possible. It is as though he or she can only arrange the facts of the past in one particular way. It is, I suppose, commonplace that amongst such people a relatively trifling misdemeanour or a small *faux pas* may cause untold misery. His narrative of his past centres on these; he thinks of it as of crucial and salient importance and behaves by reference to it. Now, if the analyst persuades him that it is a peccadillo which needs to be relegated to the periphery, its causal powers are much reduced and his life can take on another form. The causal force of these events depends upon the descriptions the sufferer gives of these. We may neutralize them by getting him to see them in another way.

The received wisdom has been that causality is extensional. It is not so in the life of the person and once this is recognized, we are on the way to a clearer vision of how causal connections are narrative-dependent in the human mind.

I shall close with a quotation from Wittgenstein which I came across after writing this chapter. It describes with extraordinary prescience the paratactic procedure identified in Barthes, and, I think, exemplifies the enormous range of Wittgenstein's ideas, too wide-ranging to be imprisoned in any of the pictures which commentators conventionally offer us.

In Freudian analysis a dream is dismantled, as it were. It loses its original sense *completely*. We might think of it as of a play enacted on the stage, with a plot that's pretty incomprehensible at times, but at times too quite intelligible, or apparently so; we might then suppose this plot torn into little fragments and each of these given a completely new sense. Or we might think of it in the following way: a picture is drawn on a big sheet of paper which is then so folded that pieces which don't belong together at all in the original picture now appear side to side to form a new picture, which may or may not make sense. (This latter would correspond to the manifest dream, the original picture to the 'latent dream thought'.)

(Wittgenstein 1980: 68)

NOTES

1   Schafer has written extensively elsewhere of this approach. Stephen Marcus (1976) illuminatingly treats Freudian case studies as examples of narrative art.
2   Grünbaum argues here that the application of psychoanalysis to single cases does not differ from the application of physical principles to single cases. See my critical discussion (Sharpe 1986).
3   Worth comparing this with the similar claim made by James Strachey in his very influential paper (1969).
4   It does seem that this paratactic procedure is a modernist aspect of the arts. Thus, though our predecessors created art which responds to this form of analysis, they presumably could not have had it in mind. It is the fractured nature of the narrative that leads Stephen Marcus to treat Freud as a modernist writer.
5   For Freud this is a matter of rendering the unconscious conscious. Do we, at this point, need to reintroduce the metapsychology? I would be inclined to argue, along with Dilman, I suspect, that at this point folk-psychology can do most of the work. That is, we can manage with those elements in Freudian psychology encapsulated in the ideas of repression, displacement and

resistance, ideas which he largely takes over from common sense. The theory of personality development, transference, repetition, compulsion, and of multiple agency within the psyche I take to be more or less speculative aspects of psychoanalysis which will only become applicable to cases as we internalize and mimic Freudian stereotypes, consciously or unconsciously.

REFERENCES

Abrams, M. H. 1953: *The Mirror and the Lamp*. Oxford.
Booth, W. 1961: *The Rhetoric of Fiction*. Chicago.
Cullers, J. 1983: *Barthes*. London.
Davidson, D. 1984: Radical interpretation, in E. Lepore (ed.), *Truth and Interpretation*. Oxford.
Farrell, B. A. 1981: *The Standing of Psychoanalysis*. New York.
Freud, S. 1963: *Leonardo*. Harmondsworth.
Grünbaum, A. 1984: *The Foundations of Psychoanalysis: A Philosophical Critique*. Berkeley, Calif.
Hartmann, H. 1958: *Ego Psychology and Adaptation*. London.
Kohut, H. 1981: *Analysis of the Self*. London.
Marcus, S. 1976: Freud and Dora: story, history, case history, in *Representations: Essays on Literature and Society*. London.
Pears, D. 1984: *Motivated Irrationality*. Oxford.
Schafer, R. 1980a: *Action and Narrative in Psychoanalysis*. New Literary History, vol. 12.
Schafer, R. 1980b: Narration in the psychoanalytical dialogue. *Critical Inquiry*. Autumn.
Sharpe, R. 1986: Psychoanalysis: science or insight. *Inquiry*, 29, 121–32.
Strachey, J. 1969: The nature of the therapeutic action of psychoanalysis. *International Journal of Psycho-Analysis*, 50, 287.
Sulloway, F. J. 1980: *Freud: Biologist of the Mind*. London.
Wittgenstein, L. 1980: *Culture and Value*, trans. P. Winch. Oxford.
Wollheim, R. 1974: The mind and the mind's image of itself, in *On Art and the Mind*. Cambridge, Mass.
Yourcenar, M. 1957: *Coup de Grace*. F.S.N.G.

PART FOUR

Psychoanalysis:
Its Evidential Support

9

Psychoanalysis: Clinical versus Experimental Evidence

EDWARD ERWIN

Two developments appear to have brightened the outlook for placing psychoanalysis on a firm scientific foundation. First, some leading methodologists have argued that causal hypotheses, and, in particular, *psychoanalytic* causal hypotheses, can be confirmed in a clinical setting. This would appear to support Freud's view that extraclinical, experimental study is unnecessary. Second, it has been argued that experimental results have now confirmed significant parts of Freudian theory.

I want to comment on these developments, beginning with the methodological arguments.

CASE STUDIES

Can uncontrolled case studies confirm non-trivial causal hypotheses? Many behaviour therapists and experimental psychologists and some philosophers of science would answer 'no'. For example, Ernet Nagel, in his classic (1959) paper on psychoanalysis, points out that use of a control group is a minimum requirement for providing cogent evidence for a causal inference. Nagel might wish to qualify his position if he were writing about the same topic today, but many reviewers of behaviour therapy outcome literature seem to agree with his point in so far as they routinely dismiss studies without a control group as having, at best, heuristic value. Even some writers sympathetic to psychoanalysis, such as

Fisher and Greenberg (1977: 15) make a blanket rejection of case reports on the grounds that there is no way to tell the good from the bad. I will refer to this view that uncontrolled case studies of non-trivial causal hypotheses are non-confirmatory as the 'sceptical view'.

How plausible this view is depends in part on what is meant by a 'nontrivial' causal hypothesis. I assume that the sceptics mean to exclude from their view such hypotheses as 'Striking the glass with the hammer caused the glass to shatter' or 'Cutting my finger with a knife caused bleeding'. They mean to include, mainly, two sorts of hypotheses: theoretical hypotheses, such as 'Phobias are caused by repressed wishes', and outcome hypotheses, such as 'This therapy produced this particular therapeutic benefit'. The sceptic need not question the logical possibility of clinical confirmation; he or she need only argue that in our world uncontrolled case studies lack the capacity for confirmation. Finally, the sceptic can allow that sometimes interesting causal claims can be *falsified* by a single case study. If I make a particularly strong causal claim that implies that in every case of disorder D, an observable characteristic, C, will be present, the failure to observe C in even one case might constitute strong disconfirming evidence for my hypothesis. The claim made by the sceptic, as I am construing his position, concerns only *confirmation*: in our world (as opposed to some possible world), uncontrolled case studies cannot confirm non-trivial causal hypotheses.

Even when restricted in the manner I have suggested, the sceptical view must face two sorts of counter-arguments that have been advanced recently. First, it has been argued that there are actual counter-examples of both a psychoanalytic and non-psychoanalytic type. Secondly, it has been argued that even if cases studies are generally not confirmatory, we can isolate the features that account for that fact and by modifying them make case studies confirmatory in the future.

Consider, first, some non-psychoanalytic counter-examples. In my book on behaviour therapy (Erwin 1978), I describe several cases of clinical confirmation of outcome hypotheses. The cases involve the use of electric shock to eliminate the self-destructive behaviour of autistic children. In each example, the child's problem behaviour was relatively stable prior to the introduction of the electric shock; the behavioural change was sudden and dramatic (e.g., in one case, the biting and headbanging of an autistic female ceased immediately after five brief shocks); and, given the cognitive deficits of the children, a placebo hypothesis was not credible. These cases may be isolated examples; and they may be different in kind from psychoanalytic case studies. However, if the behaviour therapy cases are genuine counter-examples, the psychoanalytic cases cannot be dismissed merely because they are case studies. An independent argument must be given. Furthermore, Paul Meehl, in a recent paper (1983), has presented two counter-examples of a psychoanalytic kind.

His first case concerns his experience as a patient while undergoing psychoanalytic training. While on his way to the University Hospital to see his analyst, Meehl saw a man and woman in their late thirties. The woman was weeping, and the husband and she looked troubled. The man carried a brown paper sack and a large Raggedy Ann doll. Seeing the doll and the couple's behaviour, and knowing that they were leaving the University Hospital, the thought occurred to Meehl that a child was very ill or possibly had just died. He then experienced a deep feeling of grief, and he began to weep uncontrollably. He continued weeping as he approached and then entered the analyst's office. The analyst, noticing his distraught state, asked him the following question: 'Were you harsh with Karen (Meehl's five-year-old daughter) this morning?' Meehl remembered that he had been, and the question was followed by an immediate and dramatic effect: the total cessation of the inner disturbed state and the weeping. Meehl writes (p. 356): 'I don't suppose anyone has experienced this kind of phenomenon in his own analysis without finding it one of the most striking direct behavioral and introspective evidences of the concepts of "mental conflict", "opposing psychic forces", and "unconscious influences" – the way in which a properly timed and formulated interpretation (sometimes!) produces an immediate dynamic and economic change, as the jargon has it.'

Meehl's second case involves a woman he treated for a full-blown physician phobia, which prevented her from having a needed physical examination for several years. The woman realized that her reaction was 'silly'; she attributed it to the psychic trauma she suffered after having a hysterectomy. After seventy-five or eighty sessions, Meehl inferred that, when the patient was a child, an examining physician had discovered that she had masturbated. In a later session, in which the patient had a fairly pronounced memory of the doctor's examining table, and intense anxiety as well as a feeling of nausea, she recalled, with only minimal assistance on Meehl's part, the physician's question about masturbation and her answer. The morning after his discovery, she made an appointment with a doctor (and apparently kept it). Meehl concludes: 'I think most fairminded persons would agree that it takes an unusual skeptical resistance for us to say that this step-function in clinical states was purely a suggestive effect, or a reassurance effect, or due to some other transference leverage or whatever (75th hour!) rather than that the remote memory was truly repressed and the lifting of repression efficacious' (1983: 358).

I think that many fair-minded persons would find Meehl's examples persuasive. I also agree that it is probably these kinds of clinical cases, where immediate and dramatic effects are observed, that persuade most Freudians. As Meehl notes, even the rare person who is familiar with the details of the Freudian experimental literature is not likely to be initially convinced by that literature; for most people, the case studies are of paramount significance. It continues to be important, then, despite the devastating criticisms of Grünbaum (1984) and others, to ask if psychoanalytic case studies either do or can have probative value. Concerning Meehl's examples, however, I side with the sceptics.

If Meehl is claiming evidential value for his clinical experiences, and not merely saying that, rightly or wrongly, they convinced him, then I disagree. I do not think that anyone *ought* to be convinced by either of his two cases.

The first case is interesting, but without further information, it is difficult to tell what caused Meehl's weeping or the subsequent abrupt change in his behaviour and affective state. I concede that it is plausible to speculate, as Meehl does, that his feeling bad, after scolding his daughter and not apologizing, contributed to his temporary emotional breakdown. When thinking about the death of the child visited by the couple, he might have been reminded of the mortality of his own daughter without consciously thinking of the scolding. However, this hardly shows that there was an 'unconscious influence' in the Freudian sense: namely, something that was not just in his preconscious but also could not enter consciousness without the help of psychoanalysis. Suppose that he had told his story to his wife and she had asked the analyst's question. Is it not possible, indeed likely, that Meehl would have remembered the scolding without the aid of analysis? Why, then, postulate 'unconscious influences' (in the Freudian sense) or 'opposing psychic forces'? He may have been influenced by something that he had temporarily forgotten, but *not* repressed, i.e. the scolding of his daughter. His abrupt regaining of his composure may be more difficult to explain, but it is difficult to explain even in psychoanalytic terms. Suppose we speak, as Meehl does later, of a sudden lifting of a repression; it is still not clear why a single question by an analyst would have such an immediate effect. If repressions were typically lifted that easily, psychoanalysis would not typically take two years or more. In addition, there are plausible rival hypotheses that cannot be ruled out without our having more information. By the time the incident occurred, Meehl was presumably already familiar with and sympathetic to psychoanalytic theory. When the analyst posed his question and Meehl remembered the scolding of his daughter, the following thought may have occurred to him: 'Yes, I *was* harsh with Karen; that is what caused my problem; now that I have had this insight, I should be able to control myself.' There are many other thoughts that might have occurred to him that could also have interfered with his weeping. Another factor of possible causal relevance is the presence of the analyst, whom Meehl may well have seen as an expert and as a figure with authority. The analyst, in effect, suggested to him that his problem had a simple solution – he had only to remember his mistreatment of his daughter – and then he should be able to regain control of himself. In the analytic setting, such a suggestion might have the right effect (the regaining of composure) whether or not any part of psychoanalytic theory is true.

I am also sceptical about Meehl's second example. Let us assume that Meehl's memory has not failed him at all and that his account of the case has omitted no crucial detail. Still, how do we know that the alleged cause of the phobia, the doctor's discovery of the child's masturbation, did occur? It was Meehl who first concluded that it did. How does he know that he did not subtly suggest to the patient that an event of this kind, or even the specific event, was at the root of her phobia? Even on the day she *seemed* to recall the doctor's questioning her about her masturbation, she did so with at least some assistance from Meehl. The patient herself, according to Meehl's account (p. 358), believed that *he* had implanted the memory; it was only later that she concluded that the 'remembered' event did occur. Second, and more importantly, even if the event did occur, what evidence is there that it played any causal role at all in her phobia? How do we rule out the possibility that the psychic trauma of the hysterectomy, which we know did occur, was sufficient to produce the phobia, and would have done so even in the absence of the childhood event? (The hysterectomy explanation may even be more plausible. If the childhood event caused the phobia, did the phobia exist before the hysterectomy? If it did, some explanation is needed as to how the patient managed to have the operation. Did she do so without having a prior examination?) Third, suppose it were true that an upsetting experience with a doctor in childhood was the cause of the phobia. There is still an unwarranted inferential leap in concluding that the experience was repressed and not simply forgotten. If one already assumes that repression is common in the aetiology of phobias, as Meehl presumably does, then the inference may seem plausible; however, if the evidence for the causal role of, and even the very existence of, repression is very weak then the inference is not warranted.

If Meehl's account of his case is not accepted, how can we explain the sudden and dramatic change in the patient? One plausible possibility is that a placebo-induced change occurred. Meehl (p. 358) points out that the patient came to believe that the early traumatic experience did lead to her phobia. After undergoing psychoanalysis for at least seventy-five sessions, she also presumably believed that discovering the root cause was likely to dissolve the phobia. It is not implausible to think that the patient became convinced, as the result of her seeming discovery, that she could now call her doctor and would not suffer great anxiety. This explanation fits with experimental data concerning the use of placebos in treating phobias (Lick 1975; Rosenthal 1980), even if the phobias in such studies are generally of a milder sort, and it does not require the several unwarranted assumptions crucial to Meehl's explanation.

The cases just discussed are of some interest if they are among the most powerful that Meehl could find after a long and distinguished career as both an analyst and an experimental psychologist, but the cogency of psychoanalytic clinical testing obviously does not depend on the soundness of these two examples. We need to ask if there are general features of psychoanalytic case studies that make them unsuitable as vehicles of confirmation. We can begin with a more basic question: What features generally make case studies of *any* sort non-confirmatory?

Alan Kazdin, a leading methodologist and behaviour therapist, has proposed (1981) that five characteristics generally account for the evidential weaknesses of case studies. The first is the use of anecdotal reports, such as the client's or therapist's uncorroborated assertion that improvement has taken place. Kazdin regards this feature as being perhaps the most important obstacle to drawing causal inferences. We obviously cannot establish that X caused Y in a given case unless we establish that Y occurred. It might also be added that, given the tendency of some eclectic clinicians to mix ingredients from various therapies, firm evidence is also needed that a particular therapy, X, was used, if our hypothesis is about X. If we rely on only anecdotal evidence, we may not know if either alleged cause or effect was present.

A second weakness of many case studies is the use of one-shot or two-shot assessments (e.g. post-treatment only or pre-treatment and post-treatment). With only one or two assessments, there is an increased difficulty in ruling out the possibility that change resulted from testing rather than treatment.

A third problematic feature of some case studies is that the problem being treated is either acute or episodic. Without experimental controls, it is more difficult in such cases to rule out the possibility that extraneous features caused any improvement. For example, if the subject is depressed some months and not others, and improves after a brief treatment, the change might well have occurred even if there had been no treatment. In contrast, it is more difficult to explain the elimination of a long-term, stable problem after brief treatment without appealing to the effects of the therapy.

A fourth feature is the presence of gradual, weak effects. Such effects are easier to explain in terms of a spontaneous remission hypothesis, or some other rival hypothesis, compared to effects that are sudden and dramatic (so-called 'slam-bang' effects).

The fifth weakness, which is present in every 'single-subject' case study, is that it involves only one subject. This feature is often taken to be relevant primarily to external validity – How do we know that what worked with one subject will work with another? – but it is also relevant to internal validity. If the event Y follows the same putative cause, X, in a number of subsequent cases, and the cases are varied in relevant respects, we may have more right to be confident that, in the first case, X and Y were causally connected.

Kazdin points out that, to some extent, the epistemic weaknesses of case studies can be eliminated without transforming such studies into experiments. For example, a therapist can collect objective data in place of anecdotal information, assess performance on several occasions rather than one, and accumulate a number of cases that are treated and assessed in a similar fashion. Where these things are done, and a relatively stable problem is being treated and slam-bang effects are observed, it may be possible to support a causal inference. A group design using a control group would then be unnecessary. If the changes Kazdin recommends are feasible, and can be made in the psychoanalytic setting, then even if the existing body of psychoanalytic case studies is of little value, future confirmation of Freudian theory may come from certain types of uncontrolled clinical case studies. Kazdin takes no stand on the possibility of shaping up psychoanalytic case studies, but Marshall Edelson (1984) has recently claimed that this can and should be done.

Here again, however, I side with the sceptics. I see at least three problems. First, I think Kazdin's list of epistemic defects is incomplete. Second, I think that it is generally not possible to eliminate the most important epistemic defects of case studies. Third, I think that there are special features of both psychoanalytic hypotheses and the psychoanalytic clinical setting that make clinical confirmation much more difficult for Freud's hypotheses than for many non-Freudian views.

As to the first point, I think we need to add to Kazdin's list of defects the presence of so-called 'placebo factors'. These include those factors in the therapeutic situation that are not part of the therapy and which could reasonably be held to account for therapeutic improvement and for certain other changes in the client. One such factor, of course, is the patient's expectation of being helped. There have been a number of studies in which clients received a credible pseudo-therapy and improved as much as clients in the treatment group and more than those receiving no treatment of any kind. For example, subjects in the Brill et al. (1964) study who received a pill placebo showed about the same amount of improvement as those in the psychoanalytically oriented treatment group. Even if a placebo treatment is not used, the simple act of making periodic contact with patients can result in considerable improvement, as occurred in the Sloane et al. (1975) study. In fact, Jerome Frank (1983) reports that in his placebo studies many patients experienced a marked drop in systematic distress following the initial interviews and *before* the placebo treatment even began. There are, then, several factors besides spontaneous remission that may plausibly explain treatment outcome as well as certain other changes in the client: these include the belief that one is receiving an effective treatment, the expectation that one will soon receive such a treatment, the decision to enter therapy and do something about one's problem, contact with the therapist, and the opportunity in the initial interview to discuss one's problem with another person.

Kazdin may have chosen not to discuss placebo factors because he does not regard them as barriers to causal inferences. In a footnote (1981: 186), he points out that the aspects of treatment that caused change in experimentation is not a question of internal validity but of construct validity. He also speaks of 'all that the treatment encompassed' (p. 186) and may be defining this notion broadly to include placebo factors. His point, then, may be this: if placebo factors are part of the therapy, then we need not rule out their influence in order to infer that the therapy was effective; we need only rule them out if we are interested in construct validity – i.e., if we are trying to determine that particular ingredients of the therapy and not others accounted for the change.

Even if Kazdin is not including placebo factors as part of a therapy, several other researchers have recently argued that placebo factors need not be controlled in deciding if a therapy is effective. For example, Cordray and Bootzin (1983) argue that placebo manipulations are important only in deciding *how* a therapy works; a therapy may still be effective, they say, even if it works only because of placebo factors. Jerome Frank (1983) takes a similar position; he holds that a placebo treatment *is* psychotherapy. In a paper in the *American Psychologist*, Critelli and Neuman (1984) distinguish between therapeutic effectiveness and what they called 'incremental' effectiveness. To establish therapeutic effectiveness, they claim, it is not necessary to show that the therapy is more effective than a placebo; that is only required if one is interested in incremental effectiveness.

For certain factors, I agree with these writers; I think it *is* plausible to say that a treatment is effective even if it works only because of placebo factors. For example, suppose that a treatment causes a change in the expectations of my client and that this change, in turn, causes improvement. I would agree that the treatment was effective and that it worked by altering the expectations of the client. However, some placebo factors, such as the client's decision to enter therapy and the initial interview, precede the start of the therapy; consequently, if they alone caused the change, then the therapy did not. A more important point, however, is this: if placebo factors are included as part of the therapy or are postulated as the sole mechanism through which the therapy works, then one runs the risk of trivializing the causal hypothesis that is being tested. For example, suppose that psychoanalysis is effective with certain patients, but only because they believe that they are receiving an effective treatment. We can say that the therapy is effective with these patients, but the claim is rather trivial if the same results could be achieved by any treatment that the patient had confidence in. Why use such an expensive, long-term treatment if the same results could be obtained through use of a sugar pill or one of the simple pseudo-therapies used in many studies of behaviour therapy? The claim of effectiveness – if it does not mean *more effective than a placebo* – is even less helpful if one is interested in defending Freudian theory. If a change occurred only because of placebo factors, then Freudian theory does not correctly explain why it occurred. I conclude, then, that if we are interested in Freudian theory or therapy, then we must include placebo factors as threats to internal validity. These factors are sources of hypotheses that are likely to rival non-trivial Freudian causal hypotheses and must be ruled out. I now turn to my second point, concerning the possibility of modifying case studies.

I agree with Kazdin that a study should not be dismissed as evidentially worthless merely because it is a case study, and that some things can be done to improve the quality of case studies. I do not think, however, and Kazdin may agree with this point, that very many clinical case studies can be improved to the point that all credible rival hypotheses can be ruled out except the causal hypothesis of interest. As Kazdin notes, we can introduce objective measures, make several assessments, and add together a number of cases of comparable treatment. However, in most cases, these changes will be necessary but not sufficient for ruling out all credible alternative hypotheses. If the other two factors that Kazdin mentions are missing, namely, a stable problem and immediate dramatic effects, it is likely that rival hypotheses will remain. However, as Kazdin notes, these two elements are normally outside the control of the investigator. If the problem being studied is a stable one and the treatment has no immediate or dramatic effect, then the investigator cannot normally alter these facts without changing the research problem. If we include placebo factors as additional sources of rival hypotheses, then the outlook for shaping up case studies is even bleaker. Such factors may not be important in a few isolated cases, such as in the treatment of autistic children, but in most case studies in clinical psychology and psychiatry, they are quite important. It is difficult to see how they can be eliminated as potential confounds unless we use a credible placebo treatment or some alternative, such as a component control design; if we introduce a control condition, however, then we no longer have an uncontrolled case study.

My third point is that even if case studies could be tidied up, using them to confirm *psychoanalytic* causal hypotheses raises additional problems. As is well known, and as I shall illustrate shortly, these hypotheses are extremely difficult to confirm even if experimental controls are introduced. It may be possible for a case study to confirm an outcome hypothesis about a simple behaviour therapy technique, such as the use of five electric shocks in a single session, but that is a weak reason for thinking that a case study can suffice for a complex procedure such as psychoanalysis, which normally takes two years or more to complete. Confirming Freud's *theoretical* hypotheses can be even more difficult; for they talk about events and processes that cannot be observed and, in some cases, occurred in the patient's distant past. I am not suggesting that the testing of such hypotheses is logically impossible, but rather that we should not infer that they can be confirmed without experimentation merely from the fact that clinical testing of some simple behaviour therapy hypotheses is possible in a few isolated cases. Finally, apart from the nature of the hypotheses, there is another important difference between the use of shock with autistic children and the use of psychoanalysis with neurotic patients. The latter situation is rife with suggestibility factors, as Professor Grünbaum has demonstrated in great detail (Grünbaum 1984), that contaminate the very data of psychoanalysis – the patient's dream reports, free associations and slips of the tongue – and engender numerous rival hypotheses that are difficult to defeat without the use of experimental controls. The psychoanalytic setting is not unique in this respect, but it is clearly different from the situation in which an autistic child's behaviour is modified in one or two sessions.

In short, I do not think that recent developments in single-subject research methodology should encourage the idea that uncontrolled case studies can be generally modified to make them suitable for confirming psychoanalytic hypotheses. First, placebo factors should be included along with the stability of a problem and weak, gradual effects as general epistemic liabilities in case studies. Second, it is normally beyond the power of an investigator to eliminate these features without introducing experimental controls. Third, there are special features of both the psychoanalytic clinical setting and psychoanalytic hypotheses that make confirmation by case study especially difficult for psychoanalysis. So, I disagree with the sceptic who denies the very possibility of uncontrolled clinical confirmation of causal hypotheses. The cases of the autistic children are counter-examples to that view. However, I remain sceptical about both the actuality and possibility of non-experimental confirmation of psychoanalytic causal views. I agree, in short, that the vindication of Freudianism requires sound and extensive experimentation.

Someone might argue, however, that experimentation is possible in the clinical setting. Marshall Edelson (1984), in fact, has claimed that single-subject experimental designs of the type used in behaviour therapy research can be used to confirm Freud's views in a psychoanalytic setting. This claim raises a different issue, given that I have been discussing only *non-experimental* research. However, I do have two brief comments. First, we cannot reasonably infer from the limited success of behaviour therapists that psychoanalysts will also be successful in using single-subject designs. As noted earlier, there are important differences between behaviour therapy outcome hypotheses and psychoanalytic causal hypotheses, as well as differences between the respective typical clinical settings. What Edelson needs to demonstrate is that specific Freudian hypotheses can be tested in the manner he recommends. He does not do that. He does offer two or three illustrations of his thesis, but, as I have argued elsewhere (Erwin 1986a), none of these is sound. Second, Adolf Grünbaum, in his recent Gifford Lectures (Grünbaum 1985), has provided some powerful arguments for thinking that Edelson's recommendations about single-subject designs are likely to prove fruitless.

I turn now to group experimental studies.

EXPERIMENTAL STUDIES

In their review of outcome studies of psychoanalytic therapy, Fisher and Greenberg are critical of much of the work that has been done so far, but do refer to six studies in support of the following conclusion: 'While we cannot conclude that the studies offer unequivocal evidence that analysis is more effective than no treatment, they do indicate with consistency that this seems probable with regard to a number of analysts and their nonpsychotic, chronic patients' (1977: 322). I am not sure how to read this conclusion, but if it implies that the studies make it probable that *analyses* – and not just individual therapists – are more effective than no treatment for some patients, then I disagree. The very criticisms that Fisher and Greenberg make of these studies, as well as criticisms made by other reviewers, show that the six studies have too many defects to make that conclusion probable. In addition, the studies did not rule out a placebo explanation of their findings.

Other recent reviews by myself (Erwin 1980b), Paul Kline (1981) and Rachman and Wilson (1980) have reached virtually the same conclusion: that there is little or no firm evidence that psychoanalytic therapy is more effective than a placebo in providing therapeutic benefits of any kind. This does not imply, of course, that the therapy is ineffective; it is likely that the right kind of controlled study has not yet been done. Some writers cite the Sloane et al. (1975) study as being well controlled, but that study did not deal with standard psychoanalytic therapy and used a minimum contact wait list control instead of a placebo group. Others have looked to the work of Smith and Glass on meta-analysis for support of psychoanalytic efficacy, but that too is a mistake. One of these two authors, Gene Glass, points out that he believes that psychoanalysis is by far the best theory of human behaviour, but adds that there exists in the Smith and Glass data base not a single study that qualifies, as he puts it, by even 'the shoddiest standards' as a satisfactory outcome evaluation of orthodox psychoanalysis (Glass and Kliegl 1983: 40).

In sum, experimental confirmation of Freudian therapeutic claims is non-existent. I turn next to the theoretical claims.

Because of the pioneering work of Paul Kline (1972, 1981), and the later work by Fisher and Greenberg (1977), it is now much easier to evaluate the experimental evidence for and against Freudian theory. These writers discuss more than 600 studies, virtually all of the relevant experimental studies published prior to 1980. Although they are critical of many of the studies, they do argue that central parts of Freudian theory have now been empirically confirmed. The philosopher B. A. Farrell (1981) and the psychologist Lloyd Silverman (1982) have also reached positive conclusions based on the experimental evidence. In contrast, I want to argue that the experimental evidence discussed by these writers fails to warrant the acceptance of even one of Freud's theoretical hypotheses.

Consider, for example, a study by Neal Miller (1948), which Farrell cites as evidence of displacement. Miller used electric shock to train two albino rats to strike each other. He then reinforced the aggressive behaviour of each rat by turning off the shock when the animals started striking each other. Later, he replaced one of the rats with a celluloid doll and found that the remaining rat struck the doll. It would be implausible to infer from this finding that 'displacement' in the Freudian sense had occurred. There is no warrant for believing that the rat's purpose in striking the doll was to protect its ego against instinctual demands of the id; a simpler and more plausible explanation is that response generalization had occurred. Consequently, if Miller's experiment is interpreted as testing a Freudian hypothesis about displacement, then confirmation was not provided; an alternative, and more plausible, rival hypothesis was not ruled out. However, Miller himself does say that the rat's behaviour could be explained as displacement *or* could be explained in stimulus–response terms. If he means that either explanation could be offered, then I agree, but, as already noted, the stimulus–response explanation would be more plausible. However, if Miller is equating the two explanations, if he is using 'displacement' to mean 'response generalization', then he did not test any Freudian hypothesis. In Freudian theory, 'displacement' does not mean *response generalization*; response generalization could occur even if there were no ego to defend against the demands of the id or super-ego.

As a second example, consider Farrell's appeal to Dixon's (1958) study of subliminal perception. In reply, I have tried to demonstrate (Erwin 1984) that Dixon's work, as well as the related perceptual defence literature, provides no firm support for the existence of either a Freudian unconscious or repression. Dixon and other writers in this area sometimes speak of 'unconscious perception', but they mean *perception without awareness*; they are not referring to a Freudian unconscious. In fact, Dixon (1971: 227) describes the tendency of some commentators to associate subliminal perception with an unconscious mind as 'quite irrational'.

All of Farrell's remaining arguments in favour of Freudian theory are criticized in a recent paper of mine in the *British Journal for the Philosophy of Science* (1984). The conclusion reached is that he has failed to show that any of the experimental literature supports Freudian theory.

Another writer who has recently appealed to experimental evidence in support of Freudian theory is Lloyd Silverman. He and his colleagues have done a series of interesting experiments that they interpret as providing evidence for the Freudian view that activating an unconscious wish increases psychopathology. Silverman's approach involves the use of subliminal stimulation to stir up unconscious Oedipal fantasies. A tachistoscope is used to present subliminal negative stimuli, such as pictures of a lion charging or a man snarling, or messages such as 'Fuck Mommy'. Controls are shown neutral stimuli such as a picture of a man reading a paper or a message such as 'People Walking'. In some experiments, Silverman and his associates claim to have increased or decreased pathology in their subjects. One of the difficulties in interpreting these experiments is that questionable tests were used to measure psychopathology. This problem was avoided in another experiment (Silverman et al. 1978) that used a simple dependent variable, 'competitive performance', as measured by scores in a dart tournament. Heilbrun (1980) reports on three attempted replications of this work; all three failed. These failures of replication by an independent investigator are important, especially because most of the studies using the Silverman technique were done by him or his colleagues or were reported in unpublished doctoral dissertations. In his reply to Heilbrun, Silverman (1982) mentions six other attempted replications, with four having positive results and two negative results. At best, the evidence is mixed, but it should be noted that all four of the positive studies are also unpublished doctoral dissertations.

In another study (Silverman, Frank and Dachinger 1974), the effectiveness of systematic desensitization is said to have been enhanced by activating unconscious fantasies. However, it is possible that what Silverman and his colleagues compared was simply a relevant stimulus (for the treatment group) and an irrelevant stimulus (in the control). To test this possibility, Emmelkamp and Straatman (1976) tried to replicate the Silverman et al. (1974) study, using a relevant stimulus in the control sessions. They failed to replicate. Condor and Allen (1980) also tried to replicate and failed (see Silverman's reply, 1982, and their comments, Allen and Condor 1982).

The utility of Silverman's work for decreasing psychopathology or enhancing therapeutic effects of other treatments is not likely to be decided until further research is published by independent investigators. Whatever results are found, however, a problem remains: Silverman relies on psychoanalytic theory to justify the assumption that his subliminal stimuli stir up unconscious fantasies; no firm independent evidence is provided that this is so. Without such evidence, what is, at most, demonstrated is that certain kinds of subliminal stimuli produce certain sorts of interesting effects. Whether this would have any bearing on psychoanalytic theory is unclear.

The most extensive discussions of the Freudian experimental literature appear in the two books I mentioned earlier, by Kline (1972, 1981) and Fisher and Greenberg (1977). These writers review pretty much the same material and agree substantially about which Freudian hypotheses have been empirically confirmed. Their main disagreement concerns a Freudian hypothesis about the aetiology of homosexuality, specifically a view about the kinds of parents who are likely to contribute to a son's homosexuality. Fisher and Greenberg find some support for this hypothesis in the experimental literature, but Kline is critical of the relevant studies. Kline, Fisher and Greenberg do not say that all of Freudian theory has been confirmed, but they agree that central parts of it have. It would be impossible to provide here an extensive examination of the evidence cited by these authors, but I have tried to do that in a paper in the Eysenck volume (Erwin 1986b). The conclusion I reach is that the experimental literature discussed by Kline, Fisher and Greenberg fails to provide strong support for *any* part of Freudian theory. The following examples are obviously not exhaustive, but are intended only as illustrations of the nature of the disagreement between Kline, Fisher and Greenberg and myself.

Kline (1981) cites the work of Kragh and his associates in support of the existence of repression and other Freudian defence mechanisms. In a typical study, Kragh and his associates use a tachistoscope to present what are called 'DMT' and 'MCT' pictures to groups of subjects at increasingly greater exposure times. One picture shows a boy with a violin, the head and shoulders of a threatening and ugly male having been inserted at the right of the boy. A parallel picture shows a young man centrally placed and an old ugly man above him. The subjects are instructed to make a drawing of what they have seen without paying any attention to whether their impression is correct or not. If they feel unable to make any kind of drawing, they are allowed to make markings instead. Kragh (1960) uses the term 'hero' to denote the person who is seen (drawn, marked) by a subject at the place of the main person in the pictures. A 'secondary' figure is the person seen at the place of the secondary person in the picture. Results are scored using Freudian defence categories. For example, a drawing is classified as 'repression' if the hero or/and the secondary figure have the quality of stiffness, rigidity, lifelessness, or of being 'disguised', or is (are) seen as an animal. What evidence does Kragh (1960) provide to show that repression is the cause of the subject's drawing the figures in this way? None at all. He simply stipulates that 'repression' and the other Freudian categories will be applied if certain kinds of drawings are made. Without such evidence, the studies of Kragh and his associates, whatever their value in distinguishing between psychiatric groups, provide no warrant for accepting the existence of any Freudian defence mechanism.

Kline (1981: 234) makes the following comment about this lack of evidence: 'Regrettably the only evidence for the validity of the DMT and MCT defence mechanism variables is effective face-validity. That is, if one examines what behaviour is actually entailed in obtaining a score for a given mechanism, one makes a value judgement that the behaviour resembles closely what Freud described as the appropriate mechanism.' One may make such a judgement, but without supporting evidence it would be unwarranted; it is not self-evident or obviously true that Kragh's subjects are caused to draw as they do by the operation of Freudian defence mechanism. The fatal flaw in Kragh's work is precisely his failure to validate his dependent measures (the DMT and MCT pictures).

Fisher and Greenberg (1977) cite various studies as evidence of the existence of castration anxiety. My main disagreement with their interpretation of these studies concerns the use of certain projective tests to measure castration anxiety. For example, one of the studies they cite (Sarnoff and Corwin 1959) assumes that certain responses to the so-called 'castration anxiety' card of the Blacky cartoons is evidence of castration anxiety. The card shows a cartoon depicting two dogs; one dog is standing blindfolded, and a large knife appears about to descend on his outstretched tail. The second dog is an onlooker to this event. It was assumed that subjects had a high degree of castration anxiety if, for example, they accepted the following statement as best describing the emotions of the onlooking dog: 'The sight of the approaching amputation is a deeply upsetting experience for the Black dog who is looking on; the possibility of losing his own tail and the thought of the pain involved overwhelm him with anxiety.' No evidence was provided that subjects accepting this statement had any degree of castration anxiety whatsoever. Without such evidence, the study cannot be taken as establishing that anyone has an unconscious fear of being castrated. Other methodological difficulties are discussed in Eysenck and Wilson (1973).

Another study (Blum 1949) also relied on the use of the Blacky cartoons. The remaining published studies of castration anxiety cited by Fisher and Greenberg (Friedman 1952; Hall and Van de Castle 1965; and Schwartz 1956) have been criticized elsewhere (Erwin, 1980a; Eysenck and Wilson, 1973). The basic difficulty with these studies is their reliance on an unwarranted assumption about what measures castration anxiety.

A good deal more needs to be said about the important work of Kline, and Fisher and Greenberg, but I think that the criticisms made in several publications (Eysenck and Wilson, 1973; Erwin 1980a, 1986b) cast considerable doubt on the proposition that a core part of Freudian theory is confirmed by the pre-1980 experimental literature.

Additional experimental work on Freudian theory has been published in the period between 1980 and the present. Some of these newer studies have been criticized by Grünbaum (1984), but others have been published only recently and have not yet been the subject of extensive critical discussion. It is possible that these newer studies will provide solid empirical support for Freudian theory, but to do that they must avoid the problems of the earlier experimental work.

These problems are generally of three kinds. First, there has been an over-reliance on projective tests, such as the Rorschach test or Blacky cartoons, the validity of which has not been independently established. Second, in some cases, the hypotheses that were tested were perhaps suggested by Freudian theory but were not genuinely psychoanalytic hypotheses. Third, even where the first two problems have been avoided, credible rivals to the Freudian hypothesis being tested were not ruled out. Whether or not the new studies avoid these problems remains to be seen.

REFERENCES

Allen, J. and Condor, T. 1982: Whither subliminal psychodynamic activation? A reply to Silverman. *Journal of Abnormal Psychology*, 9, 131–3.
Blum, G. 1949: A study of the psychoanalytic theory of psychosexual development. *Genetic Psychology Monographs*, 39, 3–9.
Brill, N., Koegler, R., Epstein, L. and Fogey, E. 1964: Controlled study of psychiatric outpatient treatment. *Archives of General Psychiatry*, 10, 581–95.
Condor, T. and Allen, G. 1980: Role of psychoanalytic merging fantasies in systematic desensitization: a rigorous methodological examination. *Journal of Abnormal Psychology*, 89, 437–43.
Cordray, D. and Bootzin, R. 1983: Placebo control conditions: tests of theory or of effectiveness? *Behavioral and Brain Sciences*, 6, 286–7.
Critelli, Joseph W. and Neuman, Karl F. 1984: The placebo: conceptual analysis of a construct in transition. *American Psychologist*, 39, 39–49.
Dixon, N. 1958: Apparent changes in the visual threshold as a function of subliminal stimulation. *Quarterly Journal of Experimental Psychology*, 10, 211–15.
Dixon, N. 1971: *Subliminal Perception: The Nature of a Controversy*. New York: McGraw Hill.
Edelson, M. 1984: *Hypothesis and Evidence in Psychoanalysis*. Chicago: University of Chicago Press.
Emelkamp, P. and Straatman, H. 1976: A psychoanalytic reinterpretation of the effectiveness of systematic desensitization: fact or fiction? *Behavior Research and Therapy*, 14, 245–9.

222   Edward Erwin

Erwin, E. 1978: *Behavior Therapy: Scientific, Philosophical and Moral Foundations*. New York: Cambridge University Press.

Erwin, E. 1980a: Psychoanalysis: how firm is the evidence? *Nous*, 14, 443–56.

Erwin, E. 1980b: Psychoanalytic therapy: the Eysenck argument. *American Psychologist*, 35, 435–43.

Erwin, E. 1984: The standing of psychoanalysis. *British Journal for the Philosophy of Science*, 35, 115–28.

Erwin, E. 1986a: Defending Freudianism. *Behavioral and Brain Sciences*.

Erwin, E. 1986b: Psychotherapy and Freudian psychology, in S. Modgil and C. Modgil (eds), *Hans Eysenck: Consensus and Controversy*. London: Falmer Press.

Eysenck, H. J. 1973: The experimental study of Freudian concepts. *Bulletin of the British Psychological Society*, 25, 261–8.

Eysenck, H. J. and Wilson, G. D. 1973: *The Experimental Study of Freudian Theories*. London: Methuen.

Farrell, B. A. 1981: *The Standing of Psychoanalysis*. New York: Oxford University Press.

Fisher, S. and Greenberg, R. 1977: *The Scientific Credibility of Freud's Theories and Therapy*. New York: Basic Books.

Frank, J. 1983: The placebo is psychotherapy. *Behavioral and Brain Sciences*, 6, 291–2.

Friedman, S. 1952: An empirical study of the castration and Oedipus complexes. *Genetic Psychology Monographs*, 46, 61–130.

Glass, G. and Kliegl. 1983: An apology for research integration in the study of psychotherapy. *Journal of Consulting and Clinical Psychology*, 51, 28–41.

Grünbaum, A. 1984: *The Foundations of Psychoanalysis: A Philosophical Critique*. Berkeley: University of California Press.

Grünbaum, A. 1985: The Gifford Lectures. Unpublished manuscript.

Hall, C. and Van de Castle, R. 1965: An empirical investigation of the castration complex in dreams. *Journal of Personality*, 33, 20–7.

Heilbrun, K. 1980: Silverman's subliminal psychodynamic activation: a failure to replicate. *Journal of Abnormal Psychology*, 89, 560–6.

Kazdin, A. 1981: Drawing valid inferences from case studies. *Journal of Consulting and Clinical Psychology*, 49, 183–92.

Kline, P. 1972, 1981: *Fact and Fantasy in Freudian Theory*. London: Methuen.

Kragh, U. 1960: The defense mechanism test: a new method for diagnosis and personnel selection. *Journal of Applied Psychology*, 44, 303–9.

Lick, J. 1975: Expectancy, false galvanic skin response, feedback and systematic desensitization in the modification of phobic behavior. *Journal of Consulting and Clinical Psychology*, 43, 557–67.

Meehle, P. 1983: Subjectivity in psychoanalytic inference: the nagging persistence of Wilhelm Fliess's Achensee question, in J. Earman (ed.), *Testing Scientific Theories*. Minnesota Studies in the Philosophy of Science, vol. X. Minneapolis: University of Minnesota Press.

Miller, N. 1948: Theory and experiment relating psychoanalytic displacement to stimulus–response generalization. *Journal of Abnormal Social Psychology*, 43, 155–73.

Nagel, E. 1959: Methodological issues in psychoanalytic theory, in S. Hook (ed.), *Psychoanalysis, Scientific Method and Philosophy*. New York: New York University Press.

Rachman, S. and Wilson, G. T. 1980: *The Effects of Psychological Therapy*. New York: Pergamon.

Rosenthal, T. 1980: Social cueing processes, in M. Hersen, R. Eisler and P. M. Miller (eds), *Progress in Behavior Modification*, vol. 10. New York: Academic Press.

Sarnoff, I. and Corwin, S. 1959: Castration anxiety and the fear of death. *Journal of Personality*, 27, 374–85.

Schwartz, B. 1956: An experimental test of two Freudian hypotheses concerning castration anxiety. *Journal of Personality*, 24, 318–27.

Silverman, L. 1982: A comment on two subliminal psychodynamic activation studies. *Journal of Abnormal Psychology*, 91, 126–30.

Silverman, L., Frank, S. and Dachinger, P. 1974: Psychoanalytic reinterpretation of the effectiveness of systematic desensitization: experimental data bearing on the role of merging fantasies. *Journal of Abnormal Psychology*, 83, 313–18.

Silverman, L., Ross, D., Adler, J. and Lustwig, D. 1978: Simple research paradigm for demonstrating psychodynamic activation: effects of Oedipal stimuli on dart-throwing accuracy in college males. *Journal of Abnormal Psychology*, 87, 341–57.

Sloane, R., Staples, F., Cristol, A., Yorkston, N. and Whipple, K. 1975: *Psychotherapy versus Behavior Therapy*. Cambridge, Mass.: Harvard University Press.

10

Freudian Theory and Experimental Evidence: A Reply to Erwin

PAUL KLINE

As an empirical psychologist I should like to make one general point about the philosophical discussion of Freudian theory. As might be expected it is philosophically sophisticated. However, it is psychologically naive and this is worrying when I hear one psychological research finding preferred to another without reference to the methods or techniques in the research. This is particularly serious when the technical quality of much psychological research in this area is low.

I should also add a further point. I feel ill at ease in discussions among so distinguished a gathering of philosophers. However, I take heart from the argument of Swift: that there is scarcely any matter of importance on which philosophers have not been entirely wrong.

As a non-philosopher and psychologist, I shall concentrate, in my response to Erwin, on the issues which he raised which were experimental. Put simply, his argument is that the experimental evidence cited by me and by Fisher and Greenberg as being in support of Freudian theory, on closer examination turns out to be flawed. Erwin cites a number of examples which are held to illustrate this thesis.

For a variety of reasons which I shall briefly enumerate, I do not believe that this case stands scrutiny. Let us first examine the arguments concerning the effectiveness of psychoanalytic therapy. I agree with his conclusions, incidentally, that no good evidence exists that it is effective. Furthermore I accept his points concerning the problems of countering the placebo effect of therapy itself and the uselessness of meta-analysis, actually for anything whatever. Why summarizing the results of a hundred bad studies can be thought to be meaningful lies beyond my grasp.

However, there is an approach to the evaluation of psychoanalytic therapy which, I believe, can overcome many of the difficulties raised by Erwin. This work and its general approach was discussed in my *Fact and Fantasy in Freudian Theory*, so that Erwin's ignoring these points is certainly not ignorance.

Briefly this approach aims not to evaluate the outcome of the psychotherapy, but the process itself. Thus before each session analysts with access to records of the previous sessions independently predict what will occur, stating their predictions together with the underlying Freudian theory. If on the basis of psychoanalytic theory therapeutic events can be predicted provided that no alternative theories could do so, then this is sound evidence for the validity of the theory. Preliminary work by Bellak (1958) is encouraging. Of course, such work could demonstrate the ineffectiveness of the theory if predictions of deteriorating behaviour were supported. Nevertheless if a theory can predict the events of psycho-therapy, I would argue that it constitutes support for it.

I now want to consider the claim explicit in part of Erwin's analysis and implicit in the rest – namely that many of the experimental findings cited in support of Freudian theory can be explained by other superior hypotheses. Where there are competing explanations the simplest is to be preferred: Occam's razor or the law of parsimony. Now in any one instance it is conceivable that the alternative explanation is no more complex than the psychoanalytic one or even more simple. However, when the not inconsiderable number of experiments held to support psychoanalytic theory is considered *in toto* and the psychoanalytic account is compared with the inevitably large number of *ad* or *post hoc* explanations, then the meaning of simple has to be carefully considered. I regard this as a severe weakness of the alternative explanations of the experimental evidence in support of psychoanalytic theory, especially – although I put myself at risk to state it here – of the philosophers who allow themselves the luxury of illustrating their points with but few examples and who are, by definition, not interested in the psychological status of these alternative explanations.

Let me illustrate my point. Both Grünbaum (1984) and Erwin cite with approval the work of Eysenck and Wilson (1973), arch-opponents of psychoanalysis whose opposition many might say amounted to pathology and was itself support for psychoanalytic claims. Now of what does Eysenck's and Wilson's (1973) book consist? It prints in full twenty or so studies that I had argued (1972) constituted experimental support for psychoanalysis and provides alternative explanations.

In some cases these alternatives were plausible and further work is necessary to choose between the rival claims. However, in others the rival explanations were so inelegant and so clearly designed with the particular experiment in mind that to regard them as real alternatives, given any knowledge of psychology, is absurd.

Let me illustrate my case. In one study by Zamansky (1958) it was shown that paranoids fixated longer at pictures of men than of women (support for their latent homosexuality). However, they did not overtly admit to liking the male pictures more than the female. It should be pointed out that fixation time is correlated with liking. Fisher and Greenberg (1977) and I both regard this finding as modest experimental support for the claim that paranoid schizophrenics are latent not overt homosexuals.

The alternative explanation postulated by Eysenck and Wilson and given the weight of Grünbaum's approval (1984: 278), is that the paranoids were naturally suspicious of the shrink and didn't wish to be labelled homosexual so they denied liking the homosexual pictures. Here we have a new variable in Human Motivation – Natural Suspicion of the Shrink. What other evidence is there for it? None. Has it been measured? No. Has it been discussed previously in clinical work? It has not. Such an explanation may be sufficient for a philosopher on logical grounds. It is not sufficient for a psychologist, at least not this psychologist. Paranoids' delusions are usually encapsulated and are not part of a general trait of suspiciousness (see Mayer-Gross, Slater and Roth 1967). If Grünbaum and Erwin examined the anti-Freudians with the rigour with which they examined the pro-Freudians, some different conclusions might be derived.

I shall now turn to the work of Kragh (1969) and his associates in Sweden, percept genetics, much of which has been well summarized in Kragh and Smith (1970). I admit to having a particular interest in this field because with a colleague in Exeter, Colin Cooper, I have carried out a number of investigations (see Kline and Cooper 1977; Cooper and Kline 1985).

Erwin argues that Kragh's DMT test, which purports to discern defences, is only face valid and that no objctive further support for its validity has been provided. This is the fatal flaw. However, let us consider the meaning of face validity. In psychometrics it refers to the appearance of a test. For example a test of cooking which included items such as 'How long do you boil an egg?' or 'Do you peel carrots?' has face validity.

However, it is not a valid test of cooking since it requires reading ability and comprehension. A most excellent Chef de Maison from Provence (highly rated by the *Observer* Colour Supplement) might well fail.

Now the face validity, which I referred to in my 1981 publication, of the DMT is of a quite different kind. In this responses are given which are or can be judged to be defences. I shall exemplify the point from our own researches. In 1977 (Kline and Cooper 1977), using the percept genetic method, in which stimuli are exposed in series at gradually decreasing shutter speeds until perception is 'veridical', we showed two slides: one a pig suckling piglets, the oral card of Corman's 1969 PN test, to which we expected oral defences, and a control card of a Harris Bacon pig. We obtained no protocols to this latter stimulus in which even the most ardent Freudian could discern defences. However, to the suckling pig responses were made which closely resembled defences. For example denial: at exposure 3, a subject said that it could perhaps be a pig feeding. At exposure 4 (a little slower, hence a little clearer) the subject said that it was definitely not feeding. Similarly in a study with the Blacky Pictures (Blum 1949) I obtained a response to the card of a defecating dog stating that you might think it was a defecating dog but it was not.

I have argued that such responses, and I can assure you that these are only examples and that they turn up with monotonous regularity in research, are examples of defences and as such support for Freudian theory. Erwin objects to this regarding it as mere stipulation that such drawings will be categorized as defences. Now actually how serious is this objection? Defences are themselves categories of responding. Suppose that all psychoanalysts in the world claimed that a response X was an example of repression, what sense would it make to argue that further evidence was needed since this was a mere stipulation? Although, of course, it is the case that not all analysts have been asked about Kragh's classification of DMT responses, nevertheless it is the case that they do appear to fit the psychoanalytic categorization. Thus face validity here is more meaningful support for the theory than it is in standard psychometric practice. Nevertheless I agree that stipulative definition is not enough and I agree with Erwin that other more objective evidence is desirable. I shall now briefly describe some more recent work that Cooper and I have carried out with the DMT, work that was reported in Cooper's Ph.D. thesis. As part of this study we subjected the DMT to an objective marking scheme for the presence or absence of descriptors. Factor analysis of these responses revealed a dimension which (a) could be found in the responses of two disparate groups, namely students and airmen, thus indicating that it was a stable phenomenon rather than some artefact of our sample or our statistical analysis; (b) correlated with pilot success; and (c) correlated with an independent measure of repression. A few comments on the findings are in order here. I have mentioned the replicability of the results, which is very important and I shall say no more about it here. However, the correlation with success in high-speed jet flying is of some significance. As you may know the DMT is used in the Scandinavian Air Forces to select jet pilots – a task which is beyond the scope of most psychological tests for they are used among an already highly selected sample. The rationale is that those pilots who defend will react that much more slowly and thus have more accidents. I should point out that these pilots are operating planes at treetop level, to evade radar detection, at around 500 mph and the flow of visual information is truly formidable. Thus our finding certainly supports this claim and defies alternative explanations of any coherence.

The independent measure of repression was based upon subliminal perception. Repression is defined by Freud as the denial of entry into consciousness, so that this subliminal work still seems to me to be a reasonable exemplar. In our study subjects were light adapted with a bright light, then put in a dark room in which glowed a disc of light. Subjects pressed a button as soon as they saw the disc. Below the level of awareness in some trials TV was shown beneath the disc, in others VD. The difference in time to see the disc in these two cases was our measure of repression. I think these findings cannot be so cavalierly dismissed by philosophers as not indicating repression, as indeed does Dixon, who was external examiner for this thesis. For all these reasons I think percept genetics cannot be summarily dismissed.

I agree with Erwin's comments about Silverman's work (e.g. 1980). It is disappointing that it has not been replicated elsewhere. However, the doubts that have been expressed about its replicability beyond the confines of Silverman's laboratories increase the likelihood that it never will be so replicated. Certainly I have been unable to obtain grant support for this work. Nevertheless, on a more hopeful note, some of the percept genetics workers in Lund have managed to replicate the findings of Oedipal guilt affecting dart playing.

I shall now turn to a topic which for some reason Erwin has not discussed in his refutation of the psychoanalytic supports. This is the hologeistic, anthropological work pioneered by Whiting and Child (1953) in Yale. The hologeistic method involves rating anthropological and ethnographic reports from a large number of societies, usually a genuine worldwide sample for variables of child rearing or indeed any aspect of society that is relevant to Freudian theory, and then examining the correlations between these variables in the light of psychoanalytic theory. By so doing the method, which is, of course, capable of putting to the test any environmental hypotheses concerning the determinants of behaviour, overcomes the objections to psychoanalytic theory that it was derived from a limited sample of humanity (nineteenth-century Vienna in the form of Jewish neurotic ladies of an uncertain age; far, far better the hooded rat) and yet it makes universal statements.

Stephens (1961) used this method to investigate the extent of the menstrual sexual taboo in a large sample of societies. The hypothesis, derived from Freudian theory, was that the length of this taboo reflected the castration anxiety among men that was current in the society. From this it was argued that child-rearing practices that were likely to induce such anxiety, for example the threat of punishment for masturbation, would be more prevalent in societies with a long menstrual sexual taboo than they would in societies with short or no taboos. Such indeed was found to be the case for nine child-rearing techniques – a highly statistically significant result. These findings support the notion of castration anxiety as a worldwide phenomenon. Similar studies of the postpartum sexual taboo, which encourages children to sleep with their mothers in the non-sexual sense of the word, have also give support for the Oedipus complex. I do not want to make excessive claims for this work. Rather I want to point out that the hologeistic cross-cultural method is a powerful means of testing psychoanalytic theory which has produced results which have not generally been impugned.

I think enough has been said to illustrate that the experimental evidence in support of Freudian theory cannot be dissolved away by philosophical analysis, however sophisticated and skilful this is. I have not either said all that might be said about this matter. Lee's (1958) work on the dreams of Zulu women was striking confirmation that in a psychoanalytically naive sample dreams did express wishes – in this case for babies among barren subjects. Freudian symbolism was found too. Only one woman dreamed of a dead snake and she was the wife of the only impotent man among the group. However, I know that this will not convince philosophers, being but an instance of the fallacy of enumerative deductionism (Edelson 1984).

Some of my experimental work on the aetiology of the oral character I will briefly mention as a last example of objective evidence. I developed two personality tests of oral traits, OPQ measuring oral pessimism and OOQ measuring oral optimism and validated them as measures of personality traits (Kline and Storey 1977). I then attempted to relate them to reality (Kline and Storey 1980). I found that scores on these questionnaires were linked to pencil biting and to food preferences, where oral optimists like gooseberry fools and bananas and cream; oral pessimists hot pickles and curry and cigarette smoking. There was nothing in the personality tests about eating, biting or food. None of these variables were linked to Eysenck's EPQ factors of Extraversion, Neuroticism and Psychoticism, the most pervasive of personality factors. Although this is not strong evidence for the theory of orality, one question must be asked: What other theory accounts for these findings? One other curious result was observed (Kline 1979). A combined score from measures of oral and anal traits was linked to neuroticism although each test was independent of it on its own. In view of Freud's metaphor (S.E. 1905, VII) that fixation was the ego leaving troops behind at various points thus weakening itself, this is an interesting finding, though I should hate to make too much of it.

CONCLUSIONS

I would like in closing to draw a few simple conclusions.

1   I think that the philosophical attacks on the status of the scientific evidence do not entirely stand scrutiny for reasons which I hope have been at least partially convincing.

2   I do not, as I hope is obvious, try to argue that Freudian theory is of itself either true or false. Rather I adopt Farrell's (1964) view that Freudian theory is really a collection of theories of which some may turn out true, others false.

3   Finally, I am saddened by one aspect of the philosophical attacks on the evidence purporting to confirm Freud. They are conducted with a scrupulosity and attention to detail which does not seem to be applied to rival theories. As I exemplified, the thinking and reasoning in Eysenck and Wilson's book (1973) is sloppy indeed and can stand not even elementary scrutiny. It suggests that there is more than an objective search for truth behind this work, a conclusion which of course was anticipated by Freud himself and would have caused him no surprise.

REFERENCES

Bellak, L. 1958: Studying the psychoanalytic process by the method of short-range prediction and judgement. *British Journal of Medical Psychology*, 31, 249–52.

232   *Paul Kline*

Blum, G. S. 1949: A study of the psychoanalytic theory of psycho-sexual development. *Genetic Psychology Monographs*, 39, 3–99.

Cooper, C. 1982: An experimental study of Freudian defence mechanisms. Unpublished Ph.D. thesis, University of Exeter.

Cooper, C. and Kline, P. 1986: The defence mechanism test. *British Journal of Psychology*, 77, 19–31.

Corman, L. 1969: *The Test PN*. Presses Universitaires de Paris.

Edelson, M. 1984: *Hypothesis and Evidence in Psychoanalysis*. Chicago: University of Chicago Press.

Eysenck, H. J. and Wilson, G. D. 1973: *The Experimental Study of Freudian Theories*. London: Methuen.

Farrell, B. A. 1964: The status of psychoanalytic theory. *Inquiry*, 4, 16–36.

Fisher, S. and Greenberg, P. R. 1977: *The Scientific Credibility of Freud's Theories and Therapy*. Hassocks: Harvester Press.

Grünbaum, A. 1984: *The Foundations of Psychoanalysis: A Philosophical Critique*. Berkeley: University of California Press.

Kline, P. 1972: *Fact and Fantasy in Freudian Theory*. London: Methuen.

Kline, P. 1979: Psychosexual personality traits, fixation and neuroticism. *British Journal of Medical Psychology*, 52, 393–5.

Kline, P. 1981: *Fact and Fantasy in Freudian Theory*, 2nd edn. London: Methuen.

Kline, P. and Cooper, C. 1977: A percept-genetic study of some defence mechanisms in the test P.N. *Scandinavian Journal of Psychology*, 18, 148–52.

Kline, P. and Storey, R. 1977: A factory-analytic study of the oral character. *British Journal of Social Pschology*, 16, 317–28.

Kline, P. and Storey, R. 1980: The aetiology of the oral character. *Journal of Genetic Psychology*, 1365, 85–94.

Kragh, U. 1969: *DMT Manual*. Stockholm: Tesforlaget.

Kragh, U. and Smith, G. 1970: *Percept-Genetic Analysis*. Lund: Gleerups.

Lee, S. G. 1958: Social influences in Zulu dreaming. *Journal of Social Psychology*, 47, 265–83.

Lee, S. G. 1953: *TAT for African Subjects*. Pietermaritzberg: University of Natal Press.

Mayer-Gross, W., Slater, E. and Roth, M. 1967: *Clinical Psychiatry*. London: Cassell.

Silverman, L. H. 1980: *A Comprehensive Report of Studies Using the Subliminal Psychodynamic Activation Method*. New York: Research Center for Mental Health.

Stephens, W. N. 1961: A cross-cultural study of menstrual taboos. *Genetic Psychology Monographs*, 64, 385–416.

Whiting, J. M. and Child, I. L. 1953: *Child Training and Personality*. New Haven: Yale University Press.

Zamansky, H. S. 1958: An investigation of the psychoanalytic theory of paranoid delusions. *Journal of Personality*, 26, 410–25.

PART FIVE

Freud and His Influence

11

Beyond Sulloway's *Freud*: Psychoanalysis minus the Myth of the Hero

FREDERICK CREWS

I

In the wake of Professor Grünbaum's Gifford Lectures, we assembled at St Andrews to continue debating how seriously psychoanalysis should be regarded as knowledge. For some of us, however, Grünbaum's previously published work already portended the correct answer. Ingenious though Freud was in system building, Grünbaum (1984) has shown that neither Freud nor any of his followers have supplied one cogent reason for adhering to any distinctively Freudian tenets. To be sure, Grünbaum as an inductivist feels compelled to add that support for this or that Freudian notion may yet be forthcoming. But readers who understand the restraints of Grünbaum's argumentative tact can readily, and justifiably, infer that after nine decades of question begging and wanton conceptual embroidery we might as well be waiting for Godot.

One advantage that Grünbaum reaps from his formal stance of patience is that he can maintain cordial rapport with the most methodologically alert analysts, those who still hope to bring the Freudian tradition into alignment with his high standards of verification. Whether such hopes are worth entertaining at all is, however, another matter – one that I will address directly before I am through. Though it seems obvious at first that the most 'reachable' Freudians deserve encouragement, surely there ought to be a statute of limitations on the postponing of judgement against a system of allegedly scientific thought for which no credible support has been mustered and whose proponents, more damningly, have consistently ducked the risk of falsification. In this paper I will try to show, through the 'case history' of a rich and important book whose author as well as whose reviewers were reluctant to contemplate the inherent character of psychoanalysis, why we would be well advised to cease temporizing and acknowledge the scientific bad faith of the entire Freudian enterprise. Psychoanalysis, I will maintain, does not consist of a sum of hypotheses each of which remains as yet unsubstantiated. Rather, it is in its heart of hearts a pseudo-science trafficking exclusively in dogma.

As someone who spent a decade inching his way from a pro-psychoanalytic stance to an opposite one, I am more than usually aware that Freudianism is internally resilient against exposure of its implausibility. The resilience lies not in intellectual virtues possessed by the theory but in the nature of its appeal to its adherents, most of whom have undergone a humbling and cathartic experience of thought reform that has no counterpart outside the realms of religious and political indoctrination. Indeed, as many observers have noted, psychoanalysis shows every sign of being not just a method and a psychology but also a faith, with all that this implies about psychic immunity from rationally based criticism. Like other faiths, Freudianism readily rebounds when confronted with seemingly fatal objections, for its believers have rendered it inseparable from their private sense of spiritual vitality and worth.[1]

Arguing directly with Freudians is thus a futile exercise if one expects to provoke deconversion experiences. But if one recognizes that the real audience for such discourse consists of uncommitted and increasingly wary bystanders, things begin to look brighter. In particular, epistemological and empirical critiques such as Grünbaum's *Foundations* and Eysenck's and Wilson's *The Experimental Study of Freudian Theories* (1973) can produce a properly cautionary effect by showing that Freudian claims have not been adequately supported by evidence, are regularly defended in a circular manner, and are inherently unlikely because they invariably brush aside explanatory possibilities that place less strain on our credulity about cause–effect relations and the known properties of the human organism. Eventually, such unanswerable demonstrations are sure to prevail.

Even so, the long hegemony of psychoanalysis has lent it an air of 'givenness' that leaves people inclined to regard any thoroughgoing critique as *ipso facto* extremist. The impression persists that at a certain moment Sigmund Freud must surely have achieved a great breakthrough in the understanding of mental illness and the dynamics of motivation. Otherwise, what has all the fuss been about for the greater part of a century? Rather than attend to the logic of a Grünbaum or an Eysenck and Wilson, many well-intentioned people will draw back and say, 'Even while acknowledging Freud's errors, we must be careful not to discard the core of precious insight that he bequeathed us.'²

To address such understandable recalcitrance we need to accompany the epistemological and empirical critique of psychoanalysis with a historical and biographical one, reconstructing, in so far as possible, the actual circumstances surrounding the birth and growth of Freud's movement. For people who are not already totally immersed in depth-psychological folklore, the 'givenness' of psychoanalysis can be combated by an understanding of the influences, intuitive leaps, evaded questions and extrarational means of persuasion that went into the founding of the Freudian era. Before 1897, after all, there was no tradition of 'Freudian insight' to lend psychoanalytic generalities an air of *a priori* plausibility. Were they warranted in the hour of their birth? Historical investigation can show, first, that Freudianism was far less original and forward-looking than most people realize; second, that its claimed basis in observation was more rhetorical than real; third, that its actual inspiration came from sources that merit our hearty distrust; and fourth, that its method of coping with apparent counter-examples was, from the outset, characteristically pseudo-scientific.

Evidence to establish those conclusions already lies at hand, no thanks to the high priests of psychoanalysis who watch over the top-secret Freud Archives in Washington, D.C. Though much about the origins of psychoanalysis remains obscure, we have an ample basis for determining whether Freud actually stumbled across a *terra incognita* or was misled by his drive toward heroic fame. Indeed, we already possess book-length studies which put that question largely beyond doubt. Among them, pre-eminent in rigour and doggedness of research, stands Henri F. Ellenberger's *The Discovery of the Unconscious* (1970), a work whose long chapter on Freud only dramatizes what the total volume makes plain, namely,the derivative and curiously atavistic position of psychoanalysis in nineteenth-century psychiatry. No one who ponders the entirety of Ellenberger's subtly ironic narrative can fail to come away with a sense that psychoanalysis was a high-handed improvisation on Freud's part.

Here, however, I want to concentrate on a successor volume to *The Discovery of the Unconscious*, a book that duly cites Ellenberger's key findings while breaking crucially important new ground of its own. Everyone who follows Freud studies is aware of Frank J. Sulloway's *Freud, Biologist of the Mind: Beyond the Psychoanalytic Legend* (1983a – a slightly revised edition of the original 1979 publication). Yet my own perusal of that book and of its reviews leaves me convinced that few early readers, or for that matter even Sulloway himself, correctly perceived either the book's limitations or its revolutionary implications.[3] I hope to show you not only that Sulloway was right about the distortions that constitute 'the psychoanalytic legend', but also that his own failure to achieve sufficient distance from that same legend left his study ambiguous in fundamental respects. This outcome is not just instructive in its own right. It deserves to be repaired in detail, for Sulloway's work, once stripped of its contradictions, offers a treasure-house of information about the empirical groundlessness of psychoanalysis in its earliest phases.

Sulloway's presentation builds upon Ellenberger's by completing the account of the issues and developments that actually shaped Freud's thought. I have in mind, for example, the prevalence of premature attempts to unify evolutionary theory, neurophysiology and psychology along biogenetic lines; the flourishing of sexological theory, with particular emphasis on infantile libido; the lingering but somewhat disreputable appeal of *Naturphilosophie*, with its proto-Freudian vitalism and instinctual polarities; and the comparable lingering of popular and Romantic notions of repression, the unconscious, sublimation and dream interpretation. Sulloway makes it clear, as Ellenberger did in smaller compass, why some of Freud's colleagues regarded him not as a shocking innovator but as a throwback to the heyday of Mesmerism.

The thesis of Sulloway's study is adumbrated in the two parts of its title. Freud, Sulloway maintains, was a 'biologist of the mind', and as such he was guided by principles that have been obscured by the psychoanalytic legend. According to the canonical account, Freud severed his intellectual roots in neuroanatomy when he founded psychoanalysis, an observational 'pure psychology' that was meant to be autonomous from, though ultimately compatible with, physical knowledge about the human brain and nervous system. The legend has credited Freud with heroic powers of introspection, of penetration into the minds of his patients, and of courage in defying the prudish timidity of his colleagues and a hostile public. We have been told in effect that without Freud we would have had no concept of the unconscious or repression or infantile sexuality, no theory of hidden meaning in dreams and myths and errors, and no hope for the cure of neurotic suffering. But Sulloway maintains that this picture constitutes a wilful 'nihilation' of Freud's actual intellectual milieu. Freud was indeed original, says Sulloway, but chiefly in synthesizing ideas from disparate sources and in stating as universal laws what others had either entertained more tentatively or long since rejected as 'old wives' psychiatry'.

This argument has many strands, only a few of which I will be able to trace below. Its core, however, is the contention that Freud, after the debacle of his early, creakily mechanistic 'Project for a Scientific Psychology', never did cease resting his mental system on premises borrowed from the physical sciences of his day. Instead, he made two moves that look initially paradoxical but bespeak considerable cunning. First, he temporarily suppressed explicit reference to his organic reasoning and maintained that he had derived psychoanalysis entirely from self-observation and from study of his patients. And second, he *expanded* his physical premises, allowing himself to be guided, after about 1895, less by energic-physiological considerations than by what Sulloway calls directional-historical ones. The early Freud focused on proximate causes within the individual organism, inquiring how the psyche and soma were interlinked. The later Freud largely replaced such causes with ultimate evolutionary ones, which he openly embraced only after psychoanalysis had gained a secure (though misleading) reputation as a clinically based psychology.

Freud broke off his 'Project', Sulloway shows, because he was defeated in his attempt to account physiologically for the far-fetched mechanism of repression, whereby a trauma suffered at, say, age three would suddenly begin producing symptoms at, say, age thirty-five. With characteristic impetuousness, Freud retained the threatened doctrine and merely shifted his grounds for believing in it. At the time he established psychoanalysis, Sulloway claims, Freud's overriding question had already become not how but *why* – for example, why sexuality should be the domain requiring massive repression and why mankind must endure a latency period before the recrudescence of libidinal aims at puberty.

If Sulloway is right, in founding psychoanalysis Freud passed from being an overtly neuroanatomical speculator about mind to being a 'cryptobiologist' – someone who put forward mentalistic hypotheses but whose hidden grounds for doing so were taken from neo-Darwinian theory about the emergence of the species. According to Sulloway the biogenetic and Lamarckian assumptions that finally surfaced in works like *Totem and Taboo* (1912–13) were already, by 1897, decisive for Freud in underwriting his leading ideas about innate bisexuality, repression and regression to developmental 'fixation points'.

Sulloway's argument may be wrong in certain particulars, but it possesses the immediate advantage of not straining our credulity in the ways required by the psychoanalytic legend. As Grünbaum reminds us, it was quite impossible for Freud to have gleaned his arcane developmental concepts from the interactions of the consulting room, much less from introspection about his own infancy. Those concepts obviously came from other available sources – and *Freud, Biologist of the Mind* shows what those sources probably were.

Sulloway demonstrates plausible continuities in Freud's career where the psychoanalytic legend has posited only inexplicable leaps. The legend tells us that Freud suddenly ceased being influenced by evolutionary and neuroanatomical science at the moment he conceived of psychoanalysis and found that it cured his patients' neuroses; that his openly Lamarckian whimsies stood completely apart from his metapsychology; and that notions like the death instinct were detachable philosophical speculations that just showed up in his texts one day, unbidden by the 'clinical evidence' which allegedly governed his more sober theorizing. Sulloway, by contrast, shows us a single Freud who kept brooding about the same fundamental problems, and he proves that the death instinct makes a kind of sense only if one adopts a 'psycho-Lamarckian' perspective – that is, if one 'sees as the major agent of evolutionary change the organism's reactions to its physiological needs' (Sulloway 1983: 408). Freud adhered to exactly that perspective, and it was indispensable not just to a few peculiarly vulnerable ideas but to his entire conception of the human species and its vicissitudes.

As Sulloway convincingly argues, Freud was not only encouraged but also decisively influenced by his friend and fellow psycho-Lamarckian Wilhelm Fliess, whom the psychoanalytic legend has stigmatized as a psychotic crank. According to the legend, Freud passed through an 'Oedipal' but intellectually inert dependence on Fliess prior to the great breakthrough of his self-analysis. But Sulloway reveals Freud to have been a loyal Fliessian in the very act of formulating such 'Freudian' notions as sexual aims dating from birth, erotogenic zones whose dominance and supersession constitute the path of normal development, fixation upon those zones when development goes awry, the mechanisms of sublimation and reaction formation, and an innate bisexuality that must be stifled with especial 'organically repressive' force in women, whose clitorises Freud took to be literally male organs. And this is to pass over more sensational but less fundamental ways in which Freud emulated Fliess – for example, in recklessly extrapolating from Fliess's numerological system and in diagnosing and gruesomely treating 'nasal reflex neuroses' in such unfortunates as the now celebrated Emma Eckstein.

A further merit of Sulloway's argument is that, once we have put aside the fiction that Freud reasoned directly from 'clinical evidence', we can nevertheless perceive that he had *some* basis for his gnostic inferences about infancy and prehistory. That is, we need not join the most intemperate critics of psychoanalysis who dismiss the entire system as a cocaine vision or an articulation of Freud's admittedly flagrant misogyny. To be sure, psychoanalytic theory does bear the morbid imprint of its author's prurient and clouded state of mind in the later 1890s. But Sulloway reminds us that Freud's thinking, though heedless in consequential ways, was at least responsive to a scientific tradition that still had many respectable adherents.

By taking due note of Freud's psycho-Lamarckian reasoning, for instance, we can absolve him of total arbitrariness in having declared *ex cathedra* that every dream vents a wish that was repressed in infancy and ultimately inherited from the phylogeny of the race. Sulloway's exposition shows us that such tenets were as logically necessary to Freud, the devoted believer in accumulated 'racial' memory and recapitulation, as they were unfounded in evidence that would count as such today. Similarly, Freud's curious optimism at the moment he felt obliged to renounce his 'seduction theory' no longer seems deranged if we bear in mind, as Sulloway urges us to, that this was the very period in which he was giving himself over to Fliess's developmental laws. Freud claimed in a letter that he had been left with nothing, but before long he had in hand a more breathtakingly speculative scheme of early repression than the one he had forsaken. Only when we have appreciated the overwhelmingly deductive nature of his suppressed reasoning can we understand why, in the absence of striking clinical success with the new Oedipal aetiology, Freud felt serenely confident that he had solved the riddle of human susceptibility to psychoneurosis.

II

My summary makes clear, I trust, that *Freud, Biologist of the Mind* constitutes a major challenge to the heroic Freud myth and thereby to psychoanalysis itself as a doctrine allegedly rooted in observation and therapeutic results. Yet the short-term fate of all such challenges seems to be a blend of misconstrual and peremptory rejection. It is true, to be sure, that Sulloway's book was immediately hailed as a classic by such diverse judges as Hans Eysenck, Rosemary Dinnage, Robert R. Holt, Arnold Bernstein, Marie Jahoda and M. Gerard Fromm; that it won the Pfizer Award in 1979 for the best American or Canadian work on the history of science; and that Sulloway has recently been granted a MacArthur Fellowship, presumably because of what he accomplished in this, his only book to date. Nevertheless, given the continuing strength of the psychoanalytic legend, we cannot be surprised to learn that many reviewers rejected Sulloway's argument out of hand while nearly all others accepted it only in a drastically weakened sense – a sense that, ironically, Sulloway himself was half-inclined to approve.[4] Regarded together, the book and its reviews show how 'legendary' expectations can take precedence over plausibly marshalled facts that point in an opposite direction.

Insofar as Sulloway's reviewers perceived his exposition to be in conflict with Freudian pretensions, they tended either to misrepresent it or to rebut it with allegations drawn from the very psychoanalytic legend that Sulloway was calling into question. Thus a good many reviewers chose to interpret Sulloway as claiming that Freud was scarcely a psychologist at all but rather, as Richard Wollheim put it in a singularly haughty dismissal in the *New York Review of Books*, 'a biologist who passed as a psychologist' (Wollheim 1979: 25; see also Brooks 1980; Chessick 1980; Hopkins 1979; Khan 1981; Lothane 1981; Wallace 1982). That was not Sulloway's point at all.[5] Again, Mark Kanzer spoke for many orthodox Freudian reviewers when he lamented, 'what Sulloway misses is that [Freud's] ultimate criterion was the clinical usefulness and validation of [his] postulates' (Kanzer 1980: 522; see also Chessick 1980; Hopkins 1979; Lothane 1981; Pollock 1981; Wallace 1982). After Grünbaum's unmasking of the contaminated data and spurious causal reasoning behind Freud's clinical inferences, not to mention Freud's own belated confessions that his therapy was largely unsuccessful, one can only smile at such piety toward the image of Freud as the empirically scrupulous healer. Yet that same piety pervaded the negative reviews, which conveyed near-shock at Sulloway's presumption in seeking to demean what George Steiner called 'a dominant presence in the spirit of the age' (Steiner 1979: 40). One reviewer after another adduced Freud's greatness as evidence against the plausibility of Sulloway's argument, as if it were unimaginable that our psychological Copernicus could be demoted to a fallible representative of his age.

To me, however, the outstanding feature of the reviews is that nearly all of them *overlooked* the most glaring weakness of *Freud, Biologist of the Mind*.[6] For, relentless though he is in tracing Freud's sources, Sulloway is inconsistent and misleading in evaluating the success with which Freud transformed those sources into adequate scientific hypotheses. At times he clearly acknowledges that a system dependent at its core on spurious doctrines cannot also be an accurate empirical science; yet elsewhere he appears to make exactly that quixotic claim. The result, I am afraid, is that even relatively unprejudiced readers have missed the revolutionary purport of Sulloway's findings.

Near the end of the book Sulloway voices the following important judgement, which appalled some of his reviewers:

Acceptance of Freud's historical debt to biology requires a rather uncongenial conclusion for most psychoanalytic practitioners, namely, that Freud's theories reflect the faulty logic of outmoded nineteenth-century biological assumptions, particularly those of a psychophysicalist, Lamarckian, and biogenetic nature. As we have seen, these assumptions were eminently plausible in Freud's day. Indeed, so plausible were they that Freud was not always aware of how much faith he placed in them or of how much his clinical observations absorbed from them 'empirical' meaning. Yet because he pursued such a bold and relentless logic in the world of scientific ideas, his thinking illuminates the power of his theoretical preconceptions in a particularly dramatic fashion . . . [S]uch 'clinical' discoveries as the abreaction of trauma seemed to Freud a direct corroboration of the bioenergetic principles that pervaded his theory of mind. Similarly, the child does appear to recapitulate the history of the race in many essential respects, but it recapitulates the embryonic, not the adult stages, as Freud and other biogeneticists had mistakenly thought . . . [M]uch that is wrong with orthodox psychoanalysis may be traced directly back to [such assumptions]. To cite a prime example, Freud claimed that no one, looking at a nursing infant, could possibly dispute the sexual nature of oral gratification in infancy – a claim that indeed can be disputed if one does not equate infantile forms of pleasure, as he did on biogenetic grounds, with animal-like sex. Time and time again, Freud saw in his patients what psychoanalytic theory led him to look for and then to interpret the way he did; and when the theory changed, so did the clinical findings.

(Sulloway 1983a: 498)

Here, I submit, we feel the full weight of Sulloway's implicit brief against Freud: psychoanalysis was founded not on observation but on deductions from erroneous dogma, and as a result the entire system can make no claim on our credence. Yet in the few remaining pages that follow this admirable summary, Sulloway writes repeatedly of Freud's 'fruitful insights' and even of his 'scientific greatness', and he concludes by saying, 'After all, Freud really was a hero' (Sulloway 1983a: 503) – a sentence that allowed many a reviewer to reassure the public that Freud's ghost had nothing to fear from Sulloway (e.g. 'Did Freud Build His Own Legend' 1979; Gifford 1980; Glazer 1980; Harvey 1982; Leonard 1979; Pruyser 1980; Robinson 1979; Strouse 1979).[7]

There is of course a sense in which Freud can be considered both erroneous and heroic. In his own self-conception he was always destined for fame, and the very fact that he was able to satisfy what Sulloway calls his 'obsessional need for intellectual immortality' (Sulloway 1983a: 217) *without* having found either a viable therapy or an accurate psychology does compel a certain awe. Yet Sulloway, while he supplies a rich fund of data and even a theoretical overview that will help future investigators understand how the Freud legend took hold, must finally be judged to have given that legend far too much credit. For throughout his book, not just in its closing pages, he heads off his own provocative insights by referring magnanimously to Freud's 'discoveries' and 'recognitions' and 'scientific gains'. And oddly, in every instance the 'discovery' at issue is thrown into doubt by Sulloway's own account of its genesis.

Take, for example, Freud's dream theory, which Sulloway shows to have been a wholly deductive construct inferred from the faulty repression aetiology of neurosis and indebted to the wildest psycho-Lamarckism. Yet here is Sulloway's summation: 'Freud's mature theory of dreaming is virtually unparalleled, even today, for the remarkable insight that it brought to bear upon the psychological mechanisms of dreaming' (p. 334). Though Freud is revealed to have derived his universal dream symbols from books like Karl Albert Scherner's *Das Leben des Traums* of 1861, Sulloway writes of 'his understanding of the frequency and the importance of symbols' (p. 337) in the universal language of dreaming. Freud is said to have 'discovered the specific *wish-fulfillment* meaning of dreams in 1895' (p. 322); later he 'came to see' the true role of dream censorship (p. 330). And having shown that the 'findings' gleaned from Freud's case histories always tagged along behind his latest theoretical passion, Sulloway none the less awards those same case histories 'considerable importance . . . in confirming his theory of dream interpretation' (p. 344). Freud's 'specific dream interpretations,' Sulloway opines, 'seem more acceptable to us than they once did to his colleagues' (p. 344).

Likewise, in the very paragraphs where he shows that Freud's notion of the id was extrapolated from his questionable dream theory (p. 329) and from the now discredited tenets of Lamarckian biogenetics (p. 365), Sulloway alludes to the 'discovery' of the id, as if that amorphous and ambiguous concept were a natural phenomenon that Freud had brought to light. Again, Freud is said to have 'grasped' and 'recognized' the meaning of slips (p. 351) – a meaning which, far from having been independently apprehended in a fresh investigation, was a mere by-product of the equally vulnerable repression aetiology. And though Sulloway's reconstruction of Freud's self-analysis plainly shows that Freud was already hunting among his memories for confirmation of Fliessian infantile sexuality, once again Sulloway writes of what Freud 'recognized', 'was able to recall', 'discovered', and 'was able to confirm' (p. 209). 'Self-analysis,' Sulloway concludes, 'finally allowed him to confirm from his own experience just how remarkably widespread the opportunities were in every *normal* childhood for both traumatic and spontaneous sexual activity' (p. 209). On the contrary, a reasonably sceptical reading of Sulloway's narrative 'confirms' only that Freud was, as usual, grasping at any pretext to turn his hunches into laws.[8]

Which Sulloway are we to believe, the one who has shown us a Freud habitually given to intellectual *ejaculatio praecox* or the one who calls Freud's major works 'a magnificent achievement, which certainly places Freud among the most creative scientific minds of all time . . .' (p. 358)? The answer is obvious. Not only does Sulloway's accumulated evidence speak more persuasively than his praise, but in later published comments he has characterized psychoanalysis as 'a highly problematic theoretical system' (Sulloway 1982a: 247) and remarked that the history of this 'narcissistic' movement 'is a fascinating example of the power that ideology can have when it becomes institutionalized within the educational mechanisms of science' (Sulloway 1983b: 36). As he wrote to me recently, 'there is nothing more dangerous than people who think they are right (and scientific) when they are not, especially after they have had eighty or ninety years to prove themselves.'[9]

Sulloway's current view of his book nevertheless differs significantly from my own. He tells me that much of the seemingly pro-Freudian language I have cited above merely characterizes Freud's own perception of what he was 'discovering' and 'recognizing'. No doubt that was the intent behind many individual passages of narrative. Yet we could be forgiven for inferring that Sulloway's explicit references to 'scientific greatness' mean what they say and provide a warrant for ascribing substance to Freud's 'recognitions' and 'discoveries'. Otherwise we are left with the paradox of a 'greatness' consisting entirely of error.

I suspect that Sulloway's confusion arose from three sources. First, he harboured the well-trained intellectual historian's awareness that scientific innovators often proceed in highly unorthodox ways and are given to loose speculation on any number of non-essential topics; thus he was determined not to be scandalized by Freud's departures from textbook inductivism. Second, in the absence of later critiques such as Grünbaum's, he was inclined to lend some credence to the analysts' clamorous arguments from 'clinical evidence'. And third, he admired Freud's synthetic vision for its sheer intricacy and scope, quite apart from its degree of empirical adequacy. Whatever his reasons may have been, however, the unfortunate result was that Sulloway failed to draw conclusions from the evidence of outright and egregious scientific malfeasance that runs through his account of Freud's conduct. We must attend to that evidence, segregated from its setting of palliative rhetoric, if we are to grasp the pseudo-scientific essence of Freud's intellectual tradition.

III

Of all Sulloway's reviewers only one, Frank Cioffi, fully understood that *Freud, Biologist of the Mind* not only exposes psychoanalytic myths but also exemplifies 'how difficult it is, even for an aspiring iconoclast, to stand upright in the presence of the Freud legend . . .' (Cioffi 1979: 504). And it was Cioffi again who posed the following important challenge, which carries us even beyond Sulloway's present assessment of Freud's standing:

Although much of what he recounts undermines it, Sulloway does not directly address the most potent and strategically necessary myth of all – the myth of Freud's superlative integrity. For the Freud myths were not devised by Freud's followers; they are no more than reiterations of accounts Freud himself had given. To depart from these would have been to impugn Freud's veracity and who, with the exception of one or two noble spirits, has been willing to do that? Certainly not Sulloway, who mealy-mouthedly concludes: 'The myths were merely [Freud's] historical due and they shall continue to live on protecting his brilliant legacy to mankind.'
Carry on lying.
(Cioffi 1979: 504)[10]

Cioffi's impugning of Freud's honesty sounds indecorous, but it is entirely justified by the biographical record that Sulloway and others have uncovered. Though Freud loved to sermonize about courageously opposing the human penchant for self-deception, it is no exaggeration to say that his psychoanalytic career was both launched and maintained by means of systematic mendacity. Sulloway's unwillingness, in 1979, to face that fact squarely rendered his argument inconclusive and even self-defeating. It is time to remedy that defect and, specifically, to understand the necessary relation between Freud's cavalier ethics and the scientific failings of his movement.

Freud's guile was truly chronic. For many years before and after he conceived of psychoanalysis, for example, he tried to erase from history his phase of fervent and destructive cocaine evangelism (Crews 1984: 11–12). In the pivotal Anna O. case he lied about Bertha Pappenheim's alleged cure by Breuer and lied again, in a maliciously self-serving story, about Breuer's flight from Pappenheim's supposed advances (Ellenberger 1970; 1972). One can add that he must also have lied to Breuer about his own fictitious cures of hysteria, for only on that basis, it appears, could Breuer have been coaxed into dusting off the thirteen-year-old Pappenheim case, about which he retained understandable misgivings, and reluctantly agreeing to collaboration with Freud in *Studies on Hysteria*.

Throughout his psychoanalytic career Freud lied about his therapeutic success, meanwhile privately confiding that such duplicity was necessary to keep his critics at bay (Crews 1984: 17). Again, having lifted key ideas from Albert Moll, Freud not only suppressed acknowledgment of his indebtedness but had the effrontery to accuse Moll of plagiarizing *him* (Sulloway 1983a: 313 + n., 315, 469). He lied to Fliess and then to the public in denying that he had 'leaked' Fliess's theory of bisexuality to Otto Weininger (Sulloway 1983a: 223–9). And he employed a blatant strategy of historical falsification in omitting from his *Autobiography* any mention of Fliess, without whose thirteen years of support and guidance psychoanalysis as we know it would never have come into existence.

Let us put together such conduct with the fetching tale Freud told about his titanic self-analysis and his persecution by fearful and prudish colleagues; with his seven-year silence before he could admit his privately recognized mistake about the seduction theory; with his recourse to tendentiously edited anecdotes and dream reports that appeared to validate his conclusions instead of merely exemplifying them (Glymour 1983); with his many dishonest references to his success as a clinician; with his anti-empirical insistence on absolute fidelity to his teachings; with his vendettas against former disciples who deviated from the prescribed line; with his denigration of opponents as sufferers from repression and resistance; and with the coercive rhetorical tactics that pervade his apologetics. We can then begin to grasp that Freud's greatest creation was not a scientific discovery but a seductive work of art, namely, the story he devised about a mythic Sigismund who had returned from the frightening psychic underworld with precious gifts for humankind.

My point, however, is not that Freud was by nature a congenital liar. It is rather that, given his determination to advance a doctrine that had literally nothing to be said in its scientific favour, he had no alternative to resorting to legend building. We cannot make adequate sense of the record, including the details that Sulloway so deftly recounts, unless we see that the arbitrariness of psychoanalysis itself dictated much of Freud's shifty behaviour.

Take, for example, Freud's Orwellian decision to obliterate Fliess's role in the formation of psychoanalytic theory. Sulloway, still inhibited by the remaining force of the psychoanalytic legend, explained that decision chiefly by reference to a general wish on Freud's part to disguise his biological premises so that psychoanalysis would appear to be an autonomous science. As some reviewers (e.g. Goldstein 1981; Himmelstein 1981; Holt 1981) noticed, such a motive does not in itself appear sufficiently pressing to have warranted a drastic falsification of the record. Yet the falsification assuredly did occur. It becomes understandable if we look more closely at the evidence that Sulloway himself provides regarding the flimsiness of Freud's 'science' at the time of his definitive quarrel and break with Fliess.

Sulloway makes it clear that Freud had to repudiate Fliess because in moving from the seduction theory to psychoanalysis proper he was bringing his thought into nearly total compatibility with Fliess's. That is, the locating of neurotic aetiology in the traumatic repression of 'normal' childhood sexuality rather than in repressed sexual abuse constituted a surrender to Fliess's account of the infant as a recapitulator of early man's adult sexual experience. Once Freud had taken that step, the pressing question was whether he had any right to put forward his exclusive authorship of psychoanalysis. As Sulloway shows, Fliess repudiated Freud because he came to believe that Freud intended to steal his ideas, only crediting Fliess with the subtheory of bisexuality which Freud had already tried unsuccessfully to appropriate as his own. If the world were ever to hear of Freud's real debt to Fliess, psychoanalysis would be revealed to have been generated by something other than Freud's genius as a diagnostician of himself and others.

The specific bone of contention at the Freud–Fliess breakup in 1900 was Fliess's theory of periodicity, which Freud had hitherto embraced with amazing credulousness (amazing, that is, to anyone who persists in regarding Freud as a prudent thinker). Even in later years Freud expressed grudging admiration for that side of Fliess's thought (Sulloway 1983a: 183). Why, then, was periodicity a sore point in 1900? The answer is that Fliess, as he himself recalled, adduced periodic processes to show Freud why 'neither sudden deteriorations nor sudden improvements were to be attributed to the analysis and its influence alone . . .' (quoted by Sulloway 1983a: 221). Fliess's argument was an explanation for Freud's therapeutic failure, and it must have incensed Freud precisely because, having told Fliess all along how badly his treatments were going, he had no effective rejoinder to propose. When Fliess refused Freud's peace offer of a collaborative book on bisexuality, Freud felt he had no choice but to bend every effort to turning Fliess into a non-person – a task he accomplished with an effectiveness that even Stalin might have envied.[11]

What ultimately concerns me here, I must repeat, is not Freud's desperate conduct *per se* but the necessary symbiosis between the unfoundedness of psychoanalytic claims and the manner in which they were – and still are – propounded. A doctrine like psychoanalysis can make its way in the world only by surrounding itself with rhetorical barbed wire, obscuring its unflattering origins and neutralizing objections through extrascientific means, either by direct slander (as in the continuing stigmatization of Fliess) or by generic diagnosis (all critics are suffering from repression) or by establishment of special epistemic barriers (only the analysed are entitled to criticize) or by the multiplying of escape clauses to forestall possible falsification. Psychoanalytic history is a rich data base for the study of all these restrictions upon intellectual give-and-take. In my opinion this is not an unhappy accident, the sign of a collective behavioural lapse that can be corrected once it has been pointed out; nor is it, as Sulloway appears to believe, a corruption of Freud's legacy; it is rather a native feature of psychoanalysis as a pseudo-science.

Here I diverge in emphasis from Grünbaum, whose well-merited polemic against Popper leads him to highlight the testability of some Freudian hypotheses. As Cioffi has urged in a trenchant and illuminating article (Cioffi 1970), it is not finally very interesting that certain psychoanalytic propositions, extracted from their context of vague auxiliary claims, can be treated as authentic hypotheses. What matters is that 'this is not the role which they have played in the lives of those who originated and transmitted them, nor of those who have since repeated, adapted or merely silently rehearsed them' (Cioffi 1970: 498). An emphasis on the potential falsifiability of some Freudian tenets obscures the more telling fact that everything about the actual propagation of psychoanalysis, from the inherent cloudiness of its concepts (Nagel 1959) through its safety nets against falsification and its cliquish means of repelling criticism, bespeaks contrariness to the empirical attitude. What marks psychoanalysis as a pseudo-science is not the unfoundedness of its propositions – a condition that could in principle be altered by events – but precisely that perennial reluctance to submit itself to the sink-or-swim ordeal of scientific evaluation.

Cioffi shows, and many other observers have confirmed, that Freud's most enduring penchant was for buttressing his dubious hypotheses with *ex post facto* provisos instead of asking himself whether they might be wrong. In part those provisos consisted of new theoretical entities and catch-all excuses, such as 'the hereditary factor' and 'the quantitative factor', which could be invoked whenever a given prediction went unfulfilled. Again, Freud coped with potential disconfirmation by brashly redefining his terms and stretching the scope of his concepts – as, for example, in *Beyond the Pleasure Principle* in his riposte to the proposal that shell-shock constitutes a challenge to the sexual aetiology of the neuroses: 'mechanical agitation [e.g., concussion in battle] must be recognized as one of the sources of sexual excitation' (S.E. 1920, XVIII: 33). And when all else failed, Freud simply invented a new mental law to cover the case at hand, blithely overlooking his own previous adherence to an opposite law or cynically calculating that no one would recall the earlier pronouncement.

Thus, as Cioffi (1970) shows, by putting disparate texts together we can infer that, according to Freud, humanitarianism stems from repressed homosexuality but is also compatible with open homosexuality; childhood trauma both is and is not a necessary condition for neurosogenesis, which also comes about either from repressed perversion or in conjunction with active perverted practices; recall of specific sexual material from infancy is both necessary and unnecessary to the undoing of a neurosis; a strict super-ego is produced by the misfortune of having either a hard, cruel father or, alternatively, an indulgent one; explicit castration threats are both required and not required for the generation of castration anxiety; the unconscious contains no contradictions but is perpetually engaged in coping with them; and Little Hans at age four owed his mental health to the sexually enlightened attitude of his parents, whose prudish falsehoods about sex brought on the same Little Hans's animal phobia at age five. Quintessential pseudo-scientist that he was, Freud could not be bothered to notice that his conflicting claims, taken together, free us from each of those claims singly; he was too busy extricating himself from one potential embarrassment after another.

Freud was already a pseudo-scientist from the hour that he published *The Interpretation of Dreams*, disingenuously invoking therapeutic success as proof of his repression aetiology and employing sheer allegorical ingenuity to paper over outrageous methodological liberties.[12] As he progressed in his career, increasingly averting his gaze from the dis-heartening realm of observation and fixing it instead on suppositions about instinct and prehistory, things only got worse. And here – in tracing Freud's increasingly reckless invocation of 'the hereditary factor' – is where we can return to Sulloway's book as an especially rich repository of evidence. Sulloway shows not only that the 'mature' Freud held genetic excuses at the ready for any case in which the predicted sexual noxae might not be forthcoming, but also that even an unpropitious-looking short-term line of inheritance could be trumped by reference to 'the antiquities of human development', which had allegedly 'stored up' erotic trouble in modern Europeans through Lamarckian memory traces of primeval traumas (S.E. 1917, XVI: 371).

The late appearance of this ultimate explanatory wild card is a sign of the mounting trouble Freud was having in justifying the relatively straightforward but no less fanciful Oedipal repression aetiology of 1897. The same reason helps to account for his theoretical turn toward fixed and universal dream symbols (which could redirect any interpretation that threatened to be non-sexual), toward masochism (which could account for a dream that seemed not to convey a wish), and toward the death instinct and the repetition compulsion (which ascribed to the organism powerful inherent tendencies justifying, among other salient phenomena, the failure of neurotics to respond dramatically to psychoanalytic treatment). Freud's eventually explicit appeal to Lamarckism at a time when that doctrine was in very broad retreat is only the most spectacular instance of his willingness to pay any price to spare his pet ideas.[13]

Freud's heirs, whom Sulloway is inclined to disprize as 'ideologizers' of psychoanalytic insight, think they have significantly improved on this lamentable record – but have they? Both the defenders and the critics of ego psychology in its multiple exfoliated forms have scanted the fundamental continuity of pseudo-scientific method throughout the Freudian tradition. Even in the act of altering some of Freud's notions, modern analysts have faithfully perpetuated his habits of supporting claims with question-begging anecdotes and further claims, of looking only for confirming rather than disconfirming signs, and of appeasing doubts by alluding to decisive factors accessible only to the anointed investigator and his peers. And when contemporary Freudians pride themselves on doing without the phylogenetic line of reasoning, as if the rest of the system were adequately determinate in its specifying of claims and consequences, they appear to be doing their best to illustrate the Freudian mechanism of denial. Apparently they feel that psychoanalysis can now survive by gradually dismantling some of its excrescent theoretical knobs and pulleys, just as it formerly survived by superadding them. Both stratagems are reprehensible dodges against long-standing and unanswerable doubts about Freud's original scientific romance. Despite some expressions of misgiving and halfway attempts at reform (e.g. Edelson 1984), the entire Freudian record from the 1890s until now is eloquently self-consistent.

I believe that the future study of psychoanalysis will be most fruitfully concentrated on the phenomenon that Sulloway, to his permanent credit, first brought to our attention: the propagating of a legend which has carried its own anti-scientific and authoritarian means of inducing belief, rejecting criticism and coping with deviation. If I am right, *Freud, Biologist of the Mind* will remain indispensable – provided, however, it is read with the precautions I have detailed above.

When Sulloway praises the sophistication of Freud's brainchild, noting that 'Freud recognized every possible combination of hereditary predisposition with environmental determinism' (1983a: 319), we must insist that the perceived sophistication was that of an overreaching system builder, not of a scrupulous empiricist or even of an error-prone one. True, Freud showed considerable imagination and subtlety in being at once genetic and environmentalist, psychological and biological in outlook. But Sulloway, I think, does not adequately recognize that this grand inclusiveness of causal reference, whereby each cited factor served in practice to safeguard the others from refutation, was already pseudo-scientific in Freud's hands before Freud himself became a sainted authority figure. Psychoanalysis did not go astray by allowing 'ideology' to become 'institutionalized within the educational mechanisms of science'. It went astray because it never adhered to the scientific spirit in the first place. If we can finally face that fact without equivocation, we will find ourselves readier not just to answer Freudian sophistries, but to greet with appropriate scepticism whatever opiate of the intellectuals awaits us next.

NOTES

1   The 'religious' apprehension of psychoanalysis was epitomized in a published letter objecting to my most recent polemic against psychoanalysis (Crews 1985). 'Surely Crews . . . would agree that there are ways of discovering truth other than the strictly objective and scientific. What of aesthetic and intuitive, personal and relational, and religious truth – of all the "reasons of the heart"? It is in the realms of the personal and "existential", the relational and "intersubjective", that the truth of psychoanalysis may be found' (Rogers 1985).

This view is so widely shared, especially among my humanist colleagues, that it deserves a careful reply. In the first place, there is no uniquely scientific way of *discovering* truth; any means will do, including being hit on the head with an apple or dreaming of snakes arrayed in rings. Let us by all means leave room for intuition. Scientific rigour properly enters the picture only when we try to ascertain whether purported laws of nature, however derived, merit our belief.

Universal propositions about mental functioning constitute such purported laws. For example, Freud's assertion that a neurosis is always the 'negative' of a perversion aspires to the status of a reliable generalization about the world we commonly experience, and as such it risks falsification – or would do so if psychoanalysts behaved less dogmatically – in exactly the same sense as a proposition about the mating habits of bees or the orbits of the planets. If, on the other hand, people like Rogers mean to assert that 'religious truth' resides in the therapeutic experience, not in the propositional content, of psychoanalysis, then their position is simply incoherent. Even the most intense experience asserts nothing and thus cannot be meaningfully characterized as 'true'.

2   See, for example, Jonathan Lieberson's review of Grünbaum's *Foundations*

in the *New York Review of Books*. Finding no cogent way to weaken Grünbaum's case, Lieberson simply decrees in conclusion, 'Nevertheless, there is something to psychoanalysis . . .' and he chides Grünbaum for not making due allowance for *future* improvements in the theory (Lieberson 1985: 28). Does it make sense to award a psychological doctrine a special 'something' that is exempt from all requirements of demonstration or to take as yet unattempted corrections of psychoanalytic theory to be reassurance that the theory itself is fundamentally sound? According to the same logic we could spare astrology from debunking by imagining a day when the ancient charts will have been brought into more exact alignment with the modern conformation of the heavens.

3   I owe thanks to Jennifer Snodgrass and to Dr Sulloway himself for supplying me with 79 reviews and other discussions in English, French, German and Italian. Dr Sulloway has also kindly offered comments on a draft of this paper.

4   I do not maintain that all negative comments on Sulloway's book have been motivated by prejudice. Some reviewers correctly noted that Sulloway gives short shrift to Freud's later career and to his non-scientific sources of inspiration, and many complained, not without reason, that he pays too little heed to the internally systemic traits of psychoanalysis as opposed to its borrowings from other fields. Still others objected to a certain grandiosity of tone, to Sulloway's favouritism toward a questionable-looking theory of birth order and creativity, and to signs of excessive reverence toward his Harvard mentor Edward O. Wilson and the controversial field of sociobiology. Of course none of these reservations diminish the importance of Sulloway's research – largely accomplished, it should be pointed out, when the author was still in his twenties.

5   As Sulloway protested in his preface to the paperback edition, Wollheim and others had chosen to attack a straw man; the actual thesis of the book is that 'Freudian psychoanalysis is a sophisticated "psychobiology"', focused squarely on the mind but drawing inspiration from evolutionary and embryological theory as well as from extant conceptions of physiology, anthropology and psychology proper (Sulloway 1983a: xv).

6   For notable exceptions see Cioffi 1979 and Hopkins 1979.

7   One can see from the sprinkling of favourable reviews by psychoanalysts why Sulloway must have been tempted to accentuate the positive in this manner. One reviewer even suggested that *Freud, Biologist of the Mind* 'be advocated as the work with which psychoanalytic candidates . . . will have to start from now on' (Pruyser 1980: 401). If this should come to pass, I hope the institutes will have the foresight to collect their students' fees in advance.

8   For discussion of Freud's unlikely self-analytic 'memories' and the cavalier logic of the conclusions he drew from them, see Crews 1984: 17–18.

9   Letter of 21 Jan. 1985; quoted with permission.

10   Sulloway's actual concluding sentence reads: 'The myths are merely his

historical due, and they shall continue to live on, protecting his brilliant legacy to mankind, as long as this legacy remains a powerful part of human consciousness' (Sulloway 1983a: 503; the myths in question are listed, explained, and challenged on pp. 489–95).

11   Of course the analogy with Stalin has its limits. Stalin was a heartless murderer, and though Fliess apparently believed that Freud literally wanted to kill him in 1900 (Swales 1982), that charge can never be proven. A further difference resides in the fact that while Stalin made up lies about his former associates in order to justify destroying them, there is no evidence that he actually came to believe those lies. Freud, by contrast, convinced himself that Fliess was Exhibit A of the rule that repressed homosexuality can bring on paranoia; indeed, he told Abraham that this aetiology had been revealed to him precisely through his effort to understand Fliess's case (Sulloway 1983a: 234–5). Here is a paradigmatic instance of the still prevalent tendency among Freudians to declare their opponents mentally disturbed – a tactic that, interestingly enough, was to become standard practice in Soviet psychiatry.

12   'Faced with the evidence that the methods on which almost all of his work relied were in fact unreliable, Freud had many scientifically honorable courses of action available to him. He could have published his doubts and continued to use the same methods, reporting his results in company with caveats. He could have published his doubts and abandoned the subject. He could have attempted experimental inquiries into the effects of suggestion in his therapeutic sessions. He did none of these things . . . Instead he published *The Interpretation of Dreams* to justify by rhetorical devices the very methods he had every reason to distrust' (Glymour 1983: 70). In Glymour's keen estimation *The Interpretation of Dreams* 'formed a turning point in Freud's life and work: half a rotation from scientist towards mountebank' (1983: 69).

13   See Sulloway 1983a: 440, and the classic discussion by Nagel, who remarks: 'Freud did not think that his conclusion, though regarded by all competent biologists as false, refuted *any* of his premises. It is therefore pertinent to ask what could refute those premises and whether they are at all refutable' (Nagel 1959: 44). Nagel here construes 'refutable' in Cioffi's sense, not Grünbaum's; that is, he sees no *disposition* on Freud's part to be dissuaded by any consideration.

REFERENCES

Bernstein, Arnold 1980: Rev. in *Modern Psychoanalysis*, 5, 97–9.
Brooks, Peter 1980: The crypto-biologist. *New York Times Book Review*, 10 Feb.: 9, 26.
Chessick, Richard D. 1980: Rev. in *American Journal of Psychotherapy*, 34, 446–7.

Cioffi, Frank 1970: Freud and the idea of a pseudo-science, in Robert Borger and Frank Cioffi (eds), *Explanation in the Behavioural Sciences*. Cambridge: Cambridge University Press: 471–99.

Cioffi, Frank 1979: Freud – new myths to replace the old. *New Society*, 50, no. 895 (29 Nov.): 503–4.

Crews, Frederick 1984: The Freudian way of knowledge. *The New Criterion*, June: 7–25.

Crews, Frederick 1985: The future of an illusion. *The New Republic*, 21 Jan.: 28–33.

'Did Freud build his own legend?' 1979: *Time*, 30 July: 51.

Dinnage, Rosemary 1979: The genius of Freud. *Observer*, 9 Dec.: 41–3.

Edelson, Marshall 1984: *Hypothesis and Evidence in Psychoanalysis*. Chicago: University of Chicago Press.

Ellenberger, Henri F. 1970: *The Discovery of the Unconscious: The History and Evolution of Dynamic Psychiatry*. New York: Basic Books.

Ellenberger, Henri F. 1972: The story of 'Anna O': a critical review with new data. *Journal of the History of the Behavioural Sciences*, 8, 267–79.

Eysenck, H. J. 1980: Freudian myths. *Books and Bookmen*, 25 Feb.: 38.

Eysenck, H. J. and Wilson, Glenn D. 1973: *The Experimental Study of Freudian Theories*. London: Methuen.

Fromm, Gerard 1980: Freud rescued from psychoanalysis. *Commonweal*, 107, 251–2.

Gifford, George E. 1980: Rev. in *Journal of the History of the Behavioral Sciences*, 16, 388–9.

Glazer, Michael 1980: Rev. in *Group*, 4, 60–1.

Glymour, Clark 1983: The theory of your dreams, in R. S. Cohen and L. Laudan (eds), *Physics, Philosophy and Psychoanalysis: Essays in Honor of Adolf Grünbaum*. Dordrecht: D. Reidel: 57–71.

Goldstein, Jan 1981: Rev. in *Journal of Modern History*, 53, 304–6.

Grünbaum, Adolf 1984: *The Foundations of Psychoanalysis: A Philosophical Critique*. Berkeley: University of California Press.

Habermas, Jürgen 1971: *Knowledge and Human Interests*, trans. Jeremy J. Shapiro. Boston: Beacon Press.

Harvey, Joy 1982: Rev. in *Journal of the History of Biology*, 15, 317–18.

Himmelstein, Jerome L. 1981: Rev. in *Theory and Society*, 10, 463–7.

Holt, Robert H. 1981: The great analyst reanalyzed. *Contemporary Psychology*, 26, 95–6.

Hopkins, Jim 1979: Killing and eating father. *New Statesman*, 98, 900.

Huxley, Francis 1980: Married to the Sphinx. *Guardian Weekly*, 6 Jan.: 21.

Jahoda, Marie 1979: From the bench to the couch. *New Scientist*, 6 Dec.: 792.

Kanzer, Mark 1980: Rev. in *Psychoanalytic Quarterly*, 49, 517–23.

Kern, Carl 1980: Freud: biologist in disguise? *Mind and Medicine*, Apr.: 1, 4, 6–7.

Khan, M. Masud R. 1981: Rev. in *International Review of Psycho-analysis*, 8, 125.

Leonard, John 1979: 'Freud, Biologist of the Mind'. *Books of the Times*, Oct.: 491–2.

Lieberson, Jonathan 1985: Putting Freud to the test. *New York Review of Books*, 31 Jan.: 24–8.

Lothane, Zvi 1981: Rev. in *Psychoanalytic Review*, 68, 348–61.

Nagel, Ernest 1959: Methodological issues in psychoanalytic theory, in Sidney Hook (ed.), *Psychoanalysis, Scientific Method and Philosophy*. New York: New York University Press: 38–56.

Pollock, George H. 1981: Rev. in *Journal of Interdisciplinary History*, 11, 517–20.

Pruyser, Paul W. 1980: Rev. in *Bulletin of the Menninger Clinic*, 44, 400–2.

Ricoeur, Paul 1970: *Freud and Philosophy*, trans. Dennis Savage. New Haven: Yale University Press.

Robinson, Paul 1979: Freud as sociobiologist. *Psychology Today*, Sept.: 97–9.

Rogers, Marc 1985: Letter to *The New Republic*, 11 Feb.: 2.

Steiner, George 1979: Freud and the myth of the leader. *Sunday Times*, Nov.: 40.

Storr, Anthony 1979: The super ego of Sigmund Freud. *Book World (Washington Post)*, 23 Sept.: 4–5.

Strouse, Jean 1979: Freud without myths. *Newsweek*, 29 Oct.: 97–8.

Sulloway, Frank J. 1982a: Profeta? No, biologo. Intervista con Frank J. Sulloway. *Panorama*, 13 Dec.: 239–52.

Sulloway, Frank J. 1982b: Freud and biology: the hidden legacy, in William R. Woodward and Mitchell G. Ash (eds), *Psychology in Nineteenth-Century Thought*. New York: Praeger: 198–227.

Sulloway, Frank J. 1983a: *Freud, Biologist of the Mind: Beyond the Psychoanalytic Legend*. New York: Basic Books. First edn, 1979.

Sulloway, Frank J. 1983b: Ideology and the control of scientific knowledge: the case of Freud and his psychoanalytic legend, in M. Ranchetti (ed.), *Psicoanalisi e storia delle scienze*. Florence: Leo S. Olschki.

Swales, Peter J. 1982: Freud, Fliess, and fratricide: the role of Fliess in Freud's conception of paranoia. Privately published by the author.

Wallace, Edwin R. 1982: Rev. in *Bulletin of the History of Medicine*, 56, 602–4.

Wollheim, Richard 1979: Was Freud a crypto-biologist? *New York Review of Books*, 8 Nov.: 25–8.

12

On the Irrelevance of Psychoanalysis to Literary Criticism

PETER LAMARQUE

I

Frederick Crews, once a leading proponent of psychoanalytic literary criticism (Crews 1966; 1975), is now an outspoken and uncompromising critic of psychoanalysis *tout court* (Crews 1980a; 1980b). In his chapter here he rejects Freudianism, in all its forms, for its 'empirical groundlessness' and seeks support for this wholesale condemnation from Frank J. Sulloway's detailed intellectual history *Freud, Biologist of the Mind*. In fact he chides Sulloway for not drawing what he, Crews, sees as the inevitable consequences of this history: that psychoanalysis is utterly discredited as 'pseudo-scientific' and that Freud himself was guilty of 'systematic mendacity'. These are strong charges. But I will leave it to others to take up the debate over Freud's credibility as a scientist.

Instead I will use the occasion of this reply to offer some reflections about psychoanalysis in relation to literary criticism: first, to recall the seductive power of psychoanalysis in this context, which perhaps accounts for Crews's own espousal of the theory, and then to cast doubt on the cogency of the *prima facie* case by showing that at best we have only parallels, not intrinsic connections, between psychoanalytic investigation and the aims of literary criticism.

My conclusion, that neither psychoanalytic theory nor its clinical methods are relevant to literary criticism, will no doubt find favour with Crews. But my argument rests on a quite different basis from his in that it depends in no way on the validity or otherwise of psychoanalysis itself.

One methodological criticism of Crews's argument is relevant for my purposes. It is this: in general questions about the history or origin of a theory and questions about its acceptability or its fruitfulness must be kept apart. Even if many of the core ideas of psychoanalysis were neither original to Freud nor forward-looking, even if the sources for the ideas merit, as Crews says, 'our hearty distrust', even if Freud's own integrity in propagating the ideas is suspect, we are not led inevitably to a rejection of the ideas in themselves. After all, it is a commonplace about scientific revolutions that wild assumptions and unscrupulous propaganda are not inimical to either truth or genius. The fruitfulness indeed of Freudian theory is often thought to be given exemplary illustration in the case of literary criticism.

It is, though, a notable feature of applications of psychoanalysis to literary criticism how little attention is given to the scientific credentials of the theory. Questions of empirical support, explanatory and predictive power, or clinical efficacy are rarely debated by proponents of psychoanalysis in criticism. I take it that a characteristic attitude is one adopted by a recent writer on the subject who describes psychoanalysis as a 'science of interpretation': 'The emphasis must be on the interpretative force of the theory instead of on a simplistic true/false analysis of what are highly subjective phenomena' (Wright 1984: 3). Indeed this writer uses the point to brush aside Crews's own objections to the scientific credibility of psychoanalysis (Wright 1984: 49). Perhaps behind this thinking – though it is not made explicit – is something like the 'hermeneutic' conception of psychoanalytic theory, as developed by Habermas (1971) and Ricoeur (1970), which rejects altogether the 'scientistic' status of the theory.[1]

There is a still broader tendency which contributes, I think, to an uneasy tolerance within the literary critical community towards psychoanalytic contributions: namely, that whatever the scientific respectability of psychoanalytic theory its application can often afford 'insights' into literary works and that as the demands of strict verification are in any case inappropriate in criticism the independent validity of the theory is not of crucial concern. In Geoffrey Hartmann's playful terms, 'passing through psychoanalysis' is widely tolerated, even among the otherwise sceptical (Hartmann 1978: viii). In the interests of openmindedness and a desire to welcome insights from any source, psychoanalytic criticism has become established as one among a number of critical approaches in the canon of accepted methods.

Against this commendable pluralism, it will be my contention that in fact so-called psychoanalytic criticism faces an inescapable predicament. Where criticism simply helps itself to the vocabulary of psychoanalysis without regard to the theory from which it arises it is not *psychoanalytic* criticism, where it makes essential use of psychoanalysis as an explanatory theory it is not psychoanalytic *criticism*.

II

The first step is to outline the *prima facie* case for the relevance of psychoanalysis to literary criticism. But straight away a caveat is in order. As Murray M. Schwartz (1978) has aptly warned: 'There are psychoanalys*es* today; there is no psychoanalysis.' Indeed the subject has become so complex that generalizations are increasingly suspect. Nevertheless, since psychoanalysis is strictly Freud's preserve,[2] by directing the bulk of my remarks to Freud's own theories and by concentrating on matters of general principle, I believe that what I have to say will have implications for the whole enterprise of 'psychoanalytic approaches' to literature.

I suggest there are five main categories under which psychoanalysis has a claim to the attention of literary critics. I will list them in ascending order of forcefulness: (1) the direct influence of Freud; (2) a shared subject matter; (3) Freudian theories of the creation and reception of literary works; (4) the attraction of psychoanalytic readings; (5) some apparently impressive analogies. At this stage my purpose is only to outline a *prima facie* case; my assessment of each category will follow in the next section.

1 *The direct influence of Freud.* Freud's enormous influence on both literature itself and literary criticism in the twentieth century is undeniable. Lionel Trilling could write of this influence in 1941: 'Much of it is so pervasive that its extent is scarcely to be determined; . . . it has been infused into our life and become a component of our culture of which it is now hard to be specifically aware' (Trilling 1972: 279). Trilling singles out for particular mention the influence on the Surrealists, Kafka, Thomas Mann and James Joyce but in fact as the century advances it becomes increasingly hard to think of any writer (of stature) who is positively not influenced by Freudian ideas. Of course this influence can take many forms and can be more or less self-conscious: from a superficial use of 'Freudian' symbols or dreams inviting interpretation as disguised wish-fulfilments to deeper thematic explorations of pathological conditions. Georg Lukács (1972) has characterized the whole of modernist literature as a 'flight into psychopathology'.

Once again, what is striking about this influence, in both its seriousness and its extent, is its independence of the standing of Freud's theories in the scientific community. This has led Joseph Margolis to the suggestion that the theories have acquired the status of a 'myth', which he defines (1980: 152) as 'a schema of the imagination which, independently of the scientific status of the propositions it may subtend, is capable of effectively organizing our way of viewing portions of the external world in accord with its distinctions'. Of course some explanation is needed for how such a 'myth' gets established but that is not primarily a philosophical inquiry.

The sheer volume of critical writing about literary works that overtly draws on Freudian ideas is further justification for calling the ideas mythic. But the exact nature of this influence on criticism takes us into later categories.

2　*A shared subject matter.* We can turn again to Trilling to express the close affinities between psychoanalysis and literature with respect to subject matter: 'the human nature of the Freudian psychology is exactly the stuff upon which the poet has always exercised his art' (1972: 276). Freud himself frequently acknowledged his debt to the poets and this must contribute significantly to the lasting appeal of psychoanalysis in literary circles.

Freud believed not only that creative writers had anticipated him in the discovery of the unconscious but that their writings could provide a valuable source of *evidence* for his own scientific treatment of the same ideas. In his essay on Wilhelm Jensen's novel *Gradiva*, for example (S.E. 1907, IX: 8), Freud asserts that 'creative writers are valuable allies and their evidence is to be prized highly'. This novel, with its archaeological motifs, provides a nice allegory of self-discovery; the emergence of the protagonist's memories and the enigmatic revelations in his dreams give an undoubtedly 'Freudian' feel to the story. Freud insists that even though the author knew nothing of his theory (of dreams and delusions), 'we have not discovered anything in his work that is not already in it'. He goes on: 'We probably draw from the same source and work upon the same object, each of us by another method. And the agreement of our results seems to guarantee that we have both worked correctly' (S.E. 1907, IX: 92).

Similar, if less detailed, appeals to literary works for support for psychoanalytic theory occur throughout Freud's writing. For example, in his discussion of parapraxes he offers instances (1901, 1916) of (deliberate) slips of the tongue in Schiller's play *Wallenstein* and in *The Merchant of Venice*. One recent commentator has even claimed that 'the poets discovered *psychoanalysis* before Freud did' (Skura 1981: 4).

I suggest that at the root of all such claims, at least that psychoanalysis and poetry have drawn from the same source, is an important feature of

Freudian theory, namely, its convergence with common sense or 'folk-psychology'.[3] Farrell remarks of this common sense:

It has . . . been familiar for centuries with ideas connected with human beings having impulses, growing up to deal with the world, developing a conscience, learning and losing self-control, with feelings of guilt and shame, and so on. In other words, common sense is familiar with those aspects of human functioning which the concepts of Id, Ego and Superego cover in their low level use.

(Farrell 1981: 216)

This goes a long way towards explaining the 'mythical' grip of Freudianism. In popularized forms it is highly congenial to folk beliefs.

Finally, there is a rather different, but complementary, assimilation of psychoanalysis to literature. This comes in the increasingly widespread inclination to treat Freud's own work as a species of imaginative writing. Hence such comments as this: 'his writings invite us to enter and experience his fantastic psychoanalytic universe imaginatively as we share the vision of great novelists like Dostoievsky, who make the sublime, the ridiculous, and the despicably criminal palpably human and immediately real to us' (Spector 1972: 183). No wonder questions of verification or scientific respectability get pushed to one side. Who would seek to verify Dostoievsky?

3 *Freudian theories of the creation and reception of literary works.* Our first two categories have focused on what might be called psychoanalysis *in* literature. The remaining categories concern psychoanalysis *of*, or *applied to*, literature. The starting point here has been clearly put by Crews himself: 'The simple fact that literature is made and enjoyed by human minds guarantees its accessibility to study in terms of broad principles of psychic and social functioning (1970: 1). Admittedly, Crews goes on to discuss why this 'simple fact' is not universally accepted by critics, but its forcefulness in the *prima facie* case is undeniable.

Psychoanalysis has a great deal to say, if not always consistently, about how literary works come to be 'made and enjoyed'. It is a legitimate, and fundamental, question in the study of human nature why fictional and imaginative writing should have the prominence it does. In an early essay on the subject, 'Creative Writers and Day-dreaming' (1908), Freud attributes to writers only the pursuit of egotistical fantasies. This view is often thought, even by psychoanalytic critics, to have had unwelcome consequences for criticism. Freud wrote:

A strong experience in the present awakens in the creative writer a memory of an earlier experience (usually belonging to his childhood) from which there now

proceeds a wish which finds its fulfilment in the creative work. The work itself exhibits elements of the recent provoking occasion as well as of the old memory.
(S.E. 1908, IX: 151)

This assertion heralded an era of crudely reductive analyses and psycho-biography. But if psychoanalytic views of creativity have become more refined they have by no means abandoned the link with personal fantasy. In the light of Freud's suggestion, in 1917, that art is 'a path that leads back from phantasy to reality' (S.E. 1917, XVI: 375) attention has come to focus on the path itself, and the peculiar disguises the fantasies take.

Psychoanalytic theory also offers an explanation of our enjoyment of imaginative writing which, Freud claims, 'proceeds from a liberation of tensions in our minds' (S.E. 1908, IX: 153), a kind of 'forepleasure' in sharing a fantasy softened by literary form. In an earlier, and subtle, essay 'Psychopathic Characters on the Stage' Freud describes our enjoyment of tragic portrayals as 'based on an illusion': the viewer's 'suffering is mitigated by the certainty that, firstly, it is someone other than himself who is acting and suffering on the stage, and, secondly, that after all it is only a game' (S.E. 1905, VII: 306). Psychoanalysis promises not only a general explanation of why we enjoy certain genres – tragedies, romances, even comedies (given Freud's theory of jokes) – but also why particular works have an enduring appeal. A common, perhaps disturbing, fantasy in an attractive disguise will ensure a lasting interest.

What is most striking is how comfortably this psychoanalytic vocabulary – 'fantasy', 'fulfilment', 'earlier experience', 'illusion', 'suffering', 'game' – dovetails with antecedently *literary* concerns. Also, of course, it is a widespread folk belief that fiction can offer 'escape' as well as 'forbidden pleasures'. Add to this the lack of alternative systematic theories of creativity and response, and psychoanalytic explanations come to seem the most natural framework for understanding the elusive *ars poetica* and its charms.

4   *The attraction of psychoanalytic readings.* Psychoanalytic interpretation of literature has both encouraged and flourished in an age of virtuosity in criticism. Novelty and ingenuity are rewarded when 'interpretation' becomes a pre-eminent mode of reading. Under pressure from formalism, the recovery of a writer's consciously intended meaning has come to seem a parochial, even inappropriate, aim in criticism. When the acceptability of an interpretation is seen instead to reside in ingenuity and 'insight', the sheer daring of some psychoanalytic readings has guaranteed them a continued attention. Freud's own suggestions, in *The Interpretation of Dreams*, about the character of Hamlet – the attempt to explain Hamlet's

hesitations in terms of repressed desires, later characterized as the Oedipus complex – have acquired almost the status of orthodoxy. Unfortunately, after Ernest Jones's more sweeping claims in *Hamlet and Oedipus* (1949), it is often forgotten how modest was Freud's own view of the interpretation: 'all genuinely creative writings are the product of more than a single motive and more than a single impulse in the poet's mind, and are open to more than a single interpretation' (S.E. 1900, IV: 206).

Perhaps not much in general can be said about the attractions of psychoanalytic readings. I will be discussing their nature and legitimacy later. Just like Freud's own interpretations of parapraxes, dreams and neurotic symptoms, they vary enormously with respect to plausibility. Certainly, there is a *frisson* to be had, even where plausibility is low, in the 'revelations' of sexuality in unexpected places; Norman Holland, for example, sees phallic symbolism in Macbeth's 'Out, out, brief candle' (1968: 111). More pertinently, psychoanalysis is often called upon to help with problem cases in criticism. One such is Shakespeare's *Measure for Measure*, which has long eluded critical understanding. A recent sympathetic reading, working from the Elizabethan pun on 'dying', is an imaginative effort to make sense of the play in psychoanalytic terms (Skura 1981: 243–70). In all such endeavours the psychoanalytic approach appears to stand foursquare with the alternatives. 'Insights' are particularly welcome where genuine puzzles present themselves.

5 *Some apparently impressive analogies.* Perhaps the most powerful appeal of psychoanalysis to literary critics, at least from a theoretical point of view, rests on a supposed similarity of aim, revolving round the ideas of interpretation and meaning. As Meredith Anne Skura has observed, 'psychoanalysis and criticism are both interpretive acts that have come of age during the same century and have been influenced by the same intellectual currents' (1981: 271). Freud's claim that parapraxes, dreams and symptoms have a *sense* which can be revealed through *analysis* certainly suggests a strong analogy with literary criticism. This impression is enhanced by the very form in which Freud presents, for example, his case histories. The fact that Freudian analyses reveal not only an underlying sense but also 'tensions', 'ambiguities', 'associations', 'symbolic meanings', and so on, will in itself predispose even the formalist critic in their favour.

There are further striking analogies. One is the distinction between manifest and latent content and another, related to this, the 'literary' mechanisms of the dream-work: condensation and displacement. The mind structures and transforms a deep or hidden thought, a meaning, into an overt, and often unrecognizable, form; analysis reverses the process and rediscovers the meaning. It is this that lies behind Trilling's grandiose assertion that 'of all mental systems, the Freudian psychology is the one which makes poetry indigenous to the very constitution of the mind' (1972: 287).

Yet another analogy can be noted arising from Freud's thesis of psychic determinism. The idea that nothing, however seemingly 'trivial', that occurs in the mind is arbitrary or undeserving of attention (S.E. 1916, XV: 26–8) seems to correspond to an established maxim of criticism which attributes a 'functionality' to all elements in a work (see Olsen 1978: 94, on the 'principle of functionality').

Finally, psychoanalysts have been impressed by analogies from the clinical context. The 'dynamic' relation between patient and analyst – involving resistance, transference, projection, concealment, etc. – has been thought (Wright 1984: ch. 6) to reflect the complex interaction between a reader and a text (or author).

I have said least about these last two categories because they will call for the most detailed scrutiny later on.

III

So much, then, for the *prima facie* case in favour of the relevance of psychoanalysis to criticism. I suggest that the main reasons why psychoanalysis has retained the attention of literary critics *without regard to its status as a scientific theory* lie within these five categories. Do they add up to an irresistible justification for a distinctive 'psychoanalytic criticism'? I think not.

The first two categories have no implications for the appropriateness of a particular critical method. They refer only to a certain kind of subject matter in literary works. Those post-Freudian works overtly influenced by Freud's writings, where the themes and symbols are self-consciously represented, are in fact the least amenable to psychoanalytic methods, where these seek to reveal unconscious meanings. A condition for understanding such works is certainly a *knowledge* of the theory, but not an *application* of it. By analogy, a patient who openly avows an Oedipus complex is not a subject for analysis.

Those pre-Freudian works which allegedly anticipate Freudian ideas, for example in 'discovering' the unconscious, do so *ex hypothesi* in a distinctive way of their own. Their 'Freudian' appearance can, I think, largely be accounted for through a combination of the folk-psychological basis of Freudianism and the influence of the Freudian 'myth' (in Margolis's sense). When a critic simply borrows the vocabulary from the 'myth' to re-describe an independently identifiable subject matter then psychoanalytic theory is not being engaged. When the emphasis is on the value of such works in supporting psychoanalysis, as with Jensen's *Gradiva* or Schiller's *Wallenstein*, then a purpose quite distinct from literary criticism is involved. In such cases it is not the psychoanalytic method that illuminates the works but the works which illuminate, or give weight to, the method. Of course if the further claim is made that the only, or the best, way of making sense of the subject matter *in the distinctive form that it takes in the work* is by applying psychoanalytic methods then the acceptability of the resulting interpretation becomes an issue in its own right, and we are into the considerations of category 4.

In category 3 I quoted a sentence from Crews to the effect that because literature is 'made and enjoyed by human minds' it must be accessible to psychological, and in this case psychoanalytic, study. The crucial objection to this, frequently made, is that those features which are accessible to psychological study are precisely not those in virtue of which the work is *literature* or *art*. Psychological explanations for the sources or effects of literature have no bearing on literary qualities *per se* and thus none on the critical investigation of those qualities.

The objection, though, cannot rest there. At a time when the very concept of literature is being called into question (e.g. in Eagleton 1983: ch. 1), it is no longer possible to take a complacent view of the 'autonomy' of literature or literary qualities. However, enough can be said, I think, to establish that psychological causes and effects will not determine critical methods.

The first step can be found in the notion that art is somehow 'depersonalized'. Crews (1970: 4) cites a version of this in Northrop Frye: 'Poetry can only be made out of other poems' (i.e. in contrast to the writer's private fantasies). A similar view appears in T. S. Eliot when he speaks of 'a continual extinction of personality' in art: 'the poet has, not a "personality" to express, but a particular medium' (1972: 73, 75). And in Jung (1972: 185) the point is aimed directly at Freud:

No objection can be raised if it is admitted that this approach amounts to nothing more than the elucidation of those personal determinants without which a work of art is unthinkable. But should the claim be made that such an analysis accounts for the work of art itself, then a categorical denial is called for. The personal idiosyncrasies that creep into a work of art are not essential; in fact the more we have to cope with these peculiarities, the less is it a question of art.

Jung goes on to speak of the artist, *qua* artist, as 'objective and impersonal'.

No doubt the rationale behind these views of a 'depersonalized' literature differs from case to case: Frye is concerned with the constraints on criticism, Eliot with the priority of 'tradition' over 'individual talent' and Jung with the role of a 'collective unconscious'. But each argument rests on a shared assumption that to consider something *as a work of art* is to accord it a special status, which is incompatible with its treatment merely as a product of psychological causes.

I think we can develop this point of view a stage further. The very concepts of 'art' and 'literature' function in a special way. They are not straightforwardly descriptive, at least in the sense of denoting 'natural' properties, either inherent features of a text (e.g. its subject matter or form) or its causal relations. There is no set of 'objective' defining characteristics. 'Art' and 'literature' are of course partly evaluative concepts but more significantly they are also 'institutional'. Literary works are only identified as such against the background of a cultural practice and conventions (see Olsen 1978: 94). Using a different terminology, they are 'culturally emergent' objects (see, e.g., Margolis 1980: ch. 3).

Here, then, lies the clue as to why so little follows from the observation that a work is 'made and enjoyed by human minds'. Just as no causal account of how a work came to be made or how it affects an audience can be sufficient for establishing that it is a work of art, so no psychological theory of those causes and effects makes it necessary to pursue a corresponding psychological investigation of the work when considered as a work of art. A simple parallel brings out the point. Consider the 'institution' of currency. No purely causal account of the manufacture of a banknote, just as no description of its physical properties, will explain its role in a system of currency. To understand its 'institutional' properties requires a quite different kind of investigation from the causal or 'scientific'.

Interestingly, this view of the institutional nature of literature need not be unacceptable to those who seek to eliminate the concept altogether; they simply draw different consequences from it. Thus some recent 'rejections' of literature have stemmed, misguidedly I believe, from the recognition that no set of objective properties can define 'literature'; other grounds for rejection have rested on the view that the cultural practice within which literature is embedded involves an outdated or undesirable ideology.[4] But strictly speaking none of this is a challenge to the *autonomy* of literature.

It is the ramifications of this autonomy that will occupy us in assessing the final two categories of the *prima facie* case. One well-known psychoanalytic theorist, Norman Holland, seems recently to have conceded the argument: 'psychoanalysis has nothing, nothing whatsoever, to tell us about literature *per se*' (quoted in Wright 1984: 67). Let us see why that must be so.

Psychoanalytic interpretations of individual works are often striking and ingenious. So why not acknowledge them as genuine contributions to literary understanding? I should emphasize that I am not attempting to legislate on what should or shouldn't be said about literary works. I am concerned simply to identify a distinctive class of judgements which constitute literary appreciation;[5] these are judgements, both interpretative and evaluative, about literature *per se*. Psychoanalytic interpretations, in contrast to the incidental use of psychoanalytic vocabulary, cannot by their very nature belong to this class. Ultimately, psychoanalysis is concerned with properties of a person, literary appreciation with properties of a work of art.

Various consequences, concerning these distinctive literary judgements, follow from the view that literary works are not constituted by objectively given properties, either features of a text (syntactic, semantic, rhetorical, structural, etc.) or causal relations with a writer or reader. One is that the judgements cannot be purely descriptive. Their aim rather is to identify or assign aesthetic purposes to the given textual features. Literary interpretation attributes aesthetic significance to elements of a text by subsuming the elements into ever wider combinative and thematic patterns. It does so in order to establish an overall aesthetic unity in the text. The patterns of significance thus revealed can be called aesthetic, rather than textual, features of the work. While they might be supervenient on, they are not reducible to, the textual features. They require a distinctive kind of judgement and discrimination for their identification. The literary understanding that results from such judgements can be considered as an end in itself; and the methods involved are *sui generis*. The validity of an interpretation on this account rests on criteria *defined internally to the practice of literary criticism*: a special kind of 'fit' is demanded between thematic pattern and text, as well as consistency, comprehensiveness, 'functionality', and so on (see Olsen 1978: ch. 5).

In contrast, psychoanalytic interpretations are concerned with significance in a quite different sense; their validity derives from a theoretical framework independent of literary practice and they assign to the elements in a text not an aesthetic function but a psychological one. Admittedly, psychoanalysis offers different models of literature for critical purposes, not all of which rely, like the fantasy model, on causal explanations.[6]

Traditionally, psychoanalytic approaches have focused either on the causes and effects of literary works or on character studies as 'case histories'. The recent comparisons between the reading process itself and psychoanalytic 'exchange' is a matter of analogy; we will return to it later.

What about the 'case history' model which seeks to apply psychoanalysis directly to characters? On the face of it this seems not to infringe either the 'depersonalized' view of literature (with regard to a writer's psychological states) or an autonomy based on the 'institutional' definition of literature. Yet an argument from autonomy is available against this model.

Skura, otherwise sympathetic to psychoanalysis, makes the first move:

for characters enmeshed in their fictional worlds, even the most sensitive and carefully descriptive psychoanalysis is out of place, though it would not be in life. My expectations about a man next door who acted like Leontes would be very different from my expectations about Leontes in *The Winter's Tale* . . . the cluster of traits can only mean what they mean in the play itself.

(Skura 1981: 41)

This is certainly right, yet it appeals to autonomy where it might seem at its most vulnerable, resting only on a distinction between characters and real people. A more powerful argument, I think, against psychoanalysing fictional characters emphasizes less their *fictional* status and more their role within a *literary* context. Freud is quite right not to be too concerned with the fictionality as such of Norbert Hanold in *Gradiva*. A psychoanalyst might quite legitimately invent and analyse a fictional case for expository purposes; Freud simply helped himself to one already available. There is nothing wrong with that. But taken as components in a literary work, Hanold's dream must be assumed to have a literary function. Now to say that the dreams have a sense in this context is, as we have seen, to say that they have a function within a pattern of meaning that unifies the work. That is a quite different kind of claim from saying that they arise from unconscious wishes in Hanold's mind.

The only complicating factor here is that we might well draw on a psychoanalytic vocabulary – repressed emotion, wish-fulfilment, etc. – to enrich our understanding of a character, as with Hanold in this example. These terms have an established place in our everyday thinking, under the influence of the Freudian 'myth'. So what marks the literary from the psychoanalytic interpretation is no longer the vocabulary used but the *purposes* attributed to the features of the text under discussion. The explanations offered for what functions are being fulfilled by textual elements (like Hanold's dreams) will differ radically.

As we turn to the final category – the impressive-seeming analogies between psychoanalysis and literary criticism – we already have all the background to establish that what we have are at best parallels only.

Beginning with the analogies from the psychoanalytic process – the dynamics of the patient/analyst relation – while it might be instructive to pursue these, it is clear that in principle the parallels within literary criticism are either purely contingent or involve independently identifiable and explicable phenomena. They are contingent where they refer to particular psychological attitudes of a reader (like emotional attachments, self-deception, etc.), they are independently identifiable where they refer to rhetorical 'strategies' in texts, such as 'invit[ing] complicity' or 'ward[ing] off understanding' (Skura 1981: 183). The devices of rhetoric are already the stock-in-trade of critics and while the parallels might be interesting they are not indispensable to critical method.

Similarly, the analogy between psychic determinism and a principle of functionality in criticism is merely superficial, in that the former is rooted in what Freud calls the '*Weltanschauung* of science' (S.E. 1916, XV: 28) while the latter is essentially linked to aesthetic unity.

What about the analogies with *meaning*? When Freud speaks of parapraxes, dreams and symptoms as having a *sense*, the word has very specific applications which are quite unlike those in literary criticism. A slip is a product of 'mutually interfering purposes', the 'disturbing purpose' being its sense. The sense of a dream is the 'latent dream thought' in the unconscious which is revealed in the manifest content only in a distorted form, as a result of 'censorship'; the process of distortion is the 'dream-work'. The sense of neurotic symptoms can be found in a traumatic memory repressed in the unconscious; to give the sense of the symptoms is to explain the 'motives' underlying the neurotic behaviour.

The difference with literary criticism is evident. We have seen it already in the two quite different claims, psychoanalytic and literary, that might be made in saying that *Norbert Hanold's dreams have a sense*. In psychoanalysis sense is essentially connected to (unconscious) states of mind. In literary criticism, sense, with its distinctive literary meaning, is essentially a complex relation, an internal connectedness, ascribed to elements in a text.

This irreconcilable difference carries over to all the seeming analogies. Interpretation in both cases involves the recovery of sense. But the aims and methods have little in common. For example, nothing comparable to 'free association', Freud's favoured route into the unconscious, is either possible or appropriate in literary criticism. This is another reason for the weakness of the analogy with patient and analyst.

The distinction between manifest and latent content again reflects the fundamental differences over sense. In literary criticism some meanings are indeed 'hidden'. But there the analogy ends. First of all, in the relevant sense, they are not hidden *in a mind*. This bald statement clearly confronts the issue of intentionalism in criticism. This is not the place to pursue that issue except to say that psychoanalysts can draw little support from literary intentionalism, at least in its refined forms, for example where 'intended meaning' is connected with such ideas as expression or 'controlling intelligence' (see, e.g., Lyas 1983). Characteristically, the intentionalist critic is proposing not so much a psychological programme for criticism as a certain kind of constraint on interpretation. Secondly, literary meanings might be 'hidden' in a variety of ways. Allegory and satire, for example, present clear literary cases of a division into manifest and hidden contents, but again not in the psychoanalytic sense. Empson-type ambiguities need to be uncovered, or 'teased out', but the sources are semantic and allusive rather than psychological. The favoured concepts of the formalist New Critics – 'tension', 'ambiguity', 'implicit meaning', etc. – all have a linguistic, not a psychological, basis (see, e.g. Beardsley 1958: ch. III).

As for literary themes, describing them as hidden or latent oversimplifies the complex relation they bear to a literary work. When Wilson Knight describes *Macbeth* as a 'profound and mature vision of evil' it is not that he has discovered evil in the play – that has always been recognized as manifest – but rather he is offering the concept of evil as an organizing principle in the play, a proposed focus for its aesthetic unity. In 1939, Edmund Wilson established the prison as a central symbol in *Little Dorrit*, identifying prison-analogies throughout the work. It has been suggested that this discovery in fact occasioned a radical revaluation of the novel (Olsen 1981). Seeing the prison as a unifying theme gave a particular sense and significance to the novel, that had been previously unnoticed.

Psychoanalytic interpretations can have the appearance of operating in the same way: 'In *Jane Eyre* . . . the manifest story about Jane's progress to adulthood is reinforced by a barely concealed female oedipal fantasy in which growing up means marrying daddy' (Skura 1981: 91). But it is crucially unclear what status this alleged fantasy is supposed to have as a latent meaning. Is it a feature of Charlotte Brontë's unconscious mind? Or the reader's? Or Jane's? A latent unconscious thought must belong to some mind or other on psychoanalytic theory. The only way a fantasy can be viewed as a property of a *text* is either by treating the text as a (behavioural manifestation of an unconscious state of mind or by seeing the fantasy as an abstracted theme identified through literary critical methods. If the former, the latent content is not *literary*, if the latter it is not *psychoanalytic*. From a literary critical point of view, one significant difference between the theme of evil in *Macbeth* or the prison in *Little Dorrit* and the theme of a female Oedipal fantasy in *Jane Eyre* is that the credibility of the latter depends on the importation of a highly contentious *theory*, in this case about the relations of fathers and daughters. The novel on its own offers virtually no folk-psychological support for this interpretation.

The analogy of the dream-work can establish no closer a connection between psychoanalysis and literary criticism than can be found in the analogy of manifest/latent content. For the dream-work is the mechanism by which a latent dream thought is transformed into a manifest dream content. Freud speaks of the main 'achievements' of the dream-work as condensation, displacement and the transformation of thoughts into visual images. Although similar kinds of mechanisms can undoubtedly be found in the creation of art, once again the function they perform there will be different. There is barely even an analogy between what the unconscious does to foil an inner censor and what a poet's conscious mind does to create an aesthetic effect.

Furthermore, the suggestion by Jacques Lacan (1977: 160) that condensation (in the dream-work) is a form of metaphor and displacement (in the dream-work) a form of metonymy is of no help to the literary critic. The direction of explanation is entirely the other way. The idea that the unconscious has a linguistic structure might help to illuminate psycho-analysis but it does nothing to illuminate the devices of poetry. Metaphor and metonymy as linguistic phenomena are much better understood than the Freudian dream-work. This is yet another example where the debt seems to run from literature to psychoanalysis, not vice versa.

IV

Literary criticism in the twentieth century has inevitably had to confront the overwhelming force of Freudianism. Psychoanalytic vocabulary has permeated the way we think about people's behaviour and hence our perceptions of art and the artist. Modern writers endlessly dally with Freudian themes. But psychoanalysis cannot subsume literary or artistic criticism. Explaining a work of art, making sense of its aesthetic qualities, is never equivalent to explaining human behaviour or states of mind. No doubt there are similarities and parallels. Perhaps even each enterprise can learn from the other. But by a curious irony the evidence seems to suggest that psychoanalysis, under the charge of 'empirical groundlessness', is at its most credible when it most closely imitates the established procedures of literary criticism.

272 *Peter Lamarque*

NOTES

I am grateful to Murray MacBeath and David Owen for comments on an earlier draft and particularly to Mary Uhl for pointing to numerous places where the text and argument could be tightened up. My thanks also to Stein Olsen for many stimulating discussions; his influence will be obvious to anyone who knows his work.

1 Serious criticisms can be found in Grünbaum 1984.
2 Other designations, like 'Individual Psychology' (Adler) or 'Analytical Psychology' (Jung) are offered for breakaway alternatives. The point is made by J. A. C. Brown (1964).
3 For an interesting discussion in relation to the case histories, see Morton 1982.
4 Both arguments appear in Eagleton 1983.
5 Here, and in what follows, I am greatly indebted to the work of Stein Haugom Olsen, particularly 1981 and 1983.
6 Richard Wollheim (1973) discusses different models, as does Skura (1981).

REFERENCES

Beardsley, M. 1958: *Aesthetics: Problems in the Philosophy of Criticism*. New York: Harcourt, Brace/World.
Brown, J. A. C. 1964: *Freud and the Post-Freudians*. Harmondsworth: Penguin.
Crews, F. 1966: *The Sins of the Fathers: Hawthorne's Psychological Themes*. New York: Oxford University Press.
Crews, F. (ed.) 1970: *Psychoanalysis and Literary Process*. Cambridge, Mass.: Winthrop.
Crews, F. 1975: *Out of My System: Psychology, Ideology and Critical Method*. New York: Oxford University Press.
Crews, F. 1980a: Analysis terminable. *Commentary*, July.
Crews, F. 1980b: The American literary critic Frederick Crews explains why he has rejected Freud. *London Review of Books*, 4 December.
Eagleton, T. 1983: *Literary Theory: An Introduction*. Oxford: Blackwell.
Eliot, T. S. 1972: Tradition and the individual talent, from *Selected Essays*, repr. in David Lodge (ed.), *Twentieth Century Literary Criticism*. London: Longman.
Farrel, B. A. 1981: *The Standing of Psychoanalysis*. New York: Oxford University Press.
Grünbaum, A. 1984: *The Foundations of Psychoanalysis: A Philosophical Critique*. Berkeley: University of California Press.
Habermas, J. 1971: *Knowledge and Human Interests*, trans. J. J. Shapiro. Boston: Beacon Press.

Hartmann, G. (ed.) 1978: *Psychoanalysis and the Question of the Text*. Baltimore: Johns Hopkins University Press.

Holland, N. N. 1968: *The Dynamics of Literary Response*. New York: Oxford University Press.

Jones, E. 1949: *Hamlet and Oedipus*.

Jung, C. G. 1972: Psychology and literature, from *Modern Man in Search of a Soul*, repr. in David Lodge (ed.), *Twentieth Century Literary Criticism*. London: Longman.

Lacan, J. 1977: The agency of the letter in the unconscious or reason since Freud, in *Ecrits: A Selection*, trans. A Sheridan. London: Tavistock.

Lamarque, P. (ed.) 1983: *Philosophy and Fiction: Essays In Literary Aesthetics*. Aberdeen: Aberdeen University Press.

Lukács, G. 1972: The ideology of modernism, from *The Meaning of Contemporary Realism*, repr. in David Lodge (ed.), *Twentieth Century Literary Criticism*. London: Longman.

Lyas, C. 1983: The relevance of the author's sincerity, in Lamarque 1983.

Margolis, J. 1980: *Art and Philosophy: Conceptual Issues in Aethetics*. Atlantic Highlands, N.J.: Humanities Press.

Morton, A. 1982: Freudian commonsense, in R. Wollheim and J. Hopkins (eds), *Philosophical Essays on Freud*. Cambridge: Cambridge University Press.

Olsen, S. H. 1978: *The Structure of Literary Understanding*. Cambridge: Cambridge University Press.

Olsen, S. H. 1981: Literary aesthetics and literary practice. *Mind*, XC.

Olsen, S. H. 1983: Criticism and appreciation, in Lamarque 1983.

Ricoeur, P. 1970: *Freud and Philosophy*. New Haven: Yale University Press.

Schwartz, M. M. 1978: Critic define thyself, in Hartmann 1978.

Skura, M. A. 1981. *The Literary Use of the Psychoanalytic Process*. New Haven and London: Yale University Press.

Spector, J. J. 1972: *The Aesthetics of Freud: A Study in Psychoanalysis and Art*. London: Allen Lane.

Trilling, L. 1972: Freud and literature, from *The Liberal Imagination*, repr. in David Lodge (ed.), *Twentieth Century Literary Criticism*. London: Longman.

Wollheim, R. 1973: Freud and the understanding of art, in *On Art and the Mind*. London: Allen Lane.

Wright, E. 1984: *Psychoanalytic Criticism: Theory and Practice*. London and New York: Methuen.

PART SIX

Psychoanalysis and Dreams

13

Psychoanalytic Dream Theory: A Critique Based upon Modern Neurophysiology

ALLAN HOBSON

INTRODUCTION AND SUMMARY

This chapter examines the interplay of physiology and psychology in the elaboration of dream theories. Freud's psychoanalytic theory is compared and contrasted with a modern alternative, the activation-synthesis hypothesis.

Freud's 1900 *The Interpretation of Dreams* (S.E. IV, V) is first shown to be based upon the incomplete and erroneous assumptions concerning the nervous system that are revealed in his 1895 'Project for a Scientific Psychology' (Freud 1954). The relevant milestone developments in subsequent neurobiology are summarized, together with their implications for the neurobiologically derived components of psychoanalysis.

The findings of modern neurophysiological studies of sleep are presented in terms of necessary revisions in psychoanalytic hypotheses and the new activation-synthesis model is elaborated. Testing the new theory can proceed using both the bottom–up and the top–down approaches of the mind–brain isomorphism agenda.

The study of dreaming is seen as a special case of the mind–body problem with its own special set of opportunities and hazards. To take advantage of opportunities and obviate hazards, a set of assumptions regarding mind–brain isomorphism is developed and discussed. The state concept is stressed and emphasis is placed upon the importance of comparing physiological and psychological states in terms of *formal processes*.

My discussion of these themes is divided into three parts. The first part reviews the general progress in neurobiology and psychology which allows Freud's abandoned 'Project for a Scientific Psychology' to be taken up anew. It is argued that the separation of psychology from neurobiology that ensued from Freud's disappointment with his 'Project' was programmatic and institutional but *not* conceptual. The intellectual translation of 1890s neurobiology into the main tenets of psychoanalytic dream theory is detailed.

The second part presents an overview of the new scientific data on the neurophysiology of REM sleep and the psychology of dreaming with special reference both to tenets of Freud's dream theory and the philosophical tasks confronting the new activation-synthesis hypothesis of dreaming.

The third part describes the general philosophical position of mind–brain isomorphism which today's scientists share with the Freud of 1890–1900.

The chapter concludes by summarizing major theoretical differences in answering the following questions:

1   What is the driving force of the dream process?
2   How do the dream images arise?
3   Why is dream content characterized by distinctly bizarre cognitive features?
4   Why is the bizarre dream content accepted as real?
5   Why are dreams forgotten?

ANTIQUE AND MODERN NEUROPHYSIOLOGY: THE
CRUCIFIXION AND RESURRECTION OF FREUD'S 'PROJECT
FOR A SCIENTIFIC PSYCHOLOGY'

In 'The Neurobiological Origins of Psychoanalytic Dream Theory' (McCarley and Hobson 1977) three related concepts are developed.

The first idea is that Freud, like many of his patients, could not break free of his own intellectual history and that he carried the assumptions of the 'Project' – incomplete and erroneous as they were – into his dream theory. As will be made clear in this section, Freud's dream theory is highly derivative of the neurobiology of 1890, his own disclaimers to the contrary notwithstanding. I will show how this translation occurred and indicate those parts of the theory which are invalidated *a priori* because they are based upon invalid assumptions about how the nervous system works.

The second idea is the concept of mind–brain isomorphism which formed the psychological basis of Freud's 'Project for a Scientific Psychology' (Freud 1954); I believe that the 'Project', put aside in 1895, can and should be taken up anew. In particular, as I will argue in the second and third parts of the chapter, the 'similarity of form' assumption of the isomorphist approach taken by Freud and many of his contemporaries is today quite useful in developing a modern psychophysiology of dreaming, the activation-synthesis hypothesis.

This line of reasoning is similar to that taken by the historian Frank Sulloway in his book *Freud, Biologist of the Mind* (1979) but, in carrying the argument further in the case of dreams, complements the even more radical historical arguments of Frederick Crews (this volume). This revisionist critique is also complementary to that of Adolf Grünbaum's point-by-point evaluation of Freud as an empirical scientist (1984). The scales fall from our eyes as we realize that Freud's literary-polemical genius was an intellectual sleight-of-hand hiding from view a simple translation into the language of psychology of neurobiological principles that are often completely wrong.

The third idea is that Freud's 'Project' failed because his knowledge of the brain was far too incomplete and inaccurate to support the elaboration of the general theory that he envisaged. Ninety years of vigorous work in neurobiology have now changed the knowledge base for this part of the task beyond recognition. See table 13.1 on p. 280.) In considering some of the important advances I will insist, however, that we are still a long way from being able to create a general theory. Instead, I will argue that a much more modest approach is indicated. I advocate a strategic focus upon those areas of neurobiology that are providing data of direct relevance to understanding the brain basis of such global mental states as waking, sleeping and dreaming.

1890–1900: a decade decisive and divisive

The decade beginning in 1890, and culminating at the turn of the century with the publication of *The Interpretation of Dreams* (S.E. IV and V) was a crucial watershed in Freud's life. At the age of 35 Freud had been forced to leave the path of a promising academic career in experimental and clinical neurology. Having been schooled in the strictly deterministic thinking of mid-nineteenth-century Vienna, he was prepared for a rigidly reductionistic approach to neurobiological science. It is ironic, but perhaps fitting, that Freud's work may now be undone by a continuation of the lines of work begun in the early phase of his own career. While many recognize that Freud was once a neurologist, it is not so widely appreciated that he actually worked in *cellular neurobiology*.

TABLE 13.1   Summary of structural and functional neurobiological concepts relevant to Freud's 'Project' which have been developed since 1895

Cajal: Neuron Doctrine
Histology of the nervous system reveals structural discreteness of the neurones; challenges assumption of continuity of structure setting stage for transformation of energy into excitatory and inhibitory signals.

Sherrington: Reflex Action
Concepts of integration, temporal and spatial summation change view of the reflex as unaltered discharge of energy into an information-processing contest.

Hodgkin, Huxley and Katz: Ionic Basis of the Action Potential
Recognition that signal transmission in nerve cells is ionic changes Freud's level of 'particles' from that of the neurons to the atomic level – charged ions are more reasonably considered to be thermodynamic units than are neurons.

Watson and Crick: Molecular Biology of the Gene
Establishment of the structure of DNA provides ubiquitous substrate for genetic information and a model for memory and obviates a need for Freud's 'omega' neurons.

Loewi, Dale and Eccles: Synaptic Transmission
Electrical signals are transformed at junction between cells into chemical messages which mediate excitation or inhibition according to their effect upon the ion channels of the postsynaptic cells. This second transformation adds unforeseen further complexity and richness to the system because of the multiplicity of chemical messengers.

The lowly crab, on which Freud did detailed neuroanatomical investigation, has in recent times become a popular preparation in the development of detailed knowledge of neuronal function. It is ironic to note that satisfaction of the criteria of proof of an inhibitory neurotransmitter has been most satisfactorily met by GABA (gamma amino butyric acid) by using the claw opener muscle of the crab. Had Freud persisted, he might have been able to make some of these important discoveries himself and he might also have been able to make use of the concept of inhibition, which was then already beginning to gain acceptance in other parts of the scientific world. Armed with the concept of inhibition, Freud would have developed his psychology quite differently.

The decade beginning 1890 was also epoch-making for neurobiology in that the great Spanish neuroanatomist Santiago Ramon y Cajal was enunciating and promulgating his neuron doctrine. The nerve cells on which Freud had worked were considered by many (including His and Kolliker) to be a syncytium, or network, *with direct physical continuity between the cellular elements*. Cajal's work clearly indicated that each individual nerve cell was a discrete unit enclosed by a membrane that made each cell physically discontinuous with the rest. This structural claim has subsequently been amply supported by the work of physiologists who have shown that each cell is functionally as well as structurally discrete. Cell-to-cell influences can be either excitatory or inhibitory depending upon the nature of the chemical substance liberated at the specialized junction between any two cells that is called the synapse (see table 13.1 on p. 280).

These two key points, the independence of the neuronal elements and the chemical specificity allowing them to exert either excitatory or inhibitory influences, were at the dawn of scientific consciousness in 1890 and do not appear to have been known to Freud as he shaped thinking about psychology in terms of neurobiology.

What was Freud's 'Project'?

After he abandoned his university position for the private practice of neurology, one of Freud's first theoretical efforts was to produce a unified psychophysiological theory. This became his 'Project for a Scientific Psychology', written from 1893 to 1895. Although Freud abandoned his 'Project', its concepts were carried into *The Interpretation of Dreams* without alterations. Freud's ideas about the nervous system thus formed the conceptual base of psychoanalysis.

The concepts of modern cellular neurobiology differ so markedly from Freud's as to force fundamental changes in psychoanalytic theory. It will be of particular interest here to emphasize this point in discussing the modern psychophysiological study of dreaming sleep. But first it may be worthwhile pointing out that Freud's goal in the 'Project' is not unlike our goal today: 'To represent psychical processes as quantitatively determined states of specifiable material particles.'

Is such a project more feasible 80 years after elaboration of the neuron doctrine? Will we now be able to avoid dualism (of the kind that now plagues psychoanalysis) by avoiding the scholastic monism of the nineteenth-century physiologists? Helmholtz and his student Brücke (who taught Freud) believed that 'neurophysiology, and consequently psychology, is governed by purely chemico-physical laws'. And we would agree that a psychology that ignores, denies, transcends or disobeys those laws is in peril of losing an important mooring. But can we really expect psychology to emerge from, or be reduced to, physico-chemical laws? Since we cannot yet specify the connection between brain and mind, we must take seriously – if only for heuristic and motivational purposes – any set of psychological postulates that is based upon phenomologic observation and shown to be both statistically reliable and experimentally testable.

If one reads *The Interpretation of Dreams* without being aware of its precedent in the 'Project', one might think that Freud developed his dream theory mainly in order to account for psychological phenomena that others had been unable to explain. Instead, it can be argued that dreams provided a sufficiently ambiguous text for Freud to translate his neurobiology into psychological language. By examining the role of 1890s brain science in shaping Freud's theory I hope to identify aspects of the theory which constitute *a priori* assumptions to which the data were fitted *post hoc*.

Disguise-censorship: the essence of Freud's dream theory

Freud's dream theory can be summarized as follows:

1   The ego (mediator between the super-ego demands of conscious and society, and the id urgings of instinct) wishes to sleep.
2   The ego thereby withdraws its cathexis from the outside world and simultaneously relaxes its vigil upon the unconscious forces in the id.
3   These unconscious forces (or their cognitive-level wishes) threaten to escape from their unconscious jail house and beat upon the door of consciousness where they are most unwelcome because, if they were to be admitted, they would by their unruliness disrupt consciousness and so terminate sleep.
4   Their uprising is often associated with the pairing of an unconscious wish with material still in consciousness from the day's previous experience, the so-called day-residue.

The motive force of dreaming is thus clearly defined by Freud as the repressed energy driving the unconscious impulse. Furthermore, one common formal aspect of dreams, the presence of recent wake-state information in dream scenarios, is explained by the pairing of the unconscious wish with the day-residue. But the most distinctive formal aspect of dreaming is not the day-residue, it is the 'bizarreness' that gives dreaming its distinctive character. By 'bizarreness', Freud was alluding to apparently nonsensical changes in time, place and person, those incongruities of dream plot, character and action, and those uncertainties of thought which have invited comparison to the psychotic states of patients with mental illness.

The bizarre features of dreams were ascribed by Freud to the dynamic transformation of the information contained with the unconscious impulse or wish. This 'latent content', the true meaning of the dream, was forbidden entry into consciousness by the censor. The censor does not wish or need to sleep, in fact can never sleep if it is to protect sleep. The latent content is thus *disguised* by the censor through a variety of functions which later were to become incorporated into Freud's theory of defence. These include displacement, condensation, symbolization and pictorialization. Thus, the bizarreness of dreams, the distinctive dream features, are only *apparently* meaningless. Their very meaninglessness was for Freud evidence of the effectiveness of the censor's effort to disguise their true meaning.

As for the amnesia for dreams, Freud dealt with it by postulating that even the transformed and noted manifest content of the dream might still be psychonoxious and was therefore subject to repression or active replacement in the unconscious from which it originally sprang. He also postulated a further *secondary elaboration* that performed a further detoxification or transformation of the unacceptable wishes in the remembering and retelling of the dream during conscious waking life.

Contrasting concepts of energy and information in antique and modern neurobiology

Let us now turn our attention to the origin of the key elements of the dream theory in Freud's neurobiology as they are revealed in the 'Project'. A key point to be grasped at once is that Freud's nervous system, equipped as it was with neither the notion of synaptic contact nor that of inhibition, was a nervous system that was incapable of cancelling either energy or information. In fact, Freud believed that the nervous system was the passive receptacle of both energy and information. We now know that neither of these ideas is correct, that the nervous system has the metabolic means of creating its own energy (though it is highly dependent upon oxygen and glucose) and the genetically derived means of creating its own information (though it is dependent upon external inputs for specific information about the outside world). It is further capable of cancelling both its own and the externally provided energy and information.

Most modern psychoanalysts agree that Freud's energy concepts are completely outmoded and must be discarded, but few seem to appreciate the degree to which they impugn informational aspects of his theory. An important aspect of Freud's reasoning was its tight inner connection. When any part is changed other parts need readjustment. This tight interdependency of theory components is characteristic of rationalistic thought generally.

I now summarize three concepts to illustrate the impact of Freud's antique neurobiology upon his dream theory.

1 *Energy source concepts.* For Freud, all of the energy within the nervous system came from the outside; there was no internal source. This is equivalent to seeing the nervous system only in terms of reflex action, that is, as a system which operates only when driven by externally provided forces. Freud was unaware that the nervous system created its own energy. Each individual neuron actually constitutes an energy pump which constantly and energetically maintains a membrane potential of 90 millivolts (mV). It is upon this membrane potential, endogenously developed and energetically maintained, that the system depends. Not only does each of the cells of the brain maintain its own energy, but each has its own spontaneous activity. That is to say, the energy is converted into information through the reversal or 'discharge' of the membrane potential that we call the 'action potentials'. The system is, thus, constantly 'talking to itself' as well as maintaining the motive force for such language. We shall see later that the nervous system is, in fact, anticipating the language of the outside world by its internal language. The erroneous notions that Freud maintained about energy sources in the nervous system made it impossible for him to recognize that the system would have its own rhythms and its own phases of activity, both internally programmed and internally regulated. This is an ironic oversight, especially in view of Freud's extensive familiarity with the theories of his one-time friend Wilhelm Fliess, who ascribed many psychic phenomena to the operation of biological rhythms.

2 *Energy flow concepts.* Not only was it impossible for Freud's nervous system to develop its own energy but, when external energy had entered the system, it was trapped there and could be dissipated only by motoric discharge. Because there was no intrinsic mechanism for the cancellation of energy, it remained forever within the system unless it was discharged in motoric action. This oversight is related, as we have pointed out, to

Freud's failure to take account of the internal metabolic sources of energy and of the emerging concept of inhibition. We now know that not only are our nervous systems capable of balancing both energy and information but that this balancing process involves cancellation of both energy and information.

3 *Energy transmission concepts*. Freud's nervous system received energy from the outside world unchanged in quality or quantity. For Freud there was no transduction of external energy (or of information) at the peripheral portals to the nervous system. Now we know that all external energy is changed by the nervous system into its own energy. This process is called transduction. Whether it be touch pressure impinging on the skin, or sound impinging on the ear drum, all external energies are transduced by the respective sensors into an internal code. (Note that we are talking about sensors not censors.) A key aspect of this energy transmission notion is that very small signals can be used by the modern nervous system whereas very large amounts of energy were necessarily involved in the transmission of Freud's untransduced external energy.

Dreaming: energetic overflow and informational transformation versus direct readout of brain activation

The impact of these interrelated concepts upon Freud's dream theory is quite clear. Freud's nervous system and the mind that it supported were completely dependent upon external energy and information. Such a system was highly vulnerable since it was subject to both invasion (by large sources of energy from the outside world) and to the constant threat of disruption (by the internally stored energy that could only be discharged in motoric action).

These ideas became crystallized in concepts of the dynamically repressed unconscious and were carried into the dream theory as the tendency for unconscious wishes to erupt during sleep when the repressive forces of the ego were relaxed. Freud's nervous system was constantly in need of checks and balances to deal with the threat of disruption from within and without, and his whole concept of psychic defence is related to this erroneous view of how the nervous system actually operates. I am not saying that the concept of defence is in itself erroneous, only that the weight that is placed upon it is excessive. If the system has its own means of producing energy, it is very likely to have its own means of regulating energy; if it has its own means of creating information, it is likely to have its own means of regulating information; and if it is protected at every sensory input gateway by transduction mechanisms, it is intrinsically immune to overload from the outside world. This property is particularly evident in newborn human infants who simply 'tune out' when they are either overloaded or not ready to process external impacts.

Modern sleep research has clearly documented the elaborate, entirely intrinsic mechanisms of 'state' control. We now know that sensory input can be internally controlled so that even the transduction mechanism does not operate alone to protect the system from overload. Three features of the modern nervous system – its intrinsic plasticity, its auto-regulation and its creativity – give us a very different set of operating principles upon which to construct a scientific psychology, including a modern dream theory. The modern system can turn itself on and off, can regulate the flow of internal information in diverse ways and can control access to the system by external information.

These are the principles that have been used in constructing the activation-synthesis hypothesis that is summarized in the next part of this chapter. In contrast to viewing dreaming as the result of an up-rush of normally repressed energy, the activation-synthesis model sees dreaming as the pre-programmed running of an intrinsic system mode. All energy and information are intrinsic to the system. There is no need for the system to discharge information or degrade information (though it could do both). Thus, the bizarre features of the dream are seen as naturally associated with the mode of operation of the system during dreaming sleep *and there is no need for an information-transformation mechanism*. Since the system is capable of selecting the 'store', or 'no store' modes, there is no need to postulate an active energy-consuming mechanism for the restoring of dream material in the unconscious. It can simply be 'no stored', that is unremembered.

To summarize this historical critique, Freud's 'Project for a Scientific Psychology' reveals a view of the nervous system which in many fundamental respects was incorrect. Many of the principles of this outmoded view of the nervous system were carried forward directly into Freud's theory of dreams and as such became the cornerstone of psychoanalysis. To the extent that psychoanalytic dream theory and psychoanalytic theory generally are derived from an outmoded neurobiology, they are in need of revision on historical grounds alone. Many important new findings of neurobiology allow us now to account for exactly the same processes that Freud was trying to deal with in more accurate and economical ways.

A NEW THEORY OF DREAMING: THE ACTIVATION-SYNTHESIS HYPOTHESIS

Definition of dreaming

Dreaming is a distinctive mental state which occurs periodically in normal human sleep. Typical dream reports include such psychological features as:

1 formed sensory perceptions (akin to hallucinations);
2 cognitive abnormalities (akin to the inconstancies and uncertainty in cognition that characterize delirium and dementia);
3 uncritical acceptance of all such unlikely phenomena as real (akin to delusions);
4 emotional intensifications (akin to those seen in panic anxiety); and
5 amnesia (akin, again, to that seen in organic syndromes).

These five remarkable features of dreaming have invited its comparison to psychotic states of mind occurring during waking in certain clinical conditions, and especially to the schizophrenic, the manic-depressive and the organic psychoses. The exploration of the neurobiological basis of dreaming therefore constitutes not only an aspect of mind–body interaction but also a model approach to the study of mental illness. In this respect, a scientifically sound dream theory could form a solid base for psychiatry as it attempts to develop a specific pathophysiology and it could supply the currently missing link between its phenomenology and the new psychopharmacology.

Physiological implications of some psychological features of dreaming

Dreams are characterized by vivid and fully formed hallucinatory imagery with the visual sensory domain predominant; auditory, tactile and movement sensations are also prominent in most dream reports. Compared with the intense involvement of these sensorimotor domains, taste and smell are under-represented and reports of pain are exceedingly rare despite the involvement of dreamers in frightening and even physically mutilating scenarios. This sensory profile suggests that specific physiologic systems are activated (or inactivated) in specific ways during REM sleep.

Dreaming is properly considered delusional because subjects have virtually no insight regarding the true nature of the state in which they have these unusual sensory experiences. The tendency is thus great to consider dream events as if they were completely real during the dream even though they are promptly recognized as fabrications when recalled in subsequent waking states. This is all the more surprising since uncritical belief in the reality of dream events must overcome the high degrees of improbability (and even physical impossibility) that are part-and-parcel of the experience.

The lack of insight that makes dreams delusional is part of a broader set of cognitive disturbances. Dreams are characterized by: marked uncertainties (with explicit vagueness); discontinuities (with unexplained changes of subject, action and setting); impossibilities (with defiance of physical law) and improbabilities; and incongruities (with social inappropriateness and cognitive illogicality). Dream characters and dream objects may be banal or be altogether fantastic and impossible collages of existing reality; they may behave normally or indulge in the most absurd, improbable or impossible actions in settings either familiar or bearing only the faintest resemblances to those of real life. To explain these unique and remarkable dream features, illogical thought processes such as *non sequiturs*, *post hoc* explanations, mythical, metaphorical and symbolic interpretations are the norm. The clear implication is that very major changes in information-processing functions of the brain are to be sought at the physiological level. See table 13.2, which contrasts the explanations of this distinctive dream feature offered by psychoanalysis and its modern alternative, the activation-synthesis hypothesis.

Memory undergoes a paradoxical intensification and suppression: recall is intensified within the dream as remote characters, scenes, events and concerns are knitted into the fanciful and evanescent fabric of the dream. Dreams can thus be said to be hypermnesic within the state itself; this increased access to memory within the state of dreaming contrasts markedly with the virtual impossibility of recovering the dream product after the state has terminated. Thus there is amnesia for the hypermnesic dream. On awakening even from a dream in progress, subjects have difficulty holding the vivid experience in short-term memory long enough to give a report or transcribe the dream. We can thus predict that the brain mechanisms of memory will be dramatically altered and disenabled during REM sleep.

Emotion fluctuates widely in association with the abnormal and vivid mental content of dreaming: anxiety, fear and surprise are common affects which undergo marked intensification during dreams. Obsessional concerns are common, with dreamers focusing their worry on nudity, missed trains, unpacked suitcases, and a host of other incomplete arrangements. Depressive affects are markedly under-represented, with shame and guilt playing a relatively small part in the drama. This implies that the brain

TABLE 13.2 Dream bizarreness: a comparison of the explanation offered by two theories – Freud's disguise-censorship hypothesis and the activation-synthesis hypothesis

	Disguise-censorship hypothesis	*Activation-synthesis hypothesis*
Evidential basis	*None*: As shown by Grünbaum, the fact that association to dream material may lead to unconscious ideas does not constitute probative evidence that dream bizarreness is a function of a psychic need to censor and disguise unconscious wishes.	*Abundant*: Modern neurophysiology reveals that the brain (hence the mind) is operating in an organically (hence psychically) altered state. Blockade of space–time–person information from world, failure of memory, overdriving of sensorimotor circuits are the necessary and sufficient substrate of dream bizarreness.
Economy of argument	*Convoluted*: Unconscious ideas must be detected by censor, decoded and recoded to transform 'latent' into manifest content. To be forgotten this material must be re-repressed into the unconscious. Theory requires a homunculus or supervisor (the censor), is a constant energy drain (repressor), and occupies large portions of memory (the unconscious).	*Simple*: The brain need only be activated under altered operating conditions (see above). The informational product of the process, being biologically insignificant, is simply not stored in memory.
Compatibility with science	*Awkward*: Many assertions incompatible with modern data, e.g. instigation by wishes incorrect; timing as instant pre-awakening incorrect; guardian of sleep function incorrect; poor recall as due to repression unlikely.	*Complete*: All assertions based upon recent findings: instigation via intrinsic physiological attraction; timing as real-time REM sleep correlate; sleep function 'guarded' by intrinsic physiology; poor recall due to simple amnesia.
Clinical implications	*Stultifying*: Brain–mind seen as closed-loop system. Fixed properties suggest strict determinism. Emphasizes repetition of non-adaptive responses. 'Interpretation' complex and arbitrary.	*Liberating*: Brain–mind seen open-loop system. Plastic properties suggest creativity and emphasize adaptive change. 'Interpretation' is simple and unambiguous.

mechanisms of anxiety, fear and surprise are up and running during REM sleep.

The definition and characterization of dreaming given here serves to differentiate it from other kinds of mental activity which may occur in sleep. Brief scenarios or fleeting images accompanied by the sensation of falling (but unsustained by a narrative plot and sequential action) characterize mentation at sleep onset. Once sleep is established, mental activity assumes a thought-like character which is usually perseverative and unprogressive as the sleeper reviews daytime activities and concerns in a persistent, repetitious manner. Such sleep 'thinking' is unaccompanied by either vivid visual imagery or by the bizarre cognitive features that we have detailed above. A severe problem limiting accurate assessment of sleep mentation early in the night is the confusion, disorientation and even confabulation that subjects manifest upon arousal. These features strongly beg comparison with the organic mental syndrome and imply marked disorganization of cerebral function.

Sustained dream scenarios occur only after the other two forms of mental activity have subsided. Dreaming then alternates with thought-like mentation at 90–100-minute intervals throughout the night. Recall of dreams and other forms of mental activity in sleep depends upon prompt awakening from the state in which the mental activity occurs; retention of such recall further depends upon the instrumental act of verbally reporting or transcribing the dream narration at the time of awakening. Already evanescent recall is rendered even more fugitive by the posture shifts and stretching that typically occur in spontaneous arousal from early morning sleep. Subjects must be trained to suppress such movements to aid recall.

Given the many factors that cloud the observational lens, the consistency and consensus that has developed regarding sleep and dream psychophysiology is the more remarkable. Indeed, it seems fair to assume that extant disagreements about phenomenology are attributable to methodological limitations, not inconsistencies of mind–brain isomorphism. Studies specifically designed to overcome the many known limitations by using expert subjects are badly needed.

The association of dreaming with REM sleep: an impressive correlation

Aserinsky and Kleitman (1953) noted that the sleep of children was punctuated by periodic activation of the EEG and by clusters of saccadic eye movement, the so-called rapid eye movements or REMs of sleep.

Dement and Kleitman (1957) confirmed the hypothesis that these periods of brain activation during sleep were correlated with dreaming as it has been defined in the preceding discussion. The intervening intervals, called non-REM sleep, were defined by EEG slow waves (indicating deactivatiôn of the brain) and by quiescence of motoric and autonomic systems.

When normal subjects were aroused from the rapid eye movement phase of sleep, they gave detailed reports of dream activity. The capacity to recall dreams appeared to be related to the nature of the awakening process; as indicated above, subjects who learned to obtain a fully aroused state without moving increased their recall capacity. Within the REM period, dream intensity tended to parallel the intensity of phasic physiological events, especially the eye movements; arousal during rapid eye movement sleep with eye movement activity yielded reports fulfilling the definition of dreaming given here in 90–95 per cent of the cases. When scored for vividness, emotionality and imagined physical activity, measures were correlated positively with the quantitative intensity of the eye movement in the REM sleep just prior to awakening. Awakening during REM sleep with ocular quiescence yielded reports of lesser intensity in about 70 per cent of awakenings. These figures dropped to 5–10 per cent when awakenings were made during non-REM sleep. Awakenings from non-REM sleep yielded reports of antecedent mental activity in about 50 per cent of the trials but a large proportion of these reports were of perseverative, thought-like mental activity. Reports qualitatively indistinguishable from dreaming were obtained from Stage One sleep at sleep onset, a phase of sleep without sustained eye movements; but these reports were quantitatively less impressive in duration and intensity then those obtained from emergent REM sleep periods later in the night.

Estimations of dream duration correlated positively with the time spent in REM sleep prior to arousal. When subjects were aroused after only 5 minutes of rapid eye movement sleep they gave shorter reports whereas after 15 minutes had elapsed reports were considerably longer and more detailed. Thus it would appear that despite intensification and contraction of duration estimates within individual dream scenarios the overall correlation between time estimation of dream duration and real time elapsed in REM sleep appears to be quite close.

To test the resistance of memory to dreams, awakenings were performed in the non-REM sleep phase at intervals following the termination of REM. The incidence of reported dreams dropped to non-REM levels within five minutes, indicating the extremely fragile state of memory and highlighting the strong state dependency of recall upon arousal from REM sleep.

Pointing out that not all REM sleep awakenings yield reports of dreaming and noting that some non-REM sleep awakenings do so, some sceptics have attacked the fundamental assumption of mind–brain isomorphism advanced here. While accepting the caveats that imperfect correlations leave room for doubt and that human physiology is still a relatively insensitive tool, it must be categorically asserted that the extant correlations are sufficiently robust to encourage hypothesis building against the rapidly advancing time when the refinement of our physiological tools will allow more critical tests of the isomorphism concept. To focus upon apparent exceptions to emerging rules when these are likely to be by-products of methodological imperfections is a non-progressive, obscurantist and fruitless enterprise.

Activation and synthesis as the cornerstones of a psychophysiological hypothesis of dreaming

The simplest and most direct approach to the correlation of dream mentation with the psychological state of the brain in REM sleep is to assume a formal isomorphism between the subjective and objective levels of investigation. As discussed in the third part of the chapter, by isomorphism I mean a similarity of form in the psychological and physiological domains. For example, it may be reasonably assumed that subjective experience of visually formed imagery implicates activation of the central visual system in a manner formally similar (if not identical) to that of the waking state. Other details of psychophysiological correlation are assumed to obey the same general law; for example, the vivid sensation of movement is assumed to be related to patterned activation of motor systems and those central brain structures subserving the perception of position of the body in space. When we look at the psychological level, it is found that powerful, highly coordinated excitatory processes are recordable in the oculomotor, vestibular and visual sensory centres.

Once so activated, the brain–mind synthesizes or constructs a unified conscious experience (the dream) by comparing the internally generated signals to mnemonic percepts, actions and affects. The rules of synthesis are as yet poorly worked out but involve such complex organizational processes as language (giving the narrative structure of reports) and non-verbal symbolic operations (giving the elaborate scenarios) which are presumably a function of 'higher' brain centres. The state of the art in cortical psychophysiology is so primitive even in the waking state that one must remain at least as vague and promissory in discussing dreaming. It may just be, however, that the scientific study of dreaming will yield the first great advances in understanding the brain basis of consciousness. This is because during the REM sleep/dreaming state, the brain–mind is off-line (input independent), movement free (output independent) and hence operating entirely on its own terms. For once, we can safely affirm Freud's 'Royal Road' assertion about the scientific utility of understanding dreaming.

Physiological mechanisms of activation and synthesis

To be fully adequate, a psychophysiological hypothesis has to account for the following processes:

1 *Activation*. The brain has to be turned on and kept internally activated to support dream mentation throughout the REM sleep episode. A possible mechanism is disinhibition of sensorimotor circuits related to cessation of activity in aminergic inhibitory neurons (see figure 13.1).

2 *Input blockade*. Input from the outside world to an internally activated brain has to be prevented in order for sleep and the illusion of dreaming to be maintained: this appears to be accomplished in at least two ways. One is presynaptic inhibition, which has also been recorded at secondary relay nuclei throughout the brain stem and thalamus. The second mechanism for excluding sensory input is occlusion, which occupies the higher levels of sensory circuits with internally generated messages.

3 *Output blockade*. The internally activated and actively deafferented brain must also quell motor outputs so as to prevent the disruption of sleep by reafferent stimulation and and so as to halt the enactment of dreamed motor commands. This appears to be accomplished by postsynaptic inhibition of final common path motorneurons in the spinal cord and brain stem: Hyperpolarizations of $10-15$ mV have been recorded intracellularly from such motorneurons. By these three processes, the brain is thus made ready to process information arising from within, to exclude data coming from without, and to not act upon the internally generated information.

4 *Internal signal generation*. It remains to provide the activated but disconnected brain with internal signals which it then processes as if they came from the outside world. This appears to occur in part by a mechanism intrinsic to brain activation: the reciprocal interaction of aminergic and cholinergic neurons in the brain stem. In most mammals, including man, the so-called PGO waves ('P' for pons, 'G' for (lateral) geniculate and 'O' for occipital cortex) present themselves as candidates

A

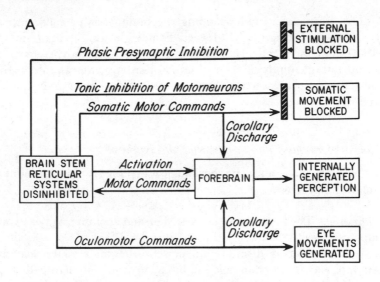

B

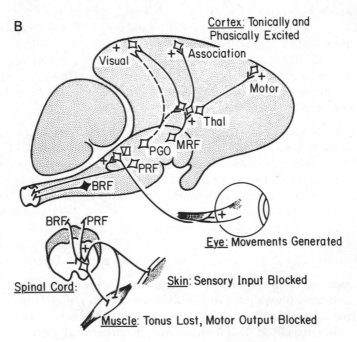

FIGURE 13.1 Mental activity in sleep: The psychophysiology of dreaming

A Systems model

As a result of disinhibition caused by cessation of aminergic neuronal firing, brainstem reticular systems auto-activate. Their outputs have effects including depolarization of afferent terminals causing phasic presynaptic inhibition and blockade of external stimuli, especially during the bursts of REM; postsynaptic hyperpolarization causing tonic inhibition of motorneurons which effectively counteract concomitant motor commands so that somatic movement is blocked. Only the oculomotor commands are read out as eye movements because the motorneurons are not inhibited. The forebrain, activated by the reticular formation and also aminergically disinhibited, receives efferent copy or corollary discharge information about somatic motor and oculomotor commands from which it may synthesize such internally generated perceptions as visual imagery and the sensation of movement both of which typify dream mentation. The forebrain may, in turn, generate its own motor commands which help to perpetuate the process via positive feedback to the reticular formation.

B Synaptic model

Some of the directly and indirectly disinhibited neuronal systems are schematized together with their supposed contributions to REM sleep phenomena. At the level of the brain stem, five neuronal tyes are illustrated: MRF = midbrain reticular neurons projecting to thalamus convey tonic and phasic activating signals rostrally; PGO = burst cells in the peribrachial region convey phasic activation and specific eye movement information to the geniculate body and cortex (pathway dashed line indicates uncertainty of direct projection); PRF = pontine reticular formation neurons transmit phasic activation signals to oculomotor neurons (VI) and spinal cord which generate eye movements, twitches of extremities, and presynaptic inhibition; BRF = bulbar reticular formation neurons and send tonic hyperpolarizing signals to motorneurons in spinal cord. As a consequence of these descending influences, sensory input and motor output are blocked at the level of the spinal cord. At the level of the forebrain, visual association and motor cortex neurons all receive time and phasic activation signals for non-specific and specific thalamic relays.

---

for an internally generated information signal arising at the level of the pontine brain stem. In association with oculomotor activity, strong pulses of excitation are conducted by reticular pathways to the thalamus and radiated via independent pathways to the visual and association cortices. It is now known that these PGO waves are generated by cellular activity which faithfully replicates the directional aspects of generated eye movements at the level of the brain stem. Thus not only is internal information generated but that information has a high degree of spatial specificity. According to the activation-synthesis hypothesis of dreaming, the now auto-activated and auto-stimulated brain processes these signals and interprets them in terms of information stored in memory.

5   *Synthesis: the weak link in the logical chain.* The motor shortcomings of the new theory are related to state-of-the-art limitations in knowledge regarding so-called higher brain functions. One way to proceed may thus be to identify important state-to-state differences in cognitive function and look to the brain for working hypotheses about the basis of the differences. For example, although the basis of the cognitive disturbances occurring in dreaming is not understood, it is tempting to see these failures as perhaps related to the cessation of activity in aminergic neurons. An arrest of aminergic neuronal activity would affect the entire brain, including the cerebral cortex, by depriving it of a tonic modulatory influence normally present in waking. I speculate that this tonic modulatory influence may be essential to attentional processes, including the capacity to organize information in a logical and coherent manner and to achieve the full self-awareness that gives waking consciousness perspective and insight.

In the combined absence of external cues and internal modulatory influences by aminergic systems, the activated forebrain interprets its internally generated signals as if they are real. There is no perspective and no insight. It may be further speculated that the synthesized dream product is unremembered owing to a similar mechanism. The activated forebrain circuits which mediate the dream experience are not instructed to keep a record of the transactions if the 'store' instruction is also mediated by the tonic modulatory influence of the aminergic interneurons upon their vast postsynaptic domain on the cerebral cortex and in those subcortical centres such as the hippocampus which are specifically implicated in memory. In waking (when aminergic neurons are active) the 'store' instruction is issued; in dreaming (where aminergic neurons are inactive) the 'store' instruction is not issued.

It is significant to note that most current models of learning and memory evoke the intervention of an aminergic interneuron. Thus, the attribution of dream amnesia to the loss of aminergic modulation is consistent with the hypotheses regarding learning and memory at the cellular level.

6   *Caveat lector.* We remind the reader that this activation-synthesis model of dreaming and reciprocal interaction theory of sleep cycle control, on which it is based, are both incomplete and controversial. They represent linked working hypotheses about the fundamental physiology of sleep and the way in which that physiology may help us to understand

unique features of the dream process. The attribution of automaticity to the control system and the features of randomness in the information generator model should not be taken to exclude the constructive nature of the synthetic process carried out by the dreaming brain. By definition, the brain/mind of each dreamer is obliged to make as much sense as is possible of its internally generated signals as the adverse working conditions of REM sleep permit. Thus, the dream product of each individual may reveal both important concerns and unique stylistic psychological features. Dreams may thus be worthy of scrutiny when one reviews life strategies. But the new theory challenges the psychoanalytic idea that the many meaningless aspects of dream mentation are the result of an active effort to disguise the meaning of unconscious wishes (which are in turn postulated to be the driving force of dreaming). Instead, it ascribes these defective cognitive properties of dreaming to unusual operating features of the internally activated, auto-stimulated brain during REM sleep. This is the heart of the theory and I hope to have convinced readers of at least the heuristic value of the new approach even if I may have failed to convert them to the specific claims of the activation-synthesis hypothesis of dreaming.

OUR COMMON CAUSE WITH FREUD: MIND–BRAIN ISOMORPHISM

Freud was convinced that the scientific explanation of mental phenomena must ultimately involve physiology and biochemistry. In abandoning the 'bottom–up' approach of the 'Project' for the 'top down' approach of psychoanalysis, he never gave up this ideal. In this section, I develop concepts that might serve to support a more supple and versatile mode of inquiry – one that could be *both* 'bottom–up' and 'top-down' at the same time. This mode of inquiry, which is called mind–brain isomorphism, assumes the same similarity of form across the domains of mind and brain that Freud anticipated in his work. A strategic emphasis is placed on the investigation of states of mind and brain, particularly the states of dreaming and REM sleep.

What is an isomorphism?

Isomorphism has a strict mathematical definition that represents the functions in two related domains with one set of equations. I am indebted to W.V.O. Quine for the following account:

Two *sets* are isomorphic if there is a one-to-one correlation of the members of the one set to the members of the other. Example: the set of all married men, in our culture, and the set of all married women. The correlation is the husband relation.

Two *relations* are isomorphic if all the things that enter into the one relation can be correlated with all the things that enter into the other relation, in such a way that always x will bear the one relation to y if and only if the correlated object x' bears the other relation to y'. Thus the correlation might be the correlation of people to their respective heads. On the strength of this correlation, the uncle relation is isomorphic to the relation that each uncle's head bears to the head of each of his nephews and nieces.

The uncle relation is dyadic, and best viewed as the set of all ordered pairs <x, y> such that x is uncle of y. There are also triadic relations, e.g. between-ness, and so on up. The notion of isomorphism carries over to any of these in obvious fashion. The correlation involved is still always dyadic, like the husband relation and the head relation in the above examples.

One speaks of isomorphism not only between a set and a set, as above, or between a relation and a relation, but also between a whole complex or system of sets and/or relations on the one hand and a matching system on the other. Thus, using again the correlation of people to their heads, we can say that the system <M, L, U> is isomorphic to the system <M', L', U'> where M is the set of all married men, L is the set of all lawyers, U is the uncle relation, M' is the relation mentioned at the end of my second paragraph.

(Quine 1985)

In practical terms, consider the visual system which quantitatively preserves spatial coordinates in its mapping of the neural transformation of retinal signals. This depends upon a retinotopic organization of the thalamic relay system and the multiple maps of visual space at the level of the cerebral cortex. As far as one can trace the signal, there is an isomorphism between external space and its representation in brain space. And this isomorphism is preserved in the perceptual product since one's estimates of length, distance, colour, etc., are reliable. We assume that the same general principles apply to higher-order operations of the mind. In dreaming, we assume, for example, that spatial parameters of the dream are isomorphic with the activation of neuronal ensembles encoding space, engendering the so-called cognitive maps.

Psychophysical isomorphism: precedents and problems

Even before Freud conceived his 'Project', a simple version of this approach was taken by Fechner, the pioneer of psychophysics, who asserted – and attempted to prove – that the intensity of sensation was a function of the stimulus intensity. An implication pursued and documented by such modern psychophysiologists as Vernon Mountcastle and Gerhard Werner is that the intensity of firing of sensory neurons is the critical intervening variable in this isomorphism.

Such simplistic assumptions often fail owing to state dependent changes in perceptual function. For example, sensation is *not* proportional to stimulus intensity during sleep. The threshold for perceived sensory stimuli shifts radically even though there is still an isomorphic encoding of stimulus strength in the rate of firing of peripheral and even central sensory neurons. In fact, the excitability of central neurons may even be amplified during sleep so that the isomorphism not only fails to describe the process but the usual relationship is paradoxically reversed.

How can the isomorphist approach survive this *bouleversement* by the radical state dependency of even the simplest psychophysical laws? Only by creating a mathematical, explicit set of laws describing central state regulation itself. This is the task of neurophysiologists studying brain states with an eye to understanding their associated mental states or vice versa since a 'top–down' is as possible as a 'bottom–up' approach. This essential task requires a revolutionary shift in scientific attitude for reasons that go far beyond the methodological problems discussed earlier and strike at the heart of the experimental method itself. Two other hurdles must be passed: one is the problem of subjectivity that confounds the characterization of mental states; the other is the unproved assumption of physiological homology between human brain physiology (which cannot be directly studied) and that of lower mammals (which can).

Characterizing mental states: the problem of subjectivity

One philosophical problem with strong impact upon the isomorphist agenda is the unconfirmable nature of all subjective experience. And this is compounded by the difficulty of access to the mind in sleep. The recent development of sleep laboratory techniques has given the study of dreaming a more instrumental and systematic character and the emerging picture has encouraged psychophysiologic integration.

It may be worth underlining this *problem of subjectivity* which is ultimately irreducible – even under the instrumental conditions of the sleep laboratory. The scientist interested in mind thus has no choice other than to accept the reports of his experimental subjects as honest, accurate and truly retrospective – all three dubious, fallible and unprovable assumptions. Can we ever be satisfied with such limitations? If not, what safeguards can our scepticism inspire? I will venture some thoughts hoping that scientific philosophers will help me to approach closure on this issue.

The first guarantee is normative and statistical. If most humans spontaneously describe formally identical mental experience in sleep as that which I take as definitive of dreaming, I can be more confident than if such reports were exceptional. Such confidence would be further increased if the subjects were disinterested, or naive (i.e. had no psychological mindedness, no education and no pet theory). The fact that dreaming occurs, and has the same form, in all cultures suggests that it is phenomenologically independent of belief systems and formally free of contamination by suggestion.

The second guarantee is the predictability found through the instrumental study of sleep. The fact that one can reliabily predict the nature of a subjective report by reading an oscilloscope (or a digital voltmeter) attached to a person's head, moves us formally as close as we ever get to objectivity in mental science. It is theoretically possible that such reports are either fabricated or arise after the experimental awakening. But even if this were the case, it would be necessary to postulate a physiologically mediated state dependency of the factitious data since the reports differ formally from one another in a systematic manner according to the pre-existing brain state.

The third guarantee is pragmatic. Here I attempt to side-step the trap of subjective doubt by having recourse to two related considerations. One is the absolute certainty that is associated with some dream recall in some subjects. Disbelieving such reports threatens, unacceptably, the whole philosophic and scientific enterprise. Such a sceptical operation of subjectivity upon subjectivity constitutes a hall of mirrors from which there is no escape were it not for the associated recognition that no other subjective experience, including instrumental operations such as the reading of an oscilloscope or a digital voltmeter (whose status also ulimately depend upon statistical reliability and predictability) has any better claim on what we call objectivity.

But objective predictability has a converse that makes such an explanation unlikely, and that is the close correspondence of the awakened subject's estimate of dream duration to the actually elapsed clock time of the pre-existing brain state. This accuracy could also be ascribed (by obsessive doubt) to post-awakening retrospection were it not for the fact that the subjective timing of external stimulus incorporation into a dream narrative also corresponds well with real clock time.

Investigative strategy and the assumption of psychological homology

The rationale and strategy taken here obviously involves another piece of fancy philosophical footwork. Without raising the unanswerable question, 'Do the cats dream?' I cannot have scientific certainty even that the brain states of the two species we wish to study are comparable. Indeed, since I can be reasonably sure they are not identical (if only because cats lack the hardware necessary for speech), we must be at least as cautious in extrapolating from the brain state of one species to that of another as we are in moving from the brain to the mind domain within a species.

The scientific evidence in favour of homology is indirect but strong. No crucial differences between the REM sleep of cats and men have yet been documented. The many shared features include:

the brain activation (implying a homologous tonic cognitive arousal);
the motoric inhibition (implying a homologous tonic suppression of output); and
the eye movements or REMs (implying a homologous internal phasic signal generator).

The recent finding that brain waves coding for eye movement directionality are common to both species would seem to clinch the phasic signal agreement.

Some hand-waving is admittedly visible in the contention that nature would probably not devise two entirely different sets of neurophysiological mechanisms for such remarkably similar behavioural syndromes. All animal models, upon which the progress of knowledge heavily depends, share this uncertainty, however, so we have the consolation of being in good scientific company. One way to gain confidence in the homology assumption is to test, in man, physiological hypotheses developed in the animal model. Positive results would at least satisfy the Jamesian pragmatist's definition of truth: it works. Such a case is provided by the demonstration that cholinergic agonists do, as predicted from animal experiments, enhance REM sleep *and* dreaming in man!

Reflexes and state: a paradigm shift?

In a paper entitled 'What Is a Behavioural State?' (Hobson 1978), I contrasted the stimulus–response paradigm (which dominates behavioural physiology as completely today as it did psychoanalysis a century ago) and the central state paradigm (which is only now emergent through research on sleep). Summarizing the arguments, the following features contrast the two paradigms:

1 The stimulus–response paradigm assumes state constancy. This *may* be true of certain highly artificial conditions imposed upon the subject by the experimenter – such as anaesthesia or decerebration – but it is *never* true of intact behaving organisms for whom dynamism is the rule. It is, however, probably not even true of those conditions on which all of modern neurophysiological knowledge is based since anaesthetic and decerebrate states clearly evolve over time both metabolically and functionally. These factors have been ignored by scientists who blindly and naively follow Claude Bernard's essential criterion of experimentation as holding all but one variable constant and then systematically varying that one. In any case, it is clear that neither the anaesthetic nor the decerebrate states can be regarded as either natural (they clearly are not) or of interest to the psychophysiologist (because sensation and/or its motoric expresions are eliminated in such states).

2 In a mathematical-statistical sense, stationarity is the problematical assumption of most experimenters who work in either the stimulus–response or the state domain. Two factors operate to upset the validity of this assumption in the experimental preparation of the greatest interest: the intact, unanaesthetized animal.

The first is habituation and is well known to stimulus–response scientists. Some become so impressed with the fact that successive stimuli elicit responses of decreasing strength (and finally no response at all) that they give up the study of sensation for the study of learning.

The second is the constant fluctuation of background activity that appears especially strongly at certain times of day and is even dramatic at all times of day, in the face of the constancy of input conditions that is an experimental designation of the Bernardian investigator. In others words, the very conditions necessary to psychophysical experimentation (input restriction and stimulus control) actually invoke dynamic changes in the system of interest. Habituation is thus the herald of sleep just as sleep is the herald of dreams!

3 Since it is a description of the rules governing the system's own dynamics that are the goal of the state scientists, one must, for a time at least, abandon the classical experimental paradigm. *The system must be allowed to run free so as to express itself clearly.* The experimenter must *do nothing* but wait and watch, a tedious, difficult and unpopular observational mode known better to ethologists than to physiologists. For

this reason, it is to be recommended that future students of behavioural physiology have ethological research experience. Interestingly, this is exactly what psychiatry, in its concern for natural behaviour, could become if only it would give up its own impulse to control states (as it does in psychopharmacology) or to interpret them by philosophically untenable theories (as it does in psychoanalysis). It is comforting to recognize that a single attitude, *expectant observation*, can unite the behavioural clinician with the behavioural scientist at this seemingly divisive moment in the history of the field.

4   The stimulus–response scientist is aided (and hindered) by the obviousness of the order of investigations appropriate to his paradigm. He begins at the receptor, proceeds to the first, then the second synaptic relay, describing the changes at each early information processing step (as if they were state independent, which they are not) and only then becomes lost in the diffusely radiating maze of central interconnections that probably, somehow, underlie sensation and perception. Some wise but unambitious colleagues side-step this issue by following the stimulus out (as motor reflex activity).

The state scientist has no such inherent structural signposts to tell him what to do first. Where (and, of course, how) do states begin and end? For states, the order sought is temporal, not spatial (since states are global) and the mechanism is an oscillator (or a clock), not a transformer (or an encoder). But there are (at least) 20 billion neurons in the brain, a daunting figure for anyone who would begin a cell-by-cell inventory! Localizing oscillators depends upon lesion studies, an unattractive method with its own problematic logical pitfalls. Destruction of the nervous system followed by functional deficit is only suggestive, not conclusive, evidence of cause. These and related concerns have recently been elaborated in detail in a discussion of the scientific tribulations of our own reciprocal interaction hypothesis (Hobson, Lydic and Baghdoyan 1986).

How can isomorphism between state levels be established?

As indicated elsewhere, I believe that the current state of knowledge limits the isomorphist approach to the most approximate, global and statistical correlations of variables from the several levels at which states are assessed. If we take dreams as our starting point, we must then focus on the formal level of analysis, leaving to the indefinite future the analysis of content (in all its narrative and syntactical richness). We thus aim at an interpretation of *dreaming* (as a universal mental process) rather than the interpretation of *dreams* (as individual mental experiences).

This about-face from the Freudian approach deserves some emphasis. I share the conclusions of Clark Glymour (1983) and of Adolf Grünbaum (1984) concerning the deficits of Freud's method of dream interpretation. Freud's method is anecdotal, *ad hoc*, internally inconsistent, uncontrolled; and it is gratuitous.

Finally, it fails even to do what is claims to do (to specify, by means of free association, the unconscious wish that motivates and determines the dream). I thus reject such an approach both as fundamentally unscientific and, in any case, as unsuited to the early stages of the isomorphic project we have adopted.

I count it as puzzling that even after 30 years of laboratory sleep research, the formal aspects of dreaming, as a psychological state, remain so ill-defined and unquantified. Two powerful traditions work against achievement of this goal:

One is psychoanalysis itself, which still claims the deep allegiance of many empirically dedicated sleep scientists. For example, in *A Grammar of Dreams*, David Foulkes (1978) follows other Freudian revisionists into the adjacent domain of linguistics in a sincere but fatally doomed effort to specify symbolic representations. Here again, I agree with philosopher Grünbaum's *Foundations of Psychoanalysis* (1984) and psychoanalyst Morris Eagle (1983) in regarding all the self-styled breakthroughs to hermeneutic paradigms as scientific regressions. I prefer the clarity and the biological inspiration of the early Freud.

The other is a radical and molecular empiricism which catalogues informational items in dream reports and neglects the *process* that organizes the items. This approach is epitomized by the Calvin Hall/Robert van de Castle 'dream bank' with its index of ten thousand dream reports each of which is itemized with respect to descriptions of dream characters (are they men, women or Martians?), plot features (are they running, jumping, standing still?), and so on. While more useful to the isomorphic agenda than any efforts at interpretation, at the narrative level this accountancy approach is at too low a level to be of real use.

A single example may help make the point: it is necessary and sufficient (for the isomorphist) to know that all well-remembered dream reports describe colour and that the common supposition that dreaming is colourless (the 'black and white' theory) is an incorrect inference related definitively and exclusively to the problems of recall (an after-the-fact memory defect). This means that no state-specific change in higher-order visual processing need be invoked – or sought – in developing a physiological state correlate for dreaming; rather a state dependent change in memory is to be postulated – and its neuronal correlate sought in experimental animal studies.

By contrast, it is neither necessary (nor even helpful) for the mind–brain isomorphist to know the incidence, in reports, of the words 'red', 'yellow', or 'chartreuse', since the higher-order physiological correlates of such specific details are unlikely to be state dependent (or discovered within our lifetime). Of course, if all colour reports were chartreuse or if a primary colour were absent we would sit up and take notice, so the approach is not, *a priori*, useless.

The choice of level that is likely to be fruitful in a state-to-state correlation is thus governed by the scientific maturity of work in one or both of the states under consideration. This limitation is severe in the case of all mental states, including dreaming, and for most physiological states except perhaps REM sleep, which may now be the most completely defined mammalian state at the behavioural and the neuronal level. In this case, it is thus the level of knowledge of the neuronal state of REM sleep which directs the contemporary state isomorphist to the appropriate psychological level in the study of dreaming. That level is the *formal* and involves a qualitative and quantitative assessment of the distinctive information-processing characteristics of the state.

Having observed certain *formal* features of the brain state in REM sleep, the mind–brain isomorphist then moves from the bottom–up to ask if there is an isomorphic set of formal features of the mind state in dreaming. Conversely, the presence of distinctive formal features of the mind state in dreaming direct a top–down quest for isomorphic features in the brain state of REM sleep. Such an approach has already proved useful in the following study of dream form:

Studies of dream movement (McCarley and Hoffman 1981). These have revealed its ubiquity in reports and its possibly distinctive character (dream subjects are never static as they often are in waking life and as they always are, in fact, when in the non-REM sleep state), there being a superabundance of curved, circular or spiral trajectories (Hobson and Hoffman 1984); this approach was suggested by the physiological finding of intense central motor system activation and by the detection of unusual signals between visuomotor coordination centres (the oculomotor, the visual sensory, the vestibular and the cerebellar).

Studies of dream sensation. These reveal a graded representation of sensory modalities ranging from one hundred per cent (vision) to zero per cent (pain) in laboratory reports (McCarley and Hoffman 1981). While we do not know how to quantify exactly the isomorphic brain state function, we would expect system activation to be very high in the case of vision (and it is) and very low in the case of pain (and it is!).

Studies of dream bizarreness (Hobson, Lydic and Bahgdoyan (1986). These have revealed that this distinctive psychological attribute is composed of (a) incongruities, (b) discontinuities, and (c) uncertainties in the domains of dream plot, dream character and dream action. Further, an analysis of the underlying cognitive processes reveals major defects in orientation, attention and memory – similar to those seen in organic syndromes. External input differentiation, parallel channel activation, and disenablement of memory systems are candidate isomorphic brain dysfunctions. The psychological data thus confirm many of the predictions of physiology and advance the isomorphist argument to a new plane.

These studies illustrate the utility of the isomorphist approach and show the value of the new theory of dreaming, whose experimental development utilizes both bottom–up and top–down approaches of the isomorphist theory. While the data cannot be said to disprove the Freudian hypothesis, they offer a simpler, more straightforward explanation of dream phenomena.

Conclusions

The foregoing discussion allows us to distinguish the major differences between Freud's psychoanalytic theory and the activation-synthesis of dreams in each of five categories:

1   *Energetics* – What is the driving force of dreaming?
    (a)   Psychoanalytic View: Day-residue pairs with unconscious wish releasing repressed energy.
    (b)   Physiologic Evidence: Pontine generator neurons are activated periodically and automatically during REM sleep.
    (c)   Activation-Synthesis: The driving force of dreaming is a basic and pre-programmed biological process of which dreaming is the psychological concomitant.
2   *Hallucinosis* – How do the images arise?
    (a)   Psychoanalytic View: Energy, released from unconscious, flows to the perceptual side of apparatus – giving rise to hallucinosis.
    (b)   Physiologic Evidence: Sensory systems are activated by pontine generator during REM sleep.
    (c)   Activation-Synthesis: Sensory perception is the information-processing concomitant of sensory system activation in REM sleep.
3   *Bizarreness* – Why is dream content characterized by such distinctive

cognitive features such as: Condensation? Displacement? Distortion? Pictorialization?

(a) Psychoanalytic View: Censor disguises basic meaning of unconscious wish to protect consciousness from disruption.

(b) Physiologic Evidence: Motor and many sensory pathways are activated in parallel, with generator speeding and slowing, and all in the absence of external input.

(c) Activation-Synthesis: The cognitive peculiarities are due to perceptual and conceptual synthesis of disparate data, arising from parallel channel activation by a brain stem pattern generator acting in the absence of external input stability.

4 *Delusional Thinking* – Why is bizarre dream content accepted as real?

(a) Psychoanalytic View: Consciousness accepts censored and distorted ideas to protect itself from the truth.

(b) Physiologic Evidence: Absence of external information, blocked by active physiological inhibition, makes reality testing impossible.

(c) Activation-Synthesis: Dereistic thinking of dreams is normal and non-significant *per se*.

5 *Amnesia* – Why are dreams forgotten?

(a) Psychoanalytic View: Preconscious represses dreams upon awakening.

(b) Physiologic Evidence: Memory system is disabled by change of state.

(c) Activation-Synthesis: Dreams are forgotten because of a simple state dependent amnesia, i.e. non-remembering.

In view of these major differences, I suggest that the interpretation of dreams using psychoanalytic principles may be unwarranted, potentially misleading and scientifically hazardous.

REFERENCES

Aserinsky, E. and Kleitman, N. 1953: Regularly occurring periods of eye motility, and concurrent phenomena during sleep. *Science*, 118, 273–4.
Dement, W. and Kleitman, N. 1957: Cyclic variations in EEG during sleep and their relation to eye movements, body motility, and dreaming. *EEG Clinical Neurophysiology*, 9, 673–90.
Eagle, M. 1983: A critical explanation of motivational explanation in psychoanalysis, in L. Laudan (ed.), *Mind and Medicine: Explanation and Evaluation in Psychiatry and the Biomedical Sciences*. Pittsburgh Series in the Philosophy and History of Science, vol. 8. Berkeley: University of California Press.
Foulkes, D. 1978: *A Grammar of Dreams*. New York: Basic Books.

Freud, S. 1954: Project for a Scientific Psychology, in M. Bonaparte, A. Freud and E. Kris (eds), *The Origins of Psychoanalysis. Letters to Wilhelm Fliess, Drafts and Notes: 1887–1902*. New York: Basic Books.

Glymour, C. 1983: The theory of your dreams, in R. S. Cohen and L. Laudan (eds), *Physics, Philosophy and Psychoanalysis*. Dordrecht and Boston: D. Reidel.

Grünbaum, A. 1984: *The Foundations of Psychoanalysis: A Philosophical Critique*. Berkeley: University of California Press.

Hobson, J. A. 1978: What is a behavioral state? in J. A. Ferrendelli (ed.), *Aspects of Behavioral Neurobiology*, 1–15. Bethesda: Society for Neuroscience.

Hobson, J. A. and Hoffman, S. 1984: Picturing dreaming: some features of the drawings in a dream journal, in M. Bosinelli and P. Cicogna (eds), *Psychology of Dreaming*. Bologna: CLUEB.

Hobson, J. A., Lydic, R., and Baghdoyan, H. A. 1986: Evolving concepts of sleep cycle generation: from brain centers to neuronal populations. *Behavioral and Brain Sciences*, 9, 371.

McCarley, R. W. and Hobson, J. A. 1977: The neurobiological origins of psychoanalytic dream theory. *American Journal of Psychiatry*, 134, 11.

McCarley, R. W and Hoffman, E. 1981: REM sleep dreams and the activation-synthesis hypothesis. *American Journal of Psychiatry*, 138, 7.

Quine, W. V. O. 1985: Personal communication.

Sulloway, F. J. 1979: *Freud, Biologist of the Mind*. New York: Basic Books.

14

Some Questions about Dreaming for Physiologists

ROGER SQUIRES

This chapter was prompted by the 1977 and 1979 articles of McCarley and Hobson and by Professor Hobson's illuminating presentation at the Gifford Conference in St Andrews. It is an encouragement to further articulation of the 'activation-synthesis hypothesis' not a philosopher's attempt to take issue with physiological theory.

ISOMORPHISM AND CAUSATION

McCarley and Hobson describe their strategy as a search for mind–body isomorphism, 'matching or mapping between operations and objects in the two conceptual systems of mind and brain' and say they don't 'view psychological events as causing physiological events or vice versa' (1979: 81). Yet the burden of their model is precisely to assert the primacy of physiological phenomena: 'The activation-synthesis hypothesis postulates that principal elements of dreams derive from a synthesis of information generated by activation of motor pattern generators and of sensory systems' (1979: 112). What are the arrows in their flow chart doing, if not indicating the direction of dependence? Only if the features of dreaming which they discuss are caused by the physiology is there any conflict with Freudian explanations of those features.

Isomorphism as such is too weak in one way, because it is consistent with coincidental similarities, and may be too strong in another, for psychological patterns may be variously matched to physiological patterns (as critics of so-called type–type identity theories have insisted). I don't want to pursue this general issue, but assume that the significant claim is that certain features of dreaming are functionally dependent on earlier physiological activity.

HOW DO DREAMS GET ORGANIZED?

McCarley and Hobson say that unstructured signals from the brain stem trigger off motor routines which, though ultimately blocked except for eye movements and twitches of the extremities, nevertheless feed back signals to the forebrain which are partially structured in the direction of ordinary activity. (The details of how structured are important.) This is so far non-visual or, at least, eyes-closed information. You see nothing (or nothing much) if you shut your eyes and move them about. Normal vision needs a richer diet for detecting visual objects. Now internal signals may simultaneously be hitting the visual cortex, but (I take it) these are random signals not subtle patterns from reflective surfaces as in perception, so we would expect something at the colour flash or phosphene level, which is what we would report if they happened to us while awake. How do we synthesize detailed and elaborate imagery from these elements? Dreams are sometimes bizarre; but this would be like watching flashing torches in the kitchen from inside a spinning washing machine!

I'm not surprised the forebrain is described as 'making the best of a bad job in producing even partially coherent dream imagery from the relatively noisy signals sent up to it from the brain stem' (Hobson and McCarley 1977: 1347). To reach the level of scenes rather than coloured lights and picture frames, an appeal has to be made to structured information already in. 'Idiosyncratic and personal elements in the dream are the ones later retrieved from the dreamer's memory because they most closely match the input' (McCarley and Hobson 1979: 116). They also suggest that memory may be directly activated by the signals. Does this imply synthesis with no matching? I'm not sure what correlations between dream features and signals could confirm this part of the story.

The synthesis, we are told (1979: 125), 'occurs in much the same fashion as it does during waking'. But if the above remarks about the poverty of the signals that we receive in dreaming sleep are right, the stored data need to play a much larger part than in normal perception. By what information processing does the forebrain select the stored scenario that most closely matches the disorganized sensory chaos? Are there millions of different scenarios waiting around in our brains to be selected as closest match? That already looks implausible. Furthermore, we know that dreams are, not memories in the ordinary sense, but relatively coherent fancies. By what physiological process does the forebrain knit together these stored elements, selected for mechanical similarity to disorganized signals, into a passable tale? It is the coherence of dreams, not their bizarreness, which poses the problem for neurophysiology.

McCarley and Hobson are concerned to prove that dreams largely reflect the physiological messages that the forebrain receives. That is the basis for their quarrel with psychoanalytic interpretation. We already have evidence of the relevant kind in the way things like clocks chiming at least sometimes seem to influence dream reports. They suggest that 'the fate of external stimuli in dream construction (in terms of the dream transformation) may be analogous to the fate of internally generated sensory stimuli . . . the dream is built on these elements, and they may be regarded as the foundation of the dream' (1979: 118). But when one looks at the way the known signals are transformed one's impression is not so much of foundation stones as of rocks which the dream current has to negotiate. An alternative to their hypothesis, presumably, would be that dream processing occurs fairly autonomously in the cortex, even if the process is triggered off from elsewhere and even if incoming signals are sometimes accommodated.

The question how dreams get organized is obviously relevant to the question whether and how much they are psychologically revealing. McCarley and Hobson seem to think they are about as revealing as our description of the view out of the window. Or perhaps our interpretation of an animated Rorschach blot. If the interesting correlations which they have researched between features of dream reports and various non-cortical physiological events hold up, then psychoanalytic interpretations of the general occurrence of *those* features is doomed. But this is a limited result. The signals to the forebrain are uncontaminated by motivation. But it has to be argued and not assumed that the synthesis of those signals is uncontaminated. I could not see how to unpack their mechanical account of the dream-organization in a plausible way. There are alternative physiological accounts which would allow the process of organization to be psychologically revealing, even expressive of hidden thoughts or fulfilling of unconscious wishes. Dreaming could even guard sleep in the sense that disturbing topics that would wake us up if explicitly treated in the dream are rendered anodyne by symbolic transformations.

Of course, I'm not claiming any of this is the case. But the idea that dreams are 'motivated' does not fall with the failure of Freud's physiology nor with the present success of Harvard's physiology. The physiological generation story had to yield to something like memory and invention in explaining the rich content of dreams. If we call that 'synthesis', it is *possible* that it proceeds mechanically as McCarley and Hobson assume. That would not just make a dent in Freud but virtually put him off the road. It is also possible, however, that synthesis is motivational. I suppose we do not have the vital physiological evidence. So I think claims to have demolished the old psychoanalytic paradigm are premature. We should not yet abandon it *in favour of* the physio-generative one. Test both – if you can.

'If the neural impetus to the dreaming state is motivationally neutral, then the corresponding or isomorphic psychological process creating the dreaming imagery cannot be described as being based on a need for disguise' (1979: 86). Wrong. It *could* be. We need to be able to track the contribution of the neural impetus to the imagery to evaluate this claim. Perhaps it is only slight. We should not move unselfconsciously from a non-motivational account of activation to a non-motivational account of synthesis.

DO WE RESPOND TO DREAMS?

In the flow chart of McCarley's and Hobson's 1979 article no response to dreams (except reporting them, which shows what the synthesis is) features at all. Eye movements, motor relays, even emotional components, are shown as dream-formative not dream-responsive. They are physiological patterns that activate the forebrain *before* it 'fits experiential data'. On this model sleep 'paralysis' does not stop us acting out our dreams; it just stops our muscles responding to automatic stimulation. The cats (Sastre and Jouvet 1977); Hendricks, Bowker and Morrison 1977) who have had the relevant immobilizing links severed and who consequently are variously active in dreaming sleep are not chasing imaginary mice or scaring potential enemies. The view of Roffwarg and associates (Roffwarg et al. 1962) that in rapid eye movements we are scanning, as it were, the events of the dream, is rejected. 'The eye movements might be initiated by giant cells but could not be generated by cortical neurons. This finding practically wrecks the scanning hypothesis and strongly favors the idea that visual cortical events are determined by events in the oculomotor brain stem' (Hobson and McCarley 1977: 1342). Similarly, the emotions we report on waking would not be occasioned by dreaming of frightening or exciting things, but that would be the way the brain incorporated physiological arousal in the dream plot. In his address at the Gifford Conference Professor Hobson speculated that 'the forebrain may, in turn, generate its own motor commands which help to perpetuate the process [synthesis from motor command signals] via positive feedback to the reticular formation' (this volume p. 295) and, in accordance with this reversal, he also described the 'output blockade' as halting 'the enactment of dreamed motor commands' so that we do not 'act upon the internally generated information' (this volume, p. 293). What is the evidence about the direction of the signals? Much of the psychological interest of the activation-synthesis model lies in the non-cognitive shaping of dreams. *Given the direction of signals from motor systems to forebrain*, the correlations between motor activity and dream features were impressive evidence against psychoanalytical accounts of those features. But if the forebrain partly shapes the motor activity the correlations are no longer clear negative evidence. The details of the neurophysiological model make all the difference.

ARE DREAMS MISINTERPRETED OR MISREPORTED?

Hobson and McCarley draw connections between the neurophysiology and the dream reports, hoping thereby to cast light on dreaming itself, which is described as a distinctive 'mental experience occurring in sleep' (1977: 1376). They face two methodological problems. First, our critical faculties in sleep are in a particularly unreliable state. We suffer from 'delusional acceptance of these phenomena [hallucinoid imagery] as "real" at the time they occur' (1977: 1336). After considering the physiology underlying attentional processes, Professor Hobson suggests we lack 'the capacity to organize information in a logical and coherent manner and to achieve the full self-awareness that gives waking consciousness perspective and insight' (this volume, p. 296). Second, our memories are also in an unusual state and are treated as fragile guides. Hobson says 'the brain mechanisms of memory will be dramatically altered and disenabled during REM sleep' (this volume, p. 288) and amnesia takes over after that. So how does he know that he is connecting features of the nervous system with features of sleeping experience rather than with features of dream reports due to poor critical judgement in sleep of what is going on and selective remembering? After all, if dreams are very different from the reports, correlations between the reports and brainstem activity will not bear on dream production in any simple way.

I hope these worries will not be dismissed as merely philosophical (by that people mean 'not worth bothering with except for a bit of fun'). How do we know that dreams are intense and vivid because sensory input is blocked (1977: 1340), yet their apparent vagueness and patchiness is because memory is inhibited? How do we know that the scene and plot shifts are due to a change in pattern of neural activation (977: 1346) rather than misinterpretation or bad reporting? How do we know that dreams are not logical and commonplace with no particular predominance of sensation or hectic activity, but that these features are highlighted by selective memory mechanisms? Or that they are totally incoherent and the coherence is introduced at the reporting stage or remembering stage? Again, it could be that anxiety is well represented in dream reports either because it is memorable (we could check with memories of, e.g., holidays abroad) or because it is connected with waking up or nearly waking up when it is more available for reporting.

The connections with brainstem activity can only be properly interpreted if we make assumptions about how these questions (and similar ones) should be answered. If we don't have the evidence to do this and leave the details of the model flexible, there is a real danger of special pleading, of giving pseudo-explanations rather like some of Freud's. For example, Hobson and McCarley (1977: 1339) advance a physiological explanation both of the higher degree of physical activity in dreams (many impulses from motor areas) and of the trouble we have moving in chase dreams ('descending inhibition of motor neurons'). It looks suspiciously as if you could explain any degree of activity with those parameters.

McCarley and Hobson say that their theory 'suggests that the primary events are sensory and motor system behavioral sequence activation and then a knitting together in a way that includes the dreamer's experience. In this view the manifest content transparently shows the impetus to the dream, in contrast to the wish fulfilment–disguise model of psychoanalytic theory' (1979: 113). How does this 'knitting together' occur? If the details of that are left flexible, the model can accommodate almost any 'correlations' between brainstem activity and dream reports. Without independent evidence for those details it would be unscientific to advance the correlations as confirmation for the general model. Dream reports cannot *bespeak* their physiological origins any more than their psychoanalytic ones.

ARE DREAMS MENTAL EVENTS IN SLEEP?

Finally, if the dream is the result of an information-processing synthesis, do we respond to it or act on it in any other way than by giving dream reports (sometimes) when we wake up? If not, it seems gratuitous to suppose there is an intermediate dream performance or presentation about which we exercise our critical faculties either well or badly during sleep. The most popular evidence for sleeping responses, if I understand it right, either occurs in the wrong sleep phase (walking and talking) or it is explicable non-motivationally (eye movements, motor twitches). So talk about states of awareness or exercises of judgement or uncritical belief in sleep or of accepting dreams as real is either speculative physiology which rather flies in the face of what is known so far, or it simply registers the potential and ill-understood connection between physical processes in sleep and strange waking impressions. One reason for the resistance to this hobby-horse is that it is natural to talk of the brain in personal terms. McCarley and Hobson, for example, say it interprets internal signals as if they are real, synthesizes the dream by comparing different information, makes 'the best of a bad job', and similar things. So we are apt to suppose people *must* exhibit judgement in sleep. Now the legitimacy and utility of homuncularizing parts of the brain are matters of debate. But I think Professor Hobson sees the postulation of superpersonal agents here as a peril to which Freudian theory succumbed (e.g. with the dream censor). Yet if the forebrain is identified with the person we have fresh problems. Are we to suppose that the dozy uncritical sleeper that McCarley and Hobson can only compare to someone in the grip of delusions and serious mental disorders is simultaneously doing a brilliant job in adverse conditions, making a coherent story from meagrely structured and chaotically abundant elements?

The remedy is to distinguish between information processing in brain science and a person's exercising judgement. When the forebrain interprets incoming signals this is presumably an electromechanical process. No question of uncritical acceptance or that it should have known better. This kind of synthesis is not (I would say) a cognitive or mental activity but a cerebral process which makes possible something which *is* mental, namely saying what you can see or reporting a dream. I realize that, with the present state of the tide, such protests are sandcastles before the oncoming waves (despite a respectable ancestry in Wittgenstein's *Blue Book* and Ryle's *Concept of Mind*). The brain scientists have claimed the world 'mental' as well as 'cognitive' and soon may claim many more. It may not matter so long as we don't lose the distinctions. It is the thought displayed by the reports which can be critically assessed, not the physiological information processing which underlies them.

Wouldn't it be simpler to *trust* dream reports unless we find reasons not to? It is an important issue whether we should treat them as *reports*. It strikes me as simpler and safer to assume we are dealing with psychological features of recently awakened subjects rather than to advance a putative psychology of sleep. Intermediate mental states may be metaphysical lumber that do no harm in philosophy: but when it comes to building a physiological model they will lead to misinterpretation and extra complications. I would like to see us guided by (or at least open to) the evidence on this rather than by intuitions of simplicity and safety, which may take their obviousness from tacit acceptance of one view or the other.

Don't the phenomena of 'lucid' dreaming, wherein people can be trained to watch dreams as they happen, signal their contemporaneous awareness by pre-arranged hand movements and even control the events of the dream, set some of these doubts to rest and confirm that the content of dreams is well reflected in waking reports? Perhaps; though there may be difficulties in the idea that someone is a simultaneous participant in and spectator of the same adventures. And there could be doubts about whether the hand movements are properly described as signals. If the further suggestion of content control is admitted, this would seem to reduce the scope for a non-motivational account and perhaps ought to make McCarley and Hobson uneasy about rejecting Freudian wish-fulfilment or censorship explanations without careful investigation. Dreams would at least be amenable to psychological interference.

THE EPICUREAN PHYSIOLOGISTS

The Roman Lucretius composed *De Rerum Natura* in the first century BC as a stylish exposition of the doctrines worked out by the Greek Epicurus and his followers two centuries earlier. The Epicureans were, as far as I know, the first to produce a non-motivational, 'activation-synthesis' explanation of dreaming and their attempt is instructive. We are impressed by the *differences* between dreams and waking events, but the main problem is to explain the striking similarities – it is the sense and coherence of dreaming that poses difficulties for a mechanical account. We naturally argue, as Lucretius did, that 'in so far as a vision beheld by the mind closely resembles one beheld by the eyes, the two must have been created in a similar fashion' (Latham 1951: 153). Now Lucretius talked of perception in terms of surface films streaming from objects into our eyes, but on any account I take it that the signals received by us are largely organized by their sources – the people, trees, clouds which they reflect. The problem for the physiologists, then as now, is: How do internal dream signals get organized?

The Epicureans thought that the surface films that explained perception got into the body through non-sensory channels and so were available as dream material. Thus the elements for dream-synthesis retained much of their daytime structure. This gives them a richer (though not a truer) start than McCarley and Hobson, whose internal signals, electrochemical impulses, have a random and unstructured origin in pontine brainstem activity. Lucretius tried to explain the movement in dreams by saying that successive images in different positions gave the illusion of motion (almost inventing the cinema here), but he realized there were severe limits to his explanation so long as he stayed on the activation side of the story.

'Assemblages of men, processions, banquets, battles – does nature create all these at a word and make them ready for us? . . . when in our dreams we see images walking with measured step and moving their supple limbs, why do they swing their supple arms in time with alternate legs and perform repeated movements with their feet appropriate to their shifting glances? Are we to suppose the stray films are imbued with art and trained to spend their nights in dancing?' (Latham 1951: 155). Lucretius answers that when presented with certain images we form natural expectations as to the sequel and, since there are very many stray films about, we then notice the ones we expect to see. Thus the dream story builds up in a way that reflects our knowledge and concerns, so that, as he ways, 'Whatever employment has the strongest hold on our interest or has last filled our waking hours . . . is what seems often to keep us occupied in sleep. Lawyers argue cases and frame contracts. Generals lead their troops into action. Sailors continue their pitched battle with the winds' (p. 160).

Having solved the main problem, Lucretius is then ready to explain some of the *differences* between dreaming and being awake. For example, 'Sometimes it happens that an image is not forthcoming to match our expectation: what was a woman seems to be suddenly transformed into a man before our eyes, or we are confronted by some swift change of feature or age. Any surprise we feel at this is checked by drowsy forgetfulness' (p. 156). It would be a mistake to think that bizarreness in dreams *confirmed* his general account. He had no independent evidence that in cases of bizarreness there were no suitable images around. He explained it only in the sense that he showed how it was consistent with his story about expectations and images.

Hobson and McCarley are presently in a similar position: 'the random but specific nature of the generator signals could provide abnormally sequenced and shaped, but spatiotemporally specific, frames for dream imagery; and the clustering of runs of generator signals might constitute time-marks for dream subplots and scene changes. Further, the activation by generator neurons of diffuse post-synoptic forebrain elements in multiple parallel channels might account for the disparate sensory, motor and emotional elements that contribute to the "bizarreness" of dreams' (1977: 1347). The assumption seems to be that the forebrain can make sense of certain unstructured patterns from the brain stem but that other patterns force it into a scissors and paste routine. Their model predicts bizarreness provided they make specific assumptions about the limited capacity of the forebrain to synthesize smoothly. But unless there is independent evidence for this capacity, bizarreness as such offers no confirmation of the model. They have explained it only by showing how on their account it would be possible.

Hobson and fellow researchers have surely made great strides in the physiological explanation of dreaming, which it would be absurd of me to question. But caution is needed in asserting what actually *is* evidence and how much it shows. We want to refer the *similarities* between dreaming and waking to similarities in the physiology and equally to refer *differences* to physiological differences. So unless we have some access to the mechanisms establishing what physiological features are relevant to what psychological ones, 'correlations' can be assigned either way. The flexibility of the physio-generative hypothesis with regard to the mechanics of synthesis may make it seem self-confirming, because the details can be filled in to suit the data from dream reports. Further articulation of the physiological processes in response to the latest neurophysiological data is the way to break out of this. If comparing dream 'reports' (I use the word shallow-referentially) and brainstem 'signals' (I use the word . . . Oh, what the heck!) is to produce significant matches, we need better tests for when we have struck lucky.

REFERENCES

Hendricks, J. C., Bowker, R. M. and Morrison, A. R. 1977: Functional characteristics of cats with pontine lesions during sleep and wakefulness and their usefulness for sleep research, in W. P. Koella and P. Lenin (eds), *Sleep 1976*. Basle: Karger.
Hobson, J. A. and McCarley, R. W. 1977: The brain as a dream state generator:

an activation-synthesis hypothesis of the dream process. *American Journal of Psychiatry*, 134, 1335–48.

Latham, R. 1951: Translation of Lucretius, *The Nature of the Universe*. Harmondsworth: Penguin Classics.

McCarley, R. W. and Hobson, J. A. 1979: The form of dreams and the biology of sleep, in B. B. Wolman (ed.), *The Handbook of Dreams*, Van Nostrand Reinhold.

Roffwarg, H. P., Dement, W. C., Muzio, J. N. and Fisher, C. 1962: Dream imagery: relationship to rapid eye movements of sleep. *Archive of General Psychiatry*, 7, 235–58.

Sastre, J. P. and Jouvet, M. M. 1977: Les schemes moteurs du sommeil paradoxal, in W. P. Koella and P. Lenin (eds), *Sleep 1976*. Basle: Karger.

15

The Analogy of Symptoms and Dreams: Is Freud's Dream Theory an Impostor?

HELENE SOPHRIN PORTE

DILEMMA IN *THE INTERPRETATION OF DREAMS*

What is the stimulus to a dream?

Whether dreams have meaning or not – and if so, what that meaning is – has always been of central concern to students of the mind. In his psychoanalytic thinking, Sigmund Freud took a high view of dreams. The 'exact natural sciences', he said, take a low view of the dream, disparage it, hold it in poor esteem. In particular, Freud criticized the 'medical authorities' for promoting *somatic* hypotheses of dreaming, in which dreams are held to be meaningless signals from the sleeping body to the sleeping mind. If this degrading view were the correct view, said Freud, 'it would only remain to investigate the laws according to which the organic stimuli turn into dream images'. Authorities on humanity, we are left to suppose, would have no work to do on the subject of dreaming. In chapter I of *The Interpretation of Dreams*, Freud credited Dr A. Krauss, a psychiatrist, with a codex for constructing dreams out of somatic stimuli (S.E. 1900, IV: 36–7). Krauss held that bodily perturbations – muscular, respiratory, gastric, sexual and peripheral – are transformed into cognate images by 'trans-substantiation' of sensation. A dream of flying is a trans-substantiation, in sleep, of the 'rising and falling of the lobes of the lungs'. A dream of the teeth falling out is due to a 'dental stimulus', an 'excitation of the teeth'. To find oneself without clothes in a dream is to wake up and find oneself without *bed*-clothes. The laws of association that legislate these images are simple and direct ones.

'That eminent philosopher Wundt', said Freud, subscribed to the somaticist notion that higher mental function is degraded in sleep. Not only did Wundt explain dreams as illusions constructed out of external and internal stimuli (S.E. 1900, IV: 40–1); he believed that the process of *association* in dreams is stupid and chaotic (S.E. 1900, IV: 58). In this respect Freud cited also the Frenchman L. F. A. Maury, who compared dream mentation, in the sphere of intelligence, to chorea and paralysis in the sphere of motility. Dream images, Maury said, are degradations of the faculty of reason; dream associations resemble delirium (S.E. 1900, IV: 56–9).

The idea that dream imagery is demented, inertial, or simply lunatic, was anathema to Freud. Although not necessarily high-minded, a Freudian dream issues from a high mental state. In sleep the intelligence loses no status, and somatic stimuli gain none. In chapter V of *The Interpretation of Dreams* Freud related a dream and an interpretation of his own that lucidly illustrate the status of somatic stimuli – and the state of the mind – in sleep. This is the 'Riding', or 'Boil' dream:

I was riding on a grey horse, timidly and awkwardly to begin with, as though I were only reclining upon it. I met one of my colleagues, P., who was sitting on a high horse, dressed in a tweed suit, and who drew my attention to something (probably to my bad seat). I now began to find myself sitting more and more comfortably on my highly intelligent horse, and noticed that I was feeling quite at home up there. My saddle was a kind of bolster, which completely filled the space between its neck and crupper. In this way I rode straight in between two vans. After riding some distance up the street, I turned round and tried to dismount, first in front of a small open chapel that stood in the street frontage. Then I actually did dismount, in front of another chapel that stood near it. My hotel was in the same street; I might have let the horse go to it on its own, but I preferred to lead it there. It was as though I should have felt ashamed to arrive at it on horseback. A hotel 'boots' was standing in front of the hotel; he showed me a note of mine that had been found, and laughed at me over it. In the note was written, doubly underlined: 'No food', and then another remark (indistinct) such as 'No work', together with a vague idea that I was in a strange town in which I was doing no work.

(S.E. 1900, IV: 229–30)

The dream, of course, is an impostor:

It would not be supposed at first sight that this dream originated under the influence, or rather under the compulsion, of a painful stimulus. But for some days before I had been suffering from boils which made every movement a torture; and finally a boil the size of an apple had risen at the base of my scrotum, which caused me the most unbearable pain with every step I took. Feverish lassitude, loss of appetite and the hard work with which I nevertheless carried on – all these had combined with the pain to depress me. I was not properly capable of discharging my medical duties. There was, however, one activity for which, in view of the nature and situation of my complaint, I should certainly have been less fitted than for any other, and that was – riding.

(S.E. 1900, IV: 230)

The dream, Freud declared, was a sort of anosognosia – 'the most energetic denial of my illness that could possibly be imagined. I cannot in fact ride . . . I have only sat on a horse once in my life and that was without a saddle, and I did not enjoy it.' In this dream Freud rode *with* a saddle – a dream-divan that looked, he admitted, like the poultice he had worn to bed to ease the pain of his boil. But the effect of the poultice, was only temporary:

The painful feelings had then announced themselves and sought to wake me up; whereupon the dream came and said soothingly: No! Go on sleeping! There's no need to wake up. You haven't got a boil; for you're riding on a horse, and it's quite certain that you couldn't ride if you had a boil in that particular place. And the dream was successful. The pain was silenced, and I went on sleeping.

(S.E. 1900, IV: 230)

I shall put aside an obvious objection to this interpretation – namely, what is Freud's *proof* that pain had intervened during his sleep? – and turn to other parts of the interpretation. The dream is not merely utilitarian. It is opportunistic as well: 'the details of the situation that was being repudiated', and the repudiating image, have been seized upon, by unconscious thoughts, for other uses. Grey – pepper and salt – is the colour of a suit owned by Freud's colleague, P.; P. was wearing it when Freud last met him. Pepper and salt, and sugar and spice – thus continue Freud's waking associations to the dream. *Spicy* food is the cause of his boil, or so the doctors have said; Freud is relieved that the cause is not *sugar* diabetes. P., it turns out, has stolen a woman patient from Freud, and P. now rides the high horse over him, even though Freud boasts that he himself perpetrated some remarkable *feats* on his patient. 'You struck me as being firmly in the saddle there', a colleague had remarked to Freud, and Freud had, in fact, felt quite at home in his patient's house, as her physician – although he admits that she was 'highly intelligent' and often took him (like Itzig, the Sunday horseman) where *she* wanted to go. Freud's dream horse is grey – like P.'s suit – but the horse, according to

Freud, 'acquired the symbolic meaning of my patient'. In spite of his *feat* of dedication to psychoanalysis, Freud fears that if he is not cured he may end up with no food, no work (S.E. 1900, IV: 231).

These interpretations, if we take Freud's word, are accessible ones, bearing on his recent and immediate experience. Plumbing deeply, Freud saw that 'the wishful situation of riding' bore on childhood quarrels with his nephew John (the son of Freud's half-brother Emmanuel, and a year older than Freud). The dream alluded to travels in Italy – to Verona and Sienna – finally, to 'sexual dream thoughts'. 'I recalled the meaning,' Freud said, 'which references to Italy seem to have had in the dreams of a woman patient who had never visited that lovely country.' Where had Freud's patient wanted to go? *Gen Italien*, she dreamed – 'to Italy'; *Genitalien*, Freud responded – 'genitals'. 'And this was connected, too,' he concluded, 'with the house in which I had preceded my friend P. as physician, as well as with the situation of my boil' (S.E. 1900, IV: 231–2).

Anybody who has read Ernest Jones's biography of Freud (1953–7) can try to finish Freud's part-interpretation of this dream. Jones stated that the children Sigmund and John had a passionate, competitive relationship, that together they would torment Freud's niece, the child Pauline. Jones assumed that this cruelty was in part erotic: in effect, consciously or unconsciously, the boys lusted together after the girl. On Freud's part, Jones concluded, this 'infantile rape fantasy' concerned not only Pauline, and later Gisela Fluss, but 'doubtless, ultimately, his mother also' (Jones 1953–7, vol. 1: 25). Thus, in a Freudian interpretation, Freud's dream may be taken to allude not simply to the Oedipus complex, but to both of its halves: to Freud's infantile heterosexuality, and to his infantile homosexuality as well.

Such an interpretation, although it is an artificial one, is true to Freud's conviction that at every level a dream is a fulfilment of a wish – and, to the extent that wishes are disturbing, a *concealed* fulfilment. The 'Riding' dream, accordingly, was stimulated by wishes. This was the case, Freud insisted, at every level of the dream's construction. At a superficial level, the dream sprang from Freud's wish not to be awakened by his boil. The boil itself was a mere goad, an *external sensory stimulus* powerless to construct a dream. It was not Freud's boil that made his dream; it was his mind's activity to wish the boil away.

Internal sensory dream stimuli

Although Freud granted a poor status to external sensory dream stimuli such as his boil, he seemed to favour *internal* sensory dream stimuli – for example, the 'nervous excitations' that Wundt claimed occurred in the retina and in the ears during sleep, producing illusory dream images and sounds (S.E. 1900, IV: 30). In Freud's view, these 'subjective' dream stimuli had 'the obvious advantage of not being dependent, like objective ones, upon external chance' (S.E. 1900, IV: 31). But they had a disadvantage, too, for 'the part they play in instigating a dream is scarcely or not at all open to confirmation' (S.E. 1900, IV: 31). The best evidence that Freud could adduce in favour of internal sensory dream stimuli was an alleged 'connection and identity' of dream images and hypnagogic hallucinations (S.E. 1900, IV: 31–3). On the basis of this evidence alone, he cautioned against underestimating the inciting power of subjective sensory dream stimuli – 'for, as we know, visual images constitute the principal components of our dreams' (S.E. 1900, IV: 33).

Given Freud's dislike of somatic theories of dreaming, his cordiality to internal sensory stimuli strikes an odd note, and his 'evidence' for such stimuli an even odder one. Clearly, Freud was not certain of the nature of internal sensory dream stimuli: were they mere nervous excitations, or were they hallucinations – perhaps even wishful hallucinations? Freud could not say; but he had to treat 'subjective' sensory stimuli kindly, for they would later emerge at the centre of his own dream theory. I refer, of course, to the *regression to sensory representation*: the movement of the dream thoughts 'backward' in the mental apparatus, away from the 'motor end', 'to the pitch of sensory vividness' (S.E. 1900, V: 542–3). As an explanation of the hallucinatory nature of dreams the regression is a plausible idea, but – as Freud himself asked with respect to internal sensory dream formation – how can it be proved?

In fact, the hypothesis of regression could not be proved or disproved in Freud's lifetime. By investigative methods now at hand, the nature of *internal sensory stimuli* to dreaming invites neurological specification. If 'subjective' sensory events occurring in dreaming sleep could be verified, should these not be brought to bear on Freud's hypothesis of the regression to visual images? Would it not be a discovery at the heart of Freud's theory, on its own ground?

In 1953 Aserinsky and Kleitman observed periodic rapid eye movements, associated with a low voltage irregular electroencephalogram, in sleeping subjects. When awakened during a period of eye movements, many subjects said that they had been dreaming. Rapid eye movement (REM) sleep was soon associated with a low voltage fast electroencephalogram – indicating high cortical activation – and muscular atonia (Dement and Kleitman 1957; Berger 1961). Dream researchers suggested that these characteristics of REM sleep could influence the form and content of dreams (Dement and Wolpert 1958; Berger and Oswald 1962). More recently, investigators have identified patterns of *subcortical* activation in REM sleep (Chu and Bloom 1973; Hobson, McCarley and Wyzinski 1975; Sakai 1980). These discoveries enlarge the domain of internal sensory dream stimuli. Dream stimuli may include not only rapid eye movements, but also brainstem motor pattern activation and excitement of the visual cortex by REM-specific activation in the pontine brain stem (Hobson and McCarley 1977). Students of Freud might grant 'low' dream stimuli such as these the same low place that Freud gave to accidental and peripheral neural dream stimuli. I submit that Freud, in good faith to his hypothesis of regression to sensory representation, could not easily do so.

Nor could Freud ignore the modern claim that REM-specific stimuli are the cause of the strangeness of dreams. It was early suggested that rapid eye movements might contribute to dream bizarreness (Pivik and Foulkes 1966). Hobson and McCarley (1977) have suggested that dream bizarreness is a direct function of the state-specific pattern of brainstem activation in REM. Freud's concept of regression parallels this hypothesis in two ways. First of all, the regression entails a *state change* in the nervous system: the 'scene of action' of dreams – their location in the psychical apparatus – is different from the location of waking thoughts. Secondly, this state change introduces 'primitive methods of expression and representation' – it *directly* introduces the breakdown of logical thinking in dreams:

If we regard the process of dreaming as a regression occurring in our hypothetical mental apparatus, we *at once* arrive at the explanation of the empirically established fact that all the logical relations belonging to the dream thoughts disappear during the dream-activity or can only find expression with difficulty.

(S.E. 1900, V: 543; italics added)

Thus, the regression to sensory representation – like Hobson's and McCarley's hypothesis of REM-specific brainstem activation – ushers in not only the sensory vividness of dreams, but also their illogicality. Freud's model and Hobson's and McCarley's both refer to 'subjective' sensory events in dreaming sleep. One can imagine that if Freud were alive today he would want to look very carefully at the neurophysiological data as they bear on his hypothesis of regression.

On the other hand, if Freud were to look with interest at any set of physiological events that might produce the manifest dream directly, the status of conflict and concealment in dream formation would fall immediately into question. In his theory of dream interpretation, Freud insisted that the strangeness and unintelligibility of dreams issue from a tendentious concealment of the dream wish (S.E. 1900, IV: 134–62).

Thus, in the 'Riding' dream the oldest, most disturbing wishes are *completely* hidden: John, Gisela and Amalie (Freud's mother) are *concealed* presences. All that we *see* in the dream is Freud's distinctly odd equestrian and gear and progress, his meeting with P., his ride into a town, his encounter, finally, with the laughing 'boots' and with the vague, penurious note, in his own handwriting, 'No food', 'No work'. If not wildly lunatic, this is at least a strange imagery in its details, and modern dream researchers would explain it in a radically different way from Freud.

As an interpreter of dreams, Freud would reject outright the notion that dream bizarreness issues directly from a state change in the nervous system, with no addition of a mechanism of concealment. And yet, Freud himself said that the mechanism of regression 'at once' explains the disintegration of logic in dreams. There seems to be a duality in Freud's dream theory – a two-sidedness that commits him to contradictory explanations of the illogicality of dreams and puts him in a genuine dilemma with respect to any straightforward explanation of that illogicality. In this chapter I shall argue that there really is a fault in Freud's dream theory, and that the origins of that fault can be understood.

THE RHETORIC AND THE MECHANISM OF DREAMS

The dream rhetoric

What is the error in the dream theory? To find out, one has to unravel the theory's construction. To this end, I have found it helpful to consider the theory in two parts: a superficial dream theory, including a rhetorical and a mechanical part, and a deeper dream theory, underlying both rhetoric and mechanism.

Freud was a master of rhetoric. He was a fine metaphorist and analogist. By the delights of his prose, we are persuaded of the truth of his theory even before we are sure what the theory is. Freud did not state the full dream theory in technical terms until chapter VII of *The Interpretation of Dreams*. Chapter VI discusses the dream-work. In the first five chapters we see shadows and plastic incarnations of the dream theory. Chapter I is Freud's review of the literature. It is not so much a review of other theories as a preview of his own, granting favour or disfavour accordingly. This chapter sets out casually, indeed parenthetically, the idea (not Freud's own) that dreams are wish-fulfilments. Chapter II takes the theory of wish-fulfilment out of parentheses, into the light. There Freud says, intimately, here is my dream, and here is its meaning. In chapter III he emerges, a self-sufficient Dante, 'from a narrow defile' to a 'high ground' of safety and certainty. He ascends from example to exposition and universality – all dreams, like the dreams of children and of geese, are wish-fulfilments. In most dreams of adults this fact is obscured, we learn in chapter IV, by *dream distortion*. Here the fecund wish meets the prudish censor. Freud's demonstration of this meeting is purely analogical – he tells us not about the mechanism of mental authority and covert activity, but about political censorship and social dissimulation. In chapter V we learn that there are no 'somatic' dreams, and no 'innocent' dreams: the true origin of dreams is in old wishes – in the tragedy of Oedipus and, with the 'secular advance of repression', Hamlet's Oedipal dilemma. These are brilliant and seductive ideas: we buy the dream machine, sight unseen.

Chapter VII weaves a more subtle rhetoric, at once highly credible and highly obscure. Chapter III's question, 'What do geese dream of?', and its answer, 'Of maize', are transparently rhetorical. Chapter VII's 'A dream is a disguised fulfilment of a wish', and its entailment, 'A dream is like a neurotic symptom', are less transparently but just as purely rhetorical. These are technical pronouncements; but on scrutiny they lack clear justification and they mask disturbing ambiguities. Freud's *technical* rhetoric is presaged in chapter I:

It seems . . . to have dawned upon some . . . writers that the madness of dreams may not be without method and may even be simulated, like that of the Danish prince . . . These . . . writers cannot have judged by appearances . . .

Thus Havelock Ellis . . . without dwelling on the apparent absurdity of dreams, speaks of them as 'an archaic world of vast emotions and imperfect thoughts', the study of which might reveal to us primitive states of the evolution of mental life.

The same view is expressed by James Sully . . . in a manner that is both more sweeping and more penetrating. His words deserve all the more attention when we bear in mind that he was more firmly convinced, perhaps, than any other psychologist that dreams have a disguised meaning.

(S.E. 1900, IV: 60)

These are attractive statements, but what do they mean? The reader is well advised to inquire into Freud's argument. What kind of dream apparatus can return the dreamer to an archaic and cognitively imperfect world of sleep and at once make him as clever as the wakeful Hamlet? As far as I can tell, Freud never revealed how a dream is at once intelligent and imperfect, wakeful and asleep. He merely said that it is so.

Nor did Freud reveal in what way, exactly, a dream is like a neurotic symptom. This is disturbing, since the analogy of dreams and symptoms is part of the bedrock of psychoanalytic theory. It is the theory's ostensible proof that the mind's inherent structure is 'neurosogenic': 'Any relatively complex dream,' Freud said, 'turns out to be a compromise produced by a conflict between psychical forces.' The analogy is present, inchoately, in the 'Project' (S.E. 1895, I: 336, 341), and is well refined in the masterly and succinct *Outline of Psycho-Analysis* (S.E. 1940, XXIII: 165–71); Freud never changed it, in its essentials, from 1895 to 1938. Is it a valid analogy?

Freud said that a dream and a symptom both originate in an 'inherent inefficiency' in the mental apparatus, to which two factors contribute (S.E. 1900, V: 597–605). The *first* factor concerns the phylogenetic and ontogenetic relationship of the *primary* and *secondary* mental processes. The primary process, briefly, is the irrational process in the mental apparatus, originating in the unconscious. Its sole aim is satisfaction. Its pursuit of satisfaction is implacable, solipsistic and direct. The primary process *wishes*, without regard for the uselessness and harm of mere wishing, and wishing ends in hallucinatory fulfilment. A new satisfaction requires merely the memory of an old one, and the sufficient building up and letting go of wishful excitation, according to the pleasure principle. It is unsurprising that in the domain of thinking, the primary process creates illogic, confusion and rearrangement, intermediate ideas and 'compromise structures'.

It is a painful thing to see one's satisfaction when in fact it is not there. Out of this 'bitter experience of life' comes the *secondary* mental process – as Santayana (1923) has called it, 'a long way round to Nirvana'. The secondary process achieves wish-fulfilment indirectly. It is cautious, sensible, dilatory. Its aim is satisfaction, and it operates according to the pleasure principle, but its method is restrictive. Constantly testing reality, the secondary process limits the development of unpleasure to the 'minimum required for acting as a signal'. Its progress to satisfaction is voluntary and mediate, sober and delicate. Secondary associations of ideas – the mode of thinking in the *preconscious* – are rational associations.

According to the first factor in symptom formation, the primary process is ontogenetically prior. The secondary process, appearing later, comes to 'inhibit and overlay' the primary one. This is a biogenetic model, describing the relation of an archaic mental apparatus to a more recent one. It is evidently a relation of inhibition and potential disinhibition. Explicitly, the primary processes are 'modes of activity of the psychical apparatus that have been freed from inhibition' (S.E. 1900, V: 605).

The second factor contributing to dreams and symptoms is an inevitable failure of dominion by the secondary process. The oldest wishes are not accessible to the secondary function, and some wishes come to be disgusting to it – though once, indeed, they were pleasurable. The preconscious turns away from what it cannot put into its own terms, and this failure of translation constitutes *repression*. But the unconscious wish lurks in readiness to insinuate itself into consciousness. When it does, 'there follows a defensive struggle',

for the Pcs. in turn reinforces its opposition to the repressed thoughts (anticathexis). Thereafter the transference thoughts which are the vehicles of the unconscious wish, force their way through in some form of compromise, which is reached by the production of a symptom.

(S.E. 1900, V: 604–5)

In sleep the compromise is not a symptom, but a dream.

The dramatic and plausible analogy of dreams and symptoms is subject in every way to Grünbaum's inductivist critique of the 'repression etiology of neurosis' (Grünbaum 1984). As Grünbaum has argued, Freud's evidence for a repression aetiology of dreams is no better than his evidence for repression as the origin of symptoms. Freud's defenders may respond that Freud's theory sustains Grünbaum's critique – that good enough proofs of the dream theory actually do exist or will be discovered. But Grünbaum has argued, more damningly, that if psychoanalysis cures symptoms, so too it must cure dreaming:

To the extent that the *analyzed* patient achieves conscious awareness of his previously repressed infantile wishes, that conscious mastery robs these very wishes of their very power to engender dreams! Hence, in proportion as the analysand's buried infantile wishes are brought to light, he should experience, and exhibit neurophysiologically (e.g., via REM sleep), a striking reduction in dream formation.

(1984: 234–5)

The proposal that psychoanalysis should, in effect, 'cure dreaming' strikes not at the adequacy of Freud's proofs, but at the integrity of the dream theory itself. If psychoanalysis cures symptoms but not dreams, then in some important way dreams and symptoms are *not* alike. And if the analogy of symptoms and dreams is a phantasm there is, in effect, no dream theory.

The dream mechanism

For those who would reject Grünbaum's critique on the ground that he is not a psychoanalyst, there is a lesson in the psychoanalytic texts themselves. To try seriously to explicate *The Interpretation of Dreams* is to make some unsettling discoveries. One of these is that Freud's dream rhetoric yields an unworkable dream apparatus. The dream machine works badly, if at all. In chapter VII Freud builds a mental apparatus (S.E. 1900, V: 536–40). He then 'sets' it to make a dream, and that dream is like a symptom (S.E. 1900, V: 540–2). But the machine, I shall argue, cannot really make a dream that is like a symptom. Freud must keep his analogy, and so he resets the dream machine to make a dream that is not like a symptom – and so on, in an elaborate vacillation that constitutes a grave *a priori* indictment of the dream theory. From the reader's point of view, this vacillation may be summarized as follows.

Beginning with the assumption that dreams and symptoms are in fact alike, one might look first for the *censor* in the dream apparatus. The prospect is promising:

Dreams are psychical acts of as much significance as any others; their motive force is in every instance a wish seeking fulfilment; the fact of their not being recognizable as wishes and their many peculiarities and absurdities are due to the influence of the psychical censorship to which they have been subjected during the process of their formation.

(S.E. 1900, V: 533)

In 1909 Freud added a confirming note: 'The kernel of my theory of dreams,' he said, 'lies in my derivation of dream-distortion from the censorship.' But how, one may ask, does the censor distort the dream?

In fact, the influence and the status of the censor are absolutely elusive. Freud said that in sleep there is a *reduction* in the censor's power. On the other hand, he added, maybe the censor can be *evaded*, 'without any reduction taking place in its power' (S.E. 1900, V: 526). Finally, he found it plausible that 'both of the factors favouring the formation of a dream – the reduction and the evasion of the censorship – are simultaneously made possible by the state of sleep' (S.E. 1900, V: 526). At the least, it is reasonable to conclude that Freud was uncertain of the censor's role in dream formation.

Yet he was clear about one accomplishment of the censorship – or was he? The dream is differently centred from the dream thoughts, he said, and *dream-displacement* is the work of the censor. It is as a consequence of displacement that the dream 'gives no more than a distortion of the dream wish which exists in the unconscious' (S.E. 1900, IV: 308). This seems clear enough.

But clarity fades to obscurity. If the *preconscious censor* – by definition the agent of the secondary process – is the agent of displacement,

displacement must be a *secondary* process. Yet displacement, along with its fellow dream-worker *condensation*, is patently a primary process. In sleep, Freud said, 'the intensities of ideas become capable of discharge *en bloc* and pass over from one idea to another' (S.E. 1900, V: 595). Condensation is the result of repeating this process; displacement is its essence. 'Processes of this kind,' Freud said, 'are scrupulously avoided in secondary thinking' (S.E. 1900, V: 602). How, then, can the censor be the agent of displacement?

But one can look at the dream machine from a different angle. A chronology of dream formation should be clarifying, and Freud did state an explicit chronology – or did he? Here is the order of events in the construction of a dream (S.E. 1900, V: 573–4). First 'the unconscious wish links itself up with the day's residues and effects a transference on to them'. The dream wish then tries to push its way to consciousness. But on its way to consciousness it meets the censorship. And so it submits to the censor's influence. 'At this point', Freud said, the dream wish 'takes on the distortion for which the way has already been paved by the transference of the wish on the recent material'. At this point the analogy to symptom formation is clear enough. When the dream wish meets the censorship it becomes like a symptom – it is 'on its way,' Freud said, 'to becoming an obsessive idea or a delusion or something of the kind'. The work of dream-disguise, we are led to assume, is done.

After the censorship the dream undergoes the regression to sensory representation – the mechanism, as I mentioned earlier, by which 'all the logical relations belonging to the dream thoughts disappear . . . or can only find expression with difficulty' (S.E. 1900, V: 543). The dream wish 'has now completed the second portion of its zigzag journey'. The 'zig' was progressive, from the unconscious to the preconscious. The 'zag' is regressive, 'from the frontier of the censorship back again to perceptions'. Curiously, it is only after the censor wreaks its distortion that the dream wish finds a way to evade the censor: 'when the . . . dream process has become perceptual, by that fact it has, as it were, found a way of evading the obstacle put in its way by the censorship and the state of sleep in the Pcs.'. Even more curiously, it is no longer clear how the dream has acquired its manifestly strange and illogical form. Is it by the censorship? Is it by the regression?

Veterans of chapter VI will notice that the condensation – so vital to the dream-work – is missing altogether from Freud's dream chronology. As he recorded this chronology he simply announced, parenthetically, that he would deal later with the question of 'compression' (S.E. 190, V: 574). This was a fatal procrastination, for when Freud got around to the condensation the censor had disappeared, and there was a new order of events in dream formation.

In the new chronology the dream wish is formed, as before, out of conscious and preconscious elements. But 'from this point onwards,' Freud said, 'the train of thought undergoes a series of transformations which we can no longer recognize as normal psychical processes and which lead to a result that bewilders us – a psychopathological structure' (S.E. 1900, V: 595). Indeed, 'intermediate ideas', 'compromises', are formed – not by the censor as agent, but by the condensation as vehicle (S.E. 1900, V: 596). The mind's energy is mobile, ebullient; 'intensities' move freely, concentrating many thoughts into one idea. Finally – disconcertingly – it is the condensation that is 'mainly responsible for the bewildering impression made on us by dreams' (S.E. 1900, V: 595).

Perhaps the condensation *is* better left until 'later', for the psychoanalytical reader is hard put to recover an analogy to symptom formation from these transformed dream processes. But if we try to retrieve the original chronology, we see that we cannot do so. The chronology has disappeared:

it seems to me unnecessary to suppose that dream-processes really maintain, up to the moment of being conscious, the chronological order in which I have described them: that the first thing to appear is the transferred dream-wish, that distortion by the censorship follows, then the regressive change in direction, and so on. I have been obliged to adopt this order in my description; but what happens in reality is no doubt a simultaneous exploring of one path and another, a swinging of the excitation now this way and now that, until at last it accumulates in the direction that is most opportune.

(S.E. 1900, V: 576)

Is *The Interpretation of Dreams*, like a Freudian dream, an impostor, presenting a seemingly clear theory to explain phenomena unclear even to Freud? Undeniably, *The Interpretation of Dreams* is a very great book. It is not a bad thing, from a literary point of view, for a book to be an impostor. Perhaps this book is not really about dreams, but about Freud's relations with his father, Jakob, who died in October 1896. Where other dreams might do as well to make a point, Freud offers dreams of filial grandiosity and paternal embarrassment; infanticide by a father; a father's grief; a father's inadvertent negligence (the famous 'Burning Child' dream of chapter VII). These build an infrastructure of dream examples, leading to the last example in the book, a patient's vision that Freud sees as the 'unfilial' castration of Kronos by Zeus. This is speculation, of course, and it is not my purpose to psychoanalyse *The Interpretation of Dreams*. I am concerned with the dream theory itself – is the *theory* an impostor?

334   *Helene Sophrin Porte*

With this question in mind, I have wondered how Freud's followers and spokesmen have understood the dream theory. The commentaries of Anna Freud (1966: 173–6) and Charles Brenner (1955: ch. 7), two of the most orthodox spokesmen, are instructive. Neither Anna Freud nor Brenner acknowleges a problem in the dream theory, but both seem compelled to solve one. Anna Freud's solution is elegant but unintelligible. The dream-work, she said, is not done by the censor at all. It is done at the censor's behest. Condensation and, indeed, displacement, belong to the id, she said. The censor – *ex machina*, one has to assume – simply uses the id for its purpose of concealment. Anna Freud offered no proof of this operation, nor any guess as to how it is accomplished.

If Anna Freud etherealized the censor, Brenner reasserts its substantive role in dream formation. But first he entertains at some length the possibility of its non-existence – the possibility that dreams are manifestly nonsensical just because they are stated in the language of the primary process. Why does Benner, a lucid and parsimonious explicator, spend time on this unpsychoanalytical possibility in an elementary textbook of psychoanalysis? Is it because Brenner is a good scholar of Freud – does he know that the role of the censor in the dream theory is never a clear one? But if the censor is not an agent in dream formation, then dreams are not analogous to symptoms. The normal exemplar of Freud's theory of mind simply disappears. Such a conclusion is not psychoanalytically acceptable. Brenner concludes – shouldering the ambiguities of the father – that dreams are bizarre *mostly* because 'the ego's defenses make them that way'.

Both Anna Freud and Brenner would make order out of disorder in the dream theory. But in trying to clarify, Anna Freud imposed a false consistency, and Brenner fortifies the theory's indeterminateness. The dream theory resists sanitation. I think that this has nothing to do with Freud's self-avowed, inexplicable, and endearing *Schlamperei* (sloppiness). Freud's is a principled uncertainty, for in fact he has two distinct and incompatible dream theories, neither of which he can abandon while maintaining the likeness of dreams and symptoms. These are the rational elements of Freud's deeper dream theory. To see the manifest theory's construction out of the latent one, it is necessary to go back to Freud's scientific 'Project', and even earlier, to his psychology of aphasia.

APHASIOLOGY AND PSYCHOANALYSIS: THE ORIGINS OF
FREUD'S DREAM THEORY

In 'Some Points for a Comparative Study of Organic and Hysterical Motor

Paralyses' (S.E. 1893, I: 157–72), Freud defined a *functional lesion*:

I shall take the phrase 'functional or dynamic lesion' in its proper sense of 'alteration in function or dynamics' – alteration of a functional property. Examples of an alteration of this kind would be a diminution in excitability or in a physiological quality which normally remains constant or varies within fixed limits.

(p. 169)

In *On Aphasia: A Critical Study* (1891), Freud attributed many of the symptoms of aphasia to *functional* change in speech association areas. This was a bold departure from Wernicke, Lichtheim, and others who ascribed aphasic symptoms to pathologic change in speech centres or to disconnections among them. In dissent, Freud invoked a mechanism of *reduced excitability* in speech *association* cortex. The effect of such a lesion, Freud said, is to breakdown the *associative structure* of speech. In disagreement with his teacher Meynert, Freud declared that perception cannot be physiologically separated from association – although psychology might invent one, there is no such *physiologic* entity as a 'simple idea'. For this neurological reason, said Freud, the cortical organization of speech is not in terms of words, but in terms of the associations among them.

In constructing his aphasiology Freud was influenced by the British neurologist John Hughlings Jackson. Jackson, whom Freud cited admiringly in *On Aphasia*, held that the speech function is organized phyletically, in two parts: an old one that is emotional and automatic, and a newer one that is intellectual and voluntary (Jackson 1873; 1874). In Freud's scheme, biologically recent modes of association take functional precedence over older ones. Clearly, the old and the new speech functions of *On Aphasia* are the precursors of Freud's primary and secondary modes of thought, and it is out of Jackson's two speech functions that Freud's two speech functions *and* the two modes of thought emerge. In Freud's psychoanalytic theory, explicitly, primary associations of ideas are governed by the 'intensities' of ideas (Jackson's emotional speech function); secondary associations are governed by volition and logic (Jackson's intellectual speech function).

The onotogenetic relation of Freud's two speech functions foreshadows the first, *ontogenetic* factor in symptom formation (p. 329 above). Accordingly, Freud characterized aphasia as a 'dis-involution', or 'retro-gression', in the developmentally established structure of speech associations. As Jones (1953–7) and Sulloway (1979) have pointed out, Freud took the notion of dis-involution from Jackson, later revising his terminology and calling it *regression*. To explain the process of dis-involution physiologically, Freud borrowed from Charlton Bastian the concept of levels of reduced excitability in the speech cortex: according to 'Bastian's modifications', the least aphasic dysfunction brought loss of the 'volitional' speech capacity; the next level loss of the 'associative' capacity; the most profound dysfunction, loss of excitability altogether. In Freud's aphasiology, regression from the newer to the older mode of speech association corresponds to Bastian's 'first level' of reduced cortical excitability. This regression produces aphasic misuse and distortion of words, or *paraphasia*, 'in which the appropriate word is replaced by a less appropriate one, which however still retains a certain relationship to the correct word; [in which] words of a similar content, or linked by frequent association, are used in place of one another' (Freud 1891: 21). 'One speaks also of paraphasia,' Freud said, 'when two intended words [are fused] into one malformation'; and 'circumlocutions by which a specific noun is replaced by a very general one [are called] paraphasias' (p. 22).

In *On Aphasia*, paraphasic distortions in speech by replacement, fusion and confusion of its elements are entirely accounted for by *regression* – by 'reduced efficiency of the apparatus of speech associations'. Thus, paraphasia – quite unlike *parapraxis* (the 'successful error' of Freud's everyday psychopathology) – is innocent of purpose or disguise. Indeed, simply by dis-involution, 'all the symptoms of paraphasia' may beset a normal person, 'in states of fatigue or divided attention or under the influence of disturbing affects' (p. 13). In *On Aphasia*, as I have said, a diminution in cortical excitability leads to paraphasia. In 'Some Points for a Comparative Study of Organic and Hysterical Motor Paralyses', it leads to *hysteria*: not simply to regression in the mode of association, but to 'abolition' and displacement of association. The hysterical paralysis of an arm, for instance,

consists in the fact that the conception of the arm cannot enter into associations with the other ideas constituting the ego of which the subject's body forms an important part. The lesion would therefore be *the abolition of the associative accessibility of the conception of the arm*. The arm behaves as though it did not exist for the play of associations.

(S.E. 1893, I: 170; Freud's emphasis)

This is because the arm is, so to speak, otherwise engaged:

the paralysed organ or the lost function is involved in a subconscious association which is provided with a large quota of affect and it can be shown that the arm is liberated as soon as this quota is wiped out.

(S.E. 1893, I: 171; Freud's emphasis)

Freud's aphasiology is based in biogenesis and regression. His hysteriology is based in displacement and repression. Evidently, in the progress from paraphasia to symptom the psychological meaning of a *functional lesion* changed in Freud's mind. Henceforth, he maintained two notions of functional alteration in the nervous system. In the evolution of his theory of neurosis, *repression* adds the critical 'second factor' in symptom formation to the first, biogenetic factor. To see the fate and continued utility of *regression*, one has only to consult Freud's nascent dream theory.

Freud's biological theory of dreaming

In fact, according to his two conceptions of 'functional lesion', Freud held two theories of dreaming. Just as paraphasia and parapraxis are distinct and incompatible events that share an exterior form, so the two kinds of dreaming are distinct and incompatible. In his long career Freud never acknowledged this duality. Instead, he worked and reworked the manifest conundrums of *The Interpretation of Dreams*. It is only in Freud's scientific 'Project' that his latent dream theory is plain – although not, as he would have it, 'free from contradiction' (S.E. 1895, I: 295).

Freud's first dream theory is one of wake–sleep *state change*. It is a model of state dependent oscillation in the relationship between the primary and the secondary processes. Waking constitutes a 'secondary' state of the brain and mind, in which the 'ego' obstructs the primary process by the quantitative mechanism of 'side-cathexis'. This impediment to hallucinatory wishing is a phylogenetic achievement: by diverting excitation from biologically older to newer networks of association, the waking ego prevents fruitless wishful hallucination and harmful 'expenditure' of defence. In *sleep* the secondary process is forgotten. The primary process goes on, unimpeded, to hallucinatory consummation. In dreams, accordingly, 'the *compulsion to associate* prevails' (S.E. 1895, I: 338; Freud's emphasis).

It is this attribute of dreaming – the *biological regression of mental activity* – that explains the illogic of dreams: 'The senselessness and illogicality of dreams,' Freud said, 'are probably to be attributed to this very same characteristic' (S.E. 1895, I: 338). Does this 'probably' intimate Freud's later ambivalence? This is a biological, or biogenetic, model of dreaming, completely described by the 'first factor' in symptom formation. Where is the second factor? Where is repression?

In *The Interpretation of Dreams* wish-fulfilment is disguised. In the biological dream model of the 'Project' dreams are fulfilments of wishes, but 'they are only not recognized as such because the release of pleasure . . . in them is slight, because in general they run their course almost without affect (without motor release)' (S.E. 1895, I: 340). In *The Interpretation of Dreams* the forgetting of dreams is tendentious. In the 'Project' dreams are forgotten, but 'this is easily explained from the fact that, for the most part, dreams follow old facilitations and thus make no change (in them), that (perceptual) experiences are held back from them and that, owing to the paralysis of motility, (dreams) do not leave traces . . . behind them' (S.E. 1895, I: 340). This is an innocent theory of dreaming – a pre-psychoanalytic theory. It is as innocent as Freud's Jacksonian aphasiology, and, I submit, exactly analogous to it. In *On Aphasia* Freud said explicitly that aphasia 'cannot be viewed independently of a broad theory of cerebral activity' (1891: 46). Although aphasia is a waking state, Freud's account of it is virtually identical to his later *biological* model of sleep and dreaming. The only difference is that sleep is a physiologic state of the whole brain: a general de-excitation of the secondary function, rather than a specifically linguistic one.

The psychoanalytical theory of dreaming

In his discussion of 'dream consciousness' in the 'Project', Freud said, in effect, that dreaming is like hysteria (S.E. 1895, I: 341–3). This is his second theory of dreaming. It is a model of wake–sleep *structural similarity*. Accordingly, absurdity in dreams mimics the absurdity of hysterical symptoms. Consciousness in dreams, as in hysteria, is piecemeal, 'discontinuous'. There is a loss of association. The absent idea is present, but it is repressed.

In the 'Project' repression entails quantitative displacement. One idea is 'denuded' of quantity, and consciousness is displaced to another idea (S.E. 1895, I: 350). Because consciousness is lacunar, the hysterical symptom is bizarre. The 'denuded' idea is inevitably a sexual one, its etiolation purposeful and specific. For dreaming, it is a loss of innocence. As an example, Freud set out a fragment of his 'Irma' dream: 'R. has given an injection of *propyl* to A. I then see *trimethylamin* before me very vividly, hallucinated as a formula' (S.E. 1895, I: 341–2). The manifest dream is unintelligible; the dream's meaning is found by uncovering 'unconscious intermediate links': 'sexual chemistry', and the sexual nature of A.'s illness. If Freud used to be a psychologist, he is a psychoanalyst now. The psychology of the aphasias has become the analysis of the neuroses, and dreams have changed character accordingly.

Hysteria is a waking state. Insofar as dreaming is like hysteria, there is no account of sleep as a distinctive condition of the brain and mind. Unlike the biological model, the psychoanalytic model of dreaming does not provide for sleeping. But Freud had to put the dreamer to sleep. He could not do away with a state change as part of his dream theory. And he could not, of course, give up the analogy of symptoms and dreams. So he simply put together the model of neurosis and the model of regression. It was a marriage of neurosis and sleep – a marriage of *waking* and sleep. It was Freud's unconscious, ingenious theory-work, and in my view it is the reason for the formidable confusions in *The Interpretation of Dreams*.

CONCLUSION

In this chapter I have claimed that Freud's analogy of symptoms and dreams is not tenable or even clear, and that its foundation is false and contrived. In a sense, this is a disappointing conclusion. If Freud's dream theory is incorrect, how will we interpret our dreams? What dream interpretation should replace a Freudian one? In partial answer, I would like to re-examine one aspect of the 'Riding' dream as a product of Freud's *sleeping* mind.

If we imagine Freud lying in bed asleep, wearing his poultice, only one thing is needed to put him on his dream horse. A sensation of *movement* would do the job. As I have mentioned, brainstem movement command is now considered to be a physiological instigator of dreaming. I believe that dreamers may experience specific types of movement command as a result of these brainstem events – for example, straightforward movement, compulsive limb movement, 'vehicular' movement, and varieties of turning movements.

Because the muscles are paralysed during REM sleep, actual movement is prohibited during dreaming. Borrowing a term that Grillner (1985) has used in another context, the dream movements to which I refer might be called 'fictive' movements. The dominant fictive movement in the 'Riding' dream is vehicular. On his horse, Freud rides straight in between two vans. Before he stops, he turns around. He tries to dismount, but he cannot do so at first – is he, perhaps, still moving? Certainly, fictive movement is not the only interesting aspect of the 'Riding' dream, but it does provide a plausible *stimulus* to this dream.

McCarley and Hoffman (1981) found that limb movement is present in a high percentage of laboratory dream reports. When Hobson and Hoffman (1984) analysed the trajectories of movement in a sample of illustrated home dream reports, they found many examples of curvilinear movement and interrupted runs of forward or oblique movements. Such movements are often present in dream reports that we have collected in our laboratory. I submit that Freud's dream image of riding conflated two stimuli. One was his awareness of the poultice that he wore as he slept. The other was the automatic activation of 'fictive' locomotion during REM. There was no wish-fulfilment or denial of affliction in the image's construction; it can be interpreted directly.

But if there is no wish-fulfilment with respect to Freud's boil, what of the deeper, disguised wish-fulfilments that Freud claims for his dream? What may be said of the 'sexual thoughts' to which Freud said his dream alludes? If the central image of 'riding' is constrained by the physiology of REM sleep, is there room for sexual allusion in the 'Riding' dream? In my view, stimuli to fictive movement in REM sleep may parallel *cortical* changes in REM that alter aspects of cognitive function in dreaming.

As brainstem movement command introduces an experience of compulsive movement, so related changes at the level of cortex may introduce a 'compulsion to associate' – the cognitive kaleidoscope of Freud's *biological* theory of dreaming. Therefore, while the 'Riding' dream's invention is explained most parsimoniously by the stimuli I have described, the dream's continuation by no means excludes sexual associations. If Freud said that his dream depicts sexual thoughts vis-à-vis his patient, or even his friend P., I would believe him. But does his dream disguise these thoughts?

In his interpretation of the 'Riding' dream Freud said, in effect, that a woman was turned into a horse, and he implied that this transformation had a sexual meaning. In thinking about this, it is fair to recall the story of Boccaccio's simpleton, Pietro, who wanted a mare to take to market. Because Pietro has only a donkey and a wife, he asks the priest, Gianni, to turn his wife into a horse. The handsome Gianni, who claims to have turned his own horse into a woman and back, arrives in his nightshirt. He sets about his work, but it is soon clear that his method of turning a woman into a horse is the method of sexual intercourse. How credulous Pietro is, as Gianni caresses his wife. Although the reader sees immediately what Gianni is doing, Pietro – still hoping for a horse – does not. I say that if Freud's dream censor is fooled by the 'Riding' dream, then the censor is almost as credulous as Pietro. Moreover, if the image of riding is determined and constrained by the state-specific physiology of REM sleep, then the dream's sexual meaning cannot be said to be *disguised* at all. If sleep accounts for the insanity of Freud's dream, we do not need neurosis to do so.

ACKNOWLEDGEMENTS

I wish to thank Frank J. Sulloway for reading the manuscript and for his fine suggestions. I thank Adolf Grünbaum, Peter Clark and Crispin Wright for the opportunity to participate in the International Conference on Psychoanalysis and the Philosophy of Mind at St Andrews. This research supported by N.I.M.H. Grants MH 16259 and MH 139.23.

REFERENCES

Aserinsky, E. and Kleitman, N. 1953: Regularly occurring periods of eye motility and concomitant phenomena, during sleep. *Science*, 118, 273–4.
Berger, R. J. 1961: Tonus of extrinsic laryngeal muscles during sleep and dreaming. *Science*, 134, 840.
Berger, R. J. and Oswald I. 1962: Eye movements during active and passive dreams. *Science*, 137, 601.
Boccaccio, G. 1977: The *Decameron*, trans. M. Musa and P. E. Bondanella. Ninth Day, Second Story. New York: W. W. Norton.
Brenner, C. 1955: *An Elementary Textbook of Psychoanalysis*. New York: International Universities Press.
Chu, N.-S. and Bloom, F. E. 1973: Norepinephrine-containing neurons: changes in spontaneous discharge patterns during sleeping and waking. *Science*, 179, 908–10.
Dement, W. C. and Kleitman, N. 1957: Cyclic variations in EEG during sleep and their relation to eye movements, body motility and dreaming. *EEG Clinical Neurophysiology*, 9, 673–90.
Dement, W. C. and Wolpert, E. A. 1958: The relation of eye movements, body motility and external stimuli to dream content. *Journal of Experimental Psychology*, 55, 543–53.
Freud, A. 1966: *The Ego and the Mechanisms of Defense*. New York: International Universities Press.
Freud, S. 1891: *On Aphasia: A Critical Study*, trans. and with an Introduction by E. Stengel. London: Imago Publishing, 1953.
Freud, S. 1895: Project for a scientific psychology. S.E. 1950, I: 283–387.
Freud, S. 1900: *The Interpretation of Dreams*: S.E. IV and V.
Freud, S. 1938, 1940: *An Outline of Psycho-Analysis*. S.E. 1940, XXIII: 141–207.
Grillner, S. 1985: Neurobiological bases of rhythmic motor acts in vertebrates. *Science*, 228, 143–9.
Grünbaum, A. 1984: *The Foundations of Psychoanalysis: A Philosophical Critique*. Berkeley: University of California Press.
Hobson, J. A. and Hoffman, S. 1984: Picturing dreaming: some features of the drawings in a dream journal, in M. Bosinelli and P. Cicogna (eds), *Psychology of Dreaming*, Bologna: CLUEB.
Hobson, J. A and McCarley, R. M. 1977: The brain as a dream state generator: an activation-synthesis hypothesis of the dream process, *American Journal of Psychiatry*, 134, 1335–49.

Hobson, J. A., McCarley, R. M. and Wyzinski, P. W. 1975: Sleep cycle oscillation: reciprocal discharge by two brainstem neuronal groups. *Science*, 189, 55–8.

Jackson J. H. 1873: On the anatomical and physiological localization of movements in the brain. *Lancet*, 18 January.

Jackson, J. H. 1874: On the nature and diality of the brain. *Medical Press and Circular*, reprinted in *Brain*, 38 (1915), 80–103.

Jones, E. 1953–7: *The Life and Work of Sigmund Freud*. 3 vols. New York: Basic Books.

McCarley, R. M. and Hoffman, E. H. 1981: REM sleep dreams and the activation-synthesis hypothesis. *American Journal of Psychiatry*, 138, 904–12.

Pivik, T. and Foulkes, D. 1966: Dream deprivation: effects on dream content. *Science*, 153, 1282–4.

Sakai, K. 1980: Some anatomical and physiological properties of pontomesencephalic tegmental neurons with special reference to the PGO waves and postural atonia during paradoxical sleep in the cat, in J. A. Hobson and M. Brazier (eds), *The Reticular System Revisited*, 427–48. New York: Raven Press.

Santayana, G. 1923: A long way round to Nirvana, or much ado about dying. *The Dial*, November.

Sulloway, F. J. 1979: *Freud, Biologist of the Mind: Beyond the Psychoanalytic Legend*. New York: Basic Books.

16

The Interpretation of Dreams

ALESSANDRO PAGNINI

Up to now Freud's epoch-making *The Interpretation of Dreams* has been considered a permanent acquisition in the field of 'science', as well as an inexhaustible source of inspiration not only for psychoanalysts and psychologists, but also for philosophers, literary critics, art theorists, and hermeneuticians of all kinds.

Very recently, reviewing a number of experimental studies on dreaming, Paul Kline found psychological confirmations of the psychoanalytic dream theory (e.g. of the notion of symbolism, which is central to it), and concluded that 'all in all . . . Freudian dream theory does not seem too wide of the mark' (Kline 1984: 85).

Likewise, the psychiatrist Mariann Horney Eckhardt, drawing up the balance of the Freudian theory of dreaming chiefly vis-à-vis current neurophysiological issues, wrote critically but, in the end, optimistically: 'Freud was the father of this exciting child – our working with dreams. But this child has grown into a fundamentally different world; it has changed scientific principles, changed culture, and gained much new experience. Freud would have to disown this emancipated child. Yet dream approach will for a long time to come carry Freud's signature' (Horney Eckhardt 1982: 66–7).

Yet, in spite of these appreciations, over the last few years a sort of storm has fallen upon Freud's *Interpretation of Dreams*. The convergent criticisms raised by Hobson, McCarley and Helene Sophrin Porte on the neuropsychiatric side, and by Grünbaum, Glymour, Moore in analytical and epistemological terms (not to mention the historical critical remarks by Sulloway, Crews and others), seem to gainsay Kline's and Horney

Eckhardt's sanguine views, and seem to make a new overall evaluation necessary.

I'll begin by considering the neurophysiological challenge as formulated in Porte's chapter and shaped in sundry recent contributions by other scholars belonging to the Harvard Medical School.

In an illuminating re-reading of Freud's early studies on *Aphasia* and of the abandoned 'Project', Porte points out that, in Freud's account of dreaming, two different models overlap and contrast. The first is a *model of wake–sleep change*, where Freud defines sleep as characterized by a fundamental regression toward a phylogenetic stage preceding the ego achievements, and where, accordingly, the 'primary process' proceeds unimpeded. On this view, as sleep is biologically *retrogressive* and physiologically inertial, so dreams are associationally inertial and hallucinatory. This model does not entail repression or disguise of any sort in the formation of dreams, and reveals that in sleep 'ego-cathexes' are broken down.

The other model – more familiar to the superficial reader of Freud – is a *model of wake–sleep structural similarity*, where dream is compared to hysteria and dreams are like hysterical symptoms (i.e. they are formed by the concealment of repressed ideas, and their absurdity mimics the absurdity of hysterical symptoms). From this perspective, state change is not essential to the comparison of sleep and wake, and there is no account of sleep as a distinctive condition of brain and mind.

Porte sees a logical and physiological incompatibility between the two models, which, at best, together form an attractive pastiche. This fact, on her account, undermines Freud's theory of dreaming (never adequately perfected, not even on the basis of his later theory of the ego and the id), and also undermines the attempts to revise it by Freud's orthodox followers (e.g. Anna Freud and Charles Brenner).

In her analysis we can recognize and separately appraise two different, albeit linked, levels: a *'philological'–historical* level, and a *theoretical–epistemological* one.

With regard to the first, we cannot but appreciate her contribution to a deeper analysis of Freud's texts, disentangling, as she so clearly does, the diverse and often contradictory concepts and patterns employed by the father of psychoanalysis.

In bringing to light many of the implications of Freud's dream theory, Porte shows that she agrees with Hobson's and McCarley's presupposition that 'Freud built his model of the mind and his hypotheses about dreaming, which appear in *The Interpretation of Dreams*, directly on the structure of his neurobiological model of the brain as developed in his

"Project for a Scientific Psychology"' (McCarley and Hobson 1977: 1220). Even though this presupposition is largely controversial (cf. Bertini and Violani 1982; Wasserman 1984), I think that the charge of inconsistency vis-à-vis the construction of Freud's dream theory, as formulated by Porte may hold, independent of a strict assumption of such standpoint.

Many authors have already recognized the significance of Jackson's model of mental functioning and, above all, of Jackson's concept of *regression* in Freud's early writings (cf. Jackson 1969; Sulloway 1979: 269ff.) but no one (not even Sulloway, who is of one mind with Porte in distinguishing two dream theories in Freud's work) suitably weighed the bearing and the consequences of this heritage with reference to Freud's later ideas and particularly to his dream theory. I now briefly sketch the kind of argument which leads Porte to the conclusion that Freud's dream theory, in its entirety, is an 'impostor'.

1   Freud has recourse exclusively to *rhetorical* and *analogical* contrivances to support his idea that dream formation is similar to the formation of hysterical symptoms. He never produces any *independent* evidence to underpin his 'discovery', and he always ignores patent inconsistencies between his *psychoanalytic* model and his *biological* assumptions.

2   In Freud's dream theory, *regression* and *repression* seem to be compelled to live together in perfect harmony, even if they are demonstrable incompatible.

3   The role of 'dream censor' is never stated consistently by Freud (e.g., it is not clear whether the dream derives its illogical and bizarre dimension from censorship or from regression; and equally it is not clear whether in dream there is *reduction* of the censor's power or simply *evasion* of it by unconscious wishes, or both). Moreover, the very 'dream censor' seems to be posited *ad hoc* by Freud to maintain the analogy beween dreams and hysterical symptoms.

4   The second model (of *wake–sleep structural similarity*) is a model of dreaming that does not provide for sleeping.

I perfectly agree with these conceptual elucidations, and I think it opportune to underline that the second model encounters remarkable problems strictly on a neurophysiological level. These problems were never taken into account by Freud and were never solved by him (perhaps 'programmatically', as argued by the advocates of a paradigmatic shift between the early *neurological* Freud and the later *psychological* one).

On the contrary I am not sure that the concept of regression (which, in the Jacksonian version, is incompatible with that of repression) is subsumed by Freud without any adjustment.

We know that Freud draws his conception of 'primary and secondary processes' from Herbart, Meynert and Jackson, but whereas, according to Meynert and Jackson, pathological phenomena (and dreams[1]) are brought forth by a *dis-involution* of the *secondary ego* which loses its own active role, in Freud's theory the emergence of a neurosis is not due to a weakening of the ego, but to a strengthening of defences against urging instinctive drives (cf. Funari 1975). Furthermore, Freud explicitly specifies that the concept of regression has three different meanings: a *topographical* one, a *temporal* one and a *formal* one. These kinds of regression are accurately differentiated, even though Freud adds (causing confusion in my opinion) that they 'are, however, one at bottom and occur together as a rule; for what is older in time is more primitive in form and in physical topography lies nearer to the perceptual end' (S.E. 1900, V: 548). And it is evident that, if the influence of Jacksonian *dis-involution* on Freudian *formal* regression is strong, none the less it is not sufficient to cover all the senses attributed to it by Freud. It may be interesting to point out, finally, that when Freud returns to this subject in 1915 – in 'A Metapsychological Supplement to the Theory of Dream' – we no longer find any hint of *formal* regression (see S.E. 1915, XIV: 227). Despite the tendency to define which we often notice in Freud when he approaches the concept of regression, there is no doubt that, at the end, it continues to inhabit the fuzziness which envelops the greater part of Freud's dealing with theoretical terms and metapsychological problems. When, near the end of this life, Freud is concerned with a case of castration fright, we cannot but feel disconcerted to read: 'The boy did not simply contradict his perceptions and hallucinate a penis where there was none to be seen; he effected no more than a displacement of value – he transferred the importance of the penis to another part of the body, *a procedure in which he was assisted by the mechanism of regression (in a manner which need not here be explained)*' (S.E. 1938, XXIII: 277; my italics). Here, surprisingly, while Freud talks of regression in a meaning shifted again from those mentioned above, he none the less refers to it as to a clearcut and fixed concept, when in reality he never conferred on it an unequivocal, stable meaning.

Briefly, it is not accurate to say that Freud drew the concept of regression directly from Jackson without modifying it. He did modify it: he rendered it vaguer and more undetermined, but perhaps consistent with the concept of repression (so as to *save* his machinery of dreaming).

Porte is right to say that Freud could not drop the model of retrogression, for he had to put the dreamer to sleep, and, if psychoanalysis was to have the dream as a cardinal exemplar of 'compromise-structure', he could not give up the model of repression. Moreover she rightly notices that Freud put regression and repression together, and kept them together to the end of his life. But I argue that the means Freud used to achieve his (ill-)unified theory of dreaming was also a noticeable shift in the sense of regression and a progressive shelving of the Jacksonian meaning.

Let us turn now to the *theoretical-epistemological* aspect of Porte's treatment. As we have just seen, Porte's historical remarks are manifestly oriented toward a *theoretical* assessment of the tenability of Freud's dream theory. The target of her severe appraisal is also the later reformulations of the dream theory by Freud and his orthodox followers. And if it is true that Freud never substantially corrected his theory after the 'Project', to consider – as she does – only Anna Freud and Charles Brenner, outstanding advocates though they are of Freud's view, is not enough to challenge *every* psychoanalytic account of dreaming.

So I will dwell upon a recent reformulation of the psychoanalytic dream theory, to see if it is possible to correct Freud's shortcomings, and to update his hypotheses, maintaining the essence of the Freudian rationale and without contradicting modern scientific findings.

Mauro Mancia is a distinguished Italian professor of neurophysiology, well known for his important experimental studies on the reticular functions of the brain stem and on its role in the physiological wake–sleep mechanism. More recently, he has been carrying on original research on pre-natal dreaming. Mancia has a peculiar characteristic, quite unusual for a neurophysiologist. He is a Freudian psychoanalyst and a member of the Italian Psychoanalytic Society. His position concerning the Freudian theory of dreaming is sketched in the final chapters of his 1980 textbook entitled *Neurofisiologia e vita mentale* (Mancia 1980). Our interest in it is enhanced when we realize that Mancia seems to start from the same neurophysiological assumptions as Hobson, McCarley, and co-workers, whose works up to 1977 Mancia discusses and accepts as 'the most interesting works in this field [the specialized field of the unitary activity of encephalic stem's cells in wake–sleep]' (1980: 254).

In his theory of dreaming, defined as an ethological–neurophysiological theory, Mancia considers the wake–sleep phases as a single instinctive behaviour, in which the non-REM phase is *preliminary* and the REM phase (D sleep) is *consummatory*.[2]

In Mancia's account, the so-called hypnogogic or Non-REM phase is characterized by thought-like experiences without hallucinations and self-representation. REM-sleep dreams occur with hallucinations and self-representation in the 'structural frame' of an activity already present in Non-REM sleep.

For Mancia there is a regular biological alternation, but also a continuity, between the two phases. Non-REM phases, in fact, offer day-residues and other contents to the elaboration of the unconscious in REM-sleep. Furthermore, during sleep, 'primary processes' take over from 'secondary processes', but the state change is not absolute. Even though they seem to work especially in Non-REM phases, in fact, in sleep 'ego-cathexes' never break down.

Mancia moves considerably away from the original formulation of Freudian dream theory. He argues, for example, that dreams are necessary to survival, and consequently sees sleep as the guardian of dream, rather than the other way round. But in his 1980 book, Mancia maintains, as far as possible, Freudian terminology (whereas, in his later writings, he seems to prefer to adopt Kleinian and above all Bionian concepts). Consistently with Freud he admits that, in dreams, there is a *displacement activity* at the expense of 'primary processes'; that censorship *weakens* to allow dreams to take shape; that 'in sleep and in dream, we notice a regression of libido towards pre-genital phases of development' (p. 293); and that 'it is necessary that in dream psychological mechanisms, together with biological ones, favour "regression" and allow dream-work to start' (pp. 290–1).

We can observe that in Mancia's psychoanalytic account of dreaming, his conception of regression seems to be restricted to the topographical and temporal meanings, and only vaguely touches on the formal one (which implies a hierarchy of functions and structures) central to Jackson's thought. On the other hand, Mancia accepts the concept of 'censor' without any specification whatever and, I dare to say, without any tangible usefulness.

This brief and approximate sketch of Mancia's theses about dreaming leads to the following considerations: (1) current neurophysiology and psychoanalysis are not in principle irreconcilable;[3] (2) as a matter of fact, they have been given a consistent formulation (e.g. by Mancia's work); (3) since it is far from my wish to transform (2) into an *argumentum ad verecundiam*, such reformulations of psychoanalysis in the light of current neurophysiology have to be directly examined and perhaps condemned, *but not on account of Freud's sins*!

Furthermore, Mancia is not the only scholar who is revising Freudian dream theory in the light of contemporary neurophysiology or in consequence of criticisms of different kinds.

The psychoanalyst Molinari rightly observes that

as to dreams, there is practically no Freudian formulation which has remained unchallenged, in a more or less articulated way, by some psychoanalyst: the status of dream censor, the prominence to be given to the secondary elaboration, the mechanism of dream-work, the dream theory regarded as fulfilment of repressed wishes, even the distinction between manifest impulses and latent psychic material have time and again been indicated. The very procedure of interpreting dream on the strength of free associations has recently been brought up for discussion again, with particular efficacy, by Franco Fornari; while David Foulkes, at the very moment he recognized himself as 'pure Freudian', with reference to the technique of free associations and of the description of dream-work, vigorously called in question the ultradeep models of unconscious motivation, inherent in the Freudian approach, by privileging a reading of dreams as language and cognitive activity.

(Molinari 1982: 160)

We can briefly recall some of the more recent criticisms of the contents of Freud's dream construction. According to Molinari (1979), for example, the very definition of dream is nowadays controversial (from a strictly neurophysiological standpoint as well); another outstanding psychoanalyst decisively banishes the concept of 'censor',[4] and other 'Freudians' prefer to substitute the concept of regression for a cognitive concept suggesting the presence of two not exclusive modalities of mental functioning.[5] If, in the end, the definition of dreams as wish-fulfilments appears extremely reductive, here is a definition by Mancia, clearly using Kleinian terms, which renders it more flexible: 'The goal of the oniric process is not so much the hallucinatory satisfaction of repressed infantile wishes, as the *representation of an internal situation*, with all its inter- and intra-systemic components. It is also linked with older experiences which have allowed the formation of internal objects' (Mancia 1985: 199–200).

One might feel the need to discuss how much of Freudian origin may be left in these recent re-readings and 'mendings' of *The Interpretation of Dreams*, even if all the authors quoted above declare themselves to be 'Freudian' psychoanalysts. But it is nevertheless evident that Freud's more or less orthodox followers have revised the psychoanalytic dream theory in more drastic (and perhaps more interesting) ways than Anna Freud or Charles Brenner.[6] So I consider that it would be opportune to speak about these scholars also, to render the 'neurophysiological' indictment against the psychoanalytic dream theory more comprehensive, updated and convincing.

I realize that, for the sake of argument, I am acting the devil's advocate and thus betraying my own real conviction that most of the criticisms Porte levels at Freud and the Freudians are more than justified. I list for example:

1   the misuse, by Freud and his followers, of *rhetorical* and *analogical*

arguments to support a hypothesis, to the neglect of *empirical* and *logical* ones;

2 the untenability (admitted by the Freudians themselves) of many concepts, such as 'regressions' or 'censor', which are central to the structure of *The Interpretation of Dreams* itself;

3 the internal inconsistency of Freud's dream theory, though this, in my opinion, was partly compensated for by Freud, at the cost of some vagueness, abstraction, and gratuitous *ad hocness*.[7]

It is my impression that if one remains tied to Freud and the spirit of his *Interpretation of Dreams* – even at the distance and with the caveats noticed in many of his followers – one will be prevented from working out a dream theory which fits the data better and is more in agreement with current scientific knowledge. The *activation-synthesis hypothesis* of dreaming which lies behind Porte's work is obviously a valuable contribution and her cogent alternative interpretation of Freud's 'Riding' dream is very stimulating. Moreover, considering the weight of the partial but probative experimental results supporting Porte's 'research program', we can say that there are good *evidential* reasons besides *epistemic* ones (e.g. promise, simplicity, etc.), to believe that the programme will be most fruitful.

Bertini's subtly stated affirmation, shared by many, that 'thanks to Freud . . . dream enters as of right within the parameters of science, even if by way of its so-called "soft" areas' (Bertini 1984: 251) seems to me disputable. It seems controversial to think of *science* in this way and (as Porte would add) it would seem to be a requirement that the area be defined such that hard science (neurophysiology and neurochemistry) allow Freud's dream theory today.

The fundamental challenge to *The Interpretation of Dreams* and to the neurobiological and psychological implications of 'wish-fulfilment' in dreaming, *avowedly supplements* – and doesn't obviate – a critical scrutiny of Freud's arguments at a purely psychological and clinical level (as Grünbaum and Hobson recognize).

There is no space here to enter upon the subject. I can only say that I consider as devastating and definitive the methodological, logical and theoretical remarks separately addressed to *The Interpretation of Dreams* by Grünbaum (1984), Glymour (1983) and Moore (1984). Together with his analytical considerations, Glymour also offers a particularly psychological and intellectual account of Freud's hectic years at the turn of the century. His conclusion is that, precisely in *The Interpretation of Dreams*, Freud went from being a 'scientist toward a mountebank' (1983: 69).

So much for the 'scientific' status of Freud's theory of dreaming. But there is a last point to consider. The historical import of *The Interpretation of Dreams* consists also in the fact that it suggested a general pattern of interpretation, a sort of Kuhnian 'examplar', which had and still has an enormous influence in the field of the arts and humanities as well as in psychoanalysis. I refer to the *manifest/latent model*, and to its implicit assumption that everything conceals something deeper or further. Moore has very perceptively characterized this attitude to a superaddition of concealment as a sort of *animistic determinism*. This very strong model had its heyday in the sixties and seventies, above all in France. Among its renowned advocates are Paul Ricoeur, Charles Mauron, and the many spokesmen of 'post-structuralism'. Lacan (1966), for example, considered *The Interpretation of Dreams* as 'the essential expression of Freud's message', and started from the Freudian comparison between dreams and rebus to develop his 'formalistic' version of the manifest/latent model (he couched it in the magic formula: 'every signifier refers to other signifiers').

Still today the model – in the Lacanian version as in other 'semiotic' or hermeneutic reformulations – widely influences Continental 'Freudianism'. It is often presented as if it were the only cognitive way to approach the human psyche, in opposition to any *scientific* and *experimental* claim on the part of whose aims are inter-subjective testing or any other kinds of *causal* account of psychical events. This model, very frequently disguised under much varied and subtle forms of interpretative thought, is now directly – even though perhaps not definitively – challenged by the recent efforts of Grünbaum (1984: 1–94), Moore (1984: 281–309), and Eagle (1984: 164–71) to get rid of hermeneutics.

So, to conclude, an overall reappraisal of *The Interpretation of Dreams* seems to lead us, with Porte, to a single verdict: impostor. But let us not worry too much. Recently the famous philosopher Hilary Putnam has written that 'we are not free to inhabit the pre-Freudian world' (Putnam 1984: 1). New contributions, however, seem clearly to contradict Putnam. Eagle, for example, sometimes suggests that Janet's or Charcot's unconscious could be, in a sense, more up-to-date than Freud's while Hobson and Porte take us back to a neglected 'pre-Freudian' Freud. But what I see as the most important aspect of this 'iconoclastic' wave is that neurobiology, together with modern psychology, linguistics and – why not – analytical philosophy, allow us to look forward to a 'post-Freudian' world.

NOTES

1 Freud himself recalls the following words by Hughling Jackson: 'Find out all about dreams and you will have found out all about insanity.'

2 The definition of dream as instinct is already present in the work of the well-known neurophysiologist Moruzzi, and has been taken into account by several important ethologists (Tinbergen, Thorpe, Hinde et al.). A substantial revision of the ethological concept of instinct is required, however. Ethologists consider instinct to be a neural mechanism of hierarchical organization, which responds to internal and external stimuli with motor responses designed to maintain the existence of individual and species. Mancia believes, however, that the concept of instinct should cover behaviour also when movement is not present and when, indeed, there is an inhibition of motor activity. Mancia's concept of instinct seems much closer to the Freudian *Trieb* ('a concept on the frontier between the mental and the somatic') rather than to that of the ethologists, which is basically centred on the neurobiological mechanism behind any behavioural act.

3 Mancia seems to accept unreservedly Hobson's and McCarley's theses that the D sleep trigger, energy source, and watch are all pontine. 'However,' he adds, 'this is a level of discourse which cannot take place at the psychoanalytic one. D sleep is one thing, with all its specific biological variants (which are the same for every individual, and have phylogenetic roots); something else is the dream experience, with its specific motivational and functional components (differing from individual to individual)' (Mancia 1985: 197; see also Wasserman 1984: 841–2). More interestingly, in my opinion, Molinari proposes the extension of the *activation-synthesis hypothesis*, as follows: 'Granted that oniric images persist during sleep, even without phasic activation, is it not possible to conceive of two types of oniric image, one *sensorial* in origin, linked to the pontine *bad job*, the other *mental*, linked that is to the "internal language" and to the interactions which would occur between "internal language" and repository of memory, even without a specific physiological triggering?' (Molinari 1982: 182–3).

4 'If what we call censorship is active during sleep, as well as during wakefulness, dream distortions are not attributable to it. Given the way the nervous system operates during sleep, this would be like saying that a child doesn't think the way an adult does because he has censored his adult mode of thought. The censorship concept is not able to deal with the complex of mental processes it is usually called on to explain' (Fossi 1984: 265).

5 I refer to the mind's *bi-logic*, as suggested by Ignacio Matte-Blanco (1982) and taken up, among others, by Bertini, who writes: 'It can be stated therefore that oniric-imaginative language (as indeed logical-rational language) crosses between wake and sleep, though assuming different aspects of expression in these two states' (Bertini 1984: 258).

6 Besides those I have quoted, several psychoanalysts have attempted to

reformulate dream theory in the light of modern biological and neurophysiological advances. Especially worthy of mention are Bourguignon, Rallo-Romero, Diatkine, Green and Hautmann.

7 Even a superficial reading of much of the work of those followers of Freud whom I have quoted leads to the recognition of a single, recurring characteristic: too often it seems that to be Freudian it's enough to use Freud's vocabulary, and that to make a theory consistent and tenable it's enough to shade the meanings of its terms (not considering the possible consequences for the theory as a whole), or, *ultima ratio*, to transform the entire theoretical edifice into a so-called 'metaphor'. Reading Mancia, for example, it is striking with what ease he equates Freudian concepts with ethological ones (e.g. the Freudian 'free energy' becomes 'the instability of instincts'), or with what ease he conflates Freudian concepts that date from after 1920, and even Klein's and Bion's ones, with those of *The Interpretation of Dreams*, as if they belong to a unified theory; or, again, with what ease he sees Freud as a forerunner of the 'evolutionary' thesis that 'sleep is the guardian of dreaming'. My remarks are in perfect agreement with several criticisms addressed to the Freudian 'cognitive style' by many authors. Holt (1965: 1972), e.g., shows that defining concepts clearly and unambiguously was generally considered erroneous by Freud. In point of fact he regarded such a procedure as a typical aspect of barren, speculative philosophical systemizations; not a typical science, which struggles along with approximations that are defined only when they are employed. And, more interestingly in connection with my argument, Holt deems that Freud was frequently fond of expanding concepts to the very limit of applicability, as if he were convinced that stretching the realm of phenomena by means of conceptual extension was a way of making them more abstract and useful.

In the light of these characterizations of Freudian 'cognitive style', I think that vicissitudes of the concept of regression itself can be more adequately understood. Such process from the narrow and determinate sense of a concept to a 'broader and hazier' one is considered a central feature of the 'methodologically defective procedures' of psychoanalytic theorizing also in the strong (even though not always convincing) attack on Freud by the philosopher Frank Cioffi (1970).

REFERENCES

Bertini, M. 1984: Il linguaggio del sogno attraverso il sonno e la veglia, in *Il linguaggio del sogno*. Florence: Sansoni.
Bertini, M. and Violani, C. (eds) 1982: *Cervello e sogno*. Milan: Feltrinelli.
Cioffi, F. 1970: Freud and the idea of a pseudo-science, in R. Borger and F. Cioffi (eds), *Explanation in the Behavioural Sciences*. Cambridge: Cambridge University Press.
Eagle, M. 1984: *Recent Developments in Psychoanalysis*. New York: McGraw-Hill.

354   *Alessandro Pagnini*

Fossi, G. 1984: *Le teorie psicoanalitiche*. Padua: Piccin.

Funari, E. 1975: *Il giovane Freud*. Florence; Guaraldi.

Glymour, C. 1983: The theory of your dreams, in R. S. Cohen and L. Laudan (eds), *Physics, Philosophy, and Psychoanalysis*. Dordrecht: Reidel.

Grünbaum, A. 1984: *The Foundations of Psychoanalysis: A Philosophical Critique*. Berkeley: University of California Press.

Holt, R. R. 1965; Freud's cognitive style. *American Imago*, 22.

Holt, R. R. 1972: Freud's mechanistic and humanistic images of man, in R. R. Holt and E. Peterfreund (eds), *Psychoanalysis and Contemporary Science*. New York: Macmillan.

Horney Eckhardt M. 1982: The structure of Freud's dream theory, in S. L. Gilman (ed.), *Introducing Psychoanalytic Theory*. New York: Brenner-Mazel.

Jackson, S. W. 1969: The history of Freud's concepts of regression. *Journal of the American Psychoanalytic Association*, 17.

Kline, P. 1984: *Psychology and Freudian Theory*. London: Methuen.

Lacan, J. 1966: *Ecrits*, I. Paris; Seuil.

Mancia, M. 1980: *Neurofisiologia e vita mentale*. Bologna: Zanichelli.

Mancia, M. 1985: Psicoanalisi e funzioni del sogno, in M. Pissacroia (ed.), *Delle psicoanalisi possibili: Bion, Lacan, Matte-Blanco*. Milan: Borla.

McCarley, R. W. and Hobson, J. A. 1977: The neurobiological origins of psychoanalytic dream theory. *American Journal of Psychiatry*, 134.

Matte-Blanco, I. 1982: Oltre i fondamenti neurofisiologici della psicoanalisi: riflessioni sugli scritti di Hobson e McCarley, in Bertini and Violani 1982.

Molinari, S. 1979: *Notazioni sulla scienza dei sogni in Freud*. Bologna: CLUEB.

Molinari, S. 1982: Formazione del sogno, modello tonico-fasico e problema mente-corpo, in Bertini and Violani 1982.

Moore, M. 1984: *Law and Psychiatry*. Cambridge: Cambridge University Press.

Putnam, H. 1984: Editoriale. *Kos*, 10.

Sulloway, F. J. 1979: *Freud: Biologist of the Mind*. New York; Basic Books.

Wasserman, M. D. 1984: Psychoanalytic dream theory and recent neurobiological findings about REM sleep. *Journal of the American Psychoanalytical Association*, 32.

Notes on the Editors and Contributors

Frank Cioffi teaches at the University of Essex where he was appointed to the Chair of Philosophy in 1973. He read philosophy and psychology at Oxford and has held posts at the Universities of Oxford, Singapore and Kent at Canterbury. Among his research interests are the character and sources of the Freud controversy and the relation between the epistemic content of folk and human culture and that of the social and behavioural sciences.

Peter Clark took his first degree in mathematics and philosophy at Manchester. He then went to the London School of Economics to take an M.Sc. in logic and scientific method, going on to take a Ph.D. there. He taught at LSE for three years, and had a year at Pittsburgh as a Research Fellow, before coming to St Andrews in 1978. His main interest is in the philosophy of science, mathematics and logic. He is currently Lecturer in Logic and Metaphysics at St Andrews University.

Frederick Crews is Professor of English at the University of California, where he has taught since 1958. He is the author of eight books, including *The Pooh Perplex*, *E. M. Forster: The Perils of Humanism*, *The Sins of the Fathers: Hawthorne's Psychological Themes* and *Out of My System: Psychoanalysis, Ideology, and Critical Method*. Since the publication of his article 'Analysis Terminable' in 1980, he has been known as a trenchant critic of the Freudian principles he once espoused. That essay and others from the past decade are published by Oxford University Press as *Skeptical Engagements* (1986).

İlham Dilman is Professor of Philosophy at the University College of Swansea. He is the author of *Sense and Delusion* (with D. Z. Phillips) (1971), *Induction and Deduction* (1973), *Matter and Mind* (1975), *Morality and the Inner Life* (1979), *Studies in Language and Reason* (1981), *Freud and Human Nature* (1983),

Freud and the Mind (1984), *Quine on Ontology, Necessity and Experience* (1984) and many articles in philosophical journals.

Morris Eagle received his B.A. from the City College of New York in 1949 and his Ph.D. in clinical psychology from New York University in 1958. He served on the faculty of the Yeshiva University in New York as Chairman of the Graduate Psychology Department and Director of Clinical Training for the Doctoral Programme in Clinical Psychology. He is currently Professor of Psychology at York University. He is the author of numerous articles in professional journals and of *Recent Developments in Psychoanalysis: A Critical Evaluation* (1984). He carries on a part-time private practice in psychoanalytically oriented psychotherapy.

Edward Erwin, Ph.D., is a Professor in the Department of Philosophy at the University of Miami. He is the author of the *Concept of Meaninglessness* and *Behaviour Therapy: Scientific, Philosophical and Moral Foundations*. He has contributed chapters on psychoanalysis and psychotherapy to such books as *Does Psychotherapy Really Help People?* and *Hans Eysenck: A Psychologist Searching for a Scientific Basis for Human Behaviour* and published papers on these topics in such journals as *The British Journal for the Philosophy of Science*, *Nous*, *Journal of Philosophy*, *American Psychologist* and the *Journal of Contemporary Psychotherapy*.

Adolf Grünbaum was born 15 May 1923 in Germany and entered the United States in 1938. He graduated from Wesleyan University, Connecticut and from Yale (with his doctorate in 1950). He research initially devoted to the philosophy of space and time led to the publication of his major treatise *Philosophical Problems of Space and Time* in 1963, and to the greatly enlarged second edition in 1970. He has produced a number of studies in the theory of scientific rationality and the falsifiability criterion. His current research interests lie in cognitive status of psychoanalytic theory to an examination of which his *Foundations of Psychoanalysis* (1984) is devoted. In 1960 he was appointed Andrew Mellon Professor of Philosophy in the University of Pittsburgh and in 1979 Research Professor of Psychiatry at that University. He was Gifford Lecturer in the University of St Andrews in 1985.

John Haldane is Lecturer in the Department of Moral Philosophy, and Research Associate of the Centre for Philosophy and Public Affairs at the University of St Andrews. He was awarded his Ph.D. by London University in 1983. His philosophical interests are wide-ranging and he has published extensively in various areas of the subject and in related disciplines including educational theory and theology. He was co-editor with Roger Squires (q.v.) and Leslie Stevenson of *Mind, Causation and Action* (1986). He was Visiting Research Fellow at the Center for Philosophy of Science, University of Pittsburgh, in 1987.

Allan Hobson is a Professor of Psychiatry at the Harvard Medical School in Boston, Massachusetts, where he directs the Laboratory of Neurophysiology. A practitioner of clinical psychiatry since 1960, Dr Hobson has been impressed with the weakness of its psychological base in psychoanalysis and by the apparent impossibility of achieving revision of theory via clinical data. For this reason he has devoted his research efforts to understanding the neurobiology of sleep, especially REM sleep, with reference to the cornerstone of psychoanalysis Freud's dream theory. In 1977, he and his colleague Dr Robert McCarley published the first systematic critique of psychoanalytic dream theory and proposed the alternative activation-synthesis hypothesis which is summarized in Dr Hobson's contribution to this book.

Jim Hopkins is Lecturer in Philosophy at King's College, London. His main research interests lie in the general area of the philosophy of mind and philosophy of psychology. He has written extensively on psychoanalysis including his substantial introduction to the volume of essays he co-edited with Richard Wollheim, *Philosophical Essays on Freud* (1982).

Paul Kline was born in 1937 and read classics at Reading University, trained as a teacher at University College, Swansea and taught classics for two years in a comprehensive school. He then took a Master's degree in education at the University of Aberdeen and became a Research Associate in the Department of Education in the University of Manchester. He then became a Lecturer in Education in the University of Exeter and in 1969 moved to the Psychology Department where he has remained ever since. His research has covered personality measurement and the scientific validation of Freudian theory. He was appointed to a Personal Chair in Psychometrics in 1985.

Peter Lamarque is Lecturer in Philosophy at the University of Stirling. He publishes in the areas of aesthetics, philosophy and literature and semantics. His present research interests are in the theory of fiction and he is currently writing a monograph on truth and fiction. He edited and contributed to *Philosophy and Fiction: Essays in Literary Aesthetics* (1983) and was Visiting Professor at the University of Tsukuba, Japan 1983 to 1984.

Michael Moore is the Robert Kingsley Professor of Law at the University of Southern California Law Center in Los Angeles. He is the author of *Law and Psychiatry: Rethinking the Relationship* published in 1984, and of numerous articles on the philosophy of science applied to psychoanalysis and psychiatry appearing in philosophical, psychoanalytic and legal journals. He has lectured on topics related to his present chapter in the Pittsburgh Series in the Philosophy of Science, the Western Ontario Series in the Philosophy of Science, as the keynote address of the 1985 Southern Society for Philosophy and Psychology, and, most recently, as the Charles Phelps Tafts Lecturer in Philosophy at the 1986 Symposium of the University of Cincinnati.

Alessandro Pagnini is Lecturer in the History of Philosophy in the University of Florence. His research interests are in the philosophy of mind with particular reference to the philosophical problems of psychoanalysis. He was a Visiting Research Fellow at the Centre for Philosophy of Science, University of Pittsburgh and is currently Secretary to the Centre for History and Philosophy of Science in the University of Florence.

Helene S. Porte was born in Columbus, Ohio and grew up in Ohio and Vermont. She studied philosophy at Mount Holyoke College and completed her doctoral work in human development at Harvard University. Currently she is a Fellow in the Clinical Research Training Program in Social/Biological Psychiatry at Harvard Medical School, working with Dr Allan Hobson in the Laboratory of Neurophysiology and is a member of the Department of Psychology at Cornell University.

Robert Sharpe is Professor of Philosophy at Saint David's University College, Lampeter, University of Wales, and author of *Contemporary Aesthetics*, (1983), and of many articles, mainly on aesthetics but also on philosophical psychology, philosophy of the social sciences, and on music.

Roger Squires was born in Nuneaton, Warwickshire, in 1940. After reading PPE at Oxford, and a postgraduate year at Brown, he returned to Oxford to study for the B.Phil. with Gilbert Ryle. He is Senior Lecturer in Logic and Metaphysics at St Andrews University, where his research in philosophical psychology seeks to understand and advance those revolutionary but fragile insights derived largely but not exclusively from Ludwig Wittgenstein's work.

Crispin Wright read moral science at Cambridge, and did postgraduate work there and in Oxford. He has taught at Oxford, London and Princeton. His main interests are in the philosophy of logic, language and mathematics. He is the author of *Wittgenstein on the Foundations of Mathematics* (1980), *Frege's Conception of Numbers as Objects* (1983) and *Realism, Meaning and Truth* (1986). Crispin Wright is Professor of Logic and Metaphysics in the University of St Andrews, and Professor of Philosophy in the University of Michigan at Ann Arbor.

List of Conference Participants

Professor David Armstrong	(Sydney)
Mr Derek Bolton	(Maudsley Hospital)
Dr Simon Blackburn	(Pembroke College, Oxford)
Dr Peter Clark	(St Andrews)
Professor F. Crews	(Berkeley)
Dr İlham Dilman	(Swansea)
Professor Morris Eagle	(York, Ontario)
Professor E. Erwin	(Miami University)
Dr John Forrester	(King's College, London)
Dr Donald Gillies	(Chelsea)
Professor Adolf Grünbaum	(Pittsburgh)
Mrs Thelma Grünbaum	(Pittsburgh)
Dr S. Guttenplan	(Birkbeck College, London)
Dr J. Haldane	(St Andrews)
Professor Allan Hobson	(Harvard)
Professor David Holdcroft	(Leeds)
Mr Jim Hopkins	(King's College, London)
Professor P. Kline	(Exeter)
Mr Peter Lamarque	(Stirling)
Ms Zinaida Lewcuk	(St Andrews)
Dr David Milner	(St Andrews)
Professor Michael Moore	(U.S.C., Los Angeles)
Dr Alessandro Pagnini	(Florence, Italy)
Mr David Pears	(Christ Church, Oxford)
Dr Helene S. Porte	(Harvard)
Dr Jonathan Potter	(St Andrews)
Dr S. L. Read	(St Andrews)

Dr R. A. Sharpe   (Lampeter)
Ms Janet Sisson   (Glasgow)
Mr J. E. R. Squires   (St Andrews)
Mr L. F. Stevenson   (St Andrews)
Dr Charles Travis   (Tilburg, Holland)
Professor John Watkins   (L.S.E., London)
Dr N. Wetherick   (Aberdeen)
Dr John Worrall   (L.S.E., London)
Professor Crispin Wright   (St Andrews)

Index

362   *Index*

Index by Isobel McLean